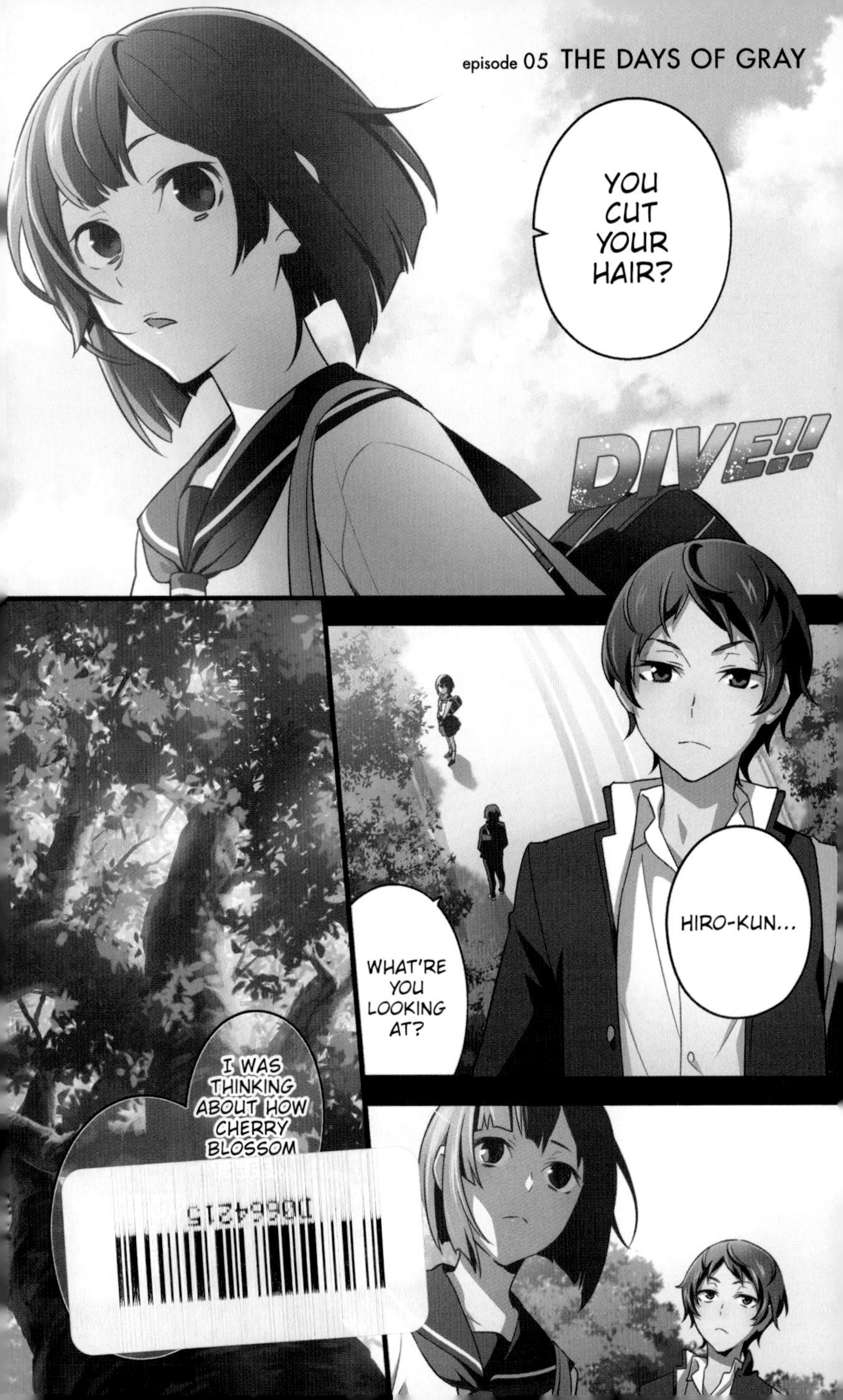

episode 05 THE DAYS OF GRAY
YOU CUT YOUR HAIR?
DIVE!!
HIRO-KUN...
WHAT'RE YOU LOOKING AT?
I WAS THINKING ABOUT HOW CHERRY BLOSSOM

episode 05 THE DAYS OF GRAY

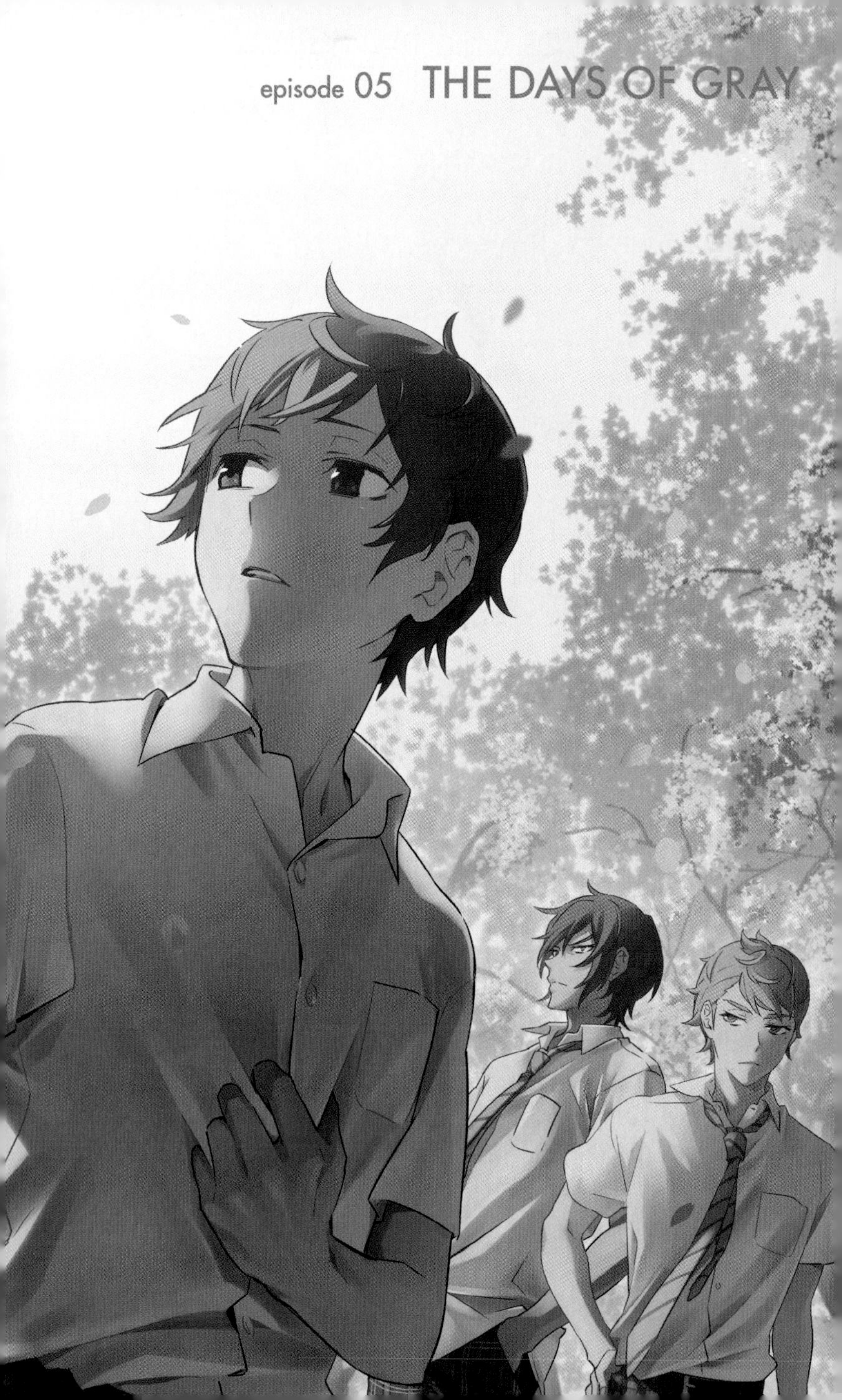

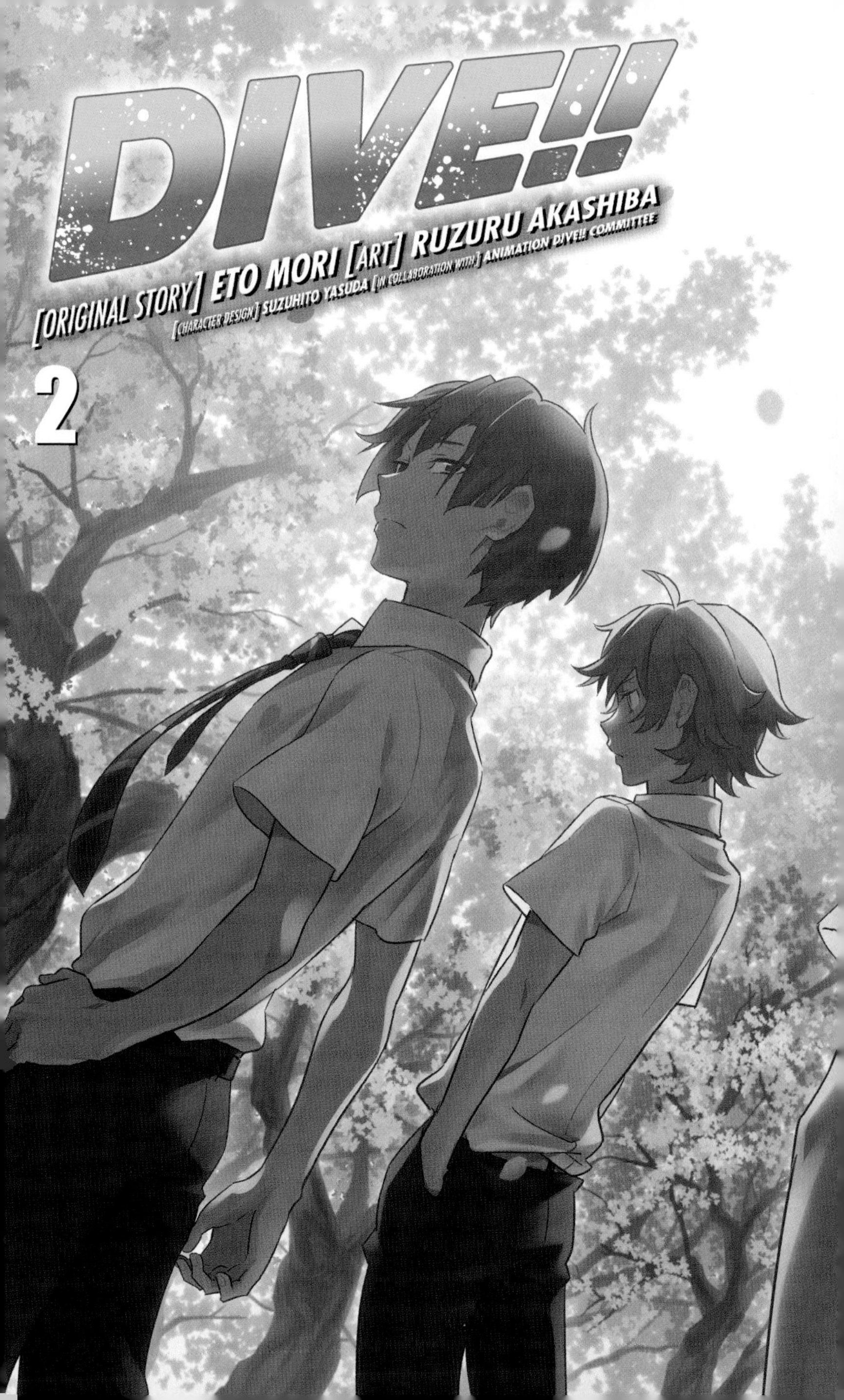
DIVE!!
[ORIGINAL STORY] ETO MORI [ART] RUZURU AKASHIBA
[CHARACTER DESIGN] SUZUHITO YASUDA [IN COLLABORATION WITH] ANIMATION DIVE!! COMMITTEE
2

CONTENTS

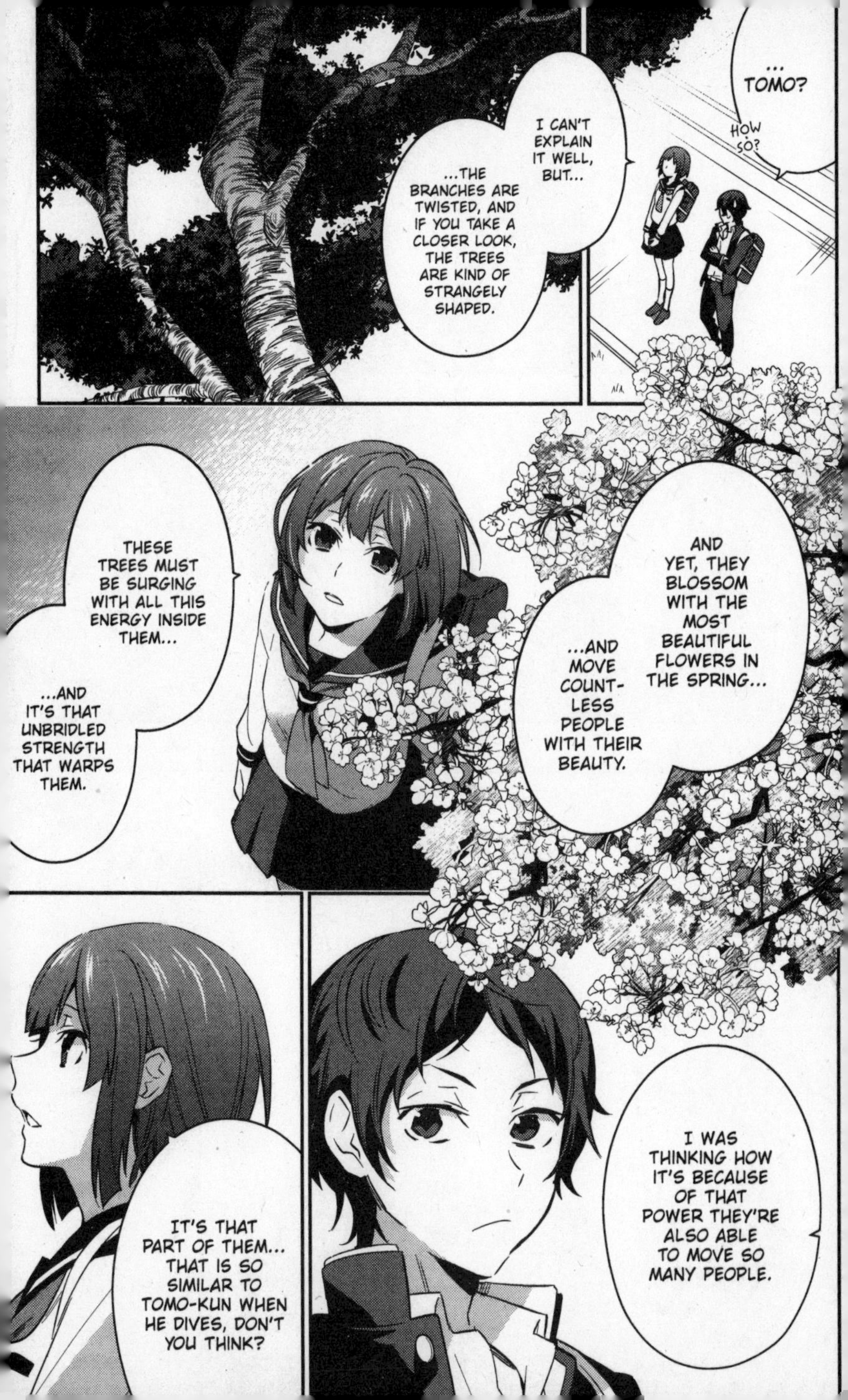

... TOMO?
HOW SO?
I CAN'T EXPLAIN IT WELL, BUT...
...THE BRANCHES ARE TWISTED, AND IF YOU TAKE A CLOSER LOOK, THE TREES ARE KIND OF STRANGELY SHAPED.
AND YET, THEY BLOSSOM WITH THE MOST BEAUTIFUL FLOWERS IN THE SPRING...
...AND MOVE COUNT-LESS PEOPLE WITH THEIR BEAUTY.
THESE TREES MUST BE SURGING WITH ALL THIS ENERGY INSIDE THEM...
...AND IT'S THAT UNBRIDLED STRENGTH THAT WARPS THEM.
I WAS THINKING HOW IT'S BECAUSE OF THAT POWER THEY'RE ALSO ABLE TO MOVE SO MANY PEOPLE.
IT'S THAT PART OF THEM... THAT IS SO SIMILAR TO TOMO-KUN WHEN HE DIVES, DON'T YOU THINK?

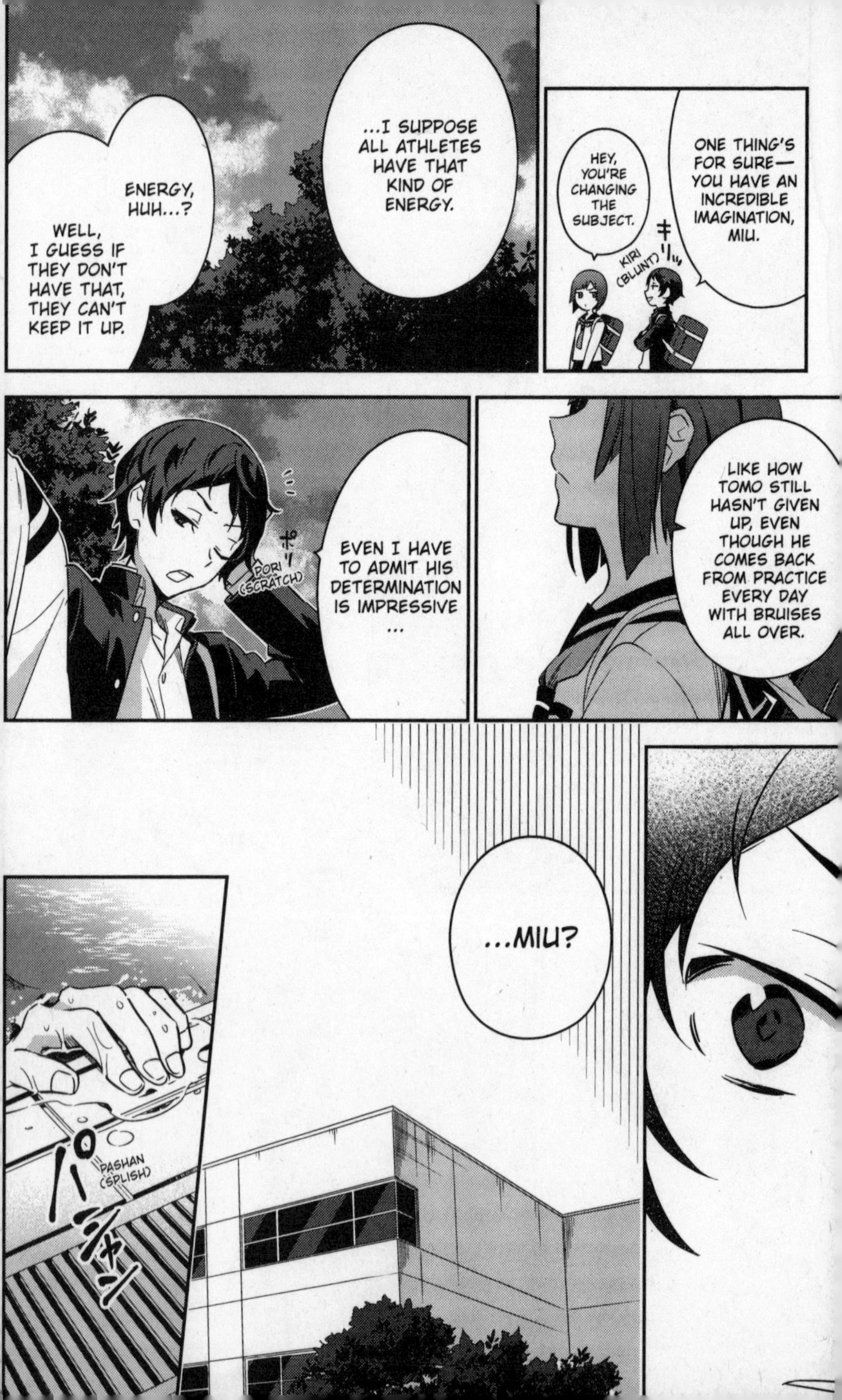
ONE THING'S FOR SURE—YOU HAVE AN INCREDIBLE IMAGINATION, MIU.
HEY, YOU'RE CHANGING THE SUBJECT.
KIRI (BLUNT)
...I SUPPOSE ALL ATHLETES HAVE THAT KIND OF ENERGY.
ENERGY, HUH...?
WELL, I GUESS IF THEY DON'T HAVE THAT, THEY CAN'T KEEP IT UP.
LIKE HOW TOMO STILL HASN'T GIVEN UP, EVEN THOUGH HE COMES BACK FROM PRACTICE EVERY DAY WITH BRUISES ALL OVER.
EVEN I HAVE TO ADMIT HIS DETERMINATION IS IMPRESSIVE ...
PORI (SCRATCH)
...MIU?
PASHAN (SPLISH)

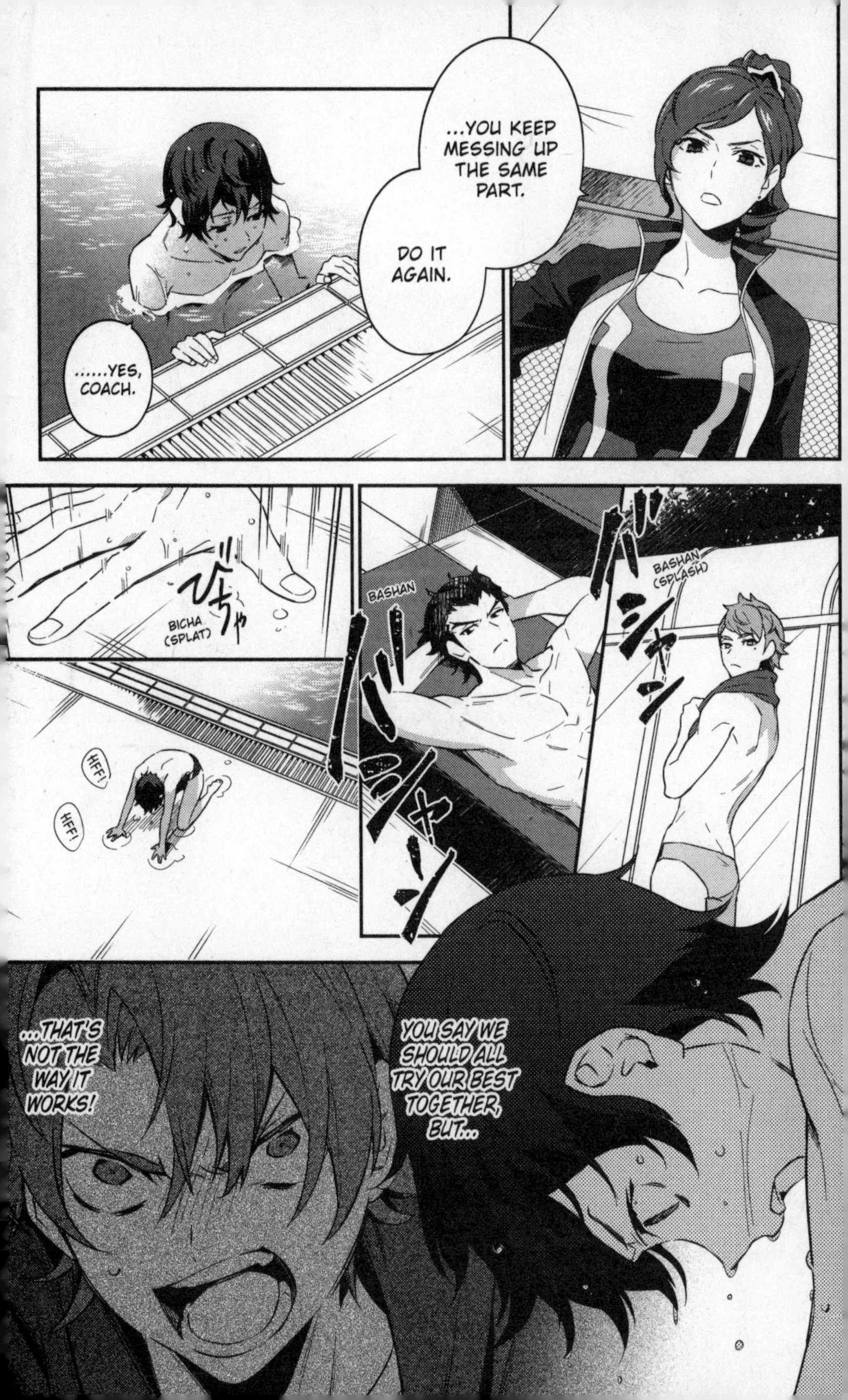
...YOU KEEP MESSING UP THE SAME PART.
DO IT AGAIN.
......YES, COACH.
BASHAN (SPLASH)
BASHAN
びちゃ
BICHA (SPLAT)
HFF!
HFF!
YOU SAY WE SHOULD ALL TRY OUR BEST TOGETHER, BUT...
...THAT'S NOT THE WAY IT WORKS!

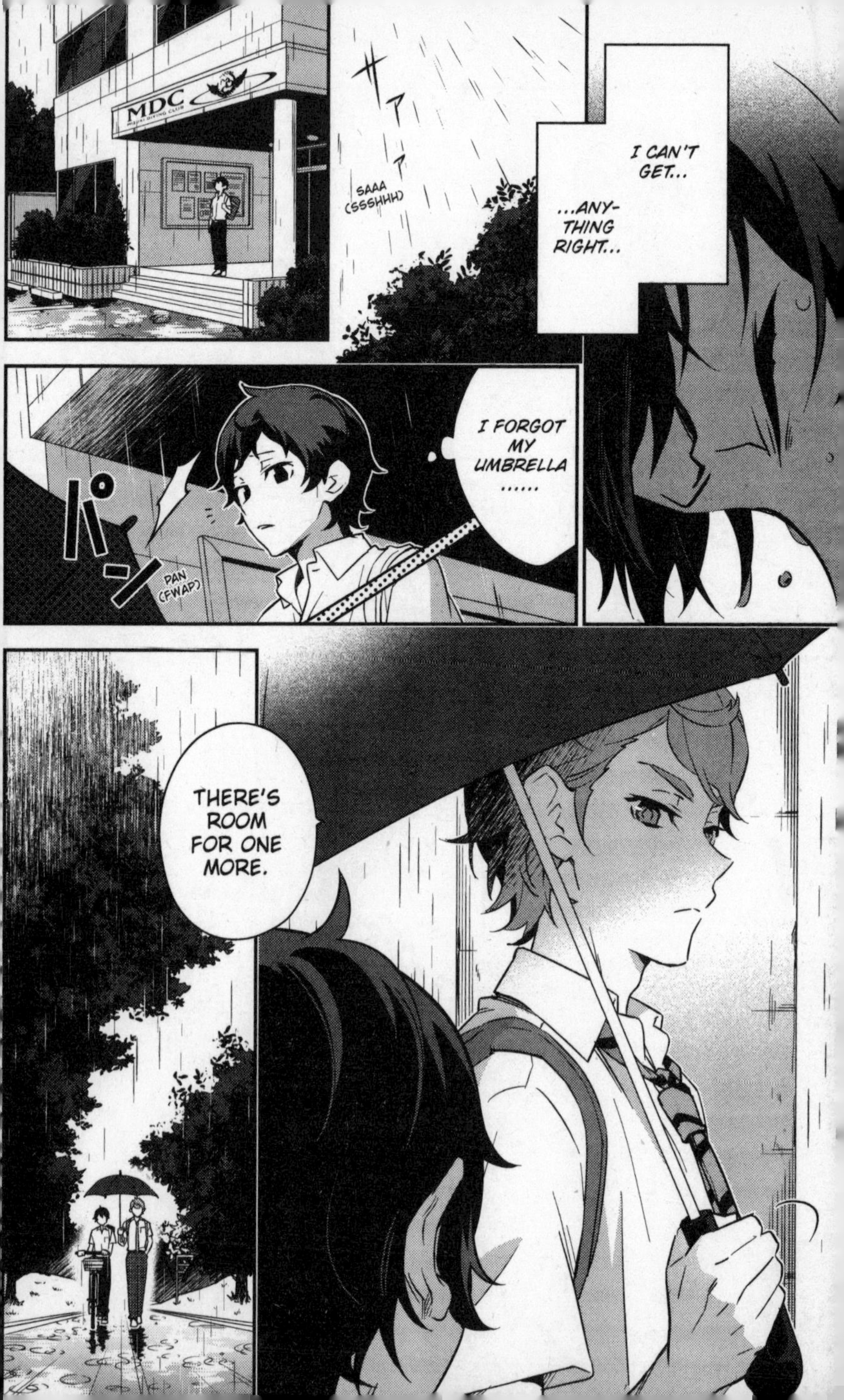

サァァ
SAAA (SSSHHH)
I CAN'T GET...
...ANY-THING RIGHT...
MDC
パーン
PAN (FWAP)
I FORGOT MY UMBRELLA ......
THERE'S ROOM FOR ONE MORE.

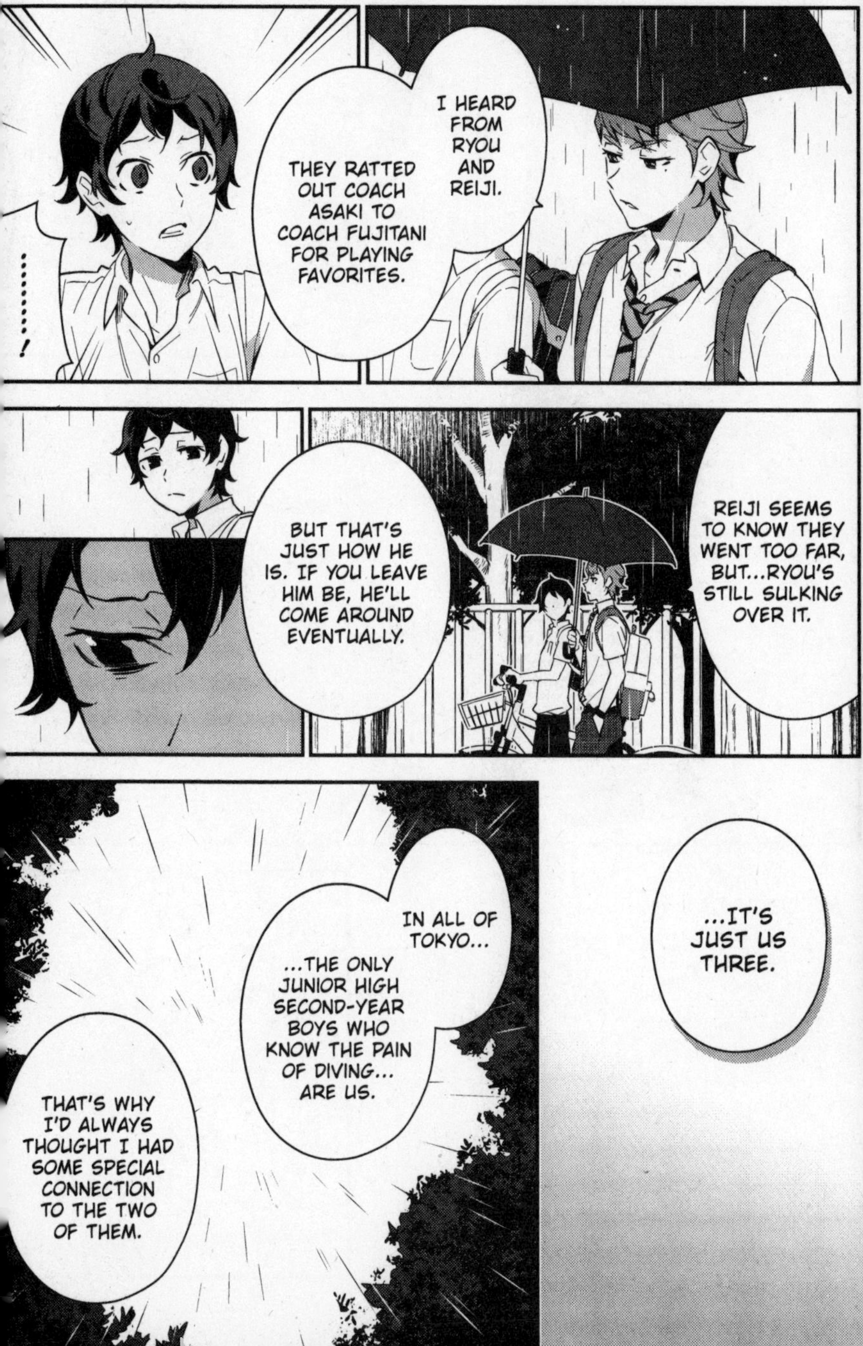
I HEARD FROM RYOU AND REIJI.
THEY RATTED OUT COACH ASAKI TO COACH FUJITANI FOR PLAYING FAVORITES.
......!
REIJI SEEMS TO KNOW THEY WENT TOO FAR, BUT...RYOU'S STILL SULKING OVER IT.
BUT THAT'S JUST HOW HE IS. IF YOU LEAVE HIM BE, HE'LL COME AROUND EVENTUALLY.
...IT'S JUST US THREE.
IN ALL OF TOKYO...
...THE ONLY JUNIOR HIGH SECOND-YEAR BOYS WHO KNOW THE PAIN OF DIVING... ARE US.
THAT'S WHY I'D ALWAYS THOUGHT I HAD SOME SPECIAL CONNECTION TO THE TWO OF THEM.

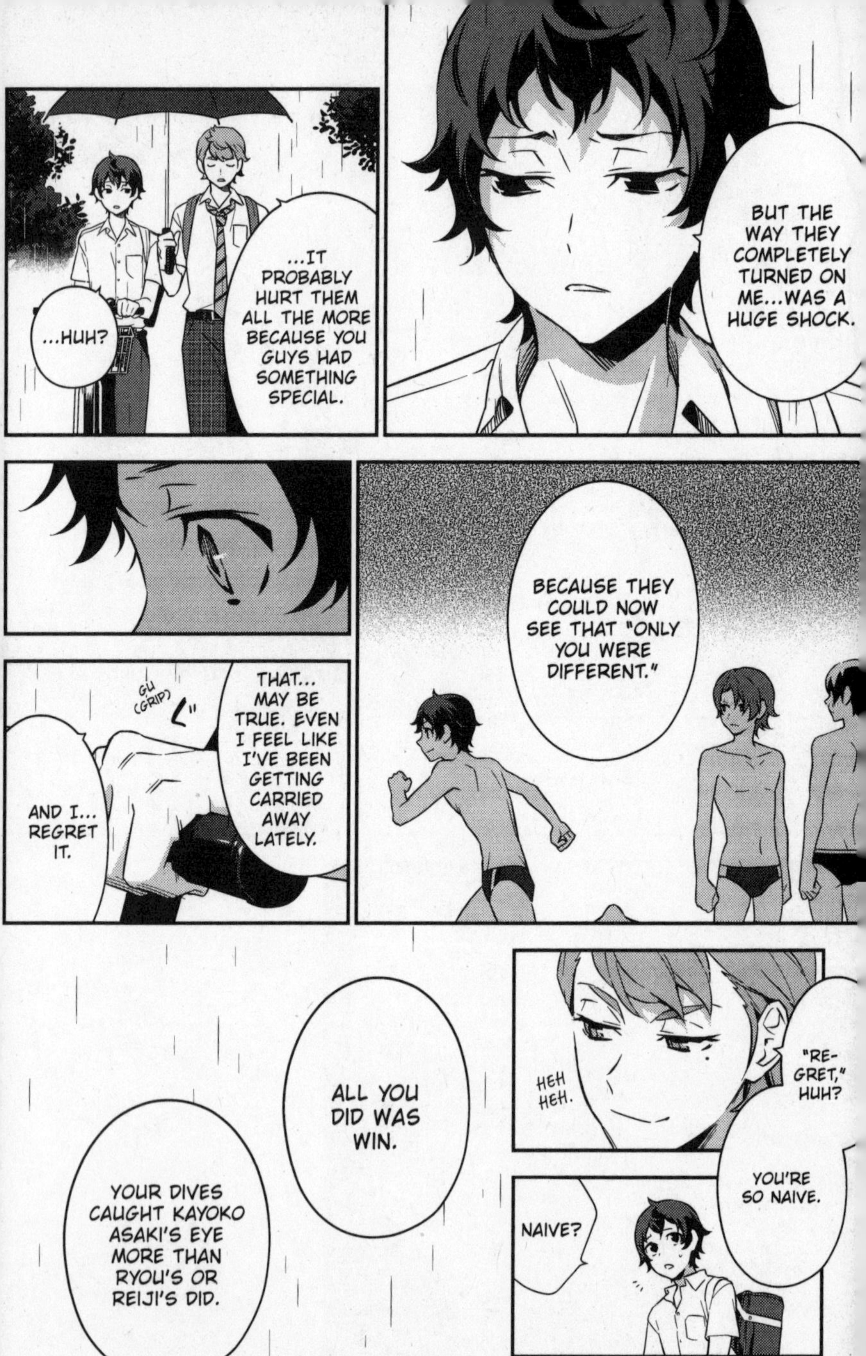
BUT THE WAY THEY COMPLETELY TURNED ON ME...WAS A HUGE SHOCK.
...IT PROBABLY HURT THEM ALL THE MORE BECAUSE YOU GUYS HAD SOMETHING SPECIAL.
...HUH?
BECAUSE THEY COULD NOW SEE THAT "ONLY YOU WERE DIFFERENT."
GU (GRIP)
THAT... MAY BE TRUE. EVEN I FEEL LIKE I'VE BEEN GETTING CARRIED AWAY LATELY.
AND I... REGRET IT.
HEH HEH.
"RE-GRET," HUH?
YOU'RE SO NAIVE.
NAIVE?
ALL YOU DID WAS WIN.
YOUR DIVES CAUGHT KAYOKO ASAKI'S EYE MORE THAN RYOU'S OR REIJI'S DID.

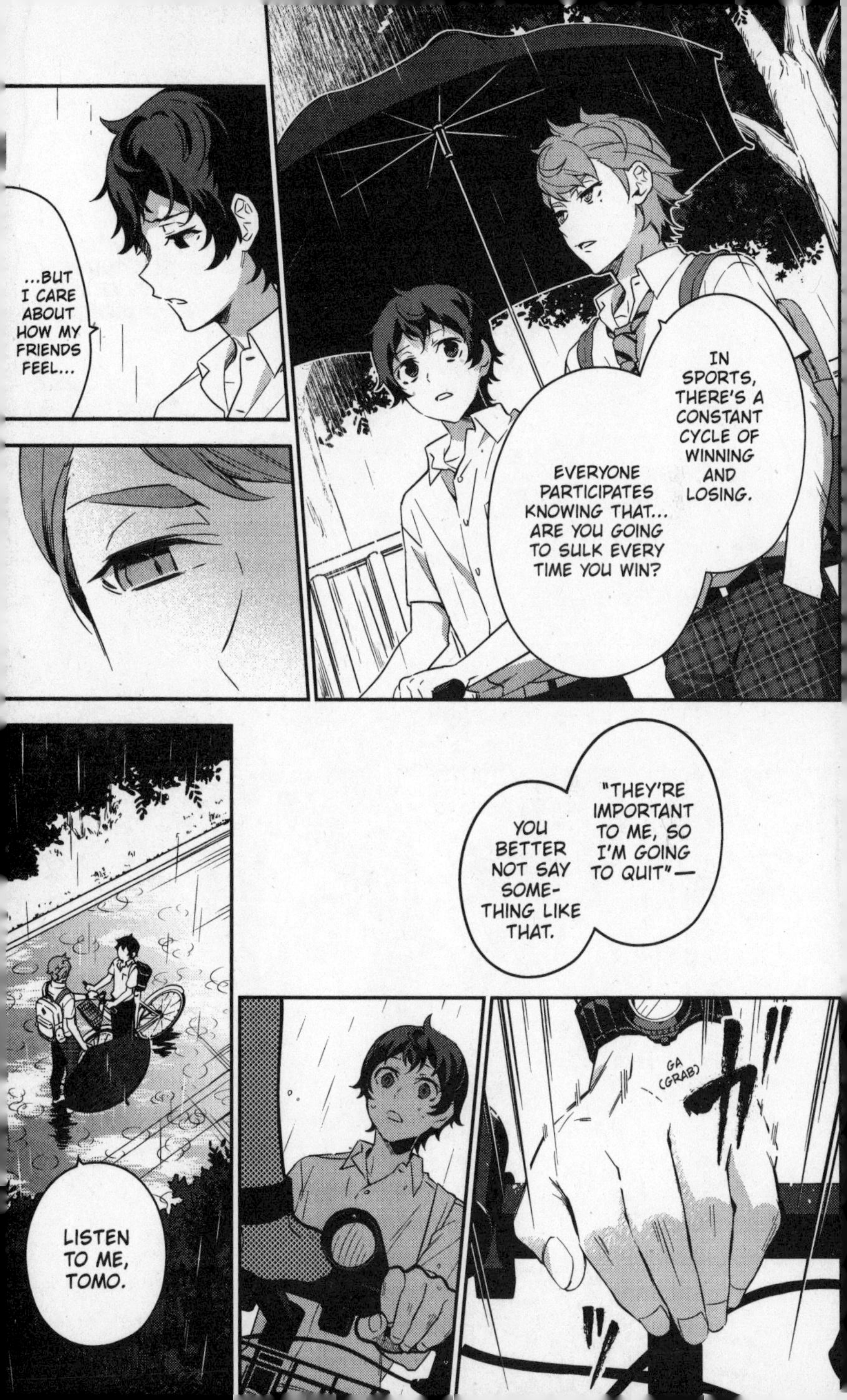
IN SPORTS, THERE'S A CONSTANT CYCLE OF WINNING AND LOSING.
EVERYONE PARTICIPATES KNOWING THAT... ARE YOU GOING TO SULK EVERY TIME YOU WIN?
...BUT I CARE ABOUT HOW MY FRIENDS FEEL...
"THEY'RE IMPORTANT TO ME, SO I'M GOING TO QUIT"—
YOU BETTER NOT SAY SOME-THING LIKE THAT.
GA (GRAB)
LISTEN TO ME, TOMO.

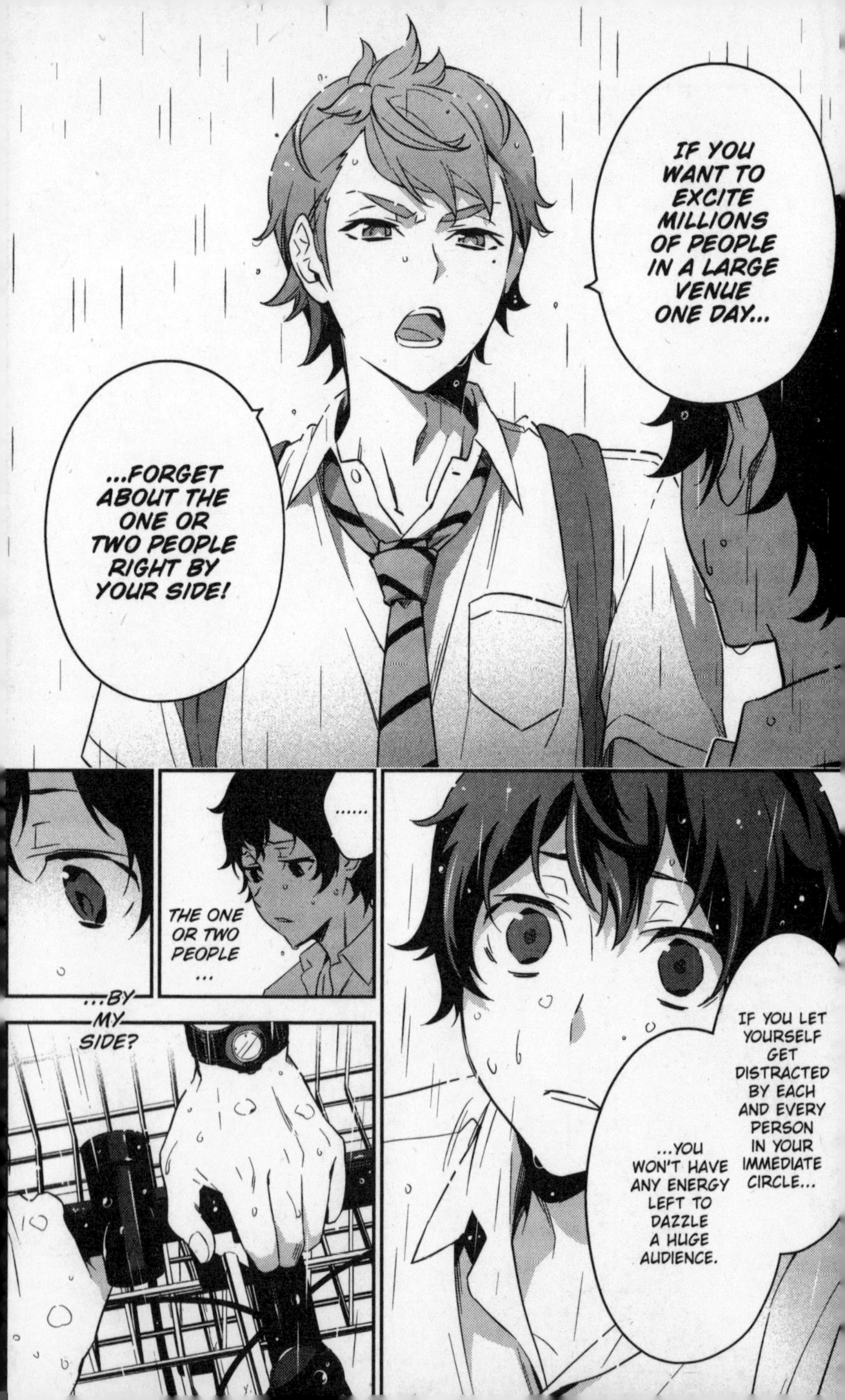
IF YOU WANT TO EXCITE MILLIONS OF PEOPLE IN A LARGE VENUE ONE DAY...
...FORGET ABOUT THE ONE OR TWO PEOPLE RIGHT BY YOUR SIDE!
IF YOU LET YOURSELF GET DISTRACTED BY EACH AND EVERY PERSON IN YOUR IMMEDIATE CIRCLE...
...YOU WON'T HAVE ANY ENERGY LEFT TO DAZZLE A HUGE AUDIENCE.
......
THE ONE OR TWO PEOPLE ...
...BY MY SIDE?

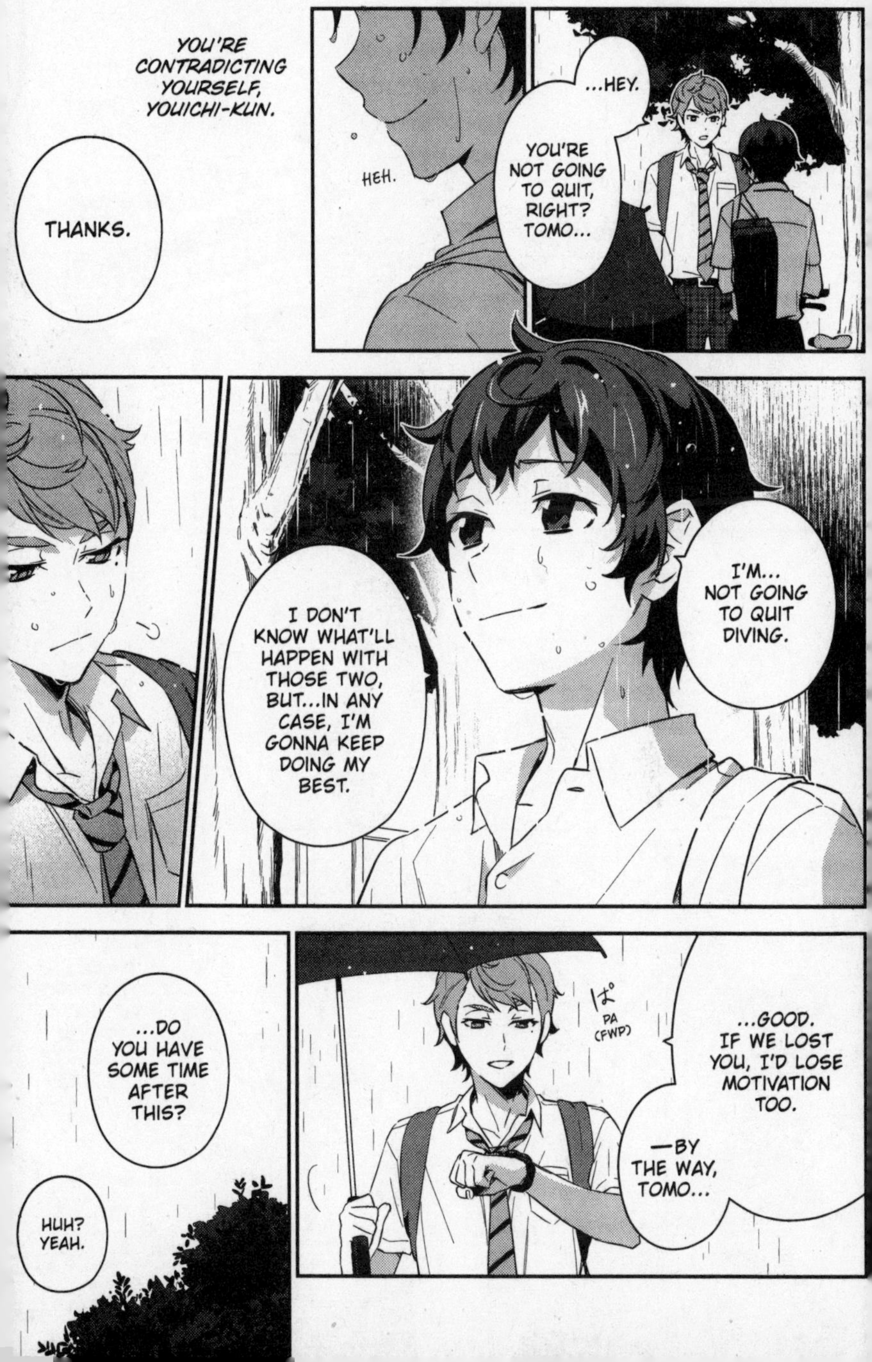
...HEY.
YOU'RE NOT GOING TO QUIT, RIGHT? TOMO...
HEH.
YOU'RE CONTRADICTING YOURSELF, YOUICHI-KUN.
THANKS.
I'M... NOT GOING TO QUIT DIVING.
I DON'T KNOW WHAT'LL HAPPEN WITH THOSE TWO, BUT...IN ANY CASE, I'M GONNA KEEP DOING MY BEST.
...GOOD. IF WE LOST YOU, I'D LOSE MOTIVATION TOO.
ぱ
PA (FWP)
—BY THE WAY, TOMO...
...DO YOU HAVE SOME TIME AFTER THIS?
HUH? YEAH.

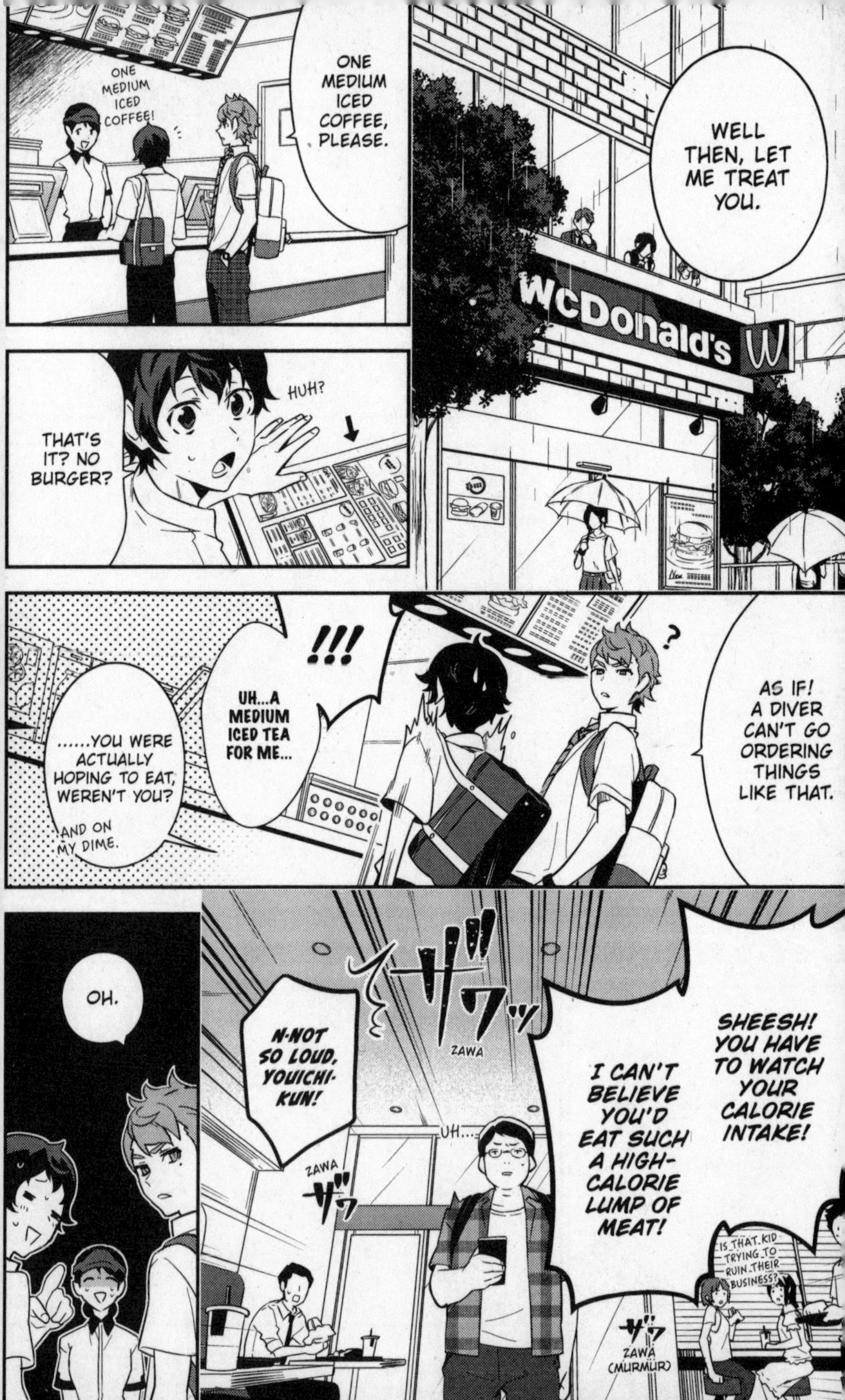
WcDonald's
WELL THEN, LET ME TREAT YOU.
ONE MEDIUM ICED COFFEE, PLEASE.
ONE MEDIUM ICED COFFEE!
HUH?
THAT'S IT? NO BURGER?
AS IF! A DIVER CAN'T GO ORDERING THINGS LIKE THAT.
?
!!!
UH...A MEDIUM ICED TEA FOR ME...
......YOU WERE ACTUALLY HOPING TO EAT, WEREN'T YOU?
AND ON MY DIME.
SHEESH! YOU HAVE TO WATCH YOUR CALORIE INTAKE!
I CAN'T BELIEVE YOU'D EAT SUCH A HIGH-CALORIE LUMP OF MEAT!
ZAWA
N-NOT SO LOUD, YOUICHI-KUN!
UH...
ZAWA
IS THAT KID TRYING TO RUIN THEIR BUSINESS?
ZAWA (MURMUR)
OH.

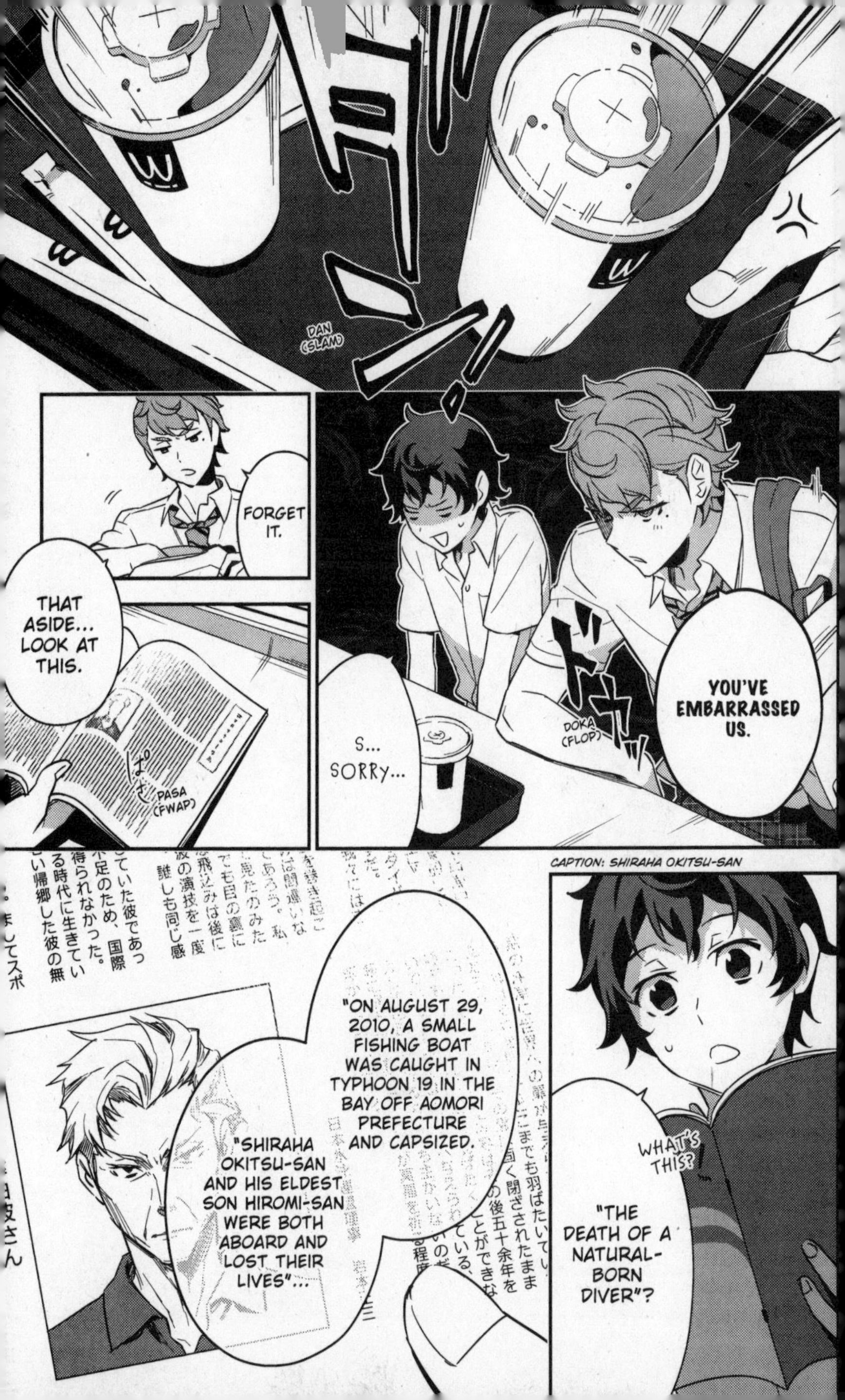
DAN (SLAM)
YOU'VE EMBARRASSED US.
DOKA (FLOP)
S... SORRY...
FORGET IT.
THAT ASIDE... LOOK AT THIS.
PASA (FWAP)
CAPTION: SHIRAHA OKITSU-SAN
WHAT'S THIS?
"THE DEATH OF A NATURAL-BORN DIVER"?
"ON AUGUST 29, 2010, A SMALL FISHING BOAT WAS CAUGHT IN TYPHOON 19 IN THE BAY OFF AOMORI PREFECTURE AND CAPSIZED.
"SHIRAHA OKITSU-SAN AND HIS ELDEST SON HIROMI-SAN WERE BOTH ABOARD AND LOST THEIR LIVES"...

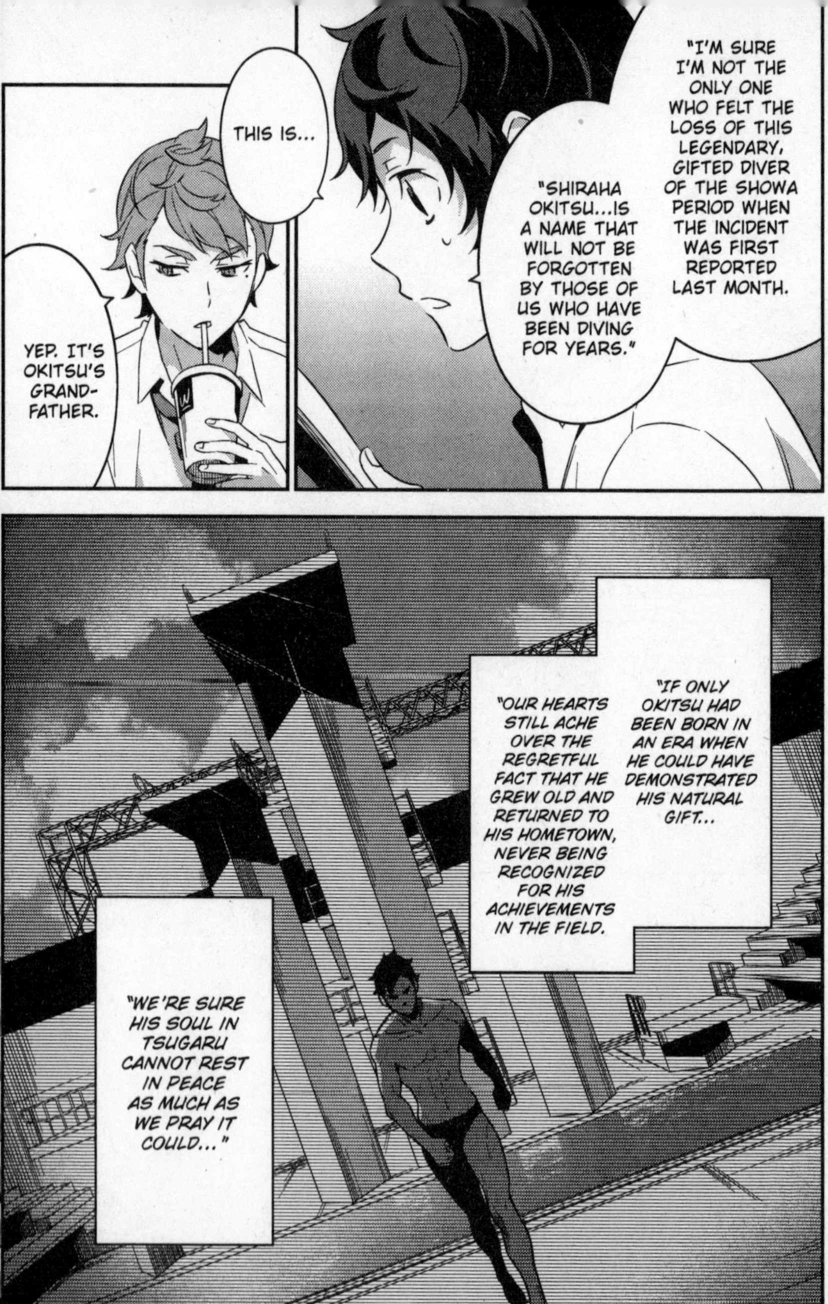
"I'M SURE I'M NOT THE ONLY ONE WHO FELT THE LOSS OF THIS LEGENDARY, GIFTED DIVER OF THE SHOWA PERIOD WHEN THE INCIDENT WAS FIRST REPORTED LAST MONTH.
"SHIRAHA OKITSU...IS A NAME THAT WILL NOT BE FORGOTTEN BY THOSE OF US WHO HAVE BEEN DIVING FOR YEARS."
THIS IS...
YEP. IT'S OKITSU'S GRAND-FATHER.
"IF ONLY OKITSU HAD BEEN BORN IN AN ERA WHEN HE COULD HAVE DEMONSTRATED HIS NATURAL GIFT...
"OUR HEARTS STILL ACHE OVER THE REGRETFUL FACT THAT HE GREW OLD AND RETURNED TO HIS HOMETOWN, NEVER BEING RECOGNIZED FOR HIS ACHIEVEMENTS IN THE FIELD.
"WE'RE SURE HIS SOUL IN TSUGARU CANNOT REST IN PEACE AS MUCH AS WE PRAY IT COULD..."

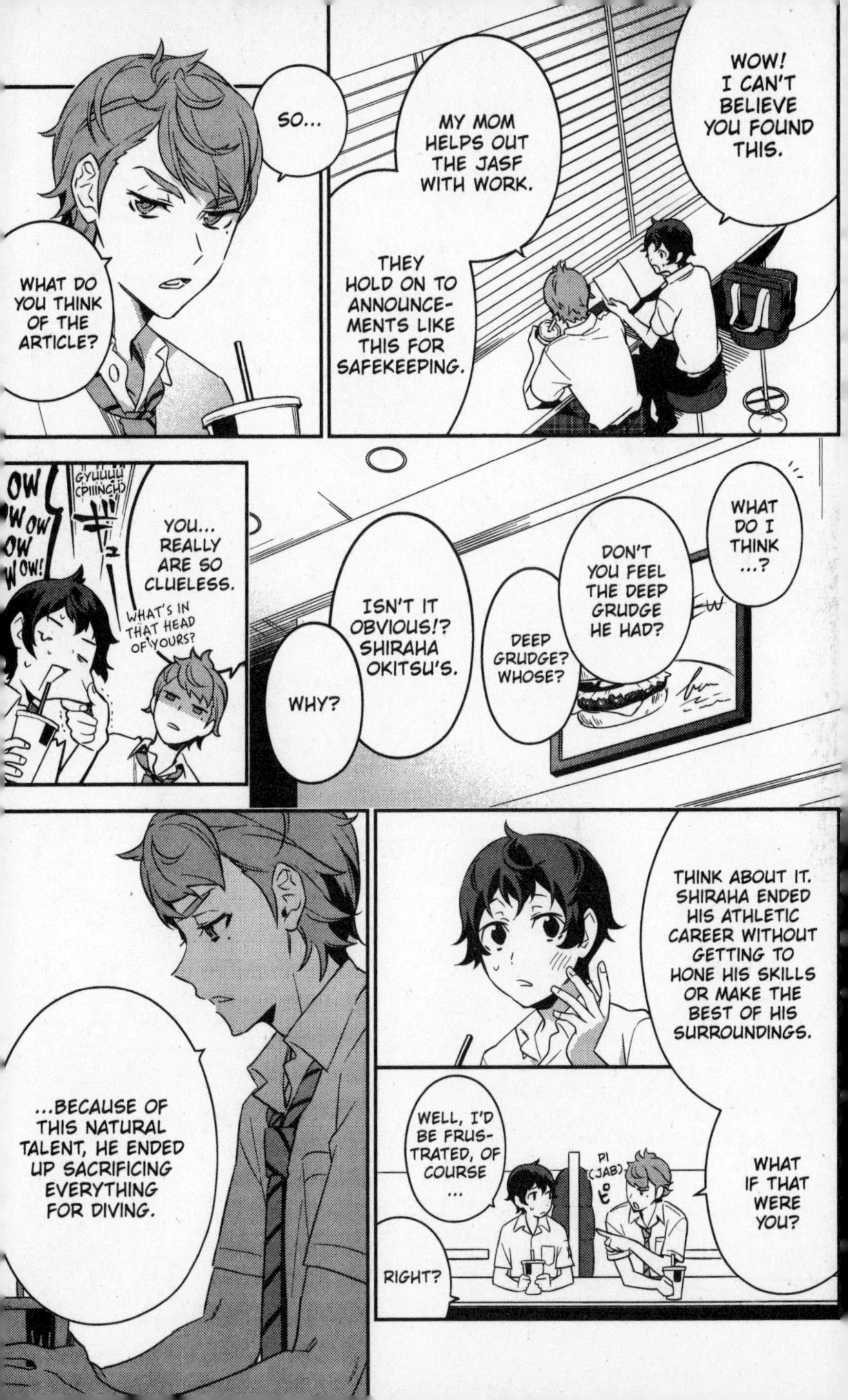

WOW! I CAN'T BELIEVE YOU FOUND THIS.
MY MOM HELPS OUT THE JASF WITH WORK.
THEY HOLD ON TO ANNOUNCEMENTS LIKE THIS FOR SAFEKEEPING.
SO...
WHAT DO YOU THINK OF THE ARTICLE?
WHAT DO I THINK...?
DON'T YOU FEEL THE DEEP GRUDGE HE HAD?
DEEP GRUDGE? WHOSE?
ISN'T IT OBVIOUS!? SHIRAHA OKITSU'S.
WHY?
GYUUUU (PIIINCH)
YOU... REALLY ARE SO CLUELESS.
OW WOW OW WOW!
WHAT'S IN THAT HEAD OF YOURS?
THINK ABOUT IT. SHIRAHA ENDED HIS ATHLETIC CAREER WITHOUT GETTING TO HONE HIS SKILLS OR MAKE THE BEST OF HIS SURROUNDINGS.
WHAT IF THAT WERE YOU?
PI (JAB)
WELL, I'D BE FRUS-TRATED, OF COURSE...
RIGHT?
...BECAUSE OF THIS NATURAL TALENT, HE ENDED UP SACRIFICING EVERYTHING FOR DIVING.

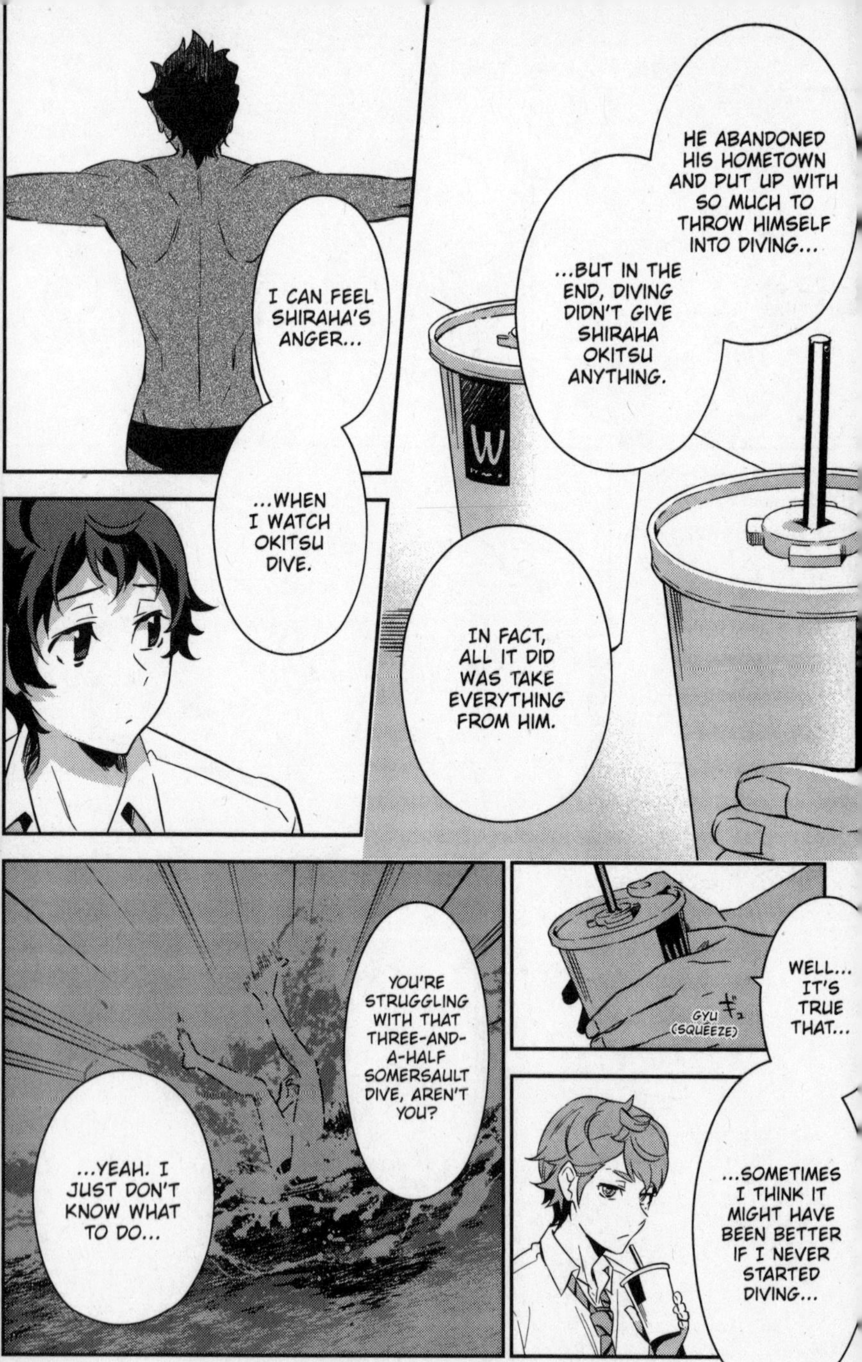
HE ABANDONED HIS HOMETOWN AND PUT UP WITH SO MUCH TO THROW HIMSELF INTO DIVING...
...BUT IN THE END, DIVING DIDN'T GIVE SHIRAHA OKITSU ANYTHING.
IN FACT, ALL IT DID WAS TAKE EVERYTHING FROM HIM.
I CAN FEEL SHIRAHA'S ANGER...
...WHEN I WATCH OKITSU DIVE.
GYU (SQUEEZE)
WELL... IT'S TRUE THAT...
...SOMETIMES I THINK IT MIGHT HAVE BEEN BETTER IF I NEVER STARTED DIVING...
YOU'RE STRUGGLING WITH THAT THREE-AND-A-HALF SOMERSAULT DIVE, AREN'T YOU?
...YEAH. I JUST DON'T KNOW WHAT TO DO...

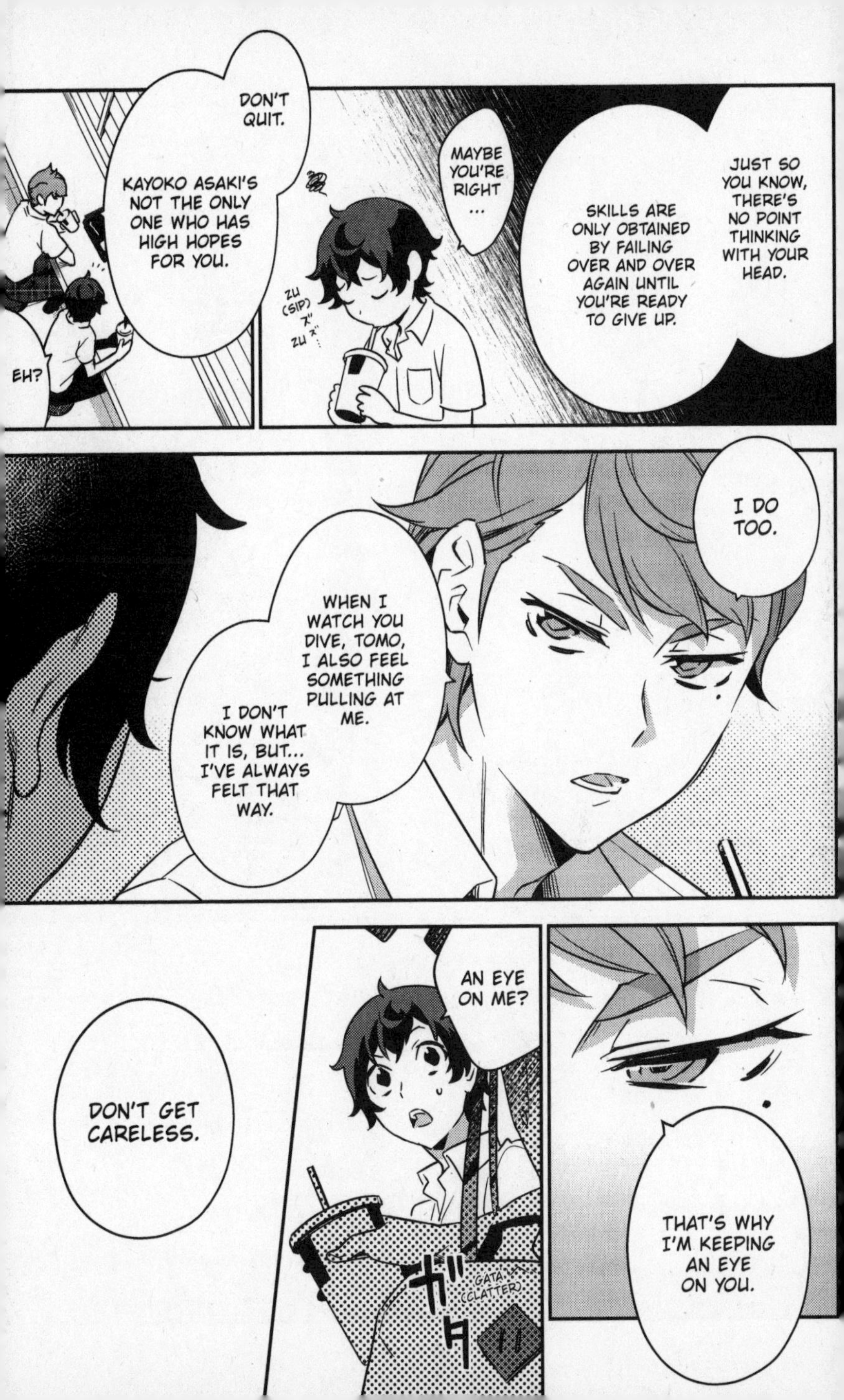
JUST SO YOU KNOW, THERE'S NO POINT THINKING WITH YOUR HEAD.
SKILLS ARE ONLY OBTAINED BY FAILING OVER AND OVER AGAIN UNTIL YOU'RE READY TO GIVE UP.
MAYBE YOU'RE RIGHT ...
ZU (SIP) ズ ZU ズ...
DON'T QUIT.
KAYOKO ASAKI'S NOT THE ONLY ONE WHO HAS HIGH HOPES FOR YOU.
EH?
I DO TOO.
WHEN I WATCH YOU DIVE, TOMO, I ALSO FEEL SOMETHING PULLING AT ME.
I DON'T KNOW WHAT IT IS, BUT... I'VE ALWAYS FELT THAT WAY.
THAT'S WHY I'M KEEPING AN EYE ON YOU.
AN EYE ON ME?
ガタ (GATA) (CLATTER)
DON'T GET CARELESS.

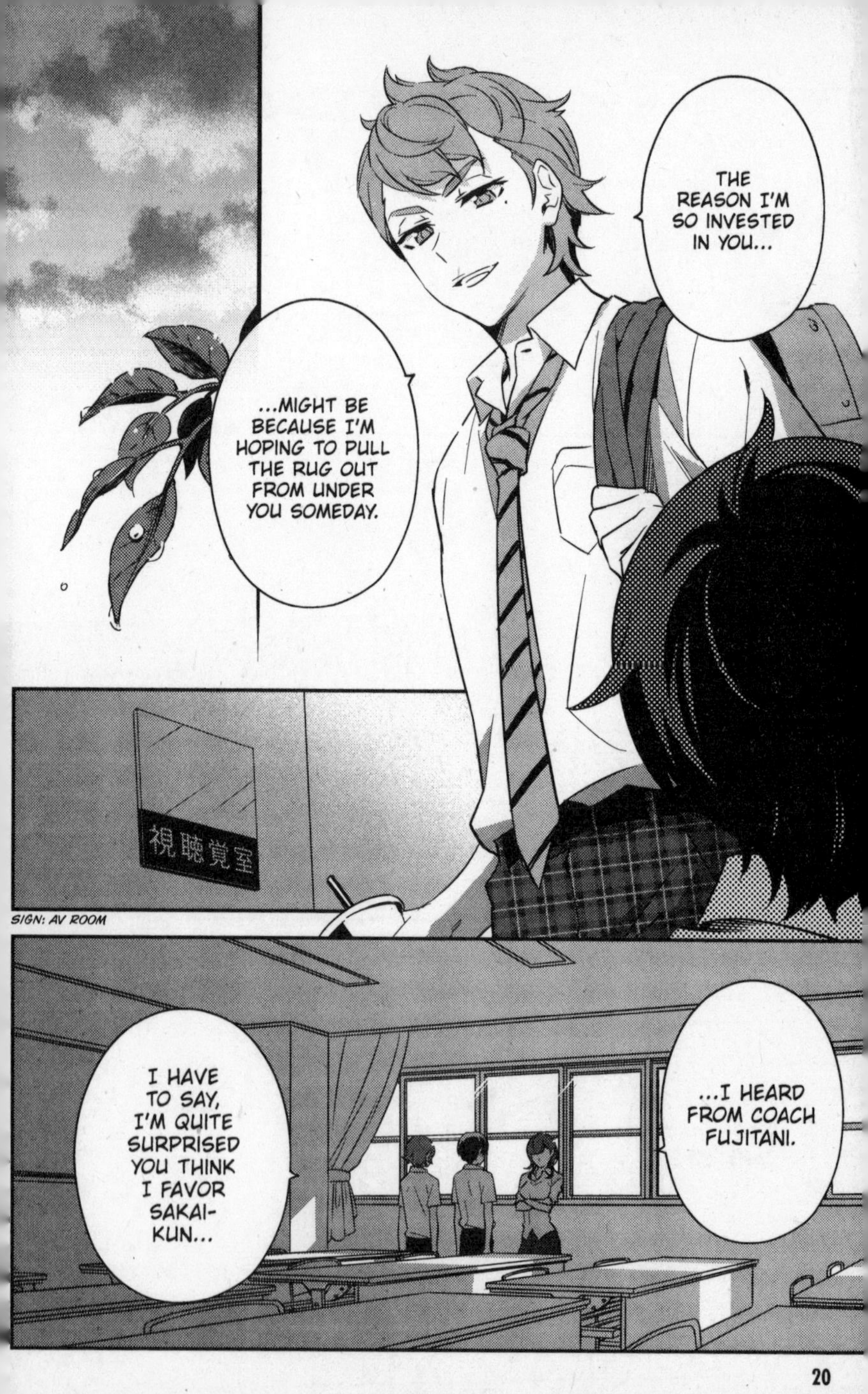
THE REASON I'M SO INVESTED IN YOU...
...MIGHT BE BECAUSE I'M HOPING TO PULL THE RUG OUT FROM UNDER YOU SOMEDAY.
視聴覚室
SIGN: AV ROOM
...I HEARD FROM COACH FUJITANI.
I HAVE TO SAY, I'M QUITE SURPRISED YOU THINK I FAVOR SAKAI-KUN...

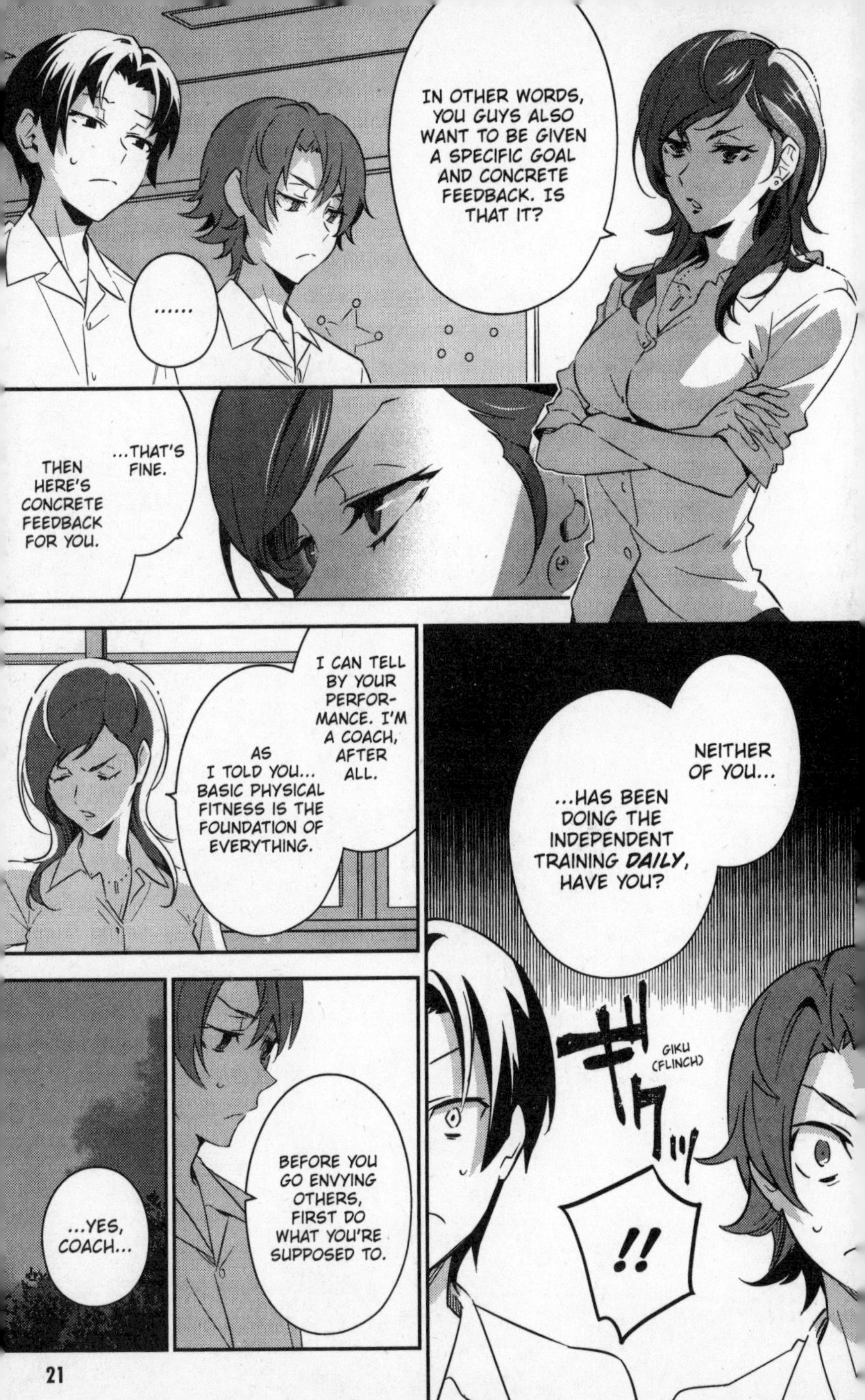
IN OTHER WORDS, YOU GUYS ALSO WANT TO BE GIVEN A SPECIFIC GOAL AND CONCRETE FEEDBACK. IS THAT IT?
......
...THAT'S FINE.
THEN HERE'S CONCRETE FEEDBACK FOR YOU.
NEITHER OF YOU...
...HAS BEEN DOING THE INDEPENDENT TRAINING ***DAILY***, HAVE YOU?
GIKU (FLINCH)
!!
I CAN TELL BY YOUR PERFORMANCE. I'M A COACH, AFTER ALL.
AS I TOLD YOU... BASIC PHYSICAL FITNESS IS THE FOUNDATION OF EVERYTHING.
BEFORE YOU GO ENVYING OTHERS, FIRST DO WHAT YOU'RE SUPPOSED TO.
...YES, COACH...

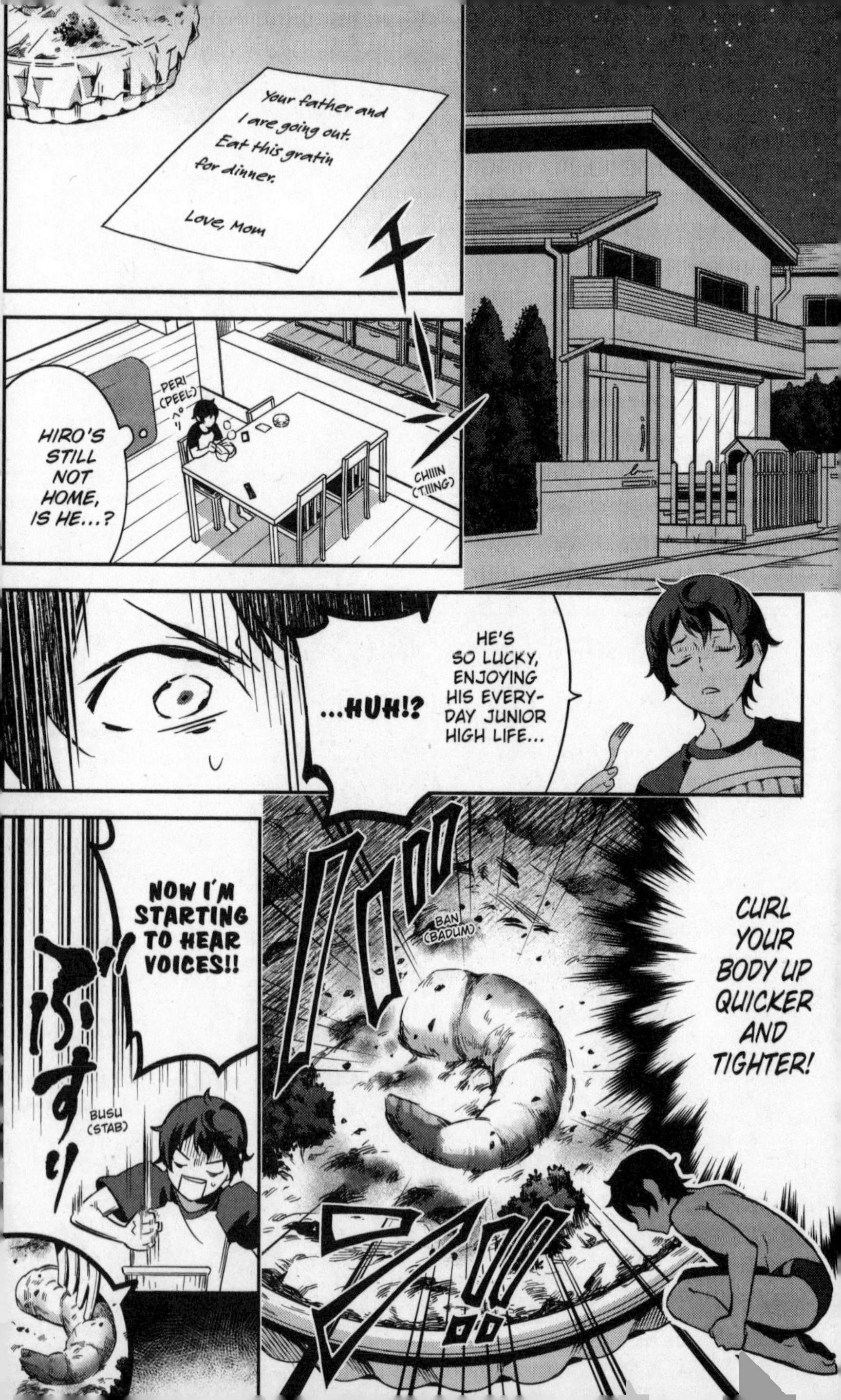
Your father and
I are going out.
Eat this gratin
for dinner.
Love, Mom
PERI
(PEEL)
CHIIIN
(TIIING)
HIRO'S STILL NOT HOME, IS HE...?
HE'S SO LUCKY, ENJOYING HIS EVERY-DAY JUNIOR HIGH LIFE...
...HUH!?
CURL YOUR BODY UP QUICKER AND TIGHTER!
BAN
(BADUM)
NOW I'M STARTING TO HEAR VOICES!!
BUSU
(STAB)

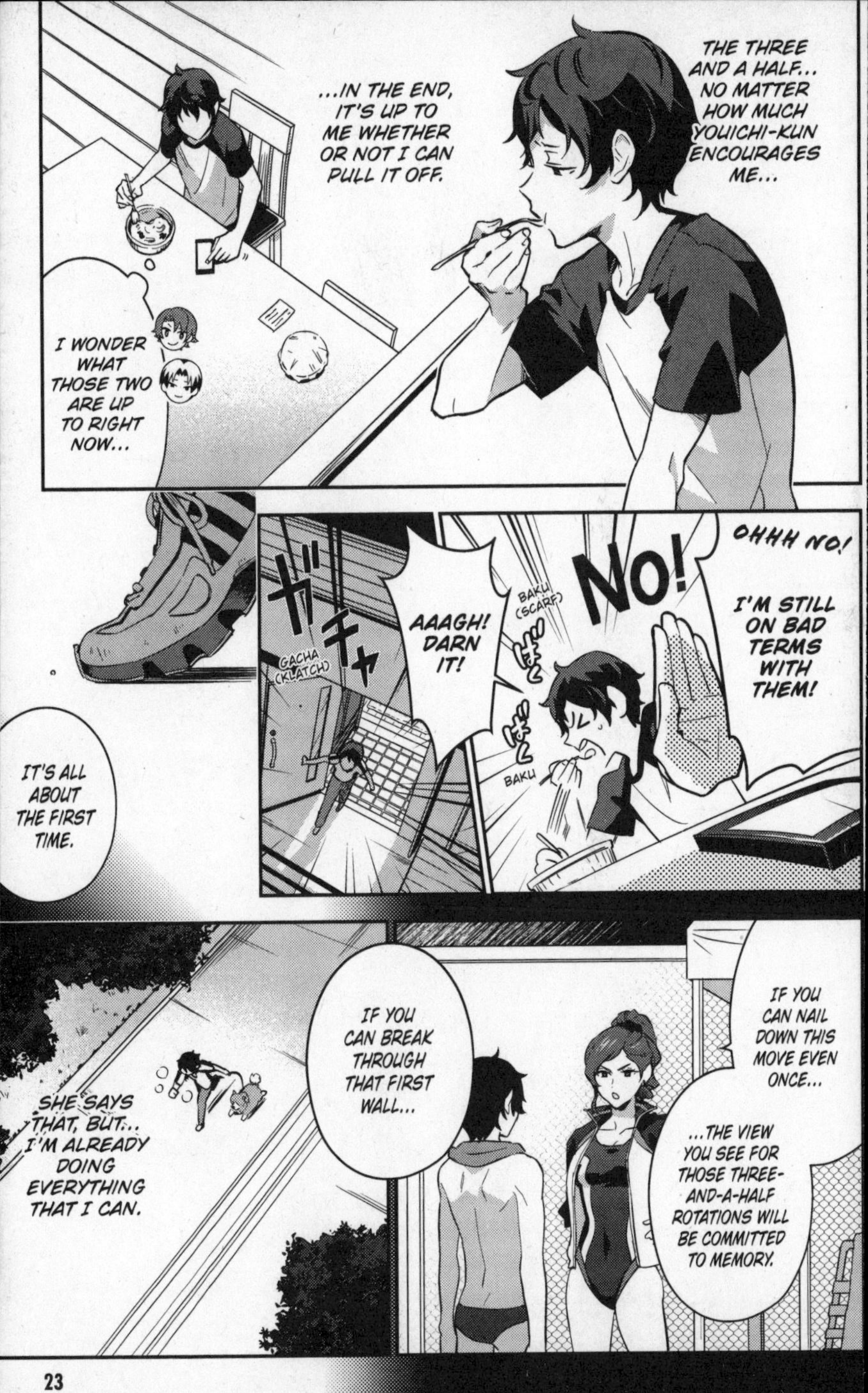
THE THREE AND A HALF... NO MATTER HOW MUCH YOUICHI-KUN ENCOURAGES ME...
...IN THE END, IT'S UP TO ME WHETHER OR NOT I CAN PULL IT OFF.
I WONDER WHAT THOSE TWO ARE UP TO RIGHT NOW...
OHHH NO!
NO!
I'M STILL ON BAD TERMS WITH THEM!
BAKU (SCARF)
BAKU
AAAGH! DARN IT!
GACHA (KLATCH)
IT'S ALL ABOUT THE FIRST TIME.
IF YOU CAN NAIL DOWN THIS MOVE EVEN ONCE...
...THE VIEW YOU SEE FOR THOSE THREE-AND-A-HALF ROTATIONS WILL BE COMMITTED TO MEMORY.
IF YOU CAN BREAK THROUGH THAT FIRST WALL...
SHE SAYS THAT, BUT... I'M ALREADY DOING EVERYTHING THAT I CAN.

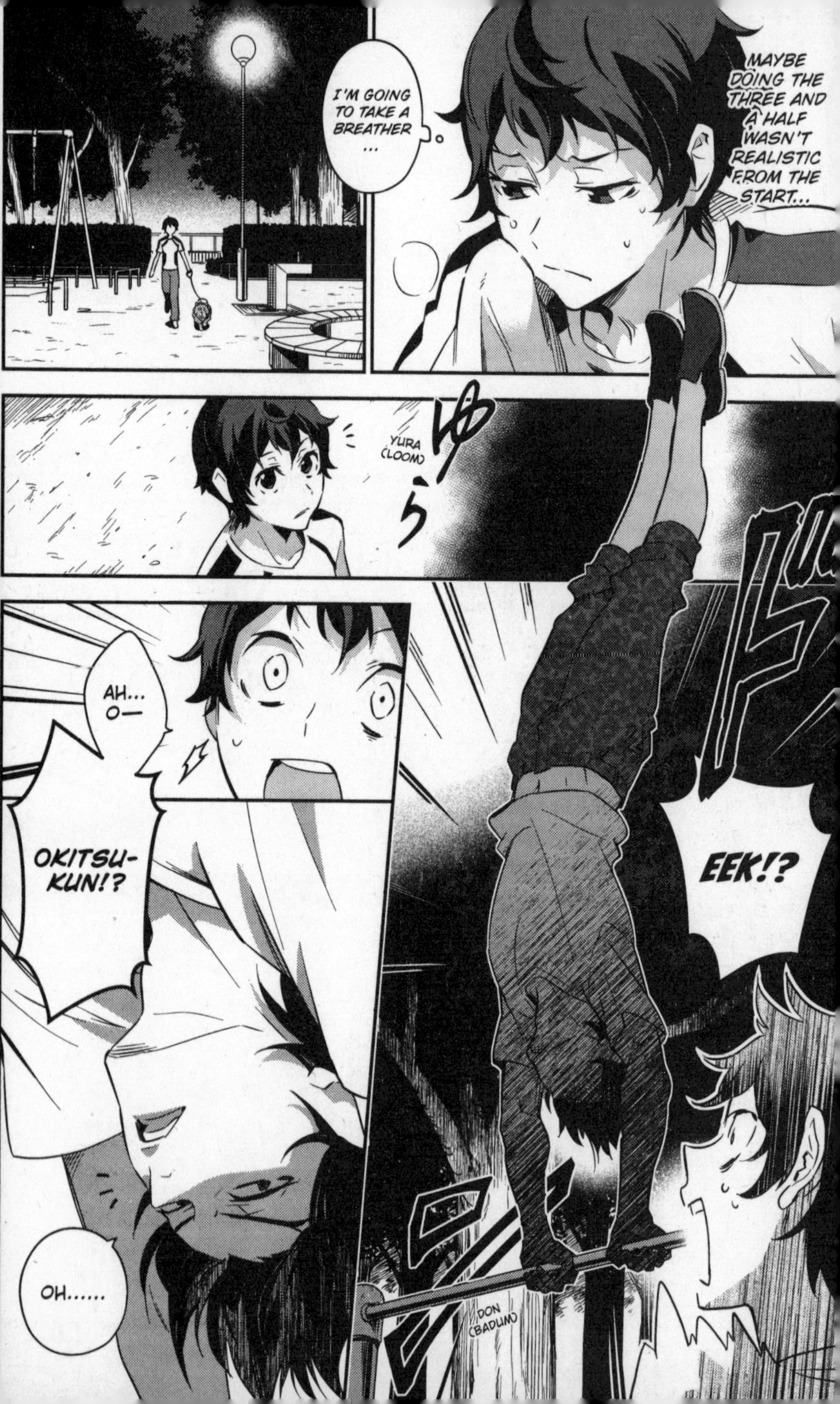
MAYBE DOING THE THREE AND A HALF WASN'T REALISTIC FROM THE START...
I'M GOING TO TAKE A BREATHER ...
ゆら
YURA (LOOM)
EEK!?
DON (BADUM)
AH... O—
OKITSU-KUN!?
OH......

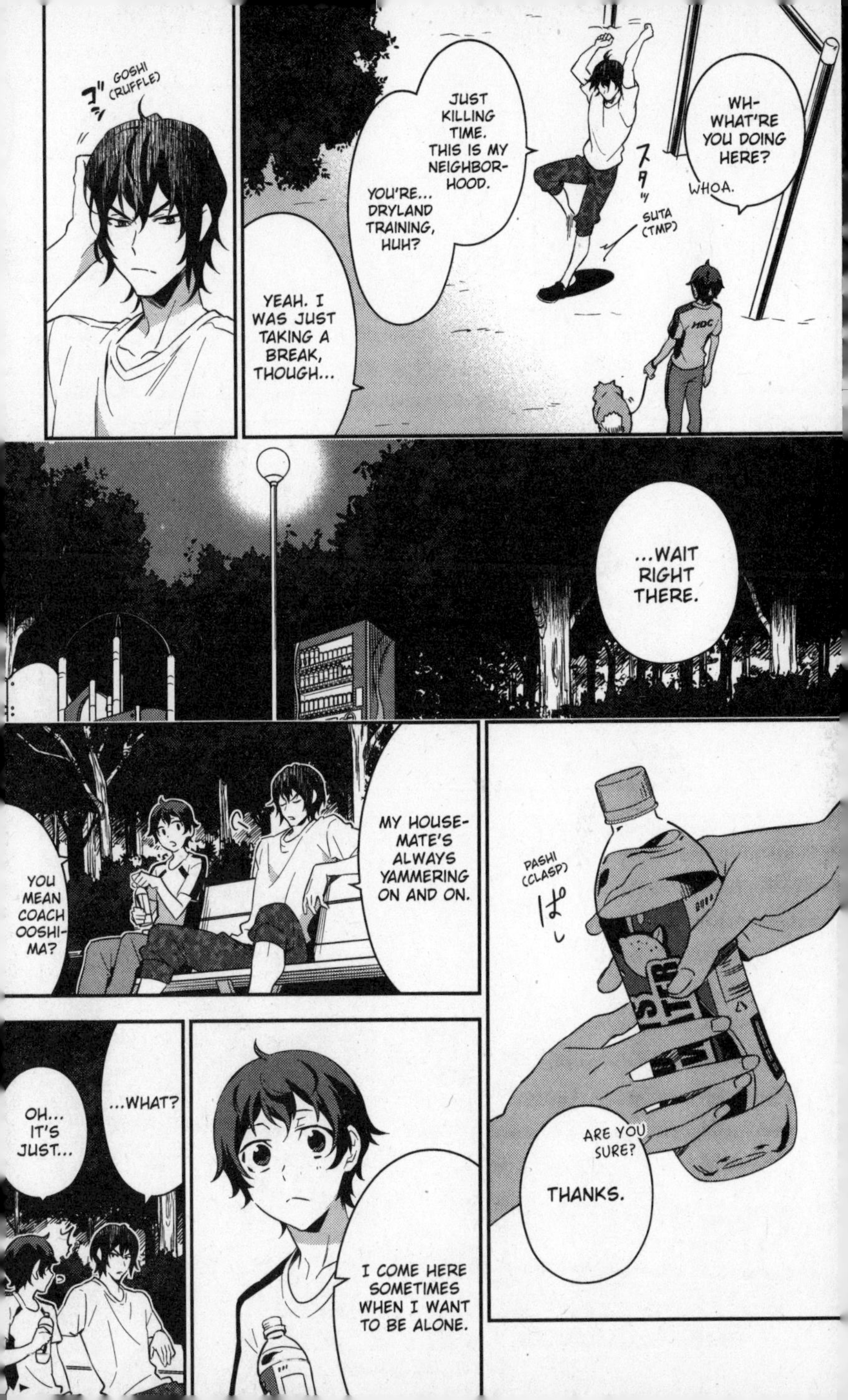
WH- WHAT'RE YOU DOING HERE?
WHOA.
SUTA (TMP)
JUST KILLING TIME. THIS IS MY NEIGHBOR-HOOD.
YOU'RE... DRYLAND TRAINING, HUH?
YEAH. I WAS JUST TAKING A BREAK, THOUGH...
GOSHI (RUFFLE)
...WAIT RIGHT THERE.
PASHI (CLASP)
ぱし
ARE YOU SURE?
THANKS.
MY HOUSE-MATE'S ALWAYS YAMMERING ON AND ON.
YOU MEAN COACH OOSHI-MA?
I COME HERE SOMETIMES WHEN I WANT TO BE ALONE.
...WHAT?
OH... IT'S JUST...

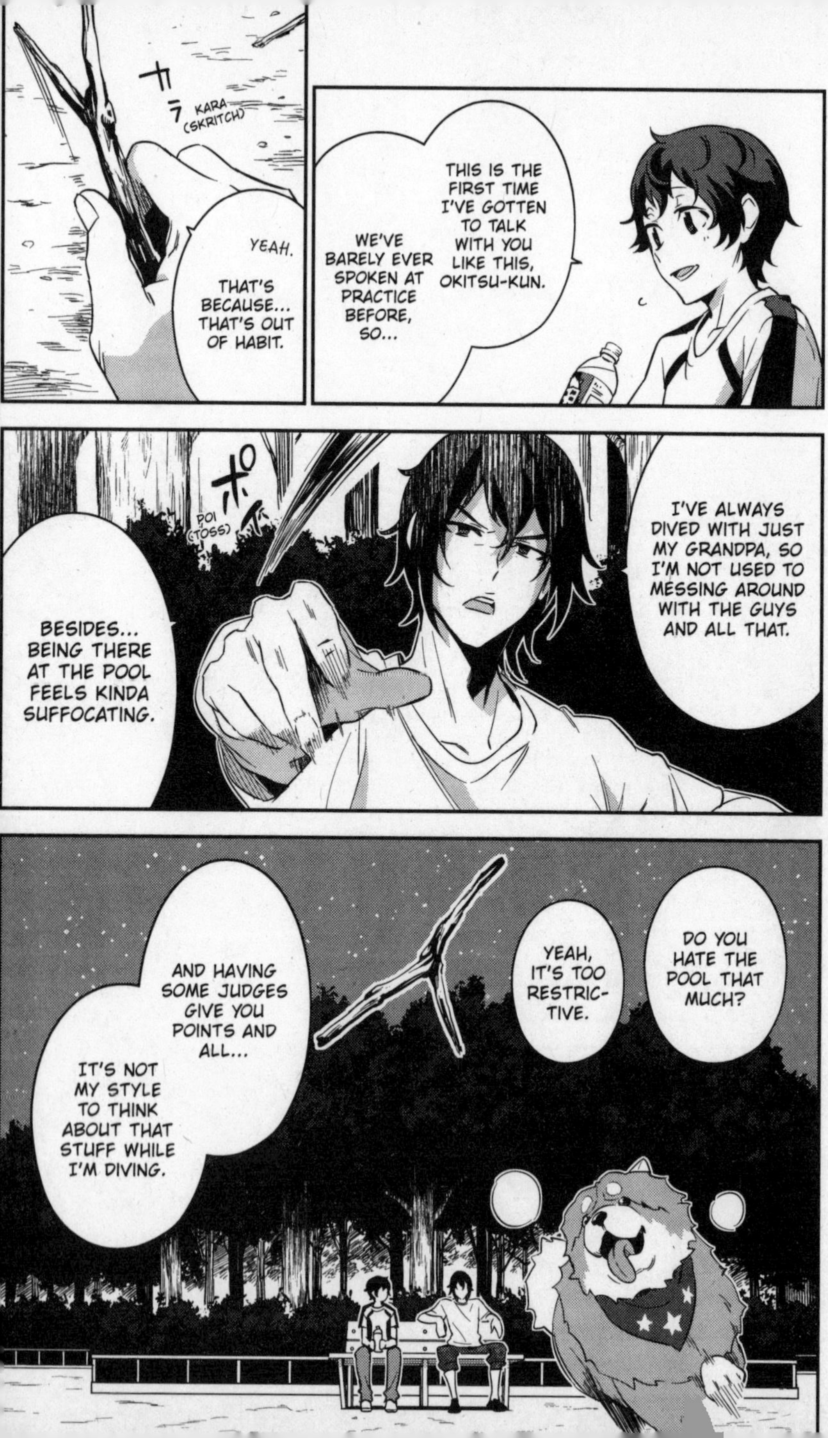
THIS IS THE FIRST TIME I'VE GOTTEN TO TALK WITH YOU LIKE THIS, OKITSU-KUN.
WE'VE BARELY EVER SPOKEN AT PRACTICE BEFORE, SO...
KARA (SKRITCH)
YEAH.
THAT'S BECAUSE... THAT'S OUT OF HABIT.
I'VE ALWAYS DIVED WITH JUST MY GRANDPA, SO I'M NOT USED TO MESSING AROUND WITH THE GUYS AND ALL THAT.
POI (TOSS)
BESIDES... BEING THERE AT THE POOL FEELS KINDA SUFFOCATING.
DO YOU HATE THE POOL THAT MUCH?
YEAH, IT'S TOO RESTRIC-TIVE.
AND HAVING SOME JUDGES GIVE YOU POINTS AND ALL...
IT'S NOT MY STYLE TO THINK ABOUT THAT STUFF WHILE I'M DIVING.

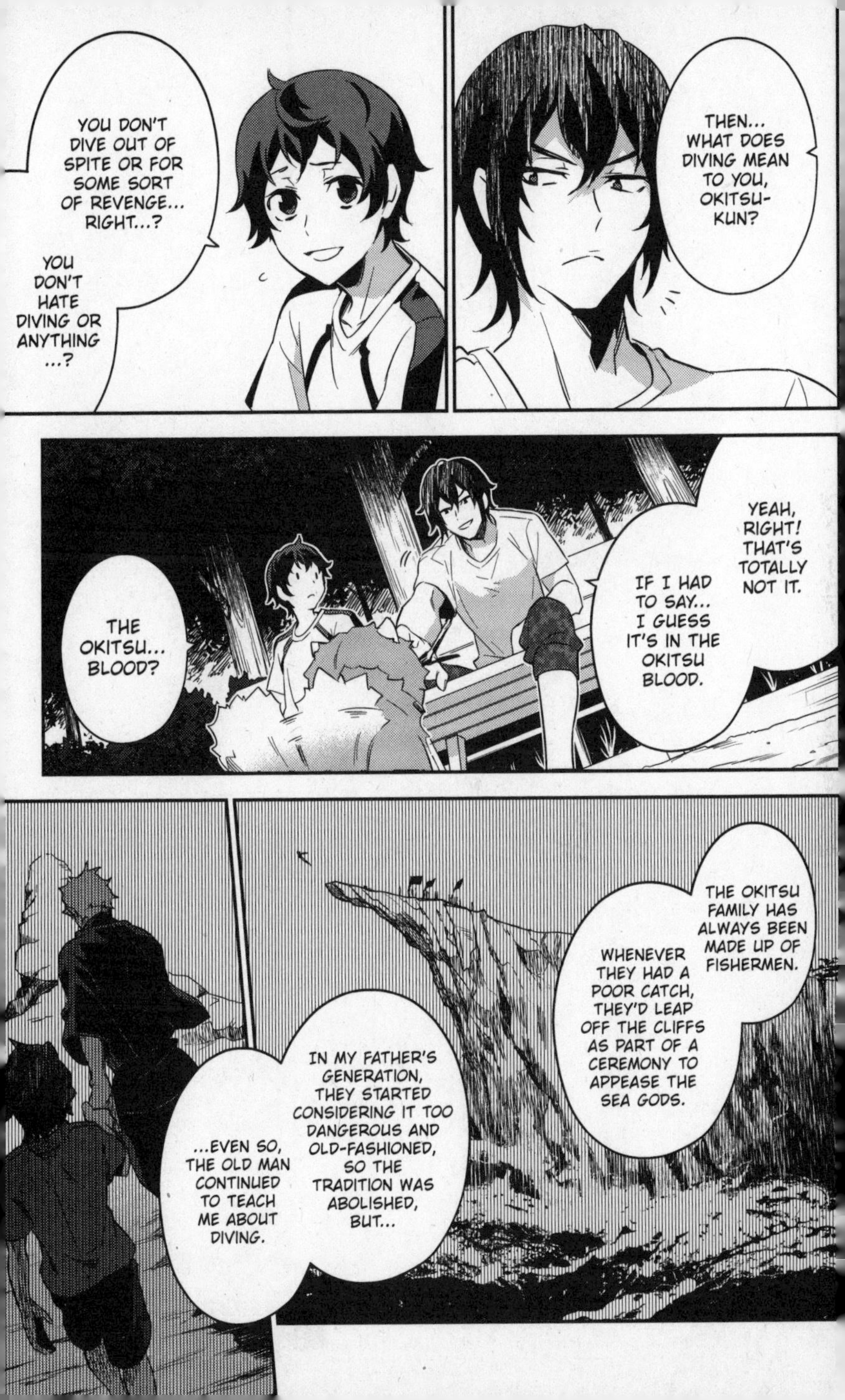
THEN... WHAT DOES DIVING MEAN TO YOU, OKITSU-KUN?
YOU DON'T DIVE OUT OF SPITE OR FOR SOME SORT OF REVENGE... RIGHT...?
YOU DON'T HATE DIVING OR ANYTHING ...?
YEAH, RIGHT! THAT'S TOTALLY NOT IT.
IF I HAD TO SAY... I GUESS IT'S IN THE OKITSU BLOOD.
THE OKITSU... BLOOD?
THE OKITSU FAMILY HAS ALWAYS BEEN MADE UP OF FISHERMEN.
WHENEVER THEY HAD A POOR CATCH, THEY'D LEAP OFF THE CLIFFS AS PART OF A CEREMONY TO APPEASE THE SEA GODS.
IN MY FATHER'S GENERATION, THEY STARTED CONSIDERING IT TOO DANGEROUS AND OLD-FASHIONED, SO THE TRADITION WAS ABOLISHED, BUT...
...EVEN SO, THE OLD MAN CONTINUED TO TEACH ME ABOUT DIVING.

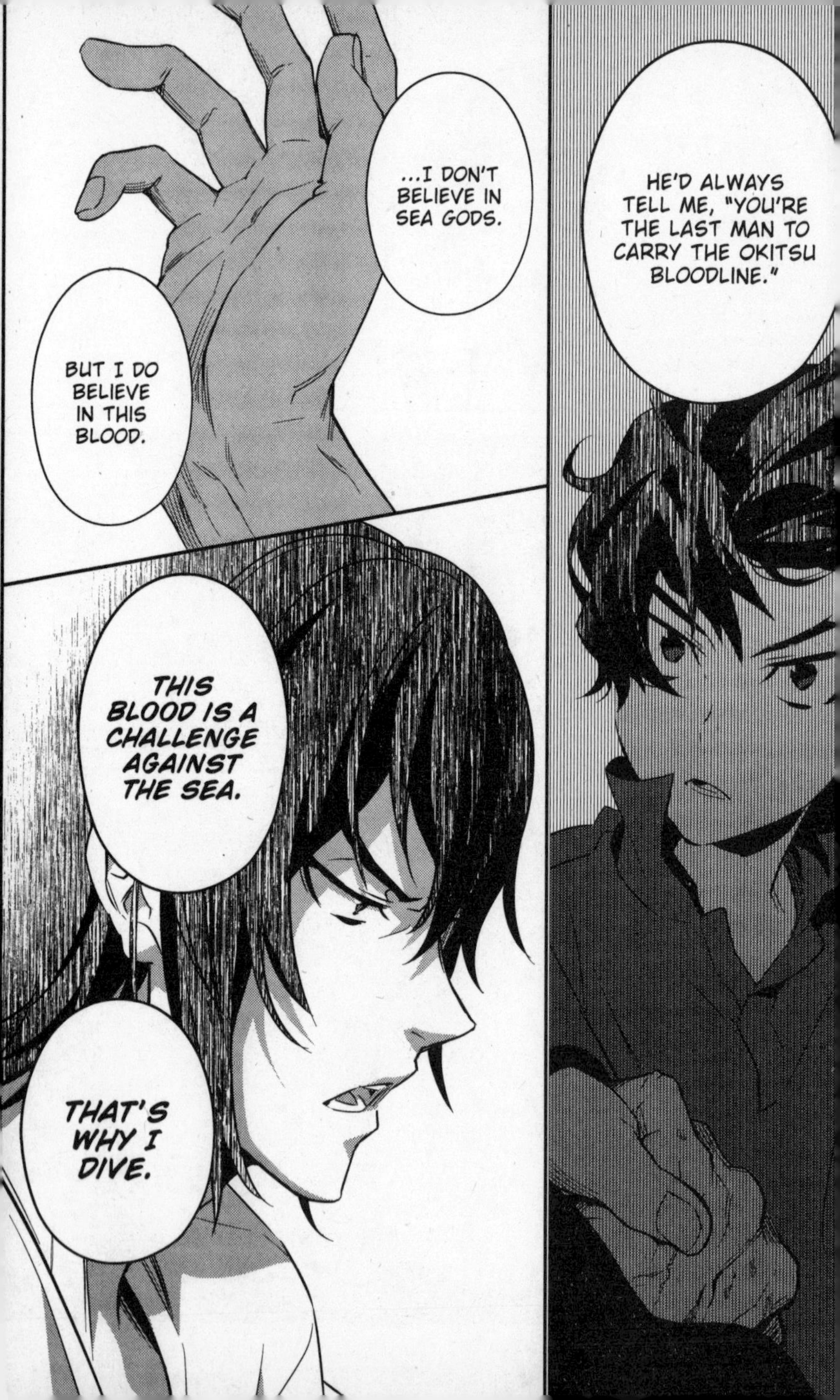
HE'D ALWAYS TELL ME, "YOU'RE THE LAST MAN TO CARRY THE OKITSU BLOODLINE."
...I DON'T BELIEVE IN SEA GODS.
BUT I DO BELIEVE IN THIS BLOOD.
THIS BLOOD IS A CHALLENGE AGAINST THE SEA.
THAT'S WHY I DIVE.

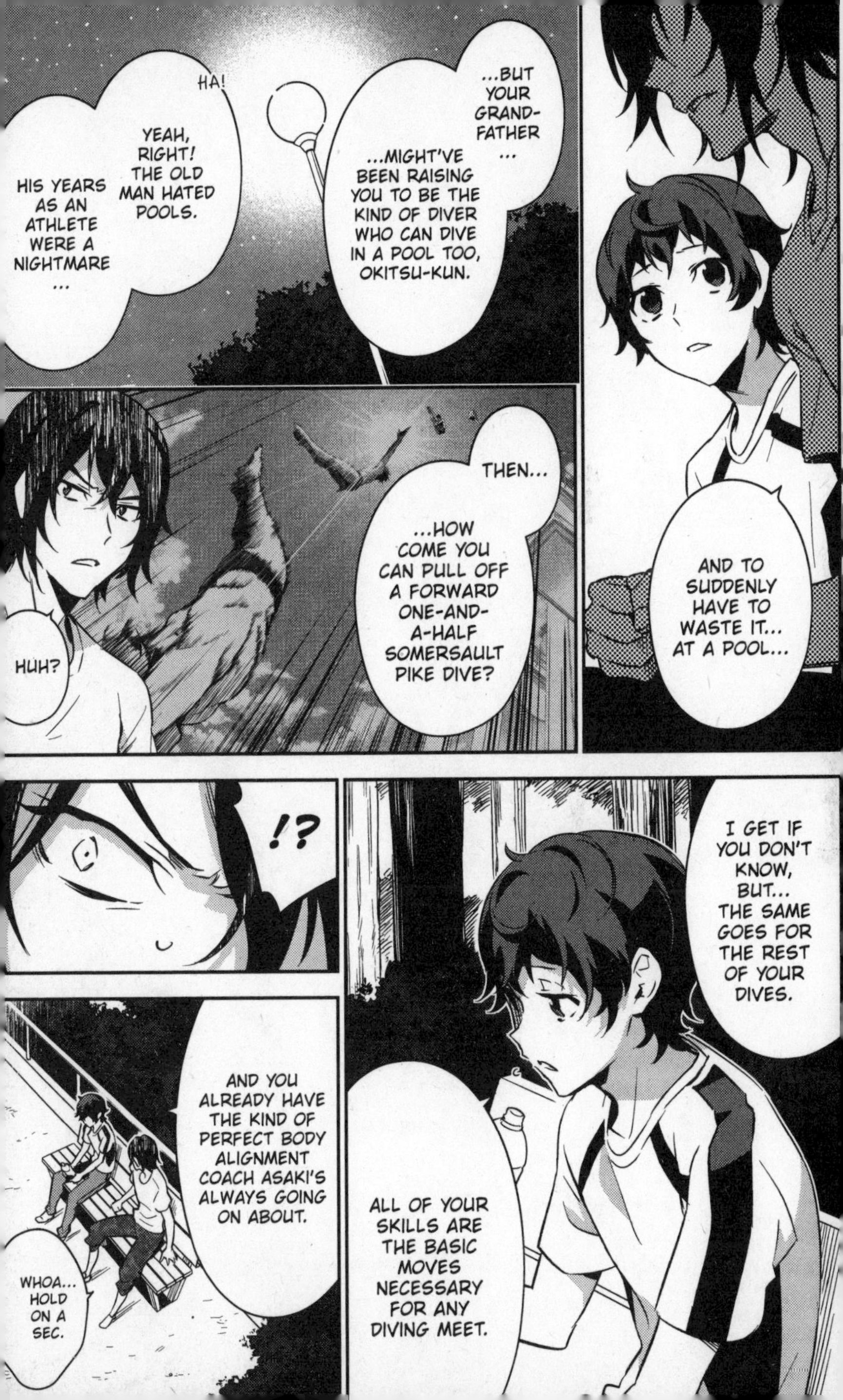
AND TO SUDDENLY HAVE TO WASTE IT... AT A POOL...
...BUT YOUR GRANDFATHER ...
...MIGHT'VE BEEN RAISING YOU TO BE THE KIND OF DIVER WHO CAN DIVE IN A POOL TOO, OKITSU-KUN.
HA!
YEAH, RIGHT! THE OLD MAN HATED POOLS.
HIS YEARS AS AN ATHLETE WERE A NIGHTMARE ...
THEN...
...HOW COME YOU CAN PULL OFF A FORWARD ONE-AND-A-HALF SOMERSAULT PIKE DIVE?
HUH?
I GET IF YOU DON'T KNOW, BUT... THE SAME GOES FOR THE REST OF YOUR DIVES.
ALL OF YOUR SKILLS ARE THE BASIC MOVES NECESSARY FOR ANY DIVING MEET.
!?
AND YOU ALREADY HAVE THE KIND OF PERFECT BODY ALIGNMENT COACH ASAKI'S ALWAYS GOING ON ABOUT.
WHOA... HOLD ON A SEC.

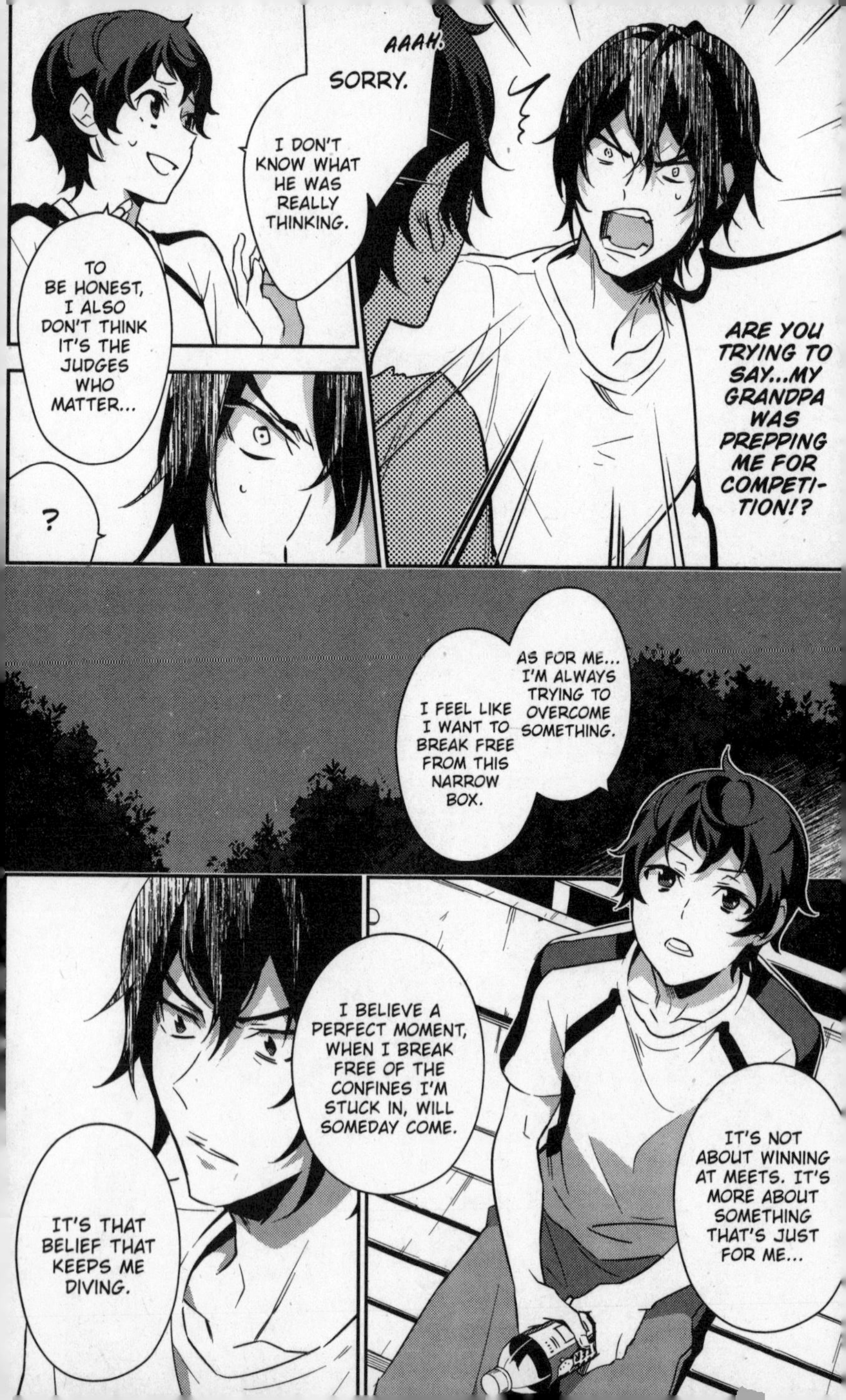
AAAH.
ARE YOU TRYING TO SAY...MY GRANDPA WAS PREPPING ME FOR COMPETITION!?
SORRY.
I DON'T KNOW WHAT HE WAS REALLY THINKING.
TO BE HONEST, I ALSO DON'T THINK IT'S THE JUDGES WHO MATTER...
?
AS FOR ME... I'M ALWAYS TRYING TO OVERCOME SOMETHING.
I FEEL LIKE I WANT TO BREAK FREE FROM THIS NARROW BOX.
IT'S NOT ABOUT WINNING AT MEETS. IT'S MORE ABOUT SOMETHING THAT'S JUST FOR ME...
I BELIEVE A PERFECT MOMENT, WHEN I BREAK FREE OF THE CONFINES I'M STUCK IN, WILL SOMEDAY COME.
IT'S THAT BELIEF THAT KEEPS ME DIVING.

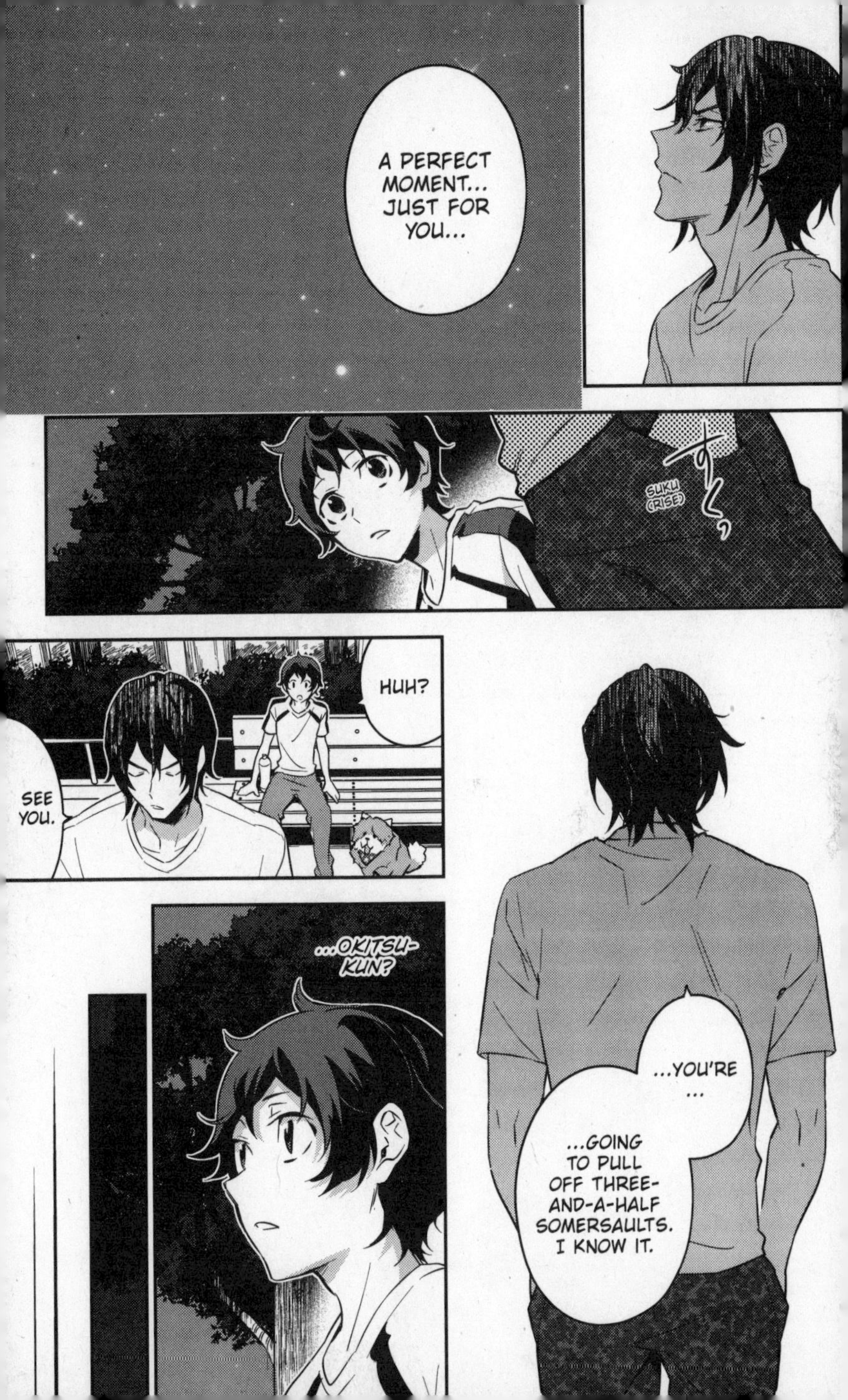
A PERFECT MOMENT... JUST FOR YOU...
SUKU (RISE)
...YOU'RE ...
...GOING TO PULL OFF THREE-AND-A-HALF SOMERSAULTS. I KNOW IT.
HUH?
SEE YOU.
...OKITSU-KUN?

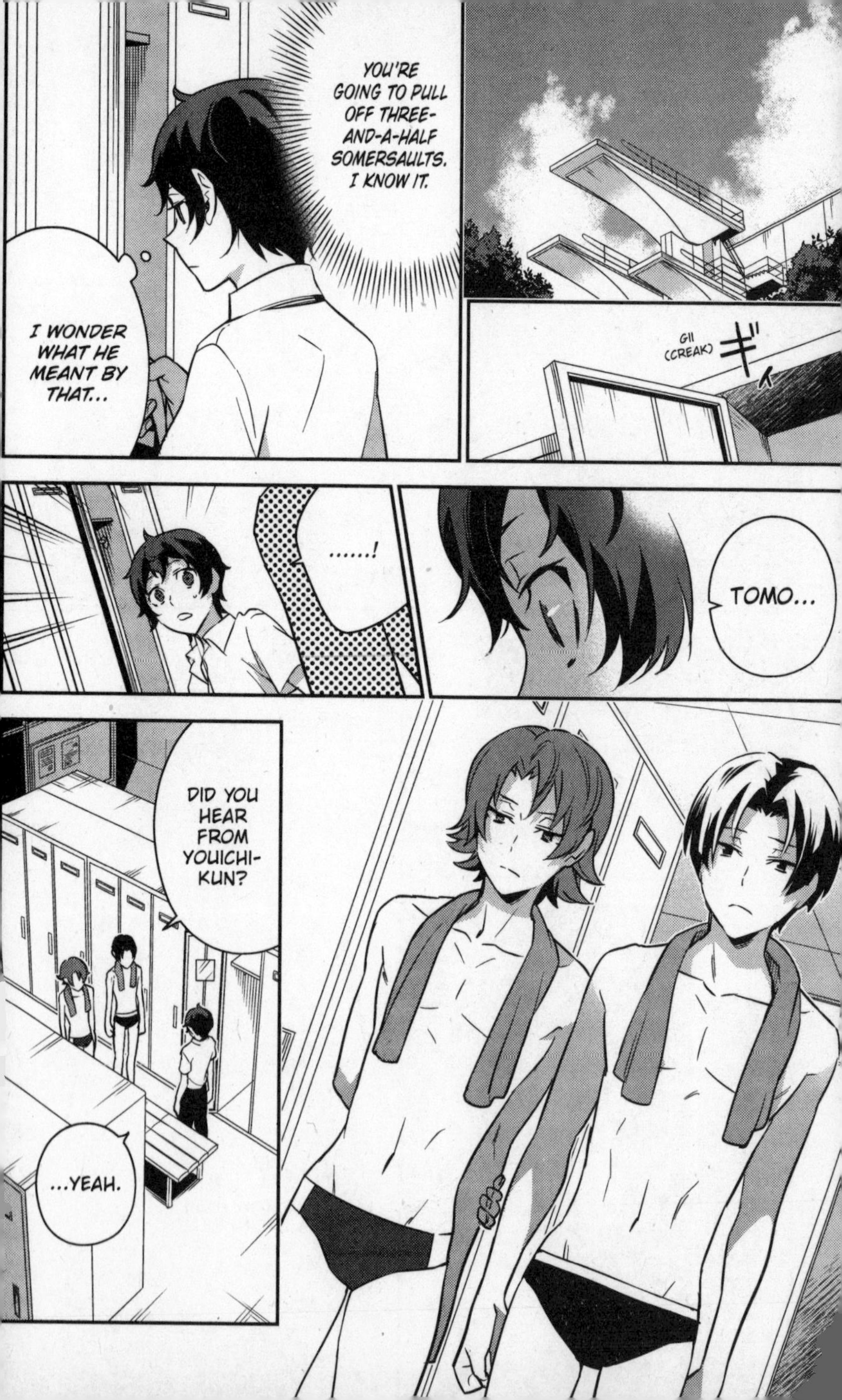
GII (CREAK)
YOU'RE GOING TO PULL OFF THREE-AND-A-HALF SOMERSAULTS. I KNOW IT.
I WONDER WHAT HE MEANT BY THAT...
TOMO...
......!
DID YOU HEAR FROM YOUICHI-KUN?
...YEAH.

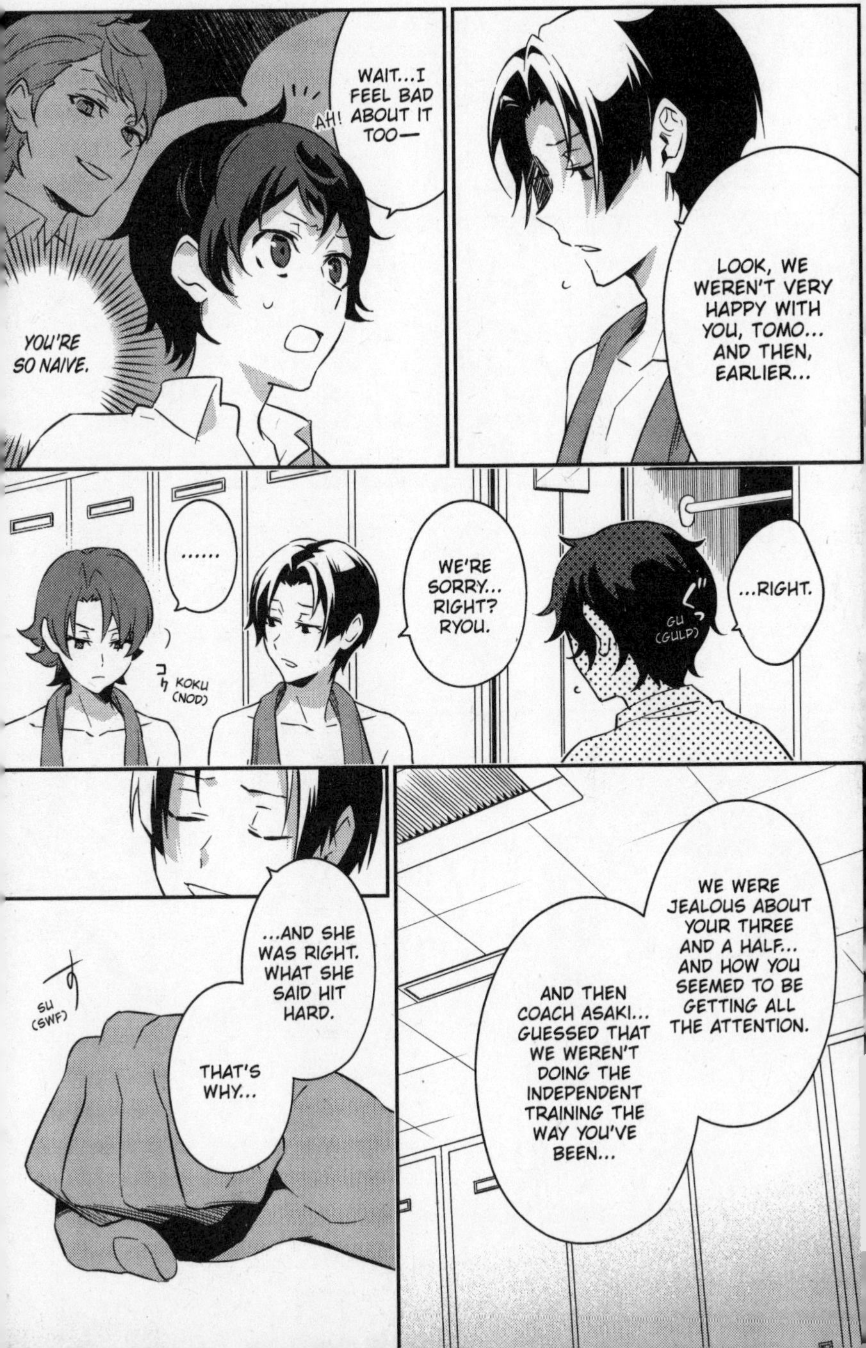
LOOK, WE WEREN'T VERY HAPPY WITH YOU, TOMO... AND THEN, EARLIER...
AH!
WAIT...I FEEL BAD ABOUT IT TOO—
YOU'RE SO NAIVE.
...RIGHT.
GU (GULP)
WE'RE SORRY... RIGHT? RYOU.
KOKU (NOD)
......
WE WERE JEALOUS ABOUT YOUR THREE AND A HALF... AND HOW YOU SEEMED TO BE GETTING ALL THE ATTENTION.
AND THEN COACH ASAKI... GUESSED THAT WE WEREN'T DOING THE INDEPENDENT TRAINING THE WAY YOU'VE BEEN...
...AND SHE WAS RIGHT. WHAT SHE SAID HIT HARD.
SU (SWF)
THAT'S WHY...

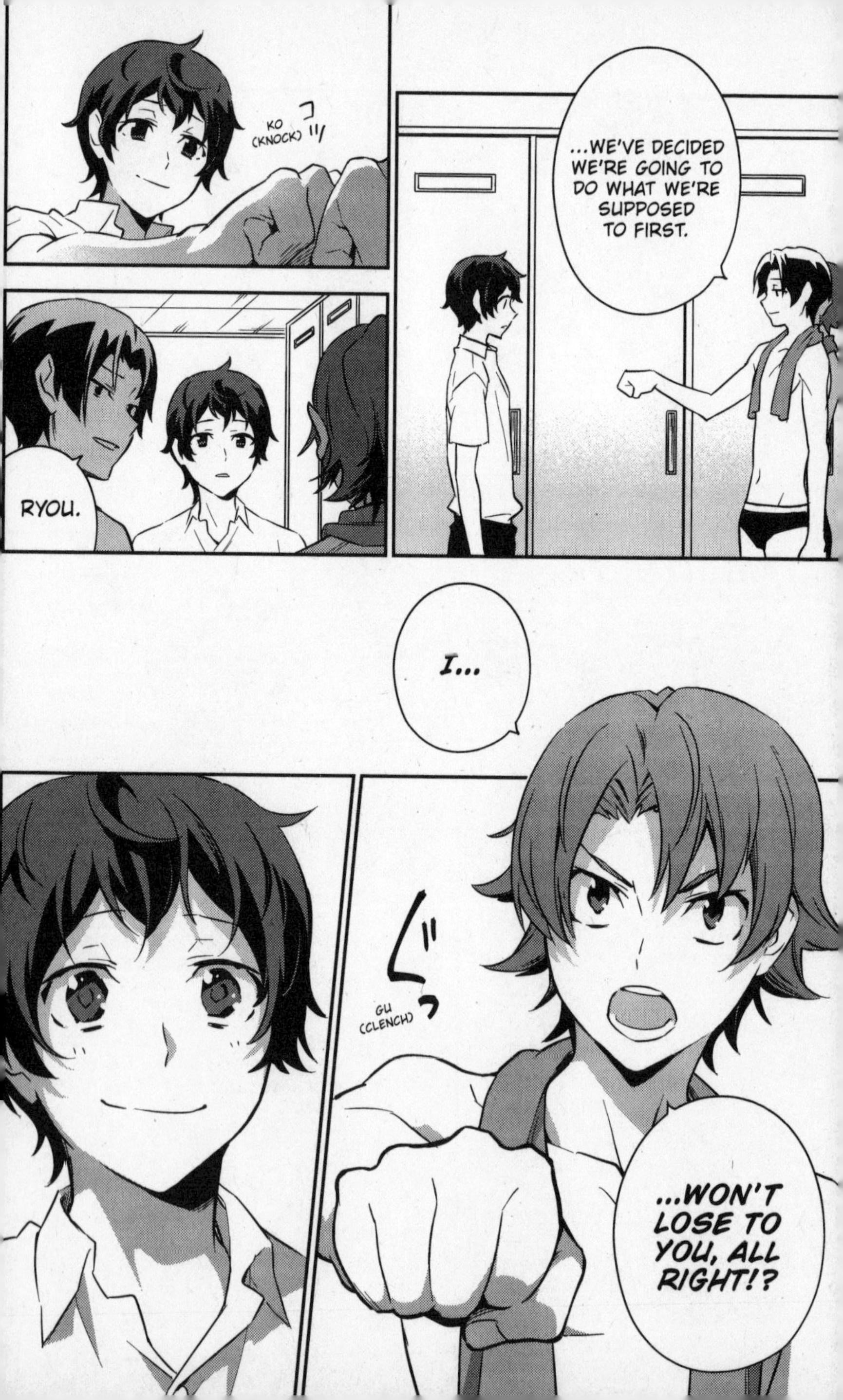
...WE'VE DECIDED WE'RE GOING TO DO WHAT WE'RE SUPPOSED TO FIRST.
KO (KNOCK)
RYOU.
I...
...WON'T LOSE TO YOU, ALL RIGHT!?
GU (CLENCH)

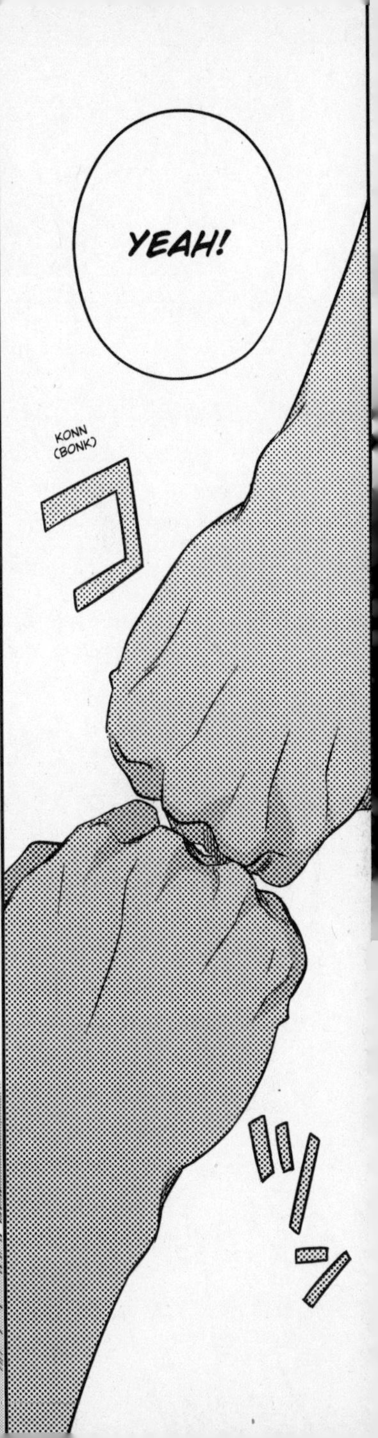
YEAH!
KONN (BONK)
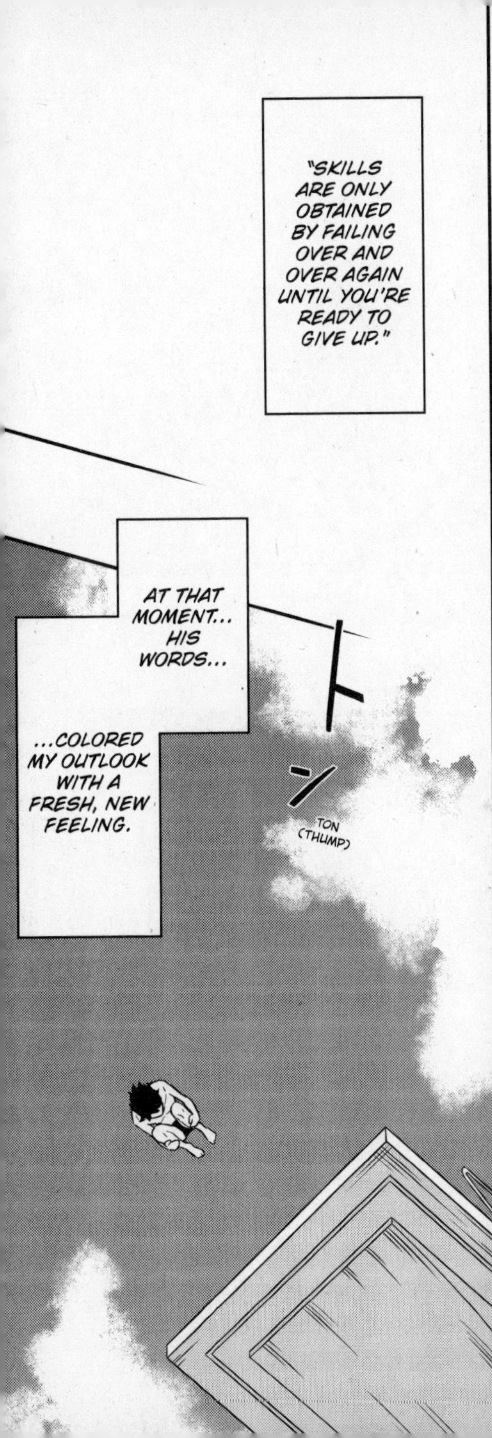
"SKILLS ARE ONLY OBTAINED BY FAILING OVER AND OVER AGAIN UNTIL YOU'RE READY TO GIVE UP."
AT THAT MOMENT... HIS WORDS...
...COLORED MY OUTLOOK WITH A FRESH, NEW FEELING.
TON (THUMP)

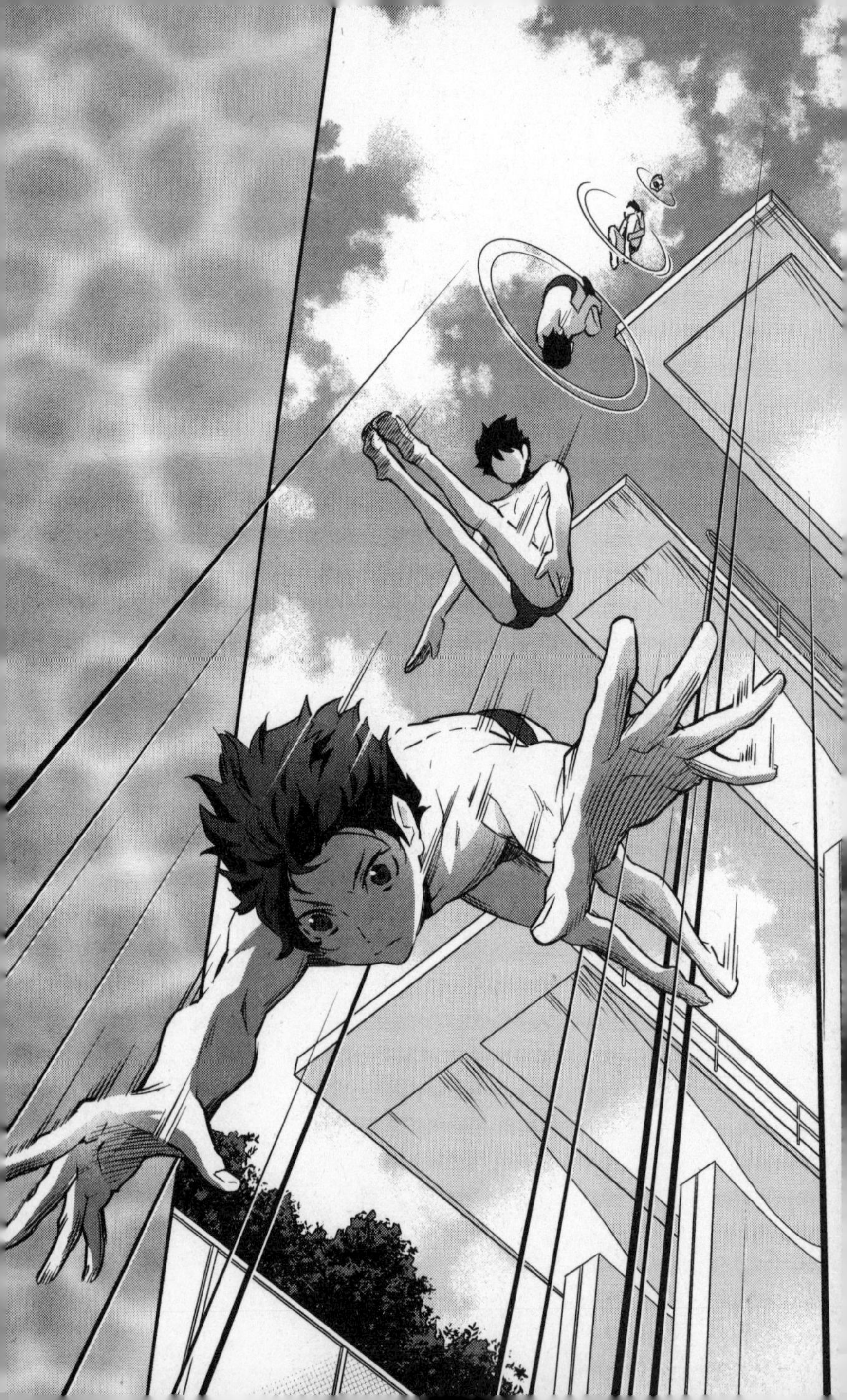

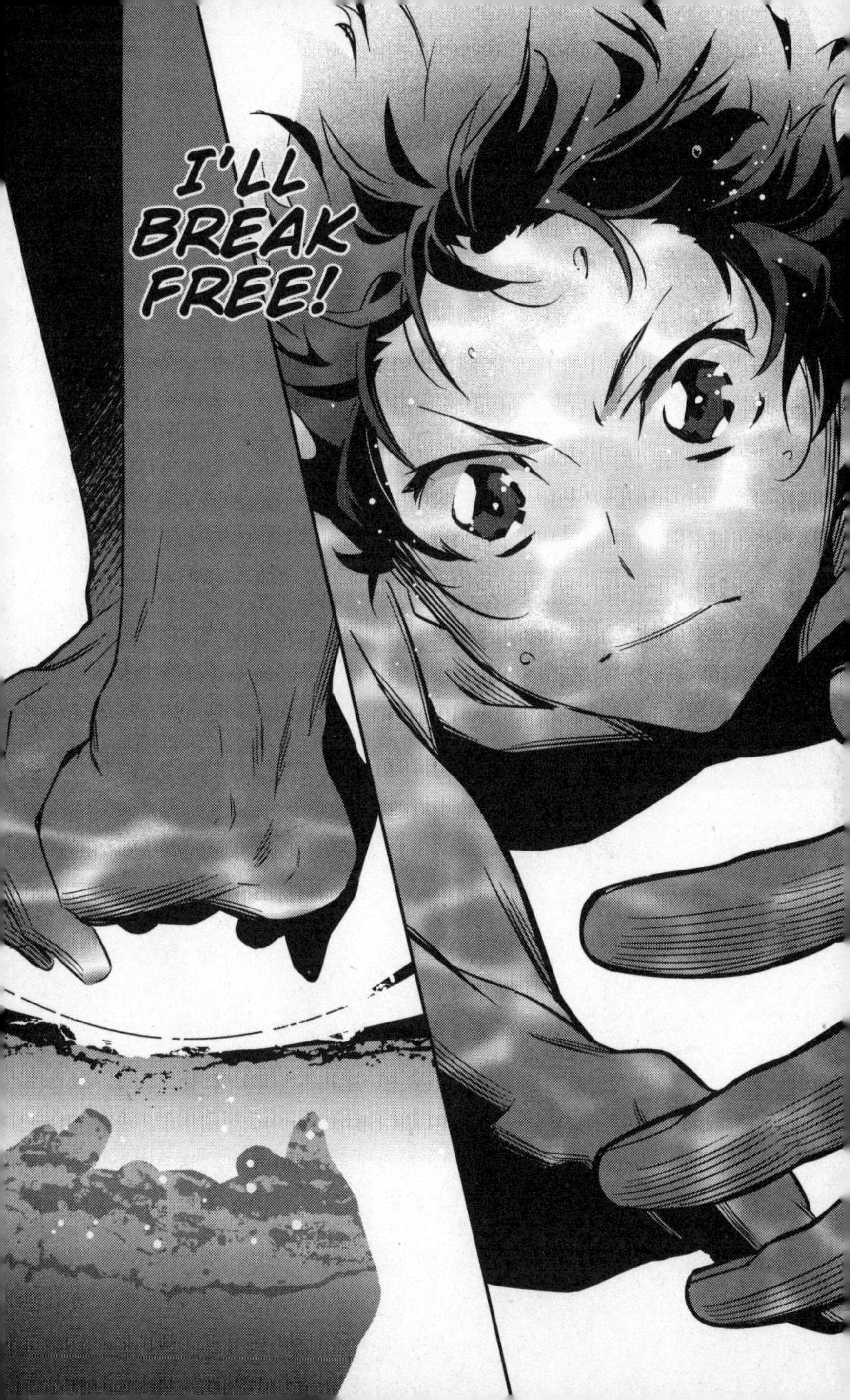
I'LL BREAK FREE!

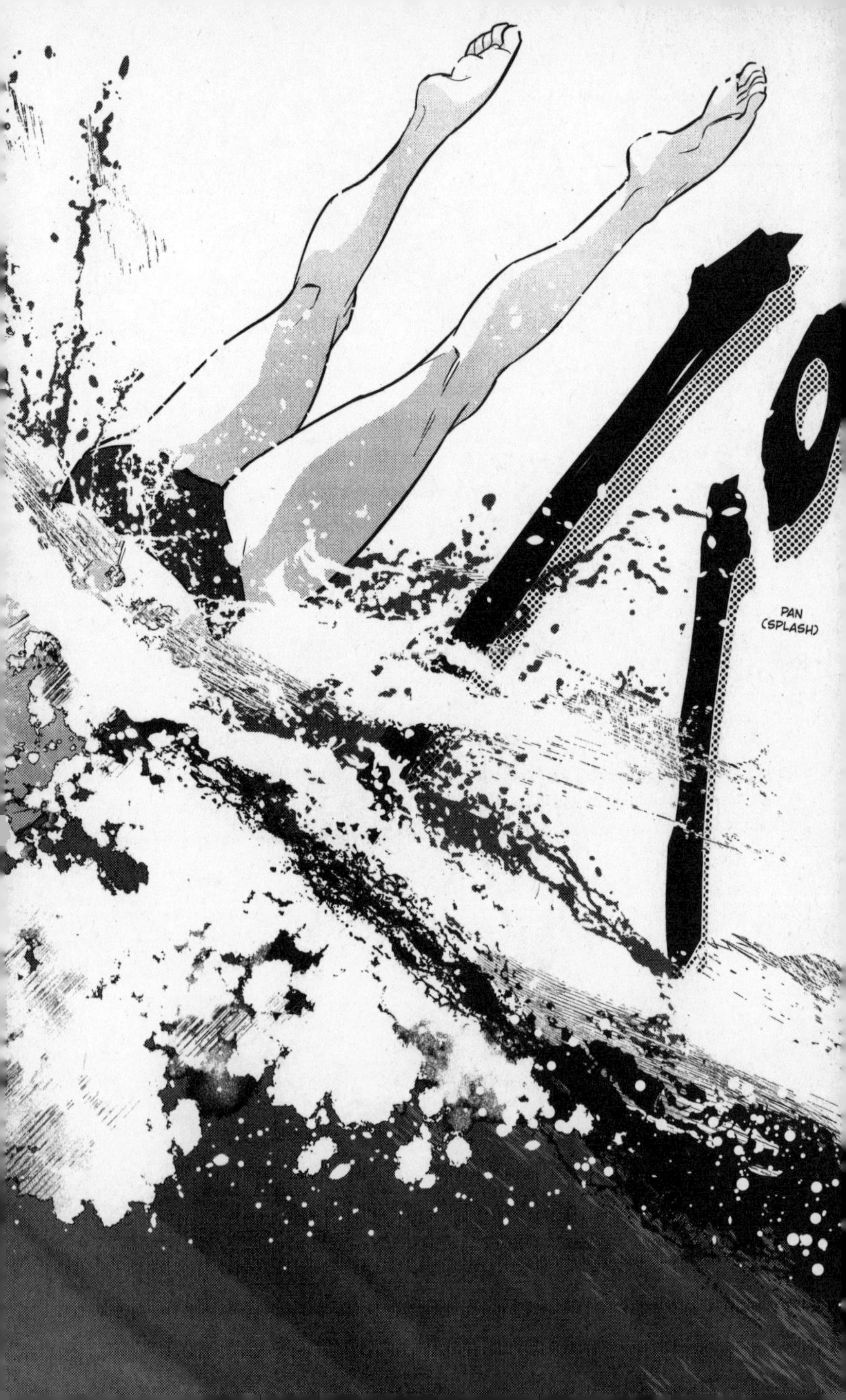
PAN
(SPLASH)

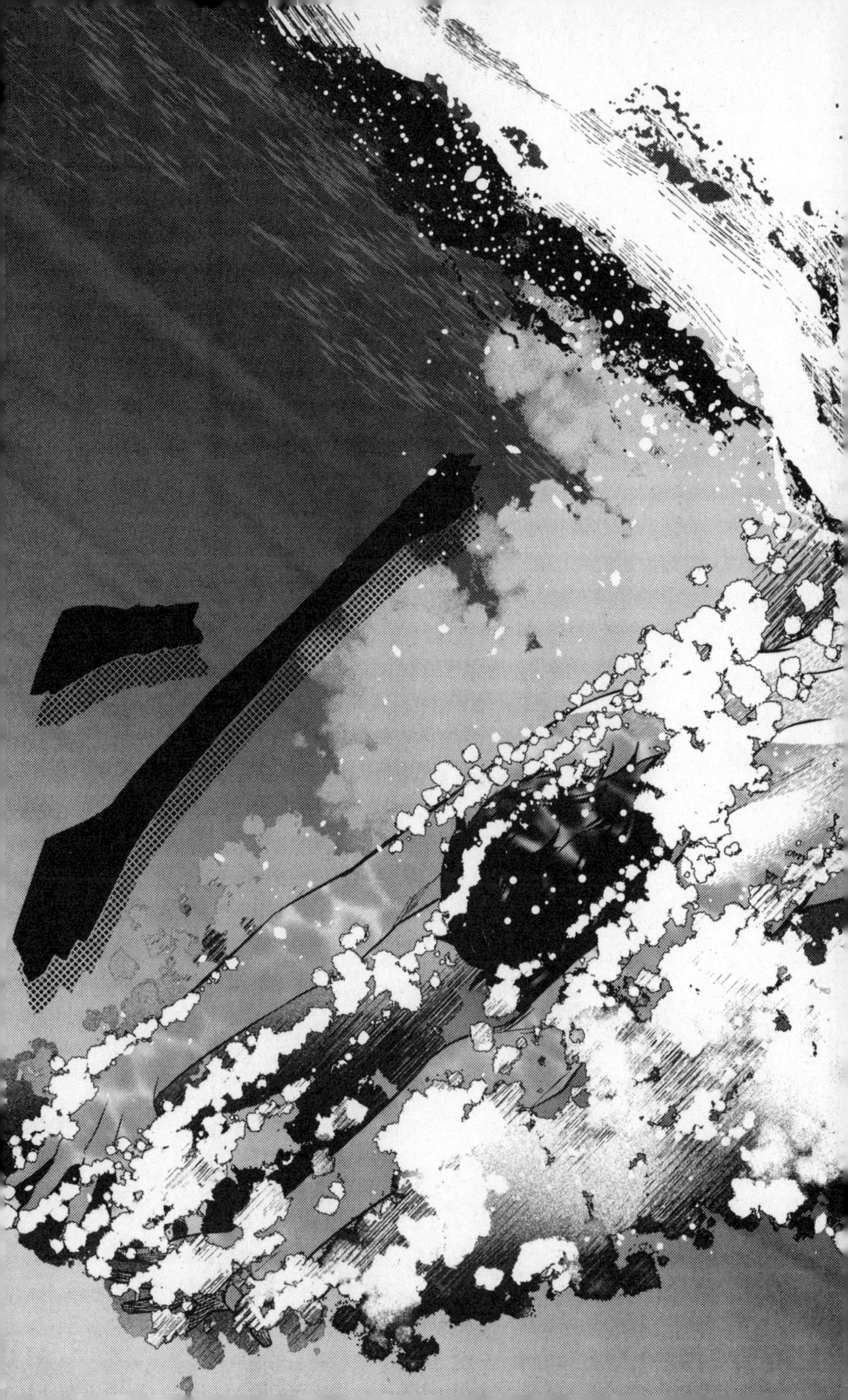

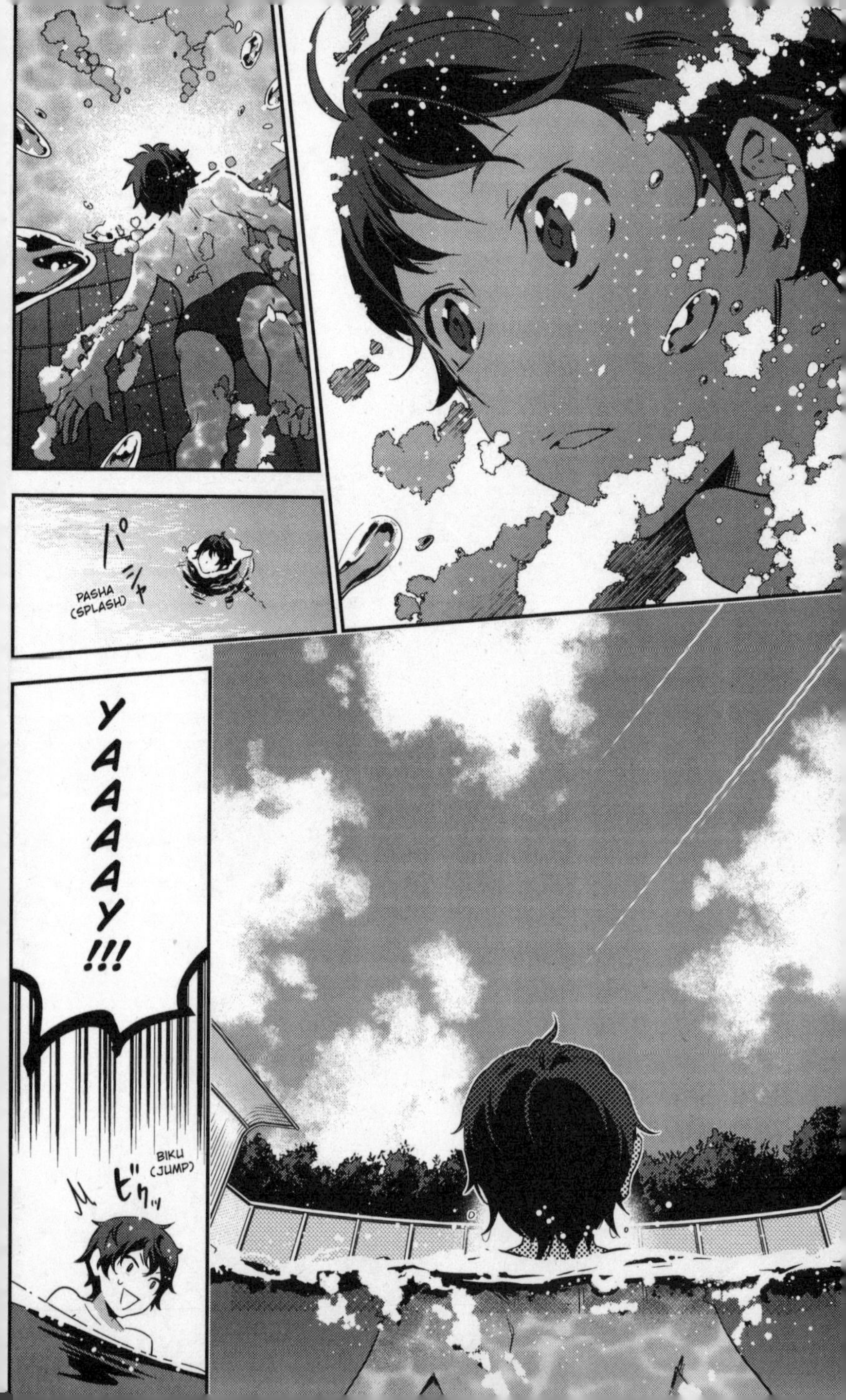
パシャ
PASHA (SPLASH)
YAAAAAY!!!
ビクッ
BIKU (JUMP)

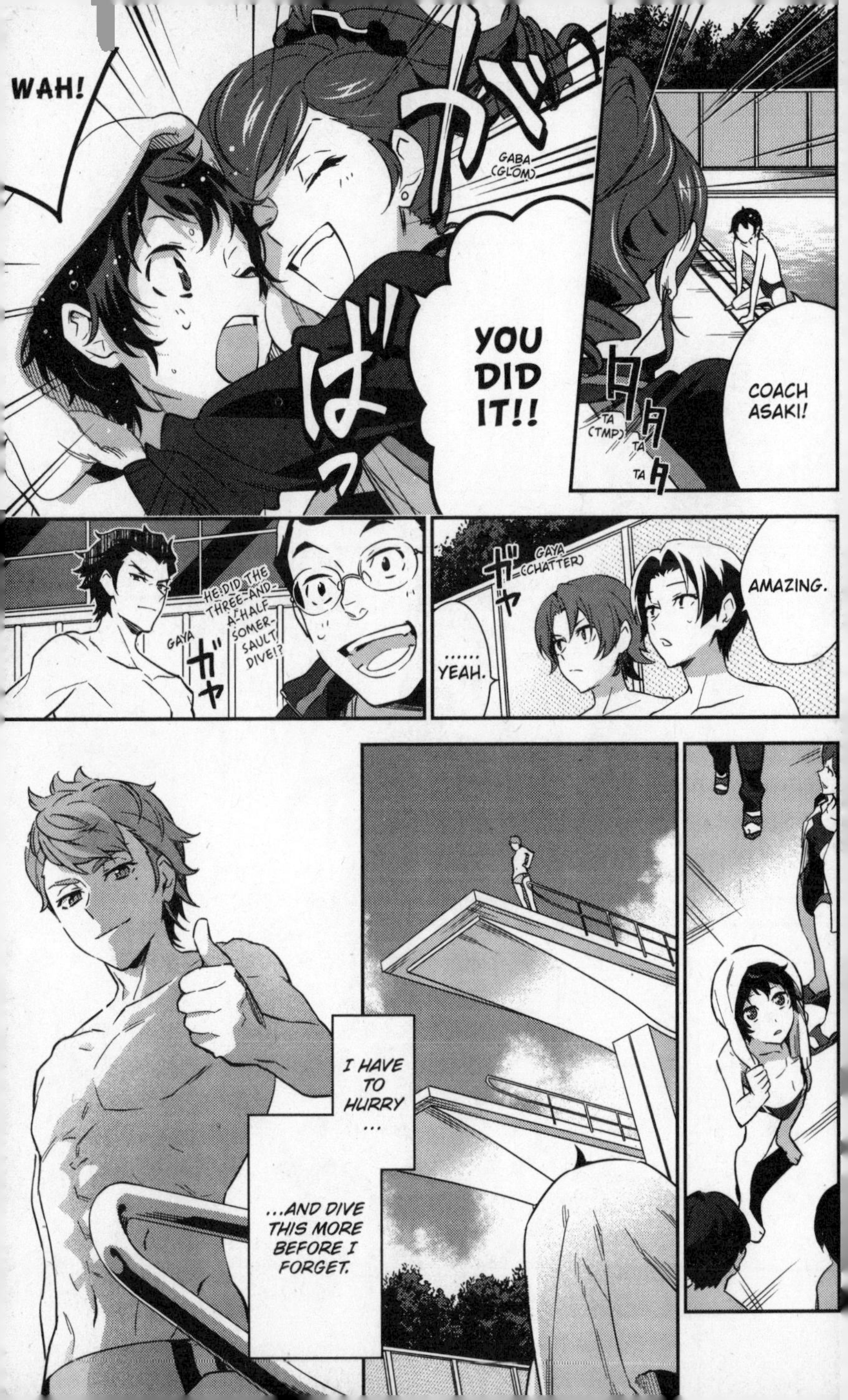
COACH ASAKI!
TA (TMP)
TA
TA
タ
タ
タ
GABA (GLOM)
YOU DID IT!!
ばっ
WAH!
AMAZING.
GAYA (CHATTER)
ガヤ
......YEAH.
HE DID THE THREE-AND-A-HALF SOMERSAULT DIVE!?
GAYA
ガヤ
I HAVE TO HURRY...
...AND DIVE THIS MORE BEFORE I FORGET.

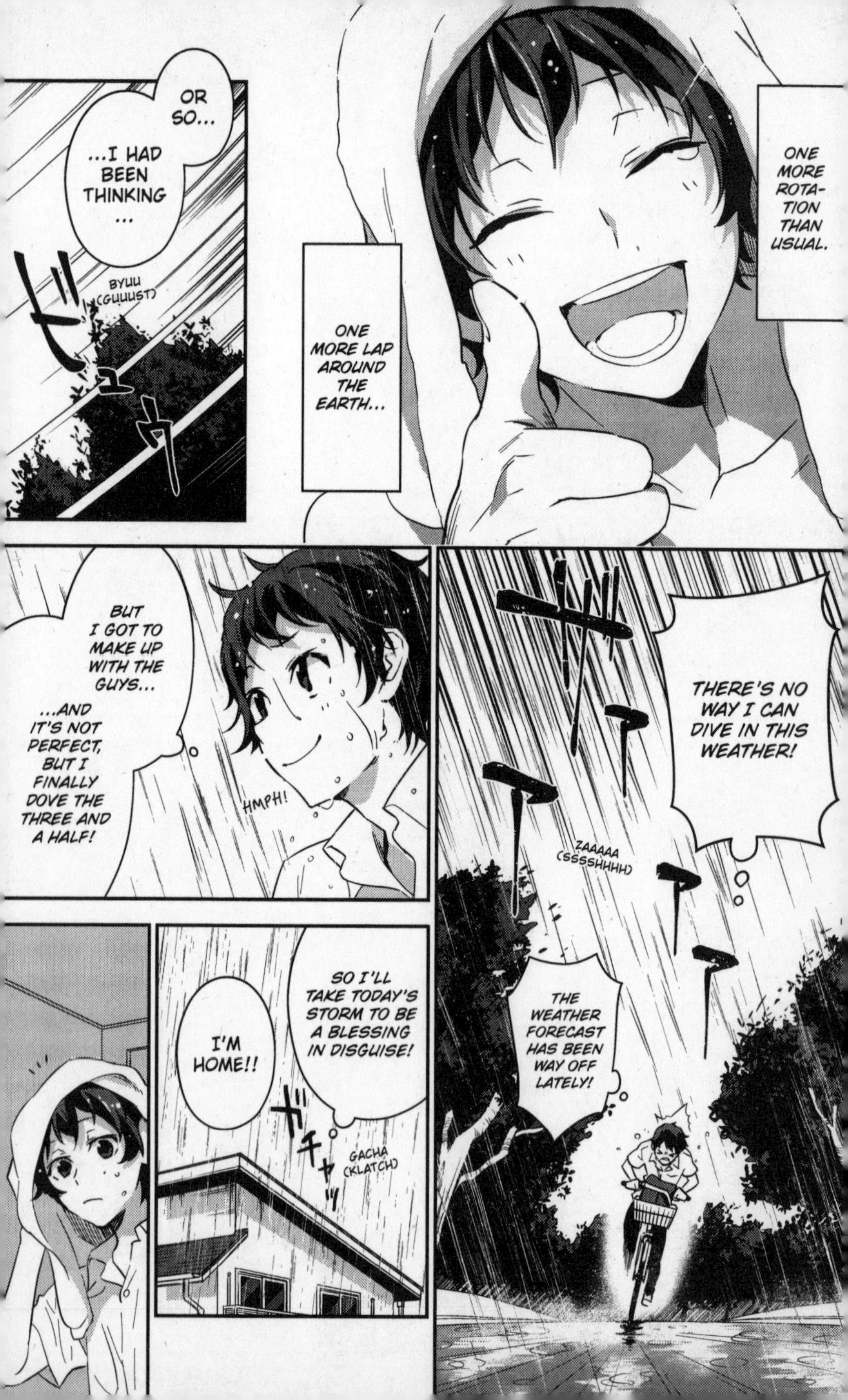
ONE MORE ROTATION THAN USUAL.
ONE MORE LAP AROUND THE EARTH...
OR SO...
...I HAD BEEN THINKING...
BYUU (GUUUST)
THERE'S NO WAY I CAN DIVE IN THIS WEATHER!
ZAAAAA (SSSSHHHH)
THE WEATHER FORECAST HAS BEEN WAY OFF LATELY!
BUT I GOT TO MAKE UP WITH THE GUYS...
...AND IT'S NOT PERFECT, BUT I FINALLY DOVE THE THREE AND A HALF!
HMPH!
SO I'LL TAKE TODAY'S STORM TO BE A BLESSING IN DISGUISE!
I'M HOME!!
GACHA (KLATCH)

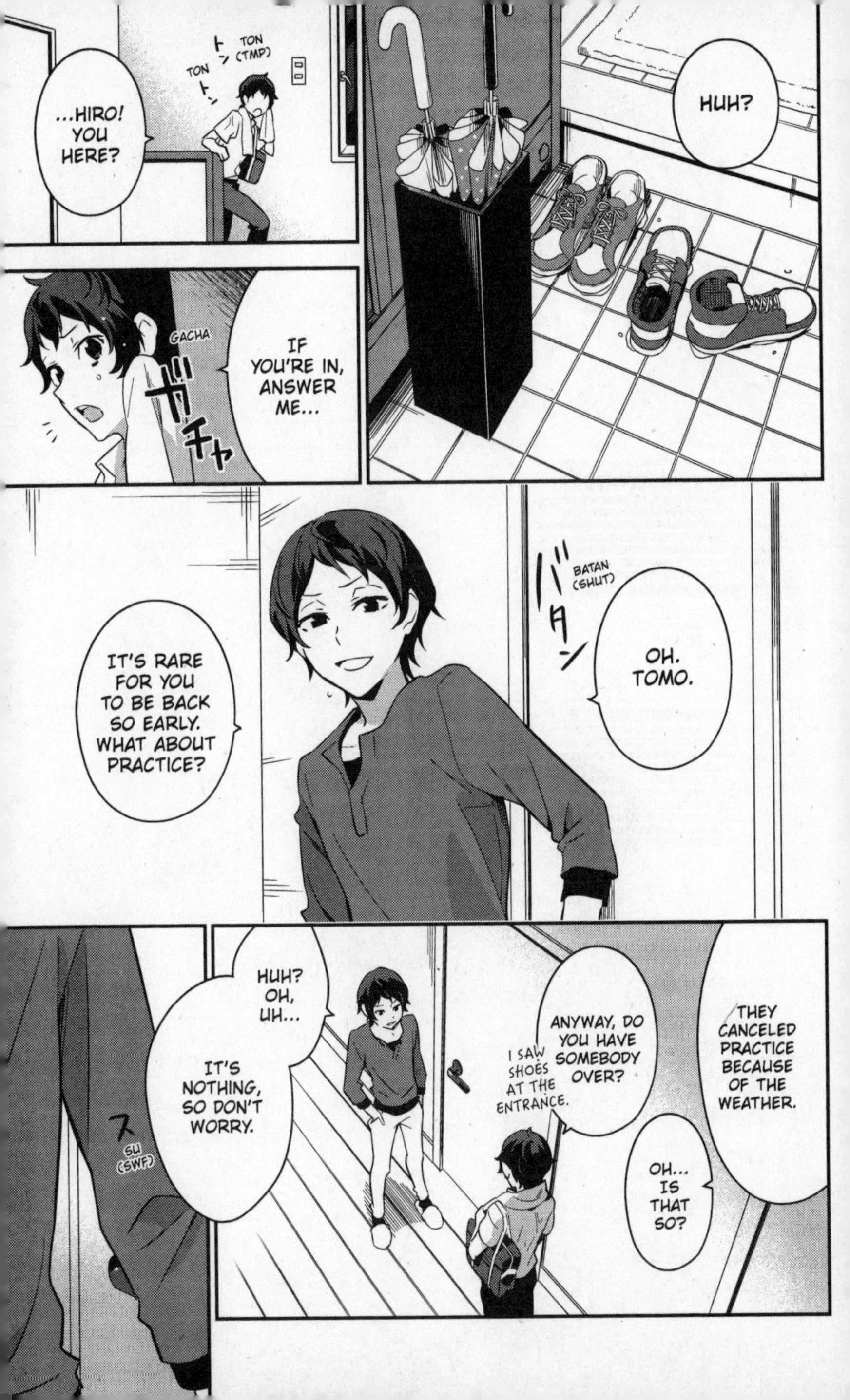
HUH?
TON (TMP)
TON
...HIRO! YOU HERE?
IF YOU'RE IN, ANSWER ME...
GACHA
BATAN (SHUT)
OH. TOMO.
IT'S RARE FOR YOU TO BE BACK SO EARLY. WHAT ABOUT PRACTICE?
THEY CANCELED PRACTICE BECAUSE OF THE WEATHER.
OH... IS THAT SO?
ANYWAY, DO YOU HAVE SOMEBODY OVER?
I SAW SHOES AT THE ENTRANCE.
HUH? OH, UH...
IT'S NOTHING, SO DON'T WORRY.
SU (SWF)

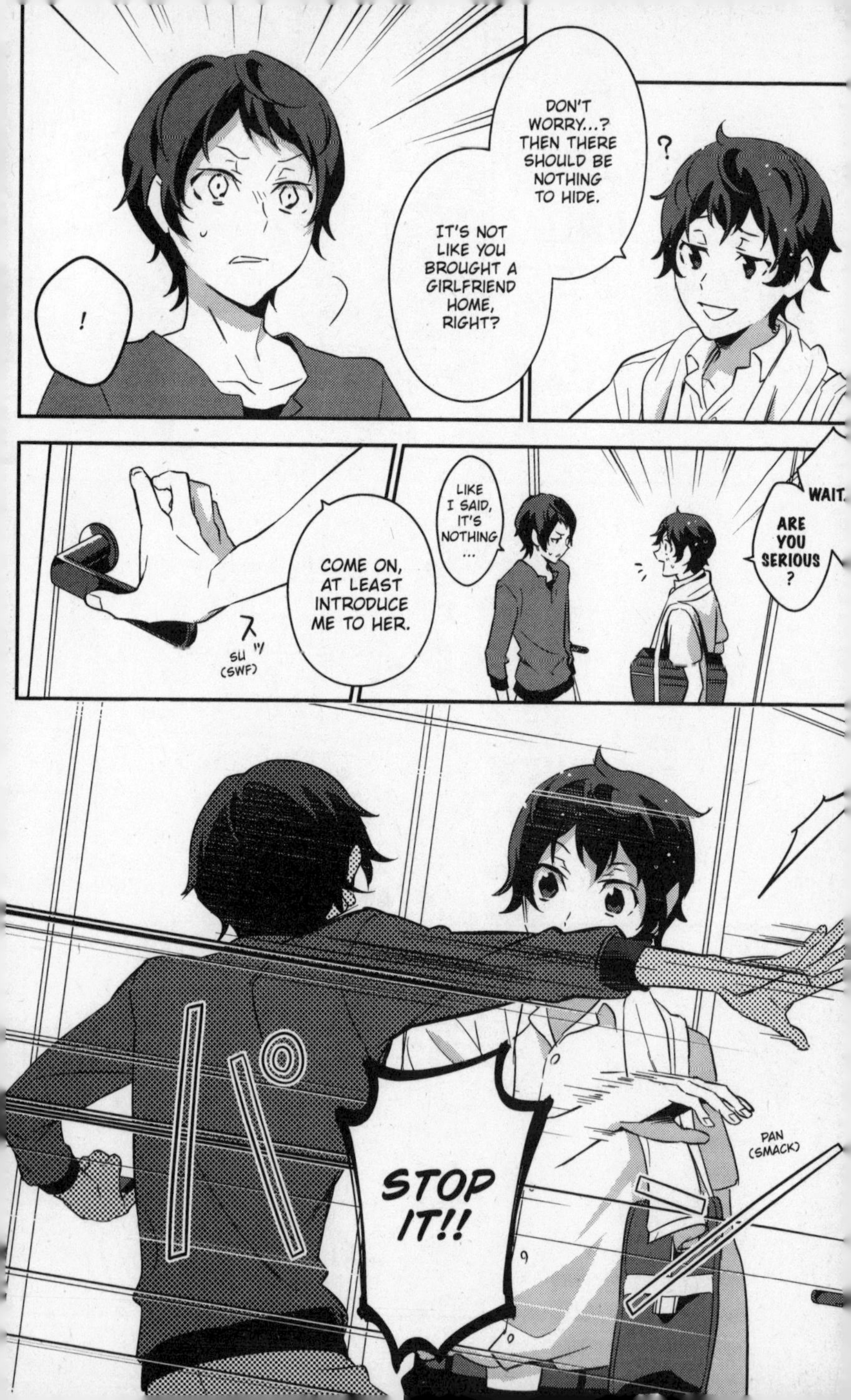
?
DON'T WORRY...? THEN THERE SHOULD BE NOTHING TO HIDE.
IT'S NOT LIKE YOU BROUGHT A GIRLFRIEND HOME, RIGHT?
!
WAIT.
ARE YOU SERIOUS?
LIKE I SAID, IT'S NOTHING...
COME ON, AT LEAST INTRODUCE ME TO HER.
スッ
SU (SWF)
PAN (SMACK)
STOP IT!!

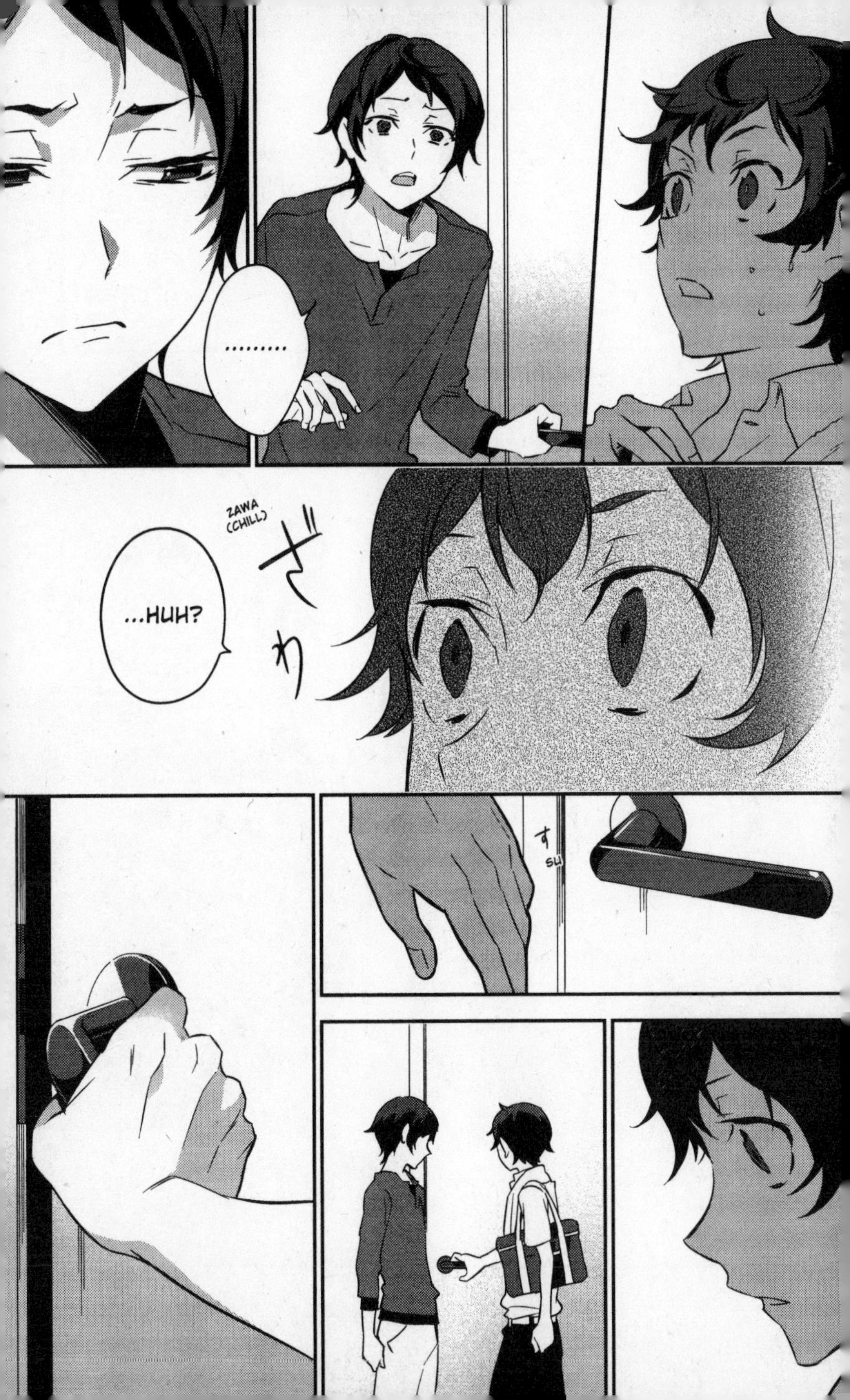
....
ざわ
ZAWA (CHILL)
...HUH?
す
SU

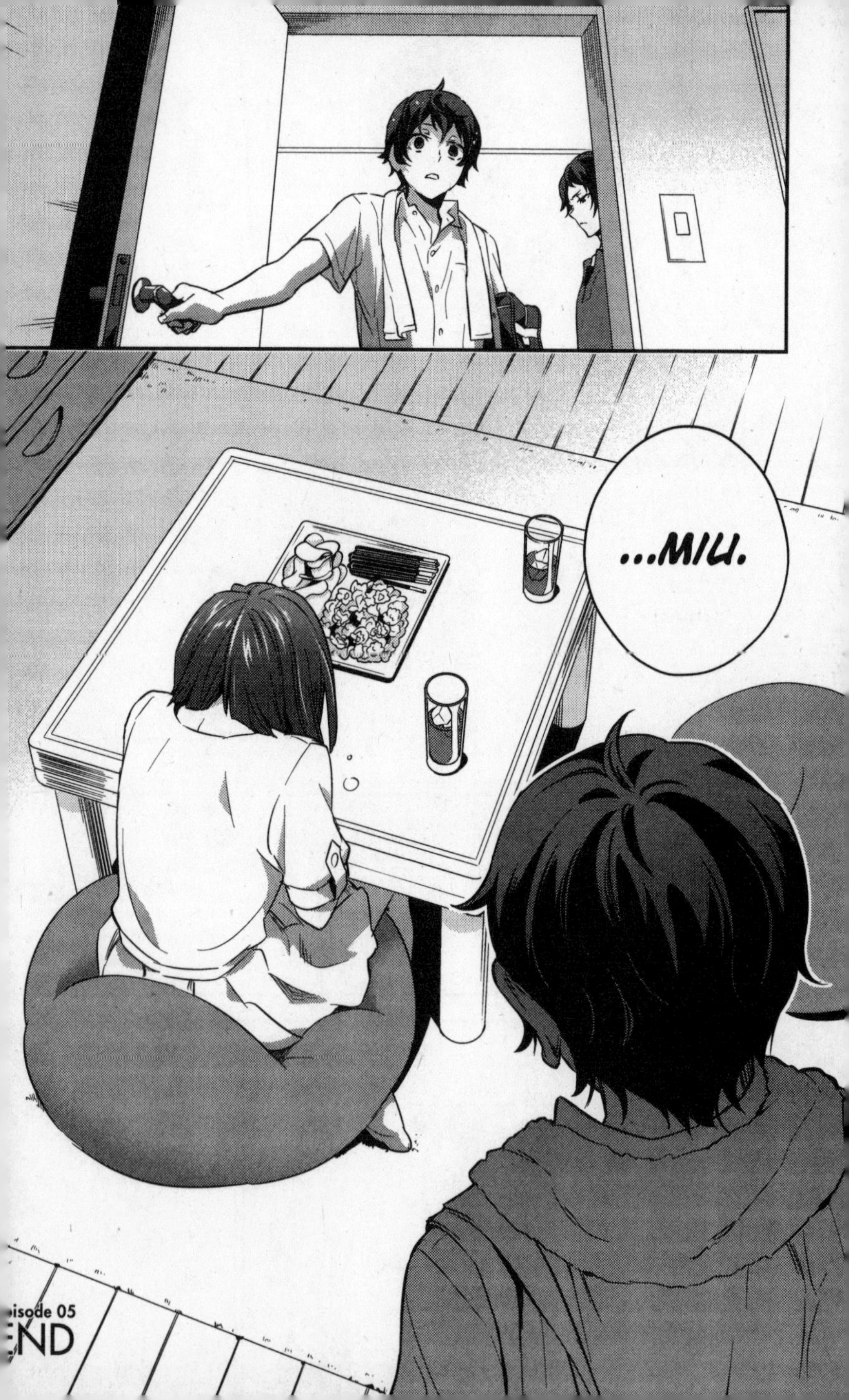
...MIU.
isode 05
ND

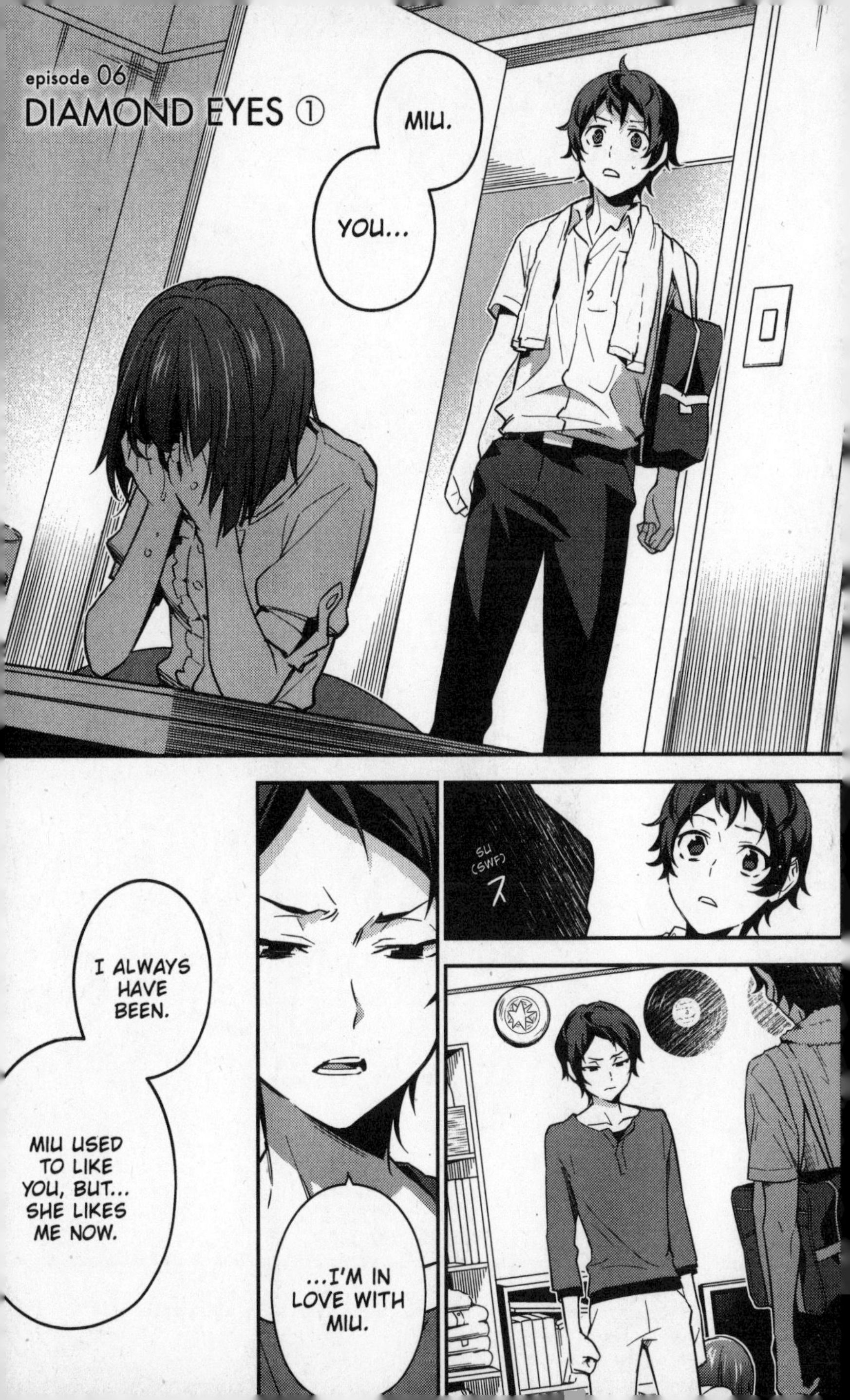

episode 06
DIAMOND EYES ①
MIU.
YOU...
SU (SWF)
ス
...I'M IN LOVE WITH MIU.
I ALWAYS HAVE BEEN.
MIU USED TO LIKE YOU, BUT... SHE LIKES ME NOW.

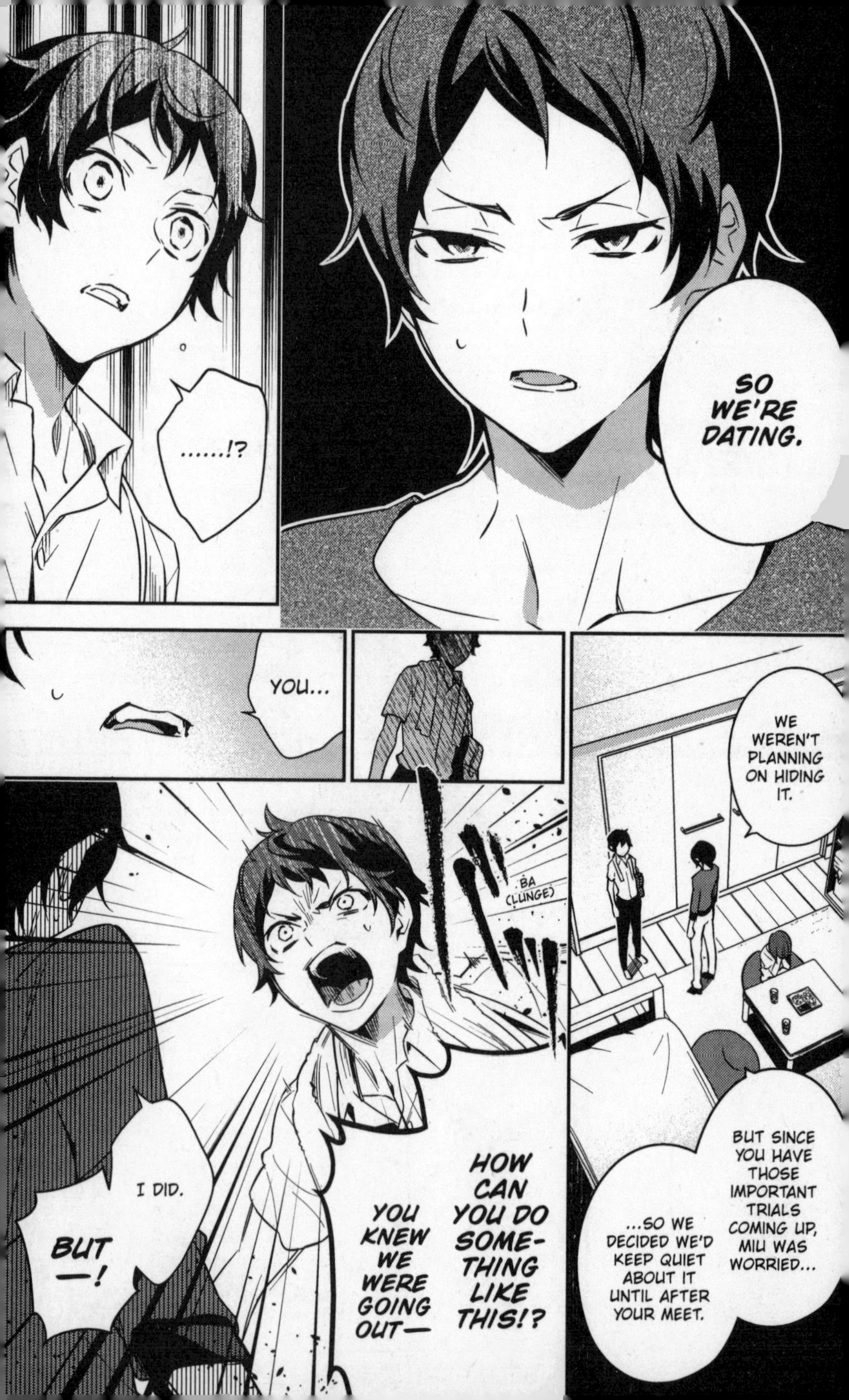
SO WE'RE DATING.
......!?
WE WEREN'T PLANNING ON HIDING IT.
BUT SINCE YOU HAVE THOSE IMPORTANT TRIALS COMING UP, MIU WAS WORRIED...
...SO WE DECIDED WE'D KEEP QUIET ABOUT IT UNTIL AFTER YOUR MEET.
YOU...
BA (LUNGE)
HOW CAN YOU DO SOME-THING LIKE THIS!?
YOU KNEW WE WERE GOING OUT—
I DID.
BUT—!

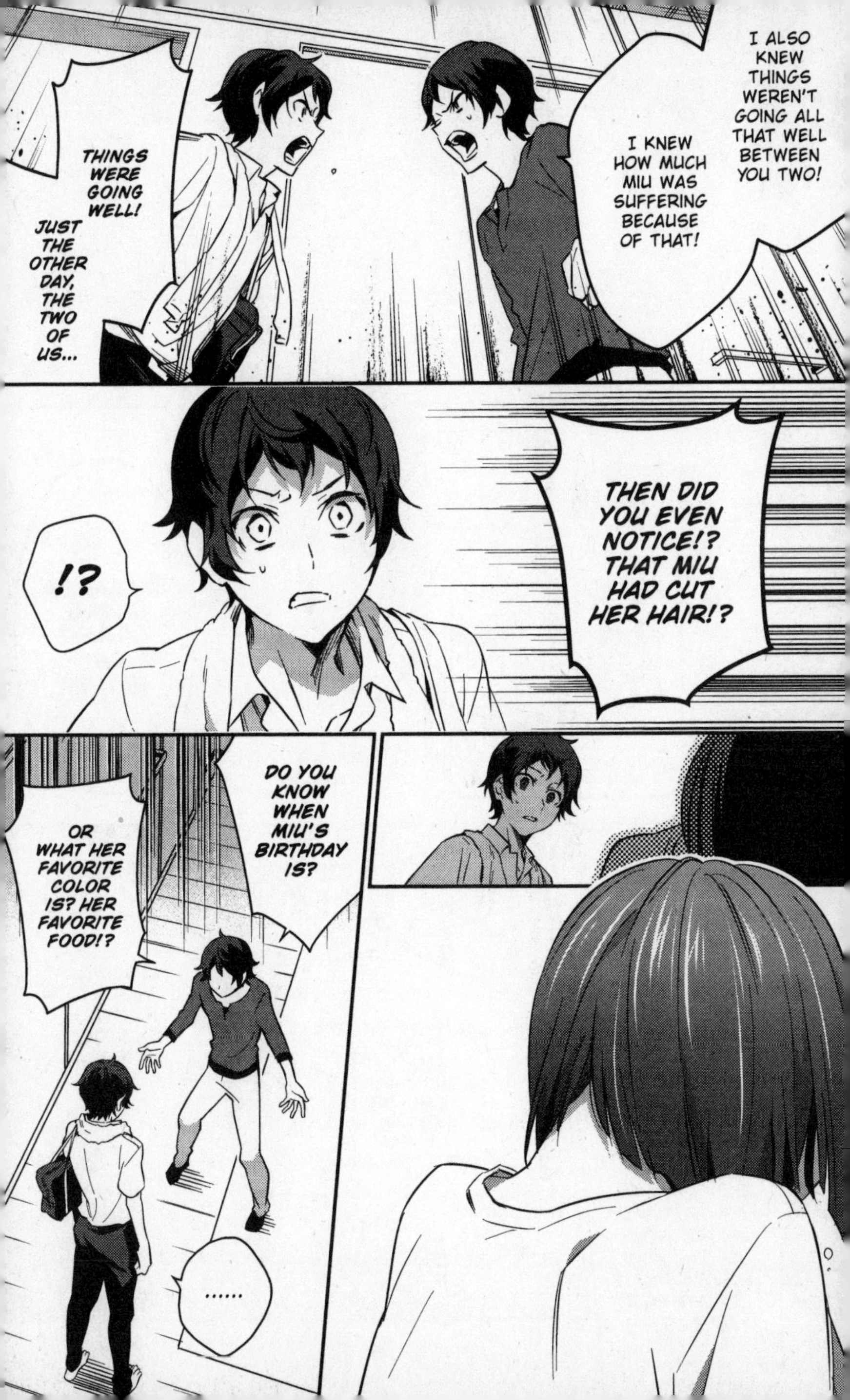
I ALSO KNEW THINGS WEREN'T GOING ALL THAT WELL BETWEEN YOU TWO!
I KNEW HOW MUCH MIU WAS SUFFERING BECAUSE OF THAT!
THINGS WERE GOING WELL! JUST THE OTHER DAY, THE TWO OF US...
THEN DID YOU EVEN NOTICE!? THAT MIU HAD CUT HER HAIR!?
!?
DO YOU KNOW WHEN MIU'S BIRTHDAY IS?
OR WHAT HER FAVORITE COLOR IS? HER FAVORITE FOOD!?
......

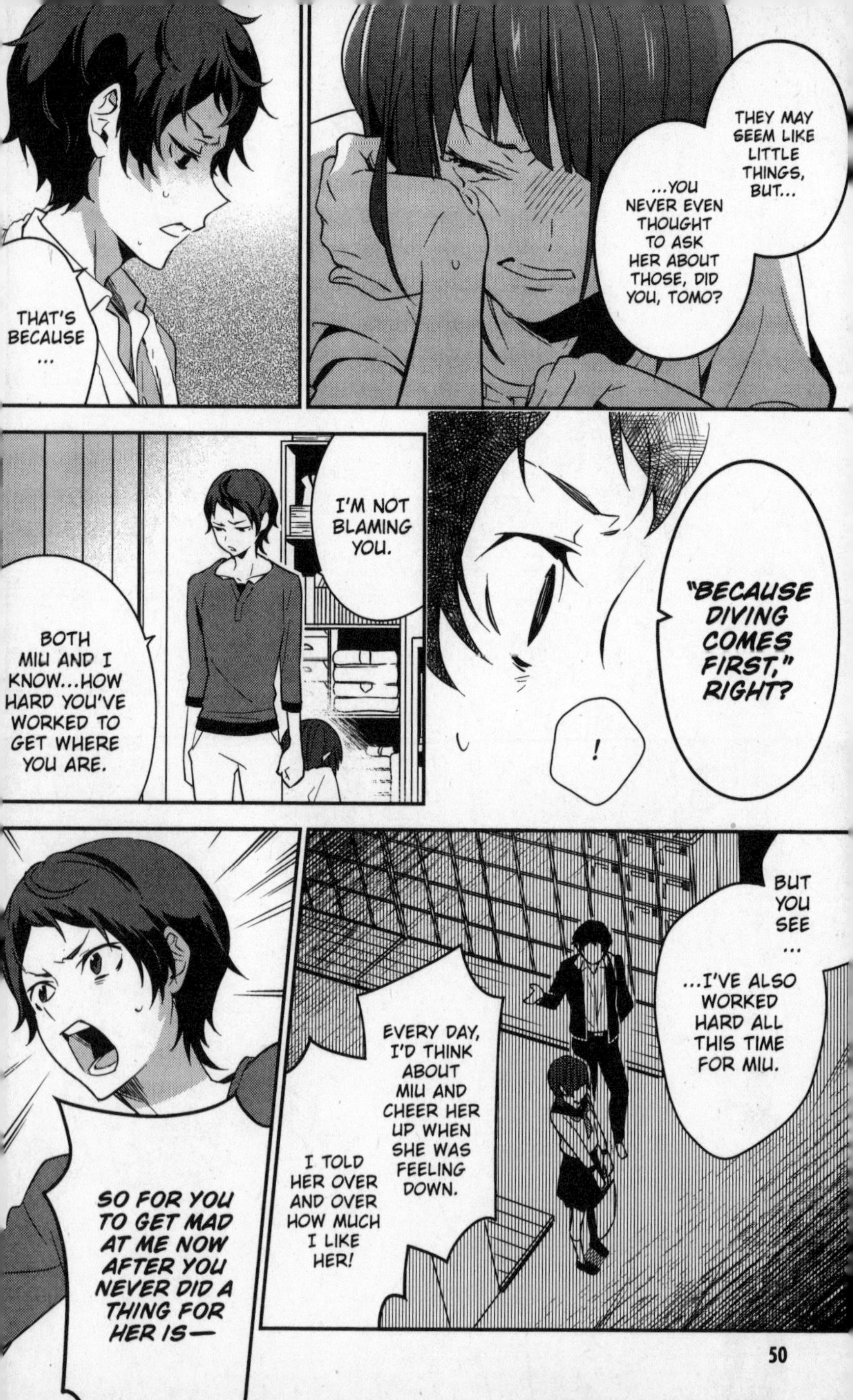
THEY MAY SEEM LIKE LITTLE THINGS, BUT...
...YOU NEVER EVEN THOUGHT TO ASK HER ABOUT THOSE, DID YOU, TOMO?
THAT'S BECAUSE ...
"BECAUSE DIVING COMES FIRST," RIGHT?
!
I'M NOT BLAMING YOU.
BOTH MIU AND I KNOW...HOW HARD YOU'VE WORKED TO GET WHERE YOU ARE.
BUT YOU SEE ...
...I'VE ALSO WORKED HARD ALL THIS TIME FOR MIU.
EVERY DAY, I'D THINK ABOUT MIU AND CHEER HER UP WHEN SHE WAS FEELING DOWN.
I TOLD HER OVER AND OVER HOW MUCH I LIKE HER!
SO FOR YOU TO GET MAD AT ME NOW AFTER YOU NEVER DID A THING FOR HER IS—

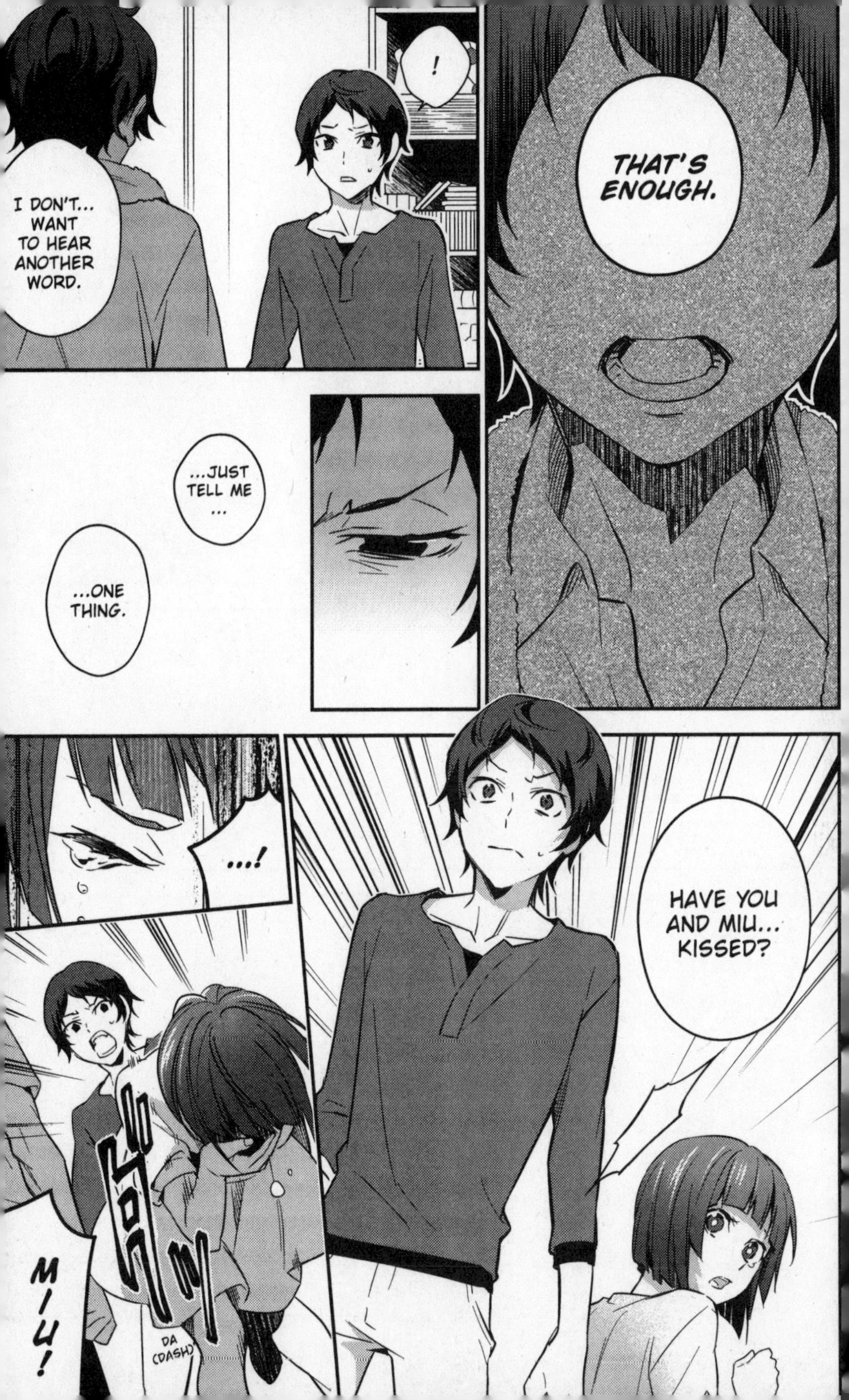
THAT'S ENOUGH.
!
I DON'T... WANT TO HEAR ANOTHER WORD.
...JUST TELL ME ...
...ONE THING.
HAVE YOU AND MIU... KISSED?
...!
MIU!
DA (DASH)

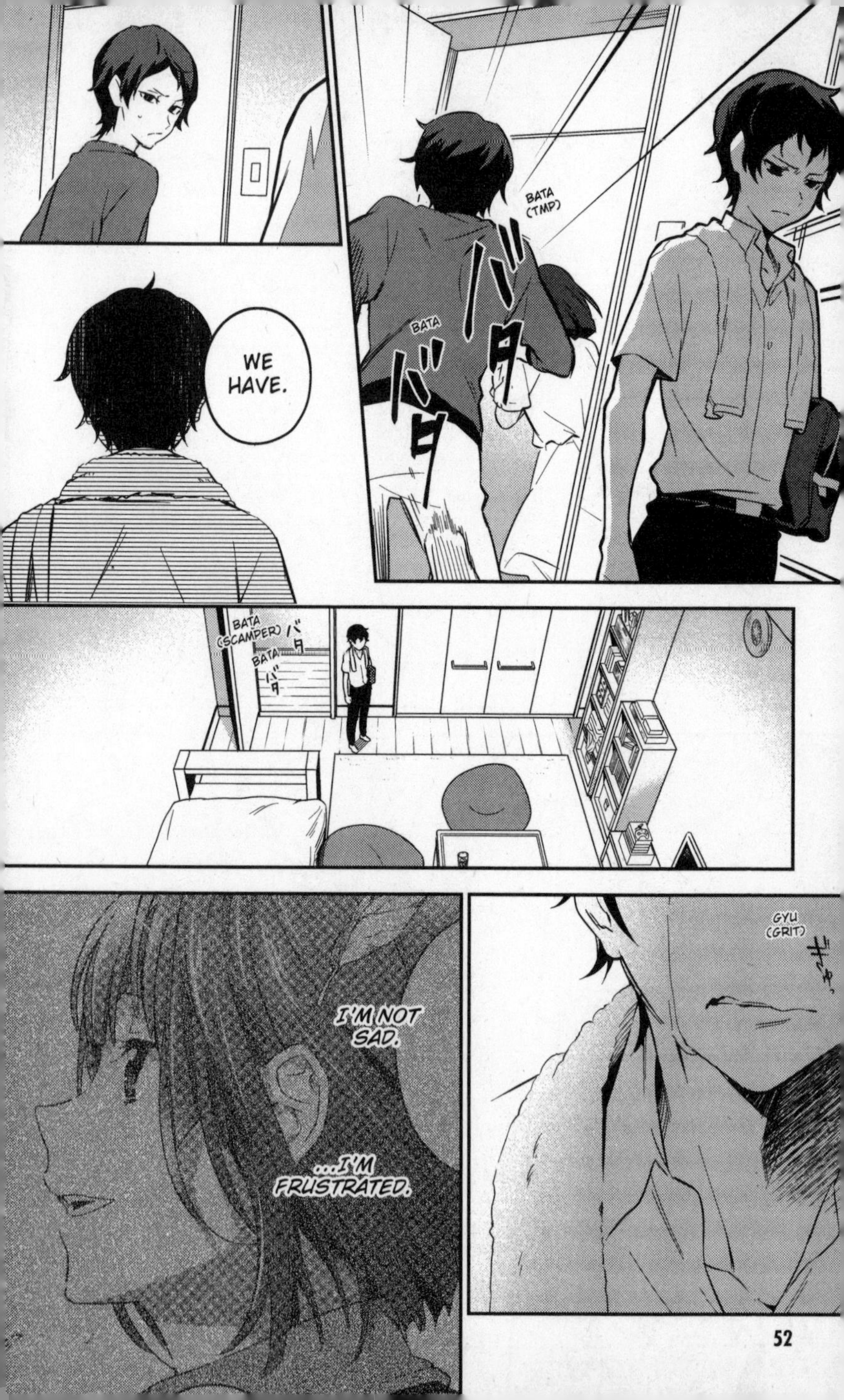

BATA (TMP)
BATA
WE HAVE.
BATA (SCAMPER)
BATA
GYU (GRIT)
I'M NOT SAD.
...I'M FRUSTRATED.

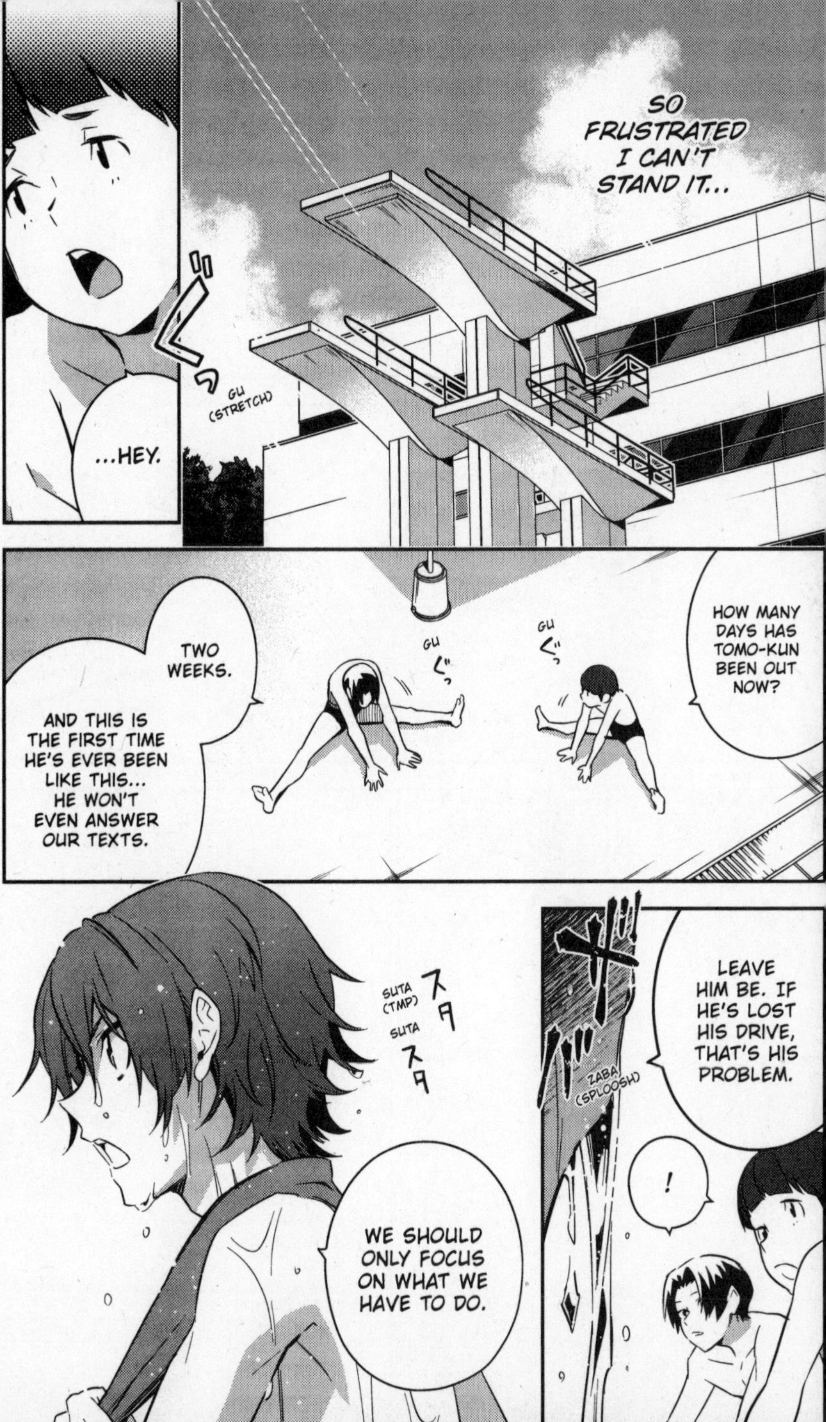
SO FRUSTRATED I CAN'T STAND IT...
GU (STRETCH)
...HEY.
HOW MANY DAYS HAS TOMO-KUN BEEN OUT NOW?
GU
GU
TWO WEEKS.
AND THIS IS THE FIRST TIME HE'S EVER BEEN LIKE THIS... HE WON'T EVEN ANSWER OUR TEXTS.
LEAVE HIM BE. IF HE'S LOST HIS DRIVE, THAT'S HIS PROBLEM.
ZABA (SPLOOSH)
!
SUTA (TMP)
SUTA
WE SHOULD ONLY FOCUS ON WHAT WE HAVE TO DO.

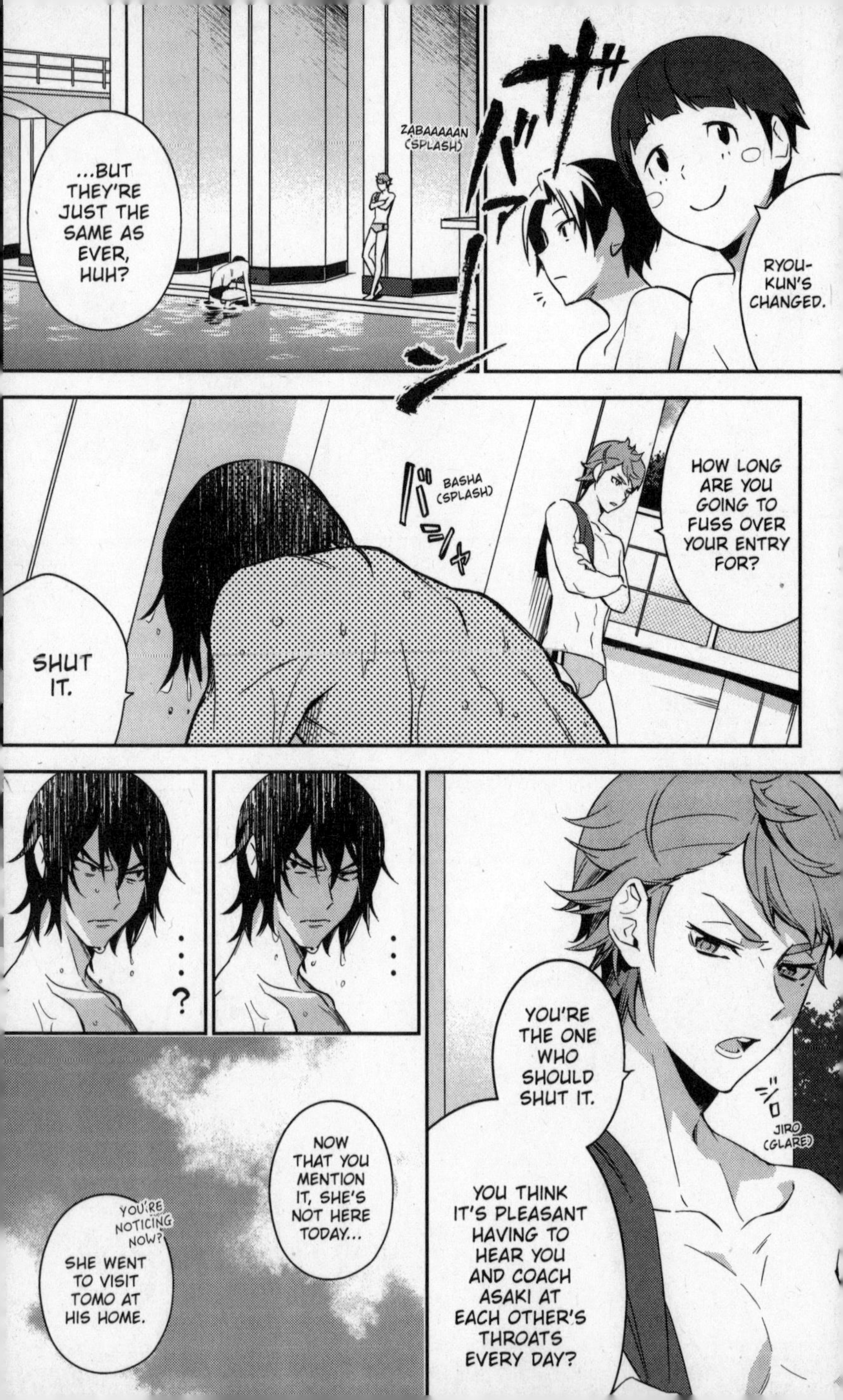
RYOU-KUN'S CHANGED.
ZABAAAAAN (SPLASH)
...BUT THEY'RE JUST THE SAME AS EVER, HUH?
HOW LONG ARE YOU GOING TO FUSS OVER YOUR ENTRY FOR?
BASHA (SPLASH)
SHUT IT.
YOU'RE THE ONE WHO SHOULD SHUT IT.
JIRO (GLARE)
YOU THINK IT'S PLEASANT HAVING TO HEAR YOU AND COACH ASAKI AT EACH OTHER'S THROATS EVERY DAY?
...
...?
NOW THAT YOU MENTION IT, SHE'S NOT HERE TODAY...
YOU'RE NOTICING NOW?
SHE WENT TO VISIT TOMO AT HIS HOME.

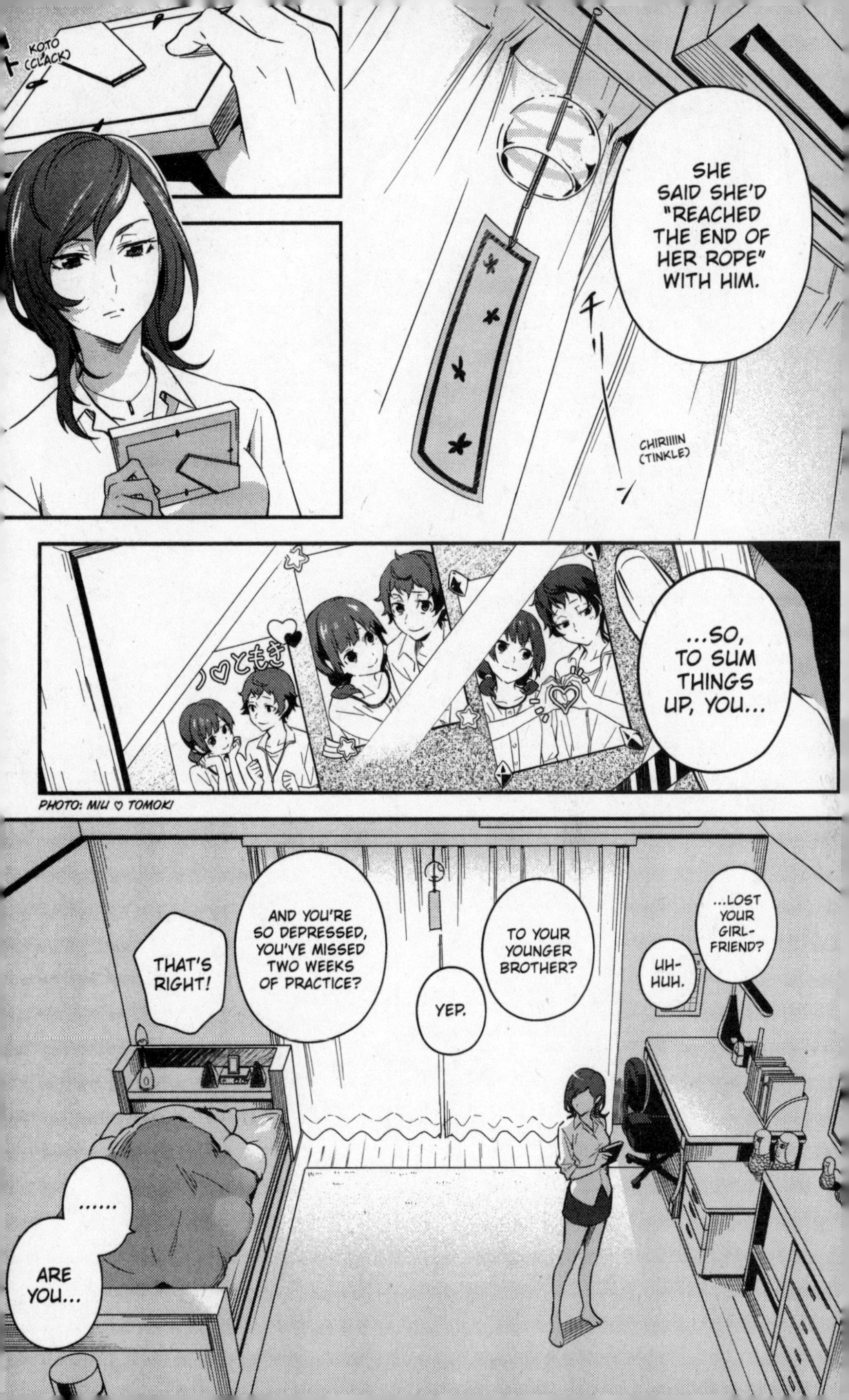
SHE SAID SHE'D "REACHED THE END OF HER ROPE" WITH HIM.
CHIRIIIIN (TINKLE)
KOTO (CLACK)
...SO, TO SUM THINGS UP, YOU...
PHOTO: MIU ♡ TOMOKI
...LOST YOUR GIRL-FRIEND?
UH-HUH.
TO YOUR YOUNGER BROTHER?
YEP.
AND YOU'RE SO DEPRESSED, YOU'VE MISSED TWO WEEKS OF PRACTICE?
THAT'S RIGHT!
......
ARE YOU...

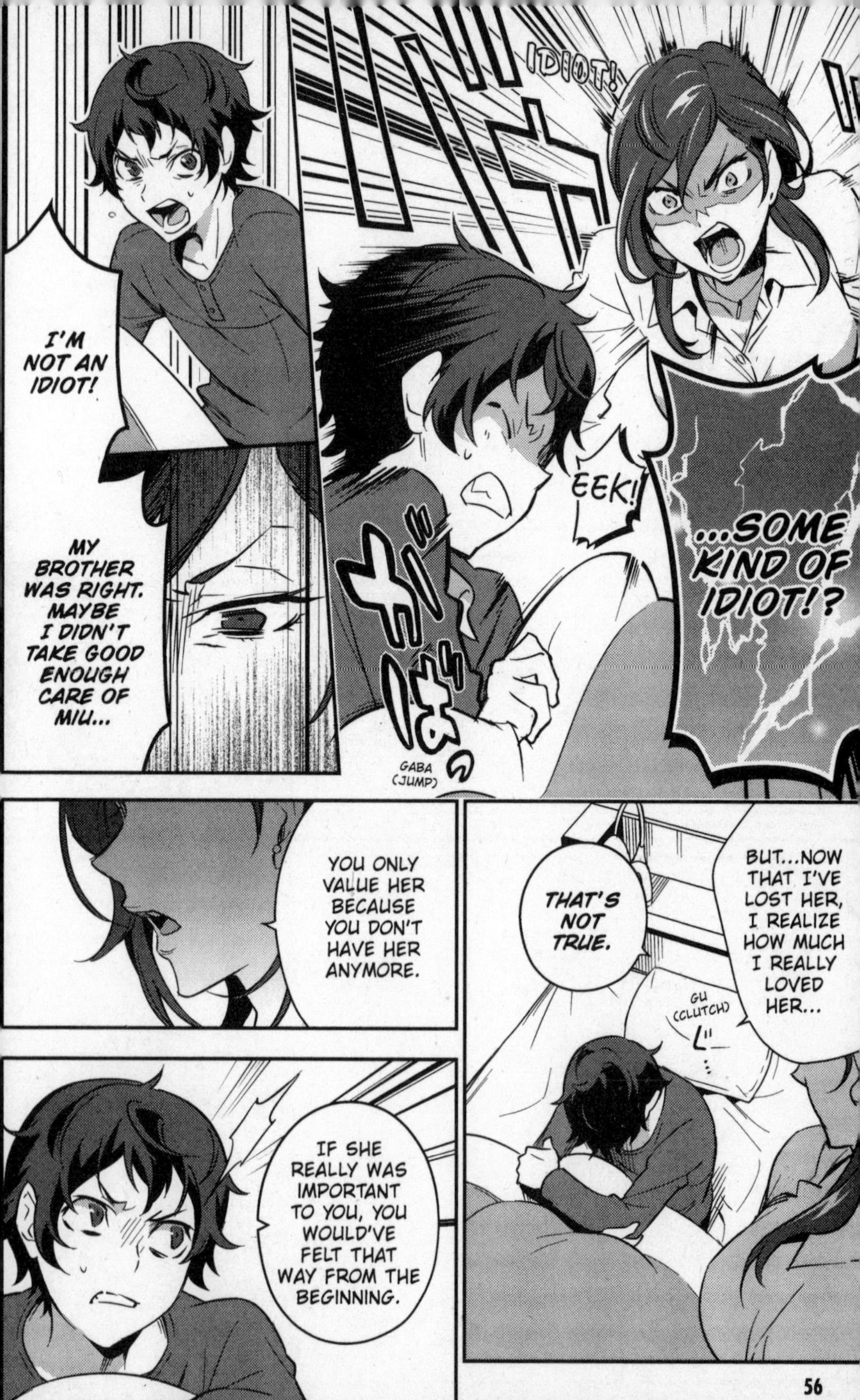
IDIOT!
...SOME KIND OF IDIOT!?
EEK!
GABA (JUMP)
I'M NOT AN IDIOT!
MY BROTHER WAS RIGHT. MAYBE I DIDN'T TAKE GOOD ENOUGH CARE OF MIU...
BUT...NOW THAT I'VE LOST HER, I REALIZE HOW MUCH I REALLY LOVED HER...
THAT'S NOT TRUE.
GU (CLUTCH)
YOU ONLY VALUE HER BECAUSE YOU DON'T HAVE HER ANYMORE.
IF SHE REALLY WAS IMPORTANT TO YOU, YOU WOULD'VE FELT THAT WAY FROM THE BEGINNING.

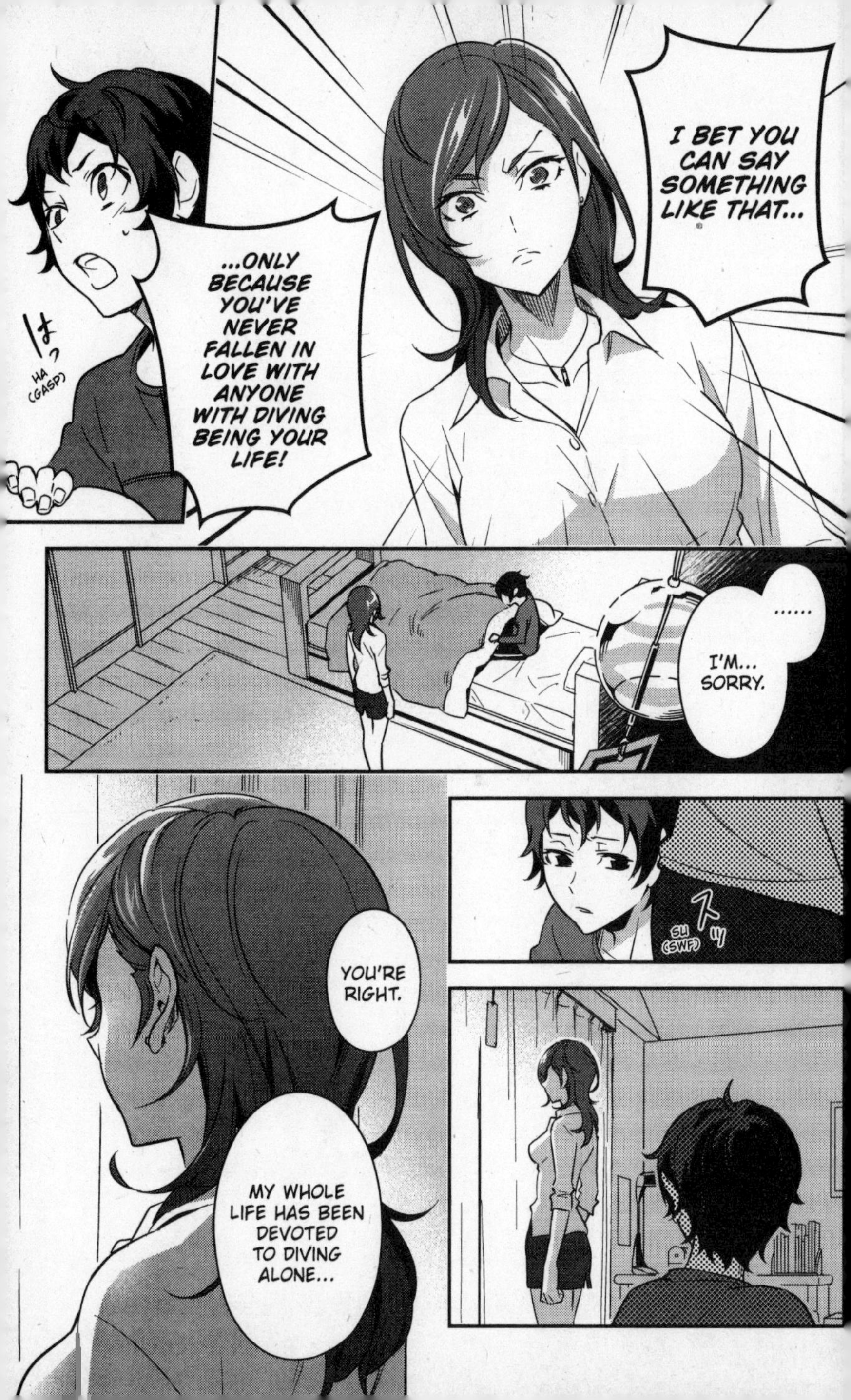
I BET YOU CAN SAY SOMETHING LIKE THAT...
...ONLY BECAUSE YOU'VE NEVER FALLEN IN LOVE WITH ANYONE WITH DIVING BEING YOUR LIFE!
はっ
HA (GASP)
......
I'M... SORRY.
スッ
SU (SWF)
YOU'RE RIGHT.
MY WHOLE LIFE HAS BEEN DEVOTED TO DIVING ALONE...

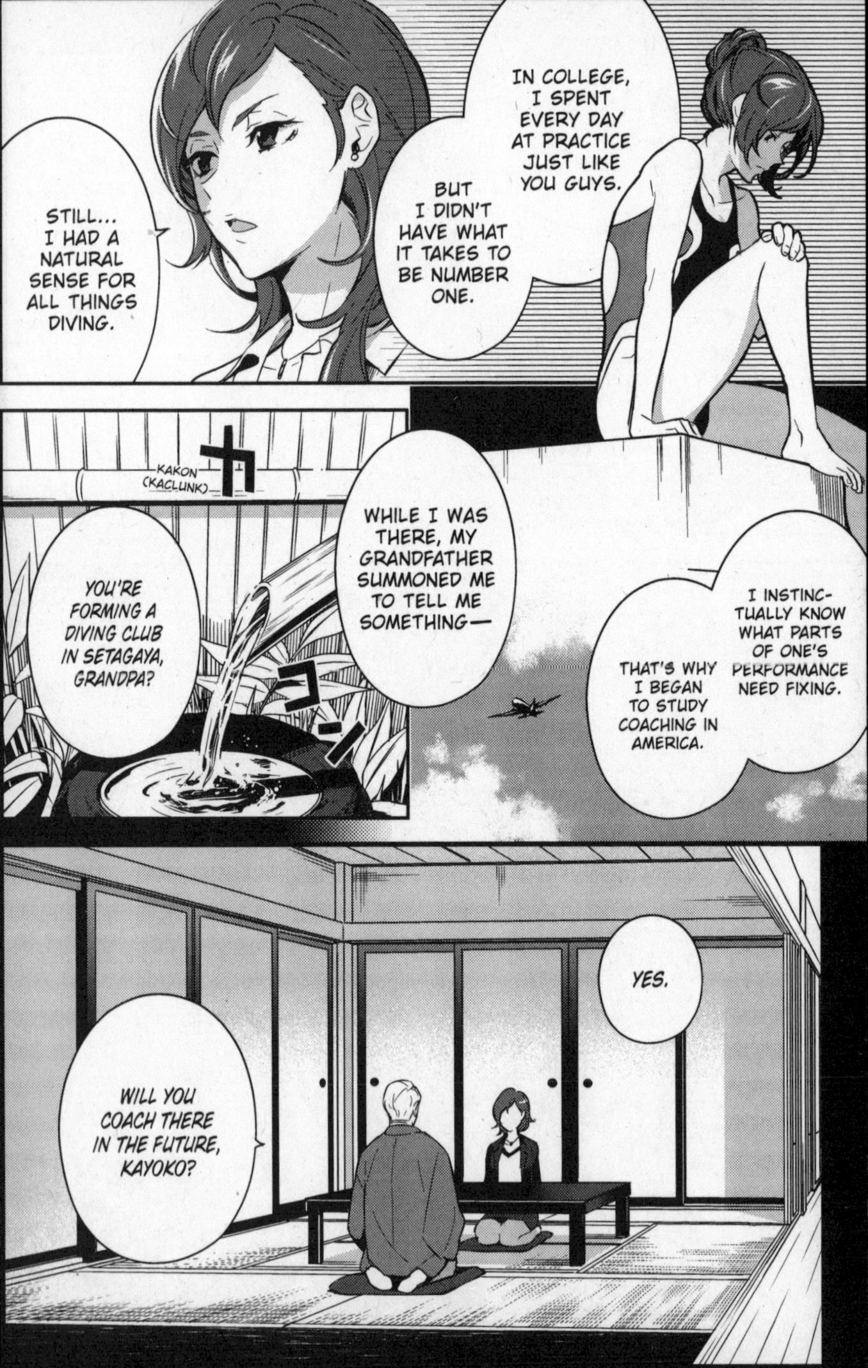
IN COLLEGE, I SPENT EVERY DAY AT PRACTICE JUST LIKE YOU GUYS.
BUT I DIDN'T HAVE WHAT IT TAKES TO BE NUMBER ONE.
STILL... I HAD A NATURAL SENSE FOR ALL THINGS DIVING.
I INSTINC-TUALLY KNOW WHAT PARTS OF ONE'S PERFORMANCE NEED FIXING.
THAT'S WHY I BEGAN TO STUDY COACHING IN AMERICA.
WHILE I WAS THERE, MY GRANDFATHER SUMMONED ME TO TELL ME SOMETHING—
KAKON (KACLUNK)
YOU'RE FORMING A DIVING CLUB IN SETAGAYA, GRANDPA?
YES.
WILL YOU COACH THERE IN THE FUTURE, KAYOKO?

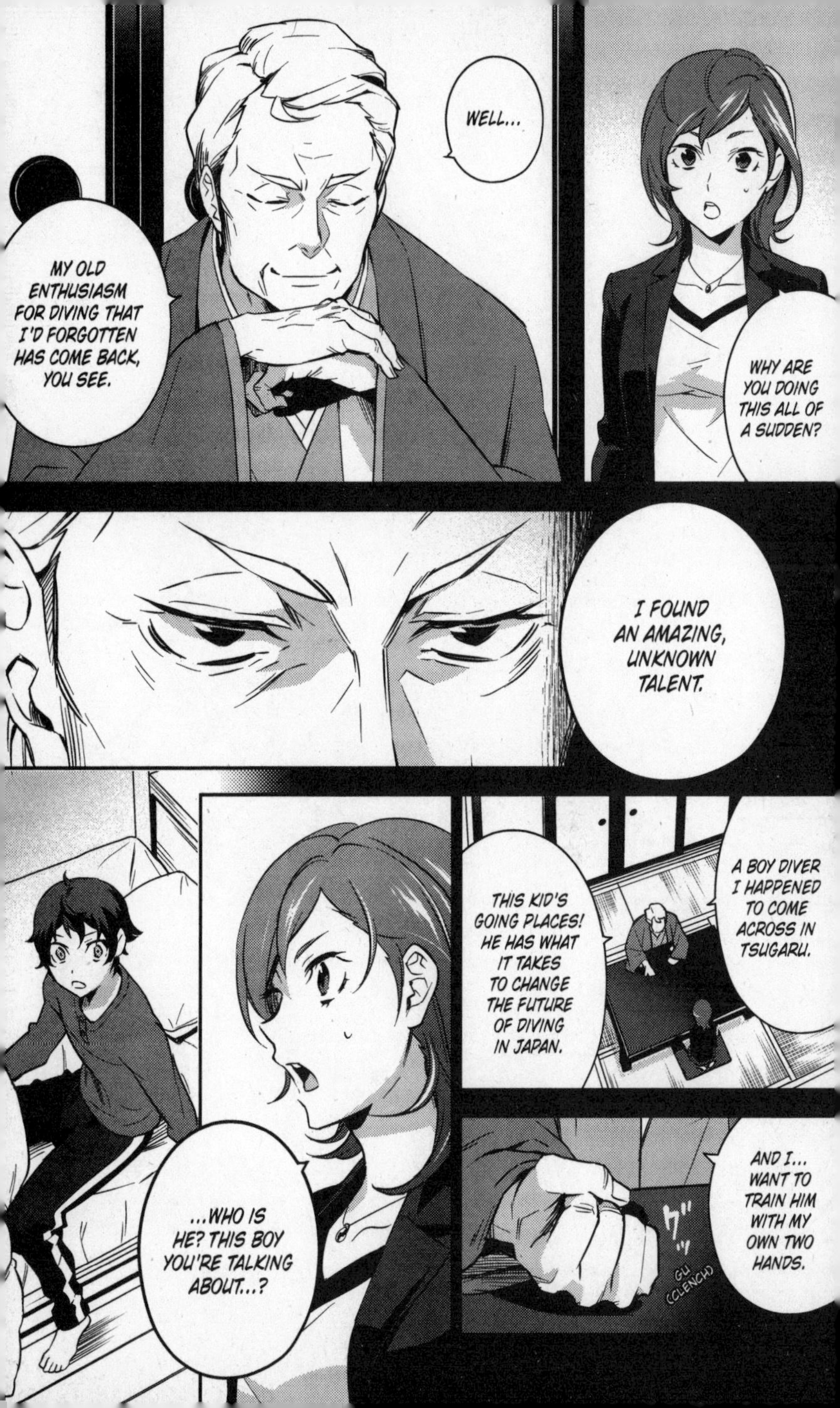
WHY ARE YOU DOING THIS ALL OF A SUDDEN?
WELL...
MY OLD ENTHUSIASM FOR DIVING THAT I'D FORGOTTEN HAS COME BACK, YOU SEE.
I FOUND AN AMAZING, UNKNOWN TALENT.
A BOY DIVER I HAPPENED TO COME ACROSS IN TSUGARU.
THIS KID'S GOING PLACES! HE HAS WHAT IT TAKES TO CHANGE THE FUTURE OF DIVING IN JAPAN.
AND I... WANT TO TRAIN HIM WITH MY OWN TWO HANDS.
グッ
GU (CLENCH)
...WHO IS HE? THIS BOY YOU'RE TALKING ABOUT...?

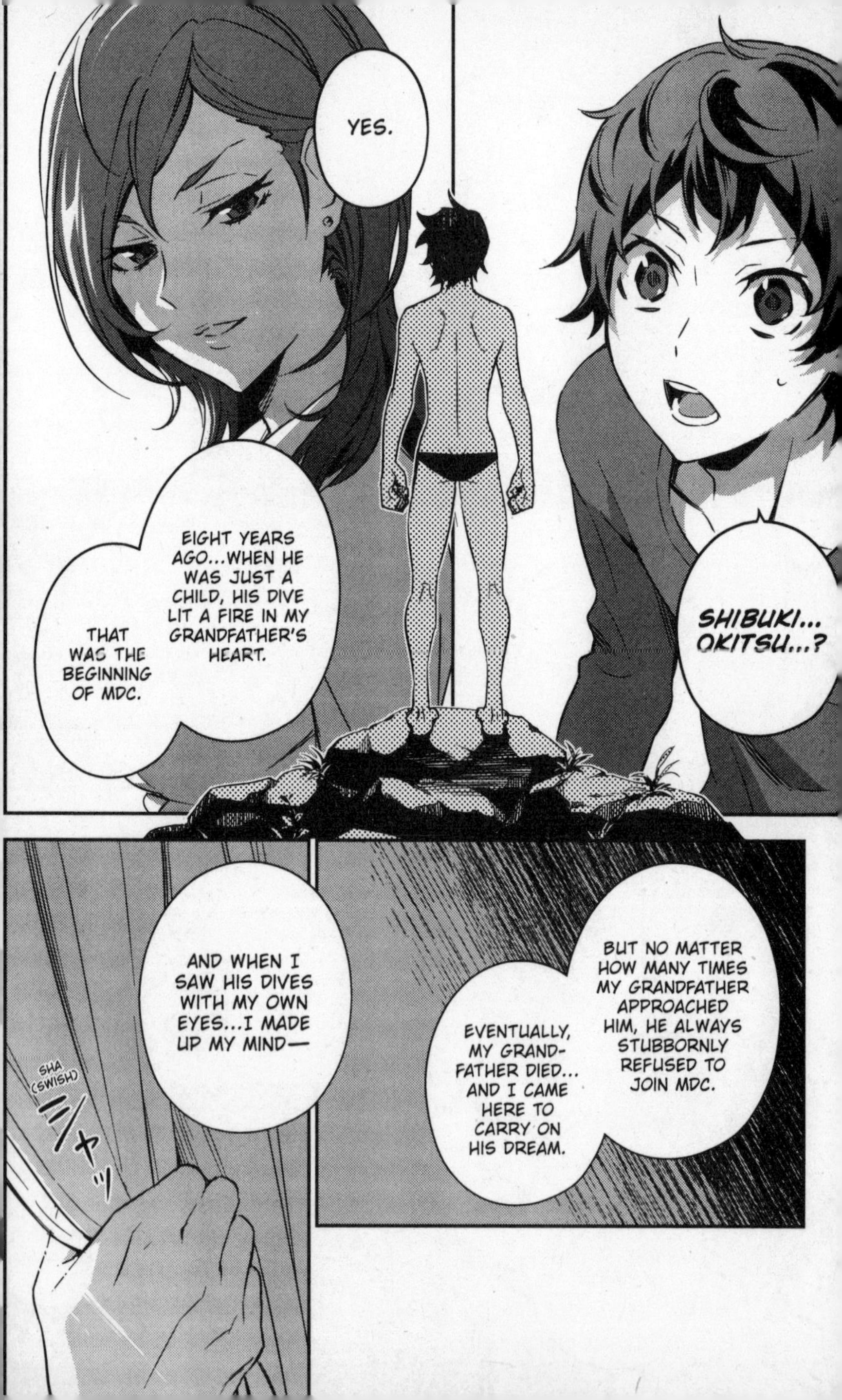
SHIBUKI... OKITSU...?
YES.
EIGHT YEARS AGO...WHEN HE WAS JUST A CHILD, HIS DIVE LIT A FIRE IN MY GRANDFATHER'S HEART.
THAT WAS THE BEGINNING OF MDC.
BUT NO MATTER HOW MANY TIMES MY GRANDFATHER APPROACHED HIM, HE ALWAYS STUBBORNLY REFUSED TO JOIN MDC.
EVENTUALLY, MY GRAND-FATHER DIED... AND I CAME HERE TO CARRY ON HIS DREAM.
AND WHEN I SAW HIS DIVES WITH MY OWN EYES...I MADE UP MY MIND—
SHA (SWISH)
シャッ

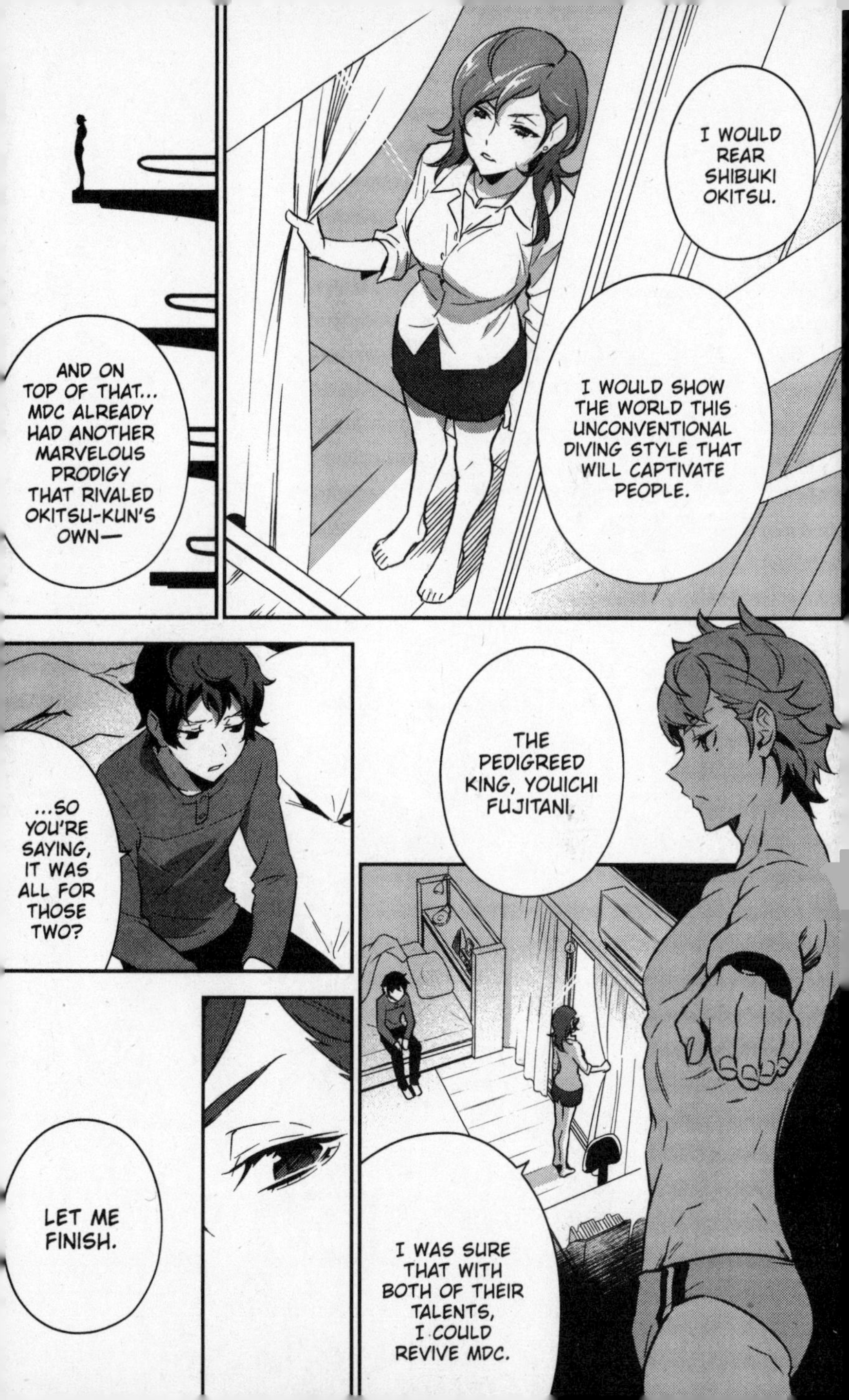
I WOULD REAR SHIBUKI OKITSU.
I WOULD SHOW THE WORLD THIS UNCONVENTIONAL DIVING STYLE THAT WILL CAPTIVATE PEOPLE.
AND ON TOP OF THAT... MDC ALREADY HAD ANOTHER MARVELOUS PRODIGY THAT RIVALED OKITSU-KUN'S OWN—
THE PEDIGREED KING, YOUICHI FUJITANI.
...SO YOU'RE SAYING, IT WAS ALL FOR THOSE TWO?
LET ME FINISH.
I WAS SURE THAT WITH BOTH OF THEIR TALENTS, I COULD REVIVE MDC.

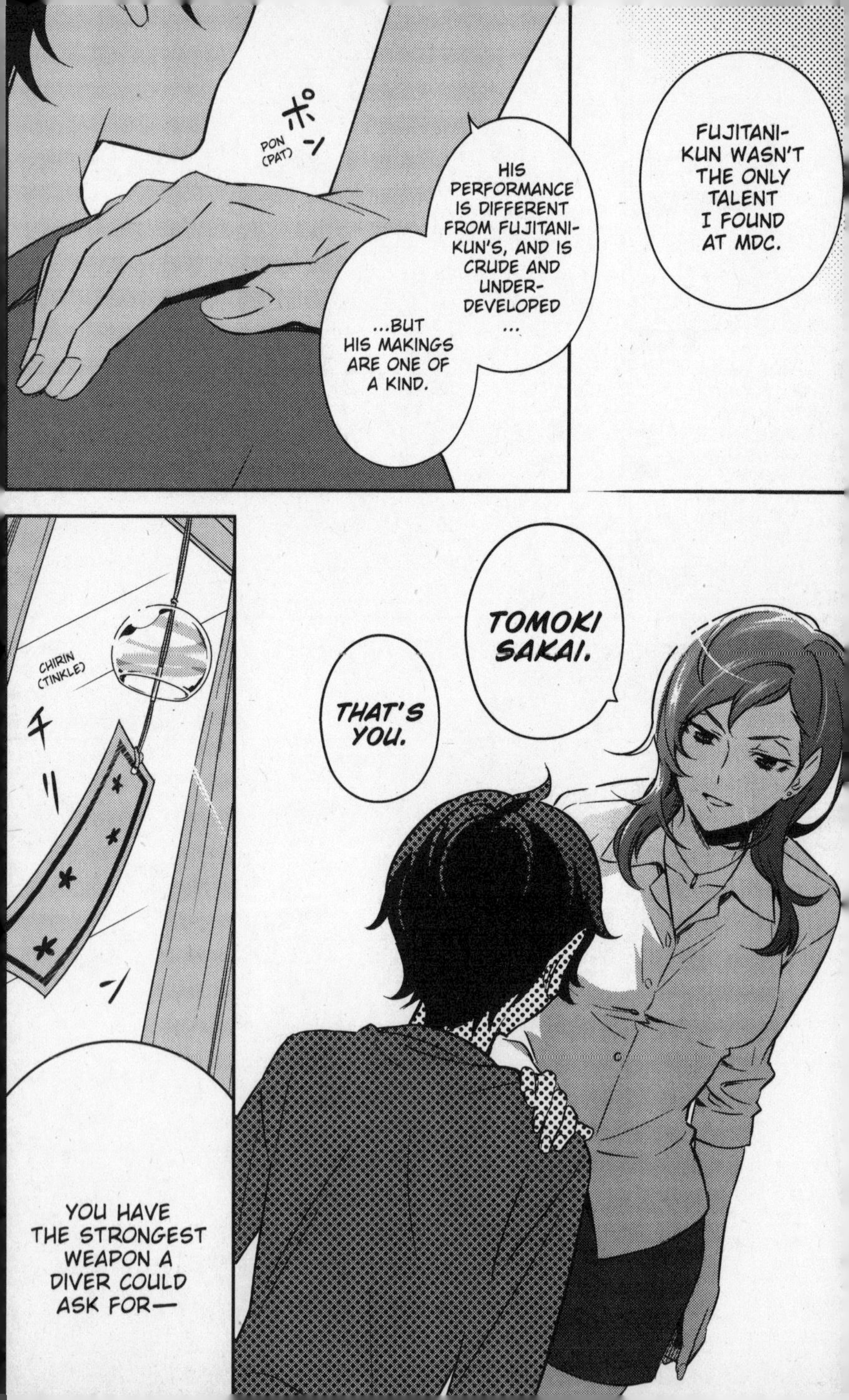
FUJITANI-KUN WASN'T THE ONLY TALENT I FOUND AT MDC.
HIS PERFORMANCE IS DIFFERENT FROM FUJITANI-KUN'S, AND IS CRUDE AND UNDER-DEVELOPED ...
...BUT HIS MAKINGS ARE ONE OF A KIND.
ポン
PON (PAT)
TOMOKI SAKAI.
THAT'S YOU.
YOU HAVE THE STRONGEST WEAPON A DIVER COULD ASK FOR—
チリーン
CHIRIN (TINKLE)

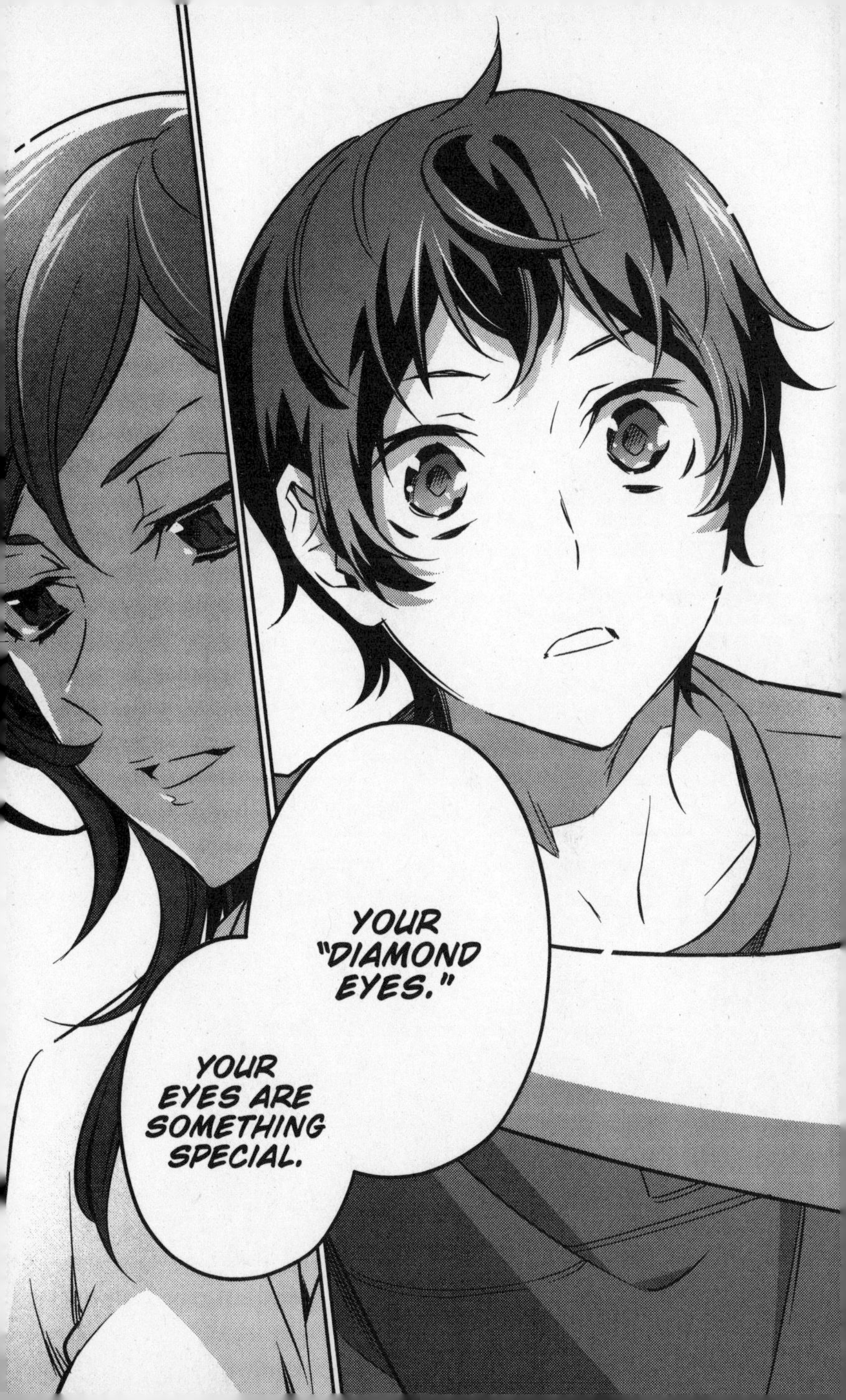
YOUR "DIAMOND EYES."
YOUR EYES ARE SOMETHING SPECIAL.

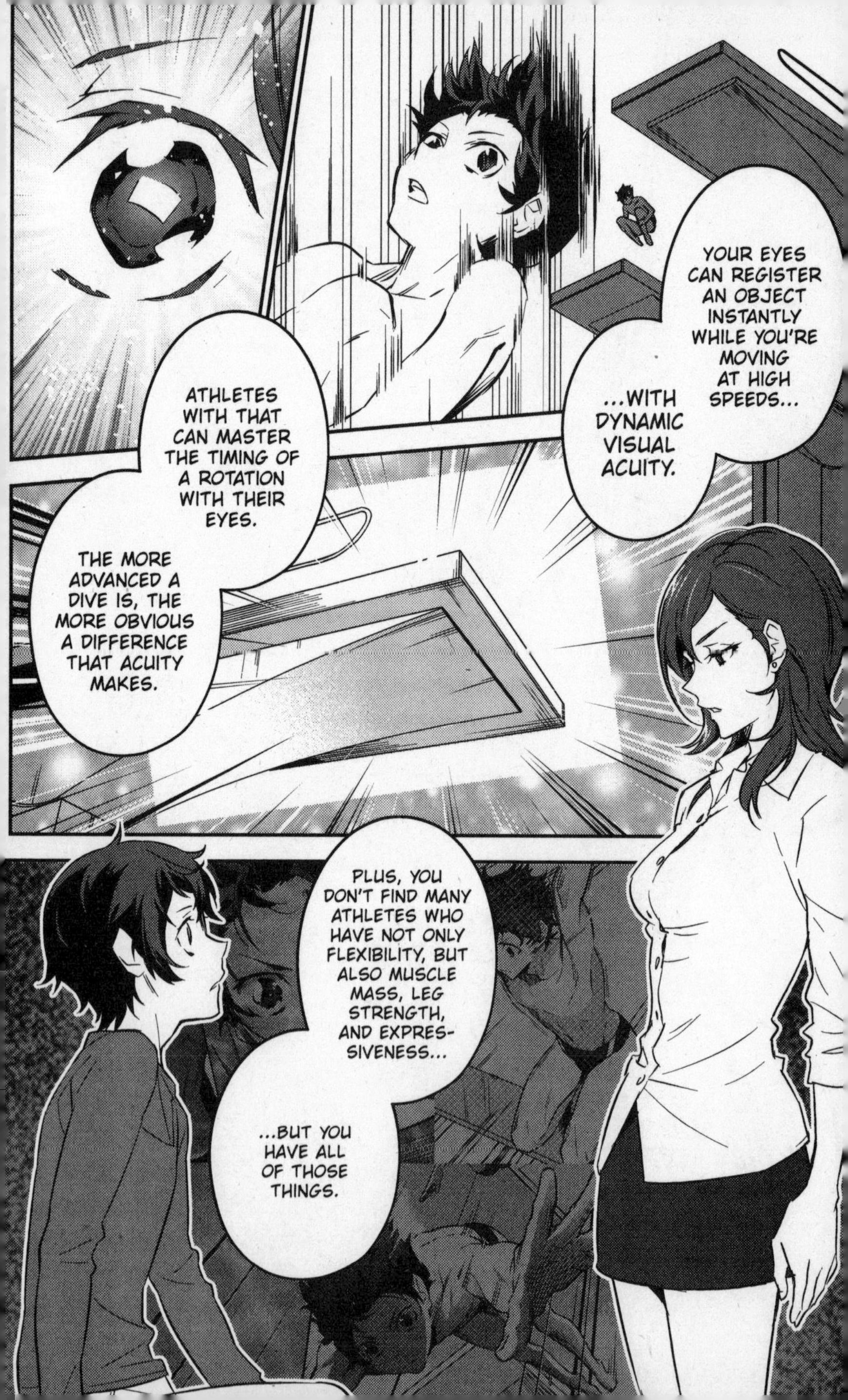
YOUR EYES CAN REGISTER AN OBJECT INSTANTLY WHILE YOU'RE MOVING AT HIGH SPEEDS...
...WITH DYNAMIC VISUAL ACUITY.
ATHLETES WITH THAT CAN MASTER THE TIMING OF A ROTATION WITH THEIR EYES.
THE MORE ADVANCED A DIVE IS, THE MORE OBVIOUS A DIFFERENCE THAT ACUITY MAKES.
PLUS, YOU DON'T FIND MANY ATHLETES WHO HAVE NOT ONLY FLEXIBILITY, BUT ALSO MUSCLE MASS, LEG STRENGTH, AND EXPRES-SIVENESS...
...BUT YOU HAVE ALL OF THOSE THINGS.

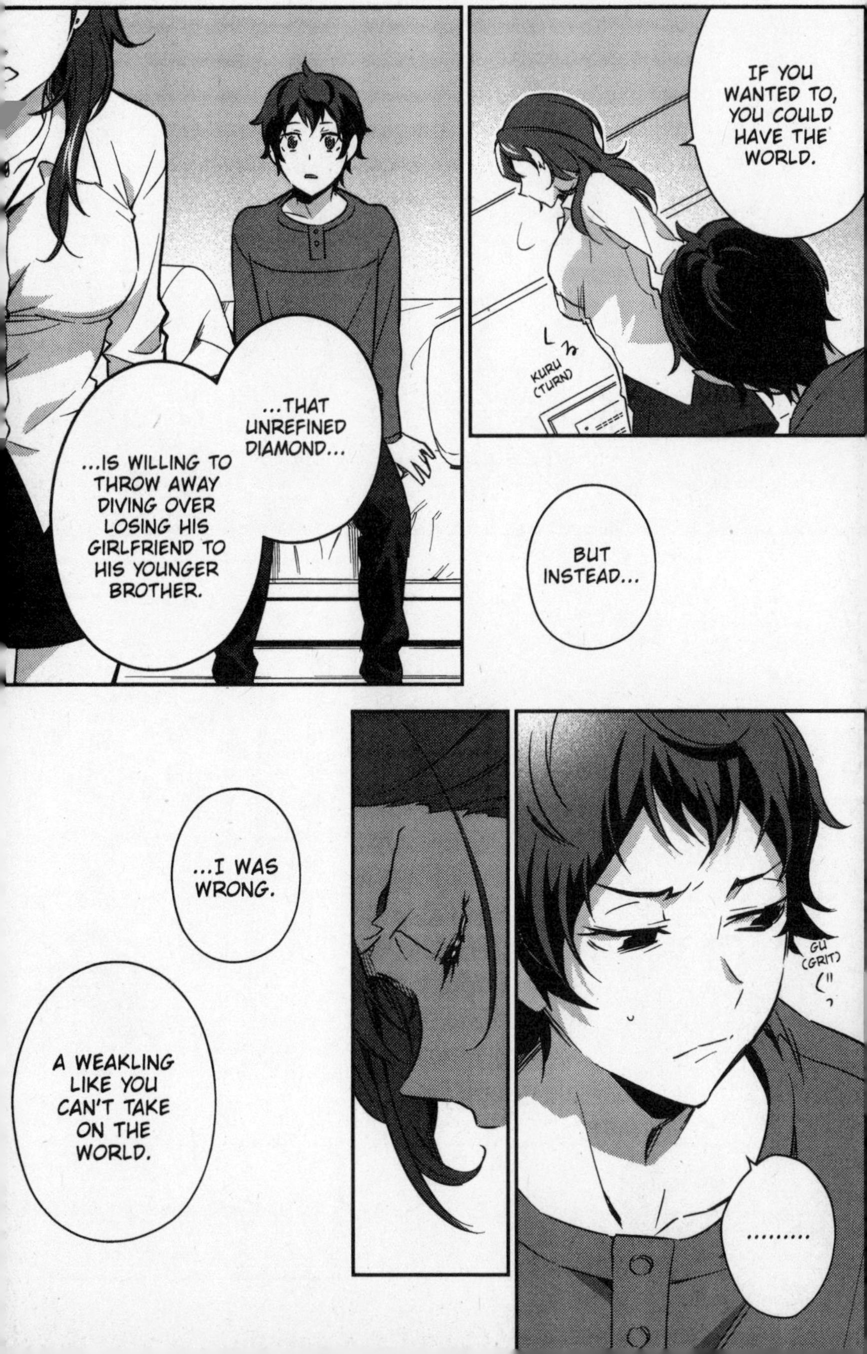
IF YOU WANTED TO, YOU COULD HAVE THE WORLD.
KURU (TURN)
...THAT UNREFINED DIAMOND...
...IS WILLING TO THROW AWAY DIVING OVER LOSING HIS GIRLFRIEND TO HIS YOUNGER BROTHER.
BUT INSTEAD...
GU (GRIT)
....
...I WAS WRONG.
A WEAKLING LIKE YOU CAN'T TAKE ON THE WORLD.

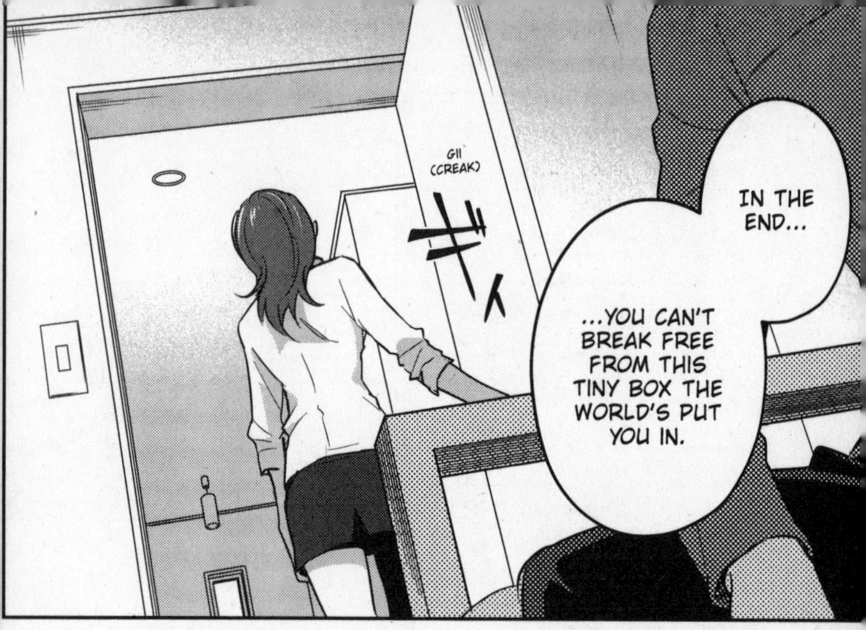
GII (CREAK)
ギィ
IN THE END...
...YOU CAN'T BREAK FREE FROM THIS TINY BOX THE WORLD'S PUT YOU IN.

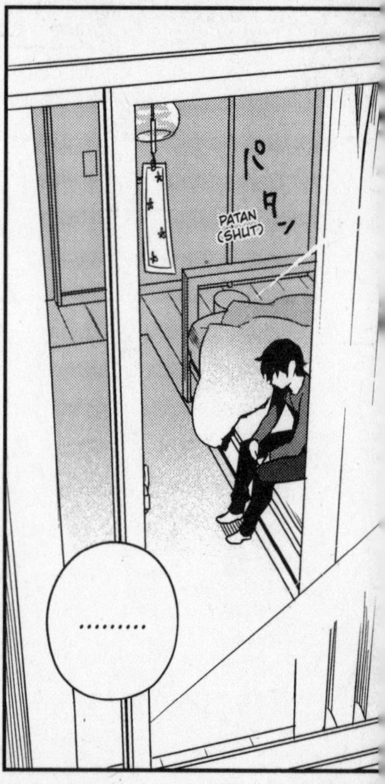
パタン
PATAN (SHUT)
....

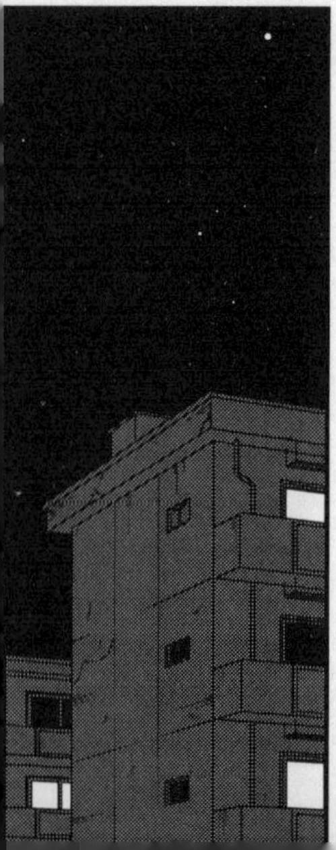

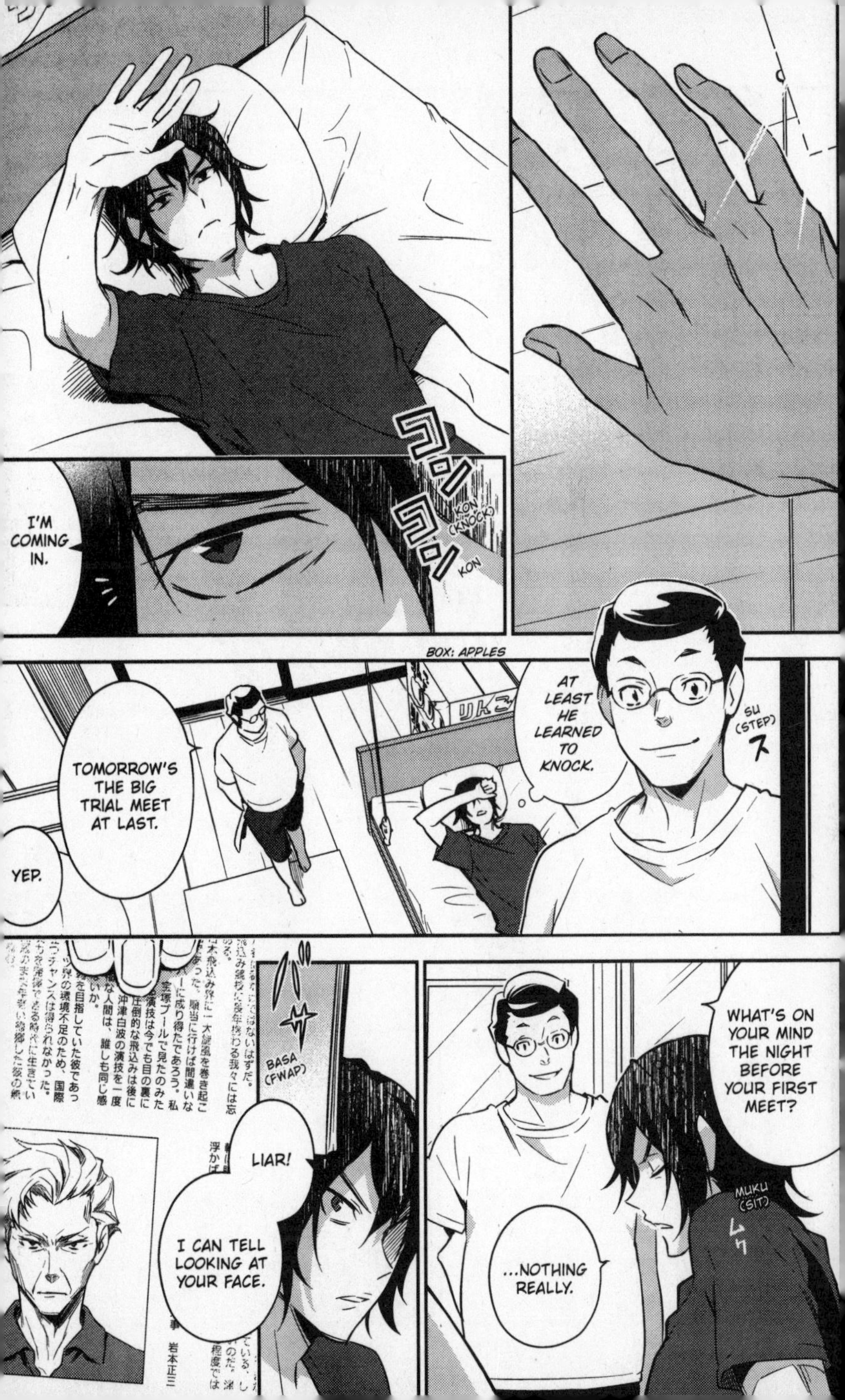
KON (KNOCK)
KON
I'M COMING IN.
BOX: APPLES
SU (STEP)
AT LEAST HE LEARNED TO KNOCK.
TOMORROW'S THE BIG TRIAL MEET AT LAST.
YEP.
WHAT'S ON YOUR MIND THE NIGHT BEFORE YOUR FIRST MEET?
MUKU (SIT)
...NOTHING REALLY.
BASA (FWAP)
LIAR!
I CAN TELL LOOKING AT YOUR FACE.

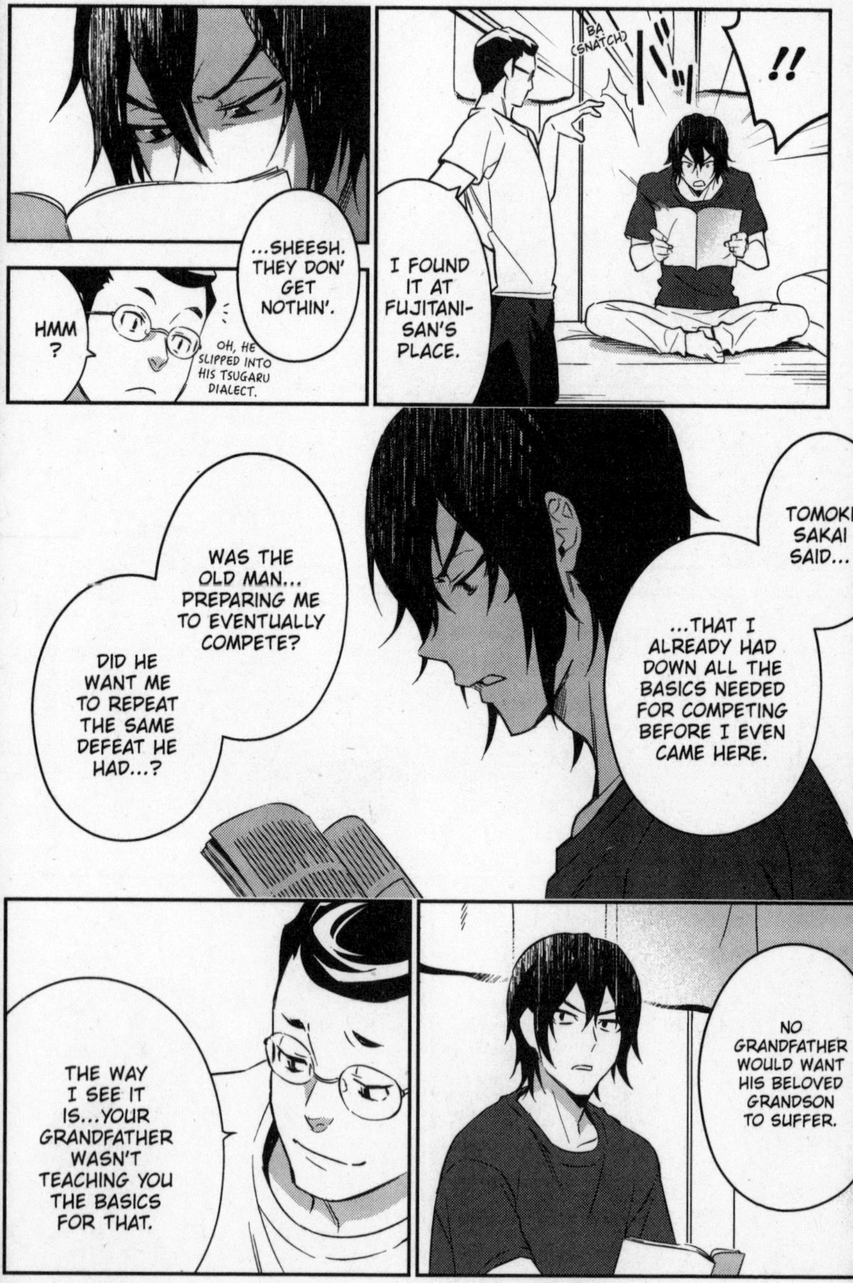
BA (SNATCH)
!!
I FOUND IT AT FUJITANI-SAN'S PLACE.
...SHEESH. THEY DON' GET NOTHIN'.
HMM?
OH, HE SLIPPED INTO HIS TSUGARU DIALECT.
TOMOKI SAKAI SAID...
...THAT I ALREADY HAD DOWN ALL THE BASICS NEEDED FOR COMPETING BEFORE I EVEN CAME HERE.
WAS THE OLD MAN... PREPARING ME TO EVENTUALLY COMPETE?
DID HE WANT ME TO REPEAT THE SAME DEFEAT HE HAD...?
NO GRANDFATHER WOULD WANT HIS BELOVED GRANDSON TO SUFFER.
THE WAY I SEE IT IS...YOUR GRANDFATHER WASN'T TEACHING YOU THE BASICS FOR THAT.

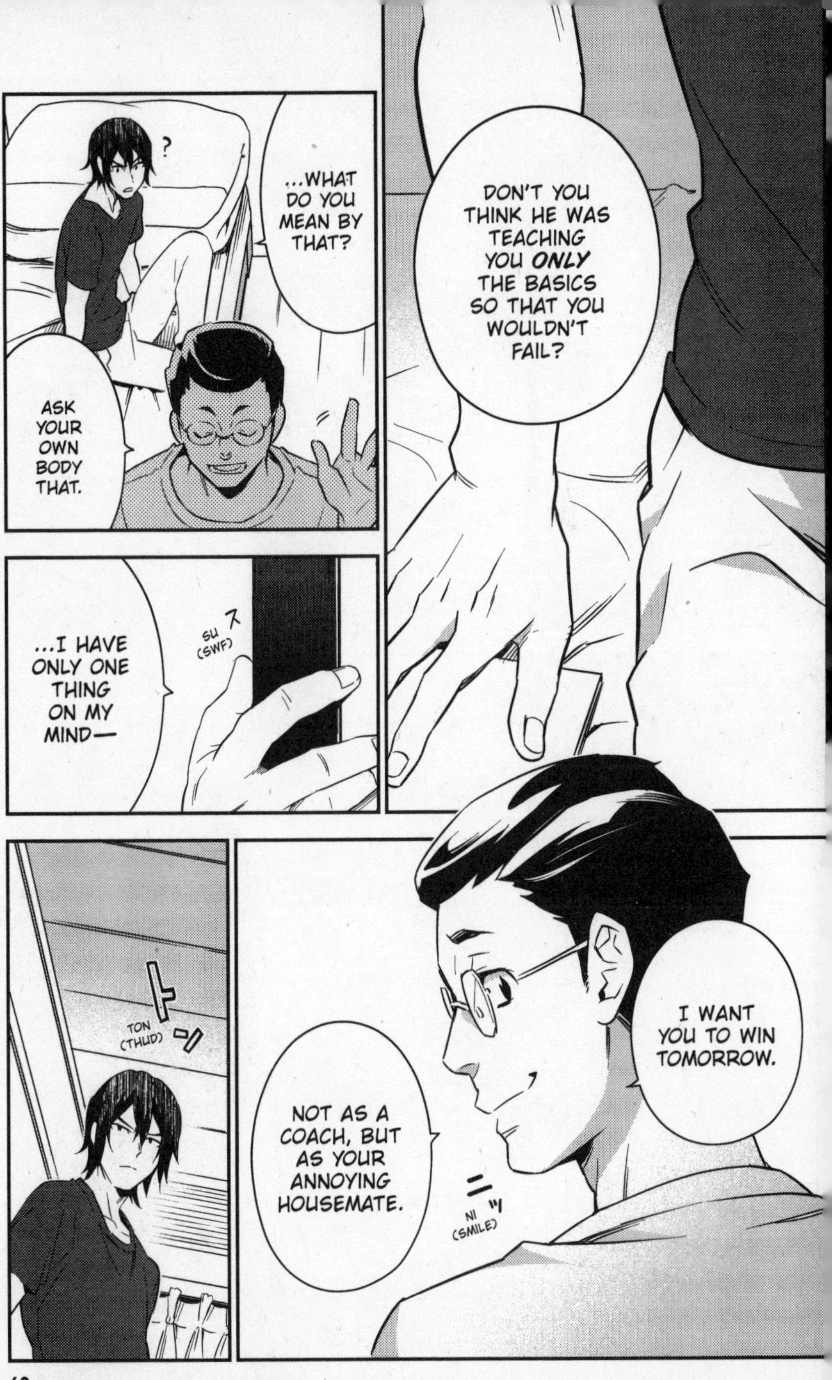
DON'T YOU THINK HE WAS TEACHING YOU ONLY THE BASICS SO THAT YOU WOULDN'T FAIL?
?
...WHAT DO YOU MEAN BY THAT?
ASK YOUR OWN BODY THAT.
ス
SU (SWF)
...I HAVE ONLY ONE THING ON MY MIND—
I WANT YOU TO WIN TOMORROW.
NOT AS A COACH, BUT AS YOUR ANNOYING HOUSEMATE.
ニッ
NI (SMILE)
トン
TON (THUD)

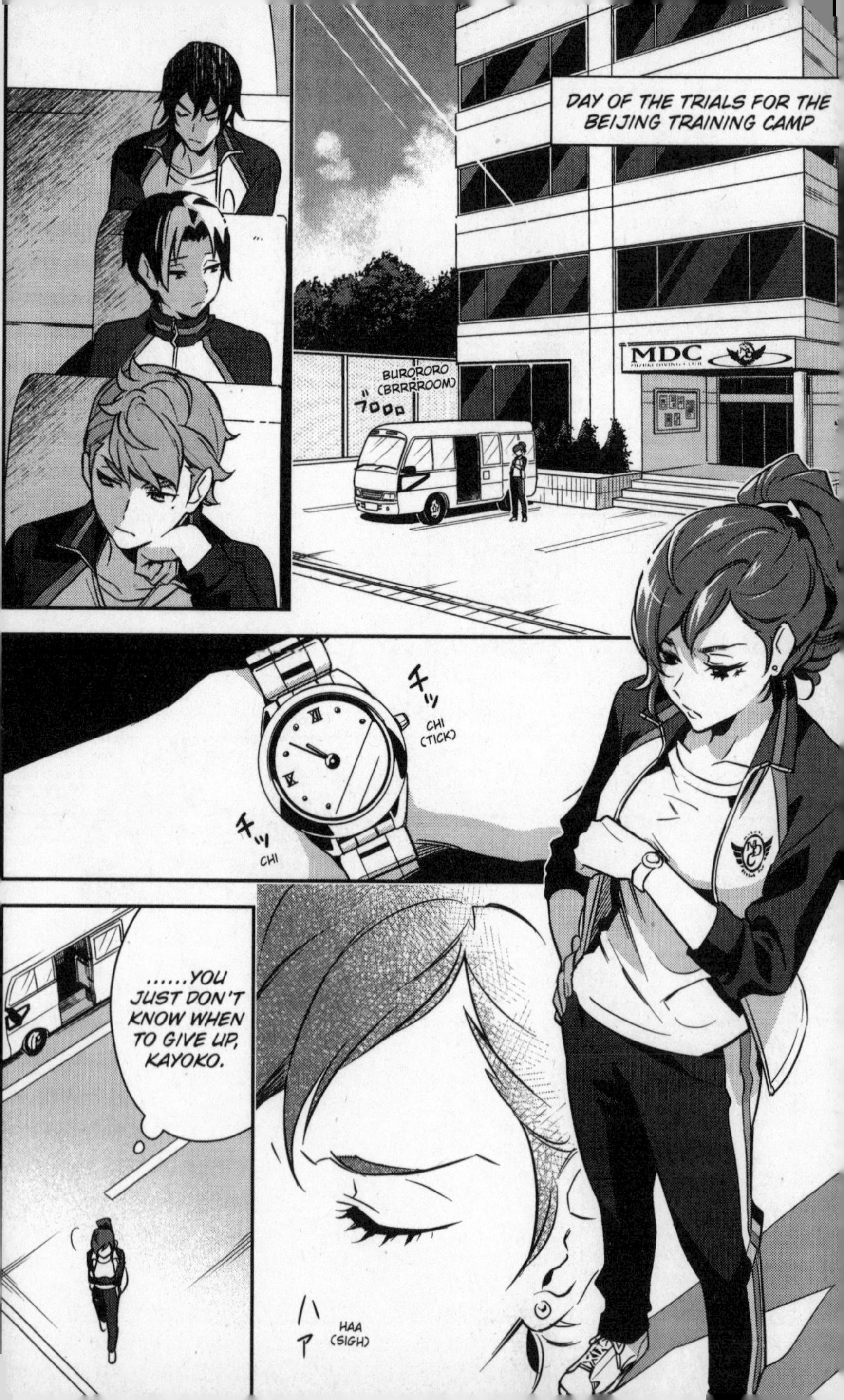
DAY OF THE TRIALS FOR THE BEIJING TRAINING CAMP
MDC
ブロロロ
BURORORO (BRRRROOM)
チッ
CHI (TICK)
チッ
CHI
ハァ
HAA (SIGH)
......YOU JUST DON'T KNOW WHEN TO GIVE UP, KAYOKO.

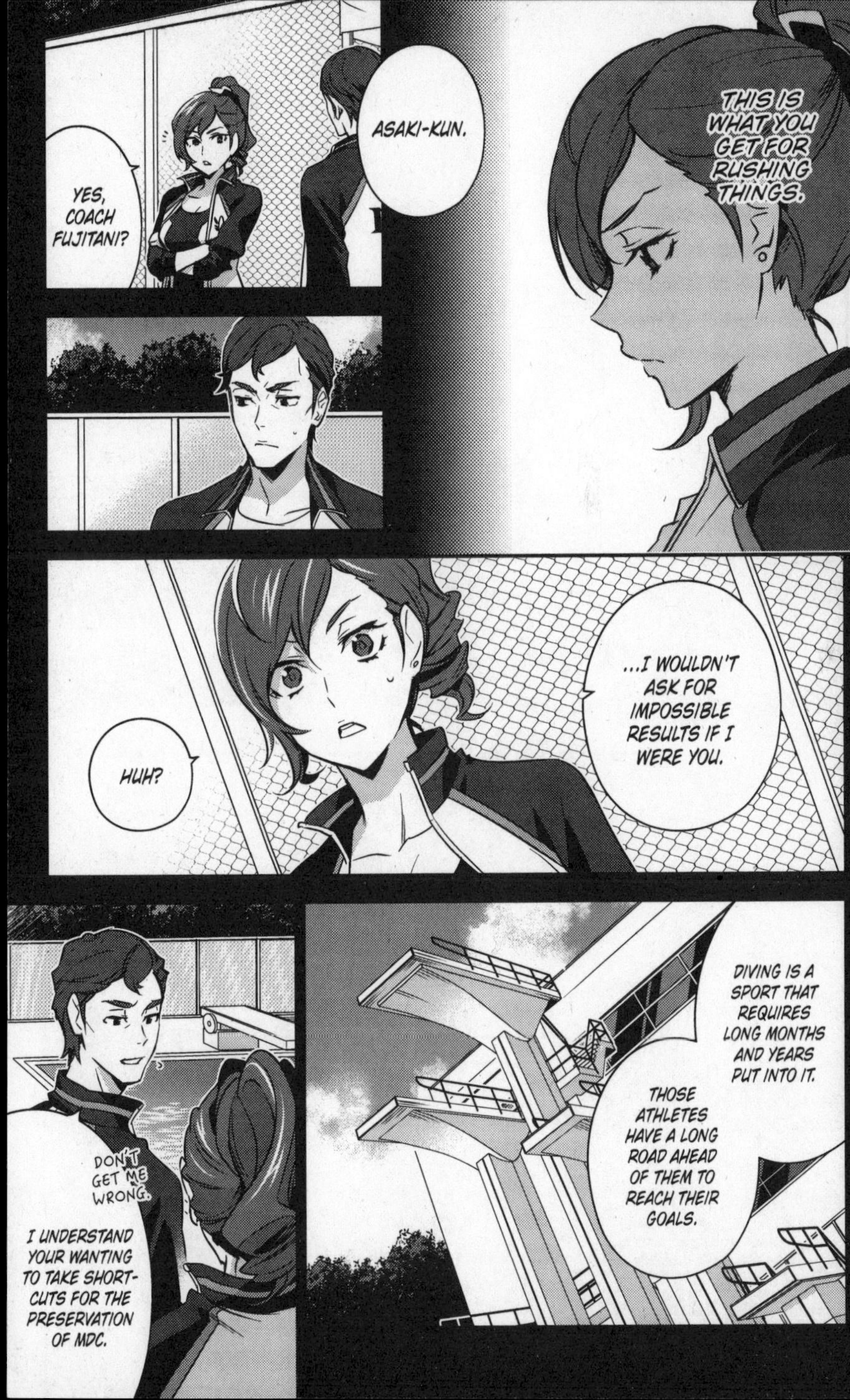
THIS IS WHAT YOU GET FOR RUSHING THINGS.
ASAKI-KUN.
YES, COACH FUJITANI?
...I WOULDN'T ASK FOR IMPOSSIBLE RESULTS IF I WERE YOU.
HUH?
DIVING IS A SPORT THAT REQUIRES LONG MONTHS AND YEARS PUT INTO IT.
THOSE ATHLETES HAVE A LONG ROAD AHEAD OF THEM TO REACH THEIR GOALS.
DON'T GET ME WRONG.
I UNDERSTAND YOUR WANTING TO TAKE SHORT-CUTS FOR THE PRESERVATION OF MDC.

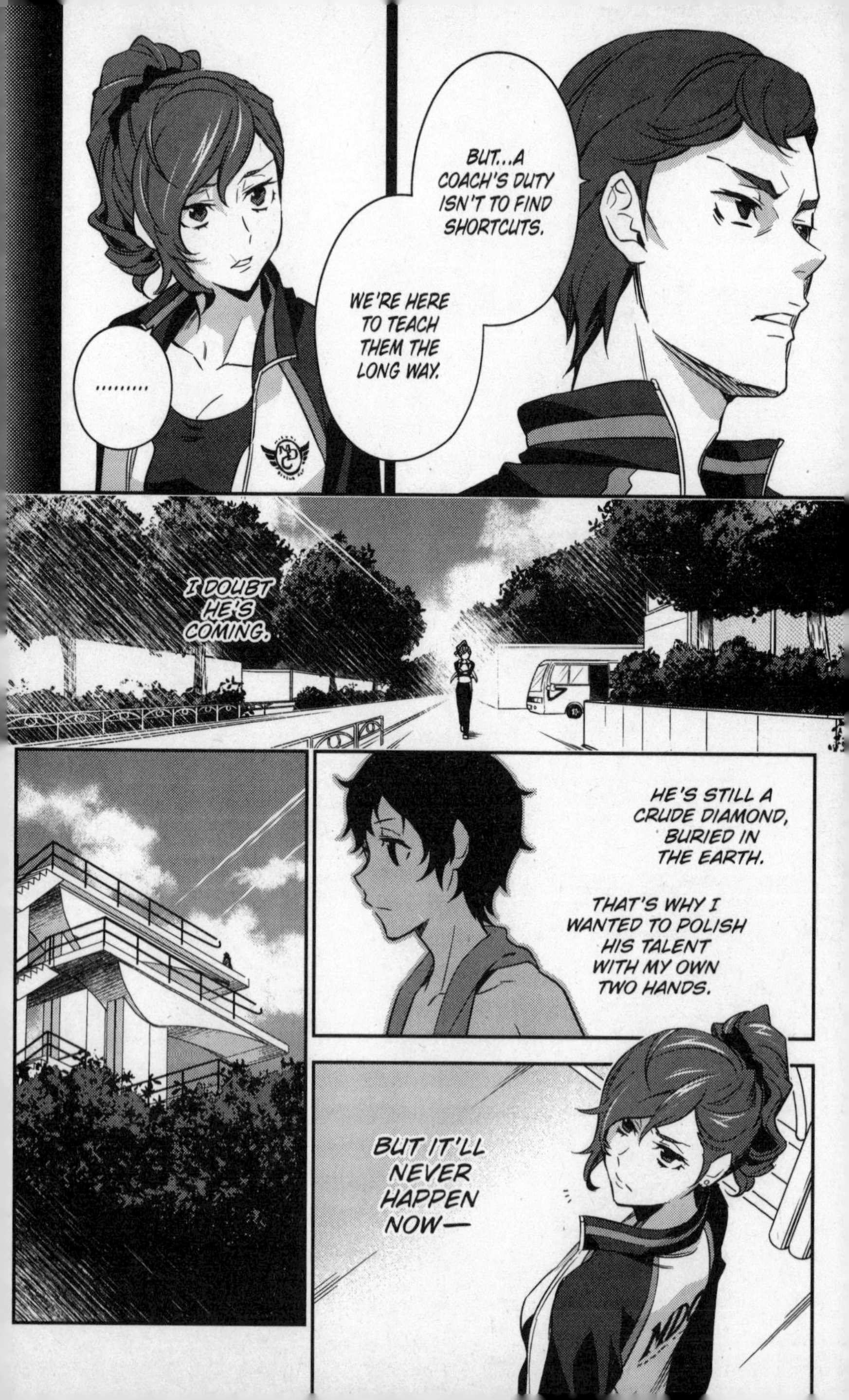
BUT...A COACH'S DUTY ISN'T TO FIND SHORTCUTS.
WE'RE HERE TO TEACH THEM THE LONG WAY.
....
I DOUBT HE'S COMING.
HE'S STILL A CRUDE DIAMOND, BURIED IN THE EARTH.
THAT'S WHY I WANTED TO POLISH HIS TALENT WITH MY OWN TWO HANDS.
BUT IT'LL NEVER HAPPEN NOW—

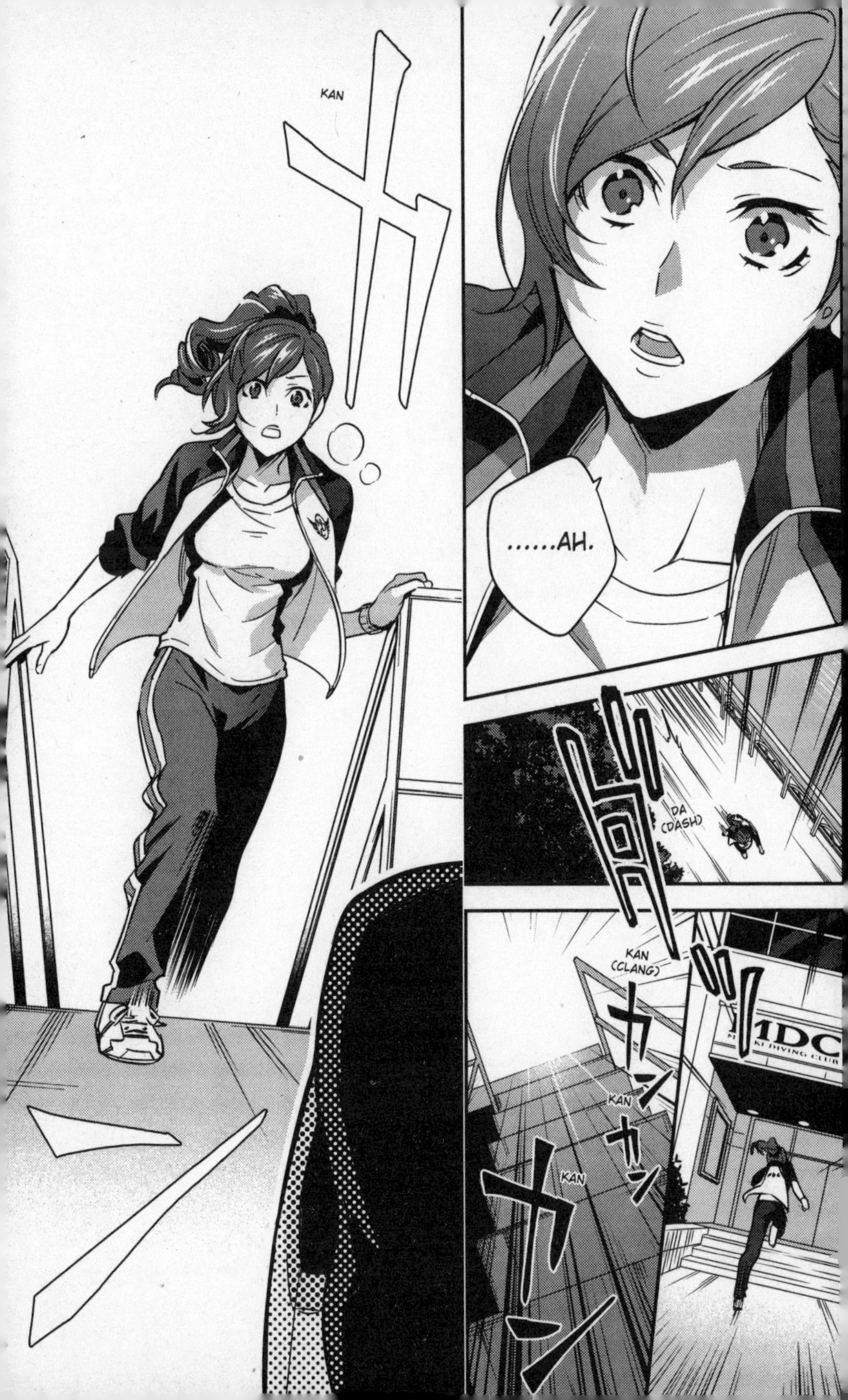

......AH.
DA
(DASH)
KAN
(CLANG)
DIVING CLUB
KAN
KAN
KAN

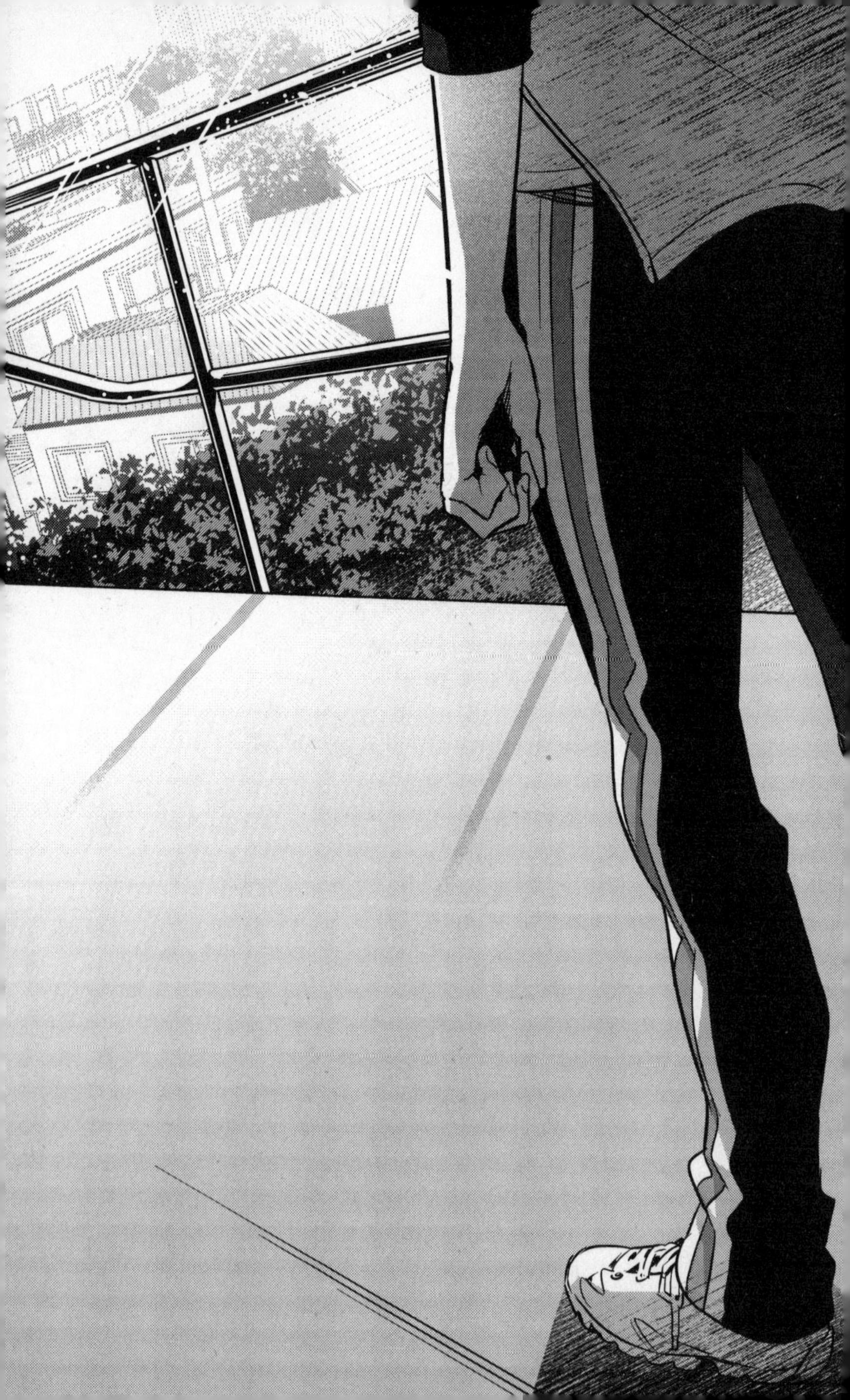

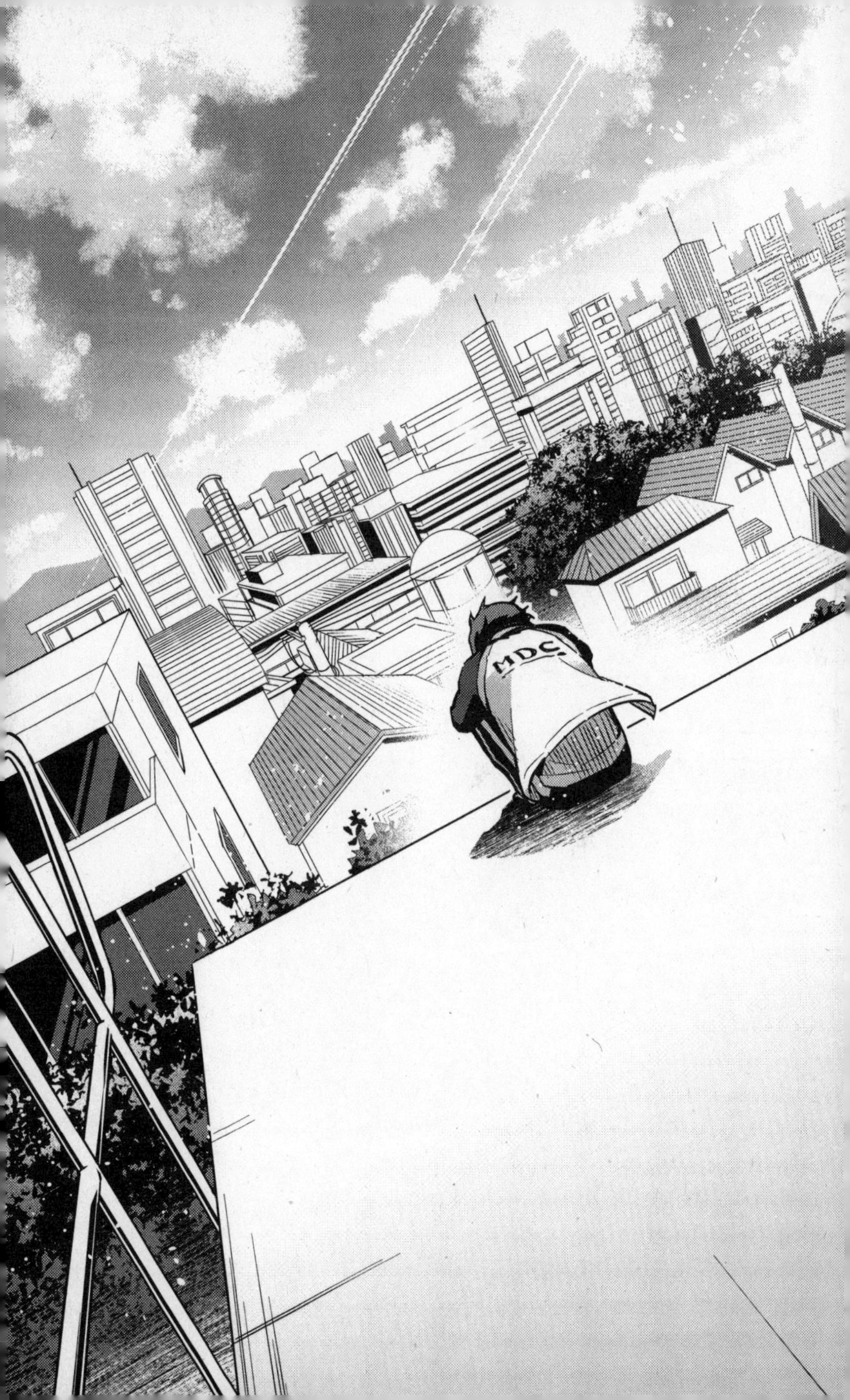
MDC

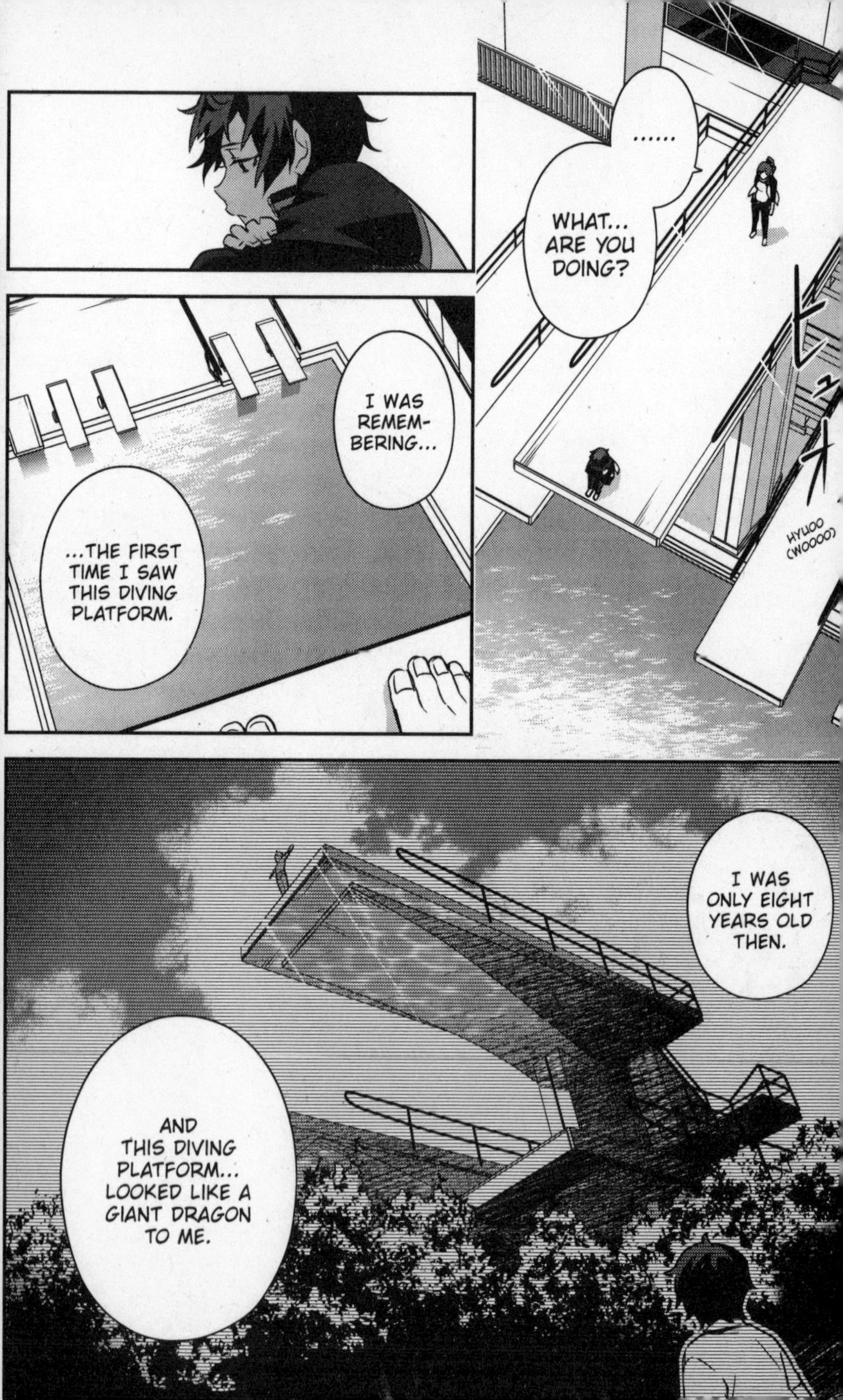
......
WHAT... ARE YOU DOING?
HYUOO (WOOOO)
I WAS REMEMBERING...
...THE FIRST TIME I SAW THIS DIVING PLATFORM.
I WAS ONLY EIGHT YEARS OLD THEN.
AND THIS DIVING PLATFORM... LOOKED LIKE A GIANT DRAGON TO ME.

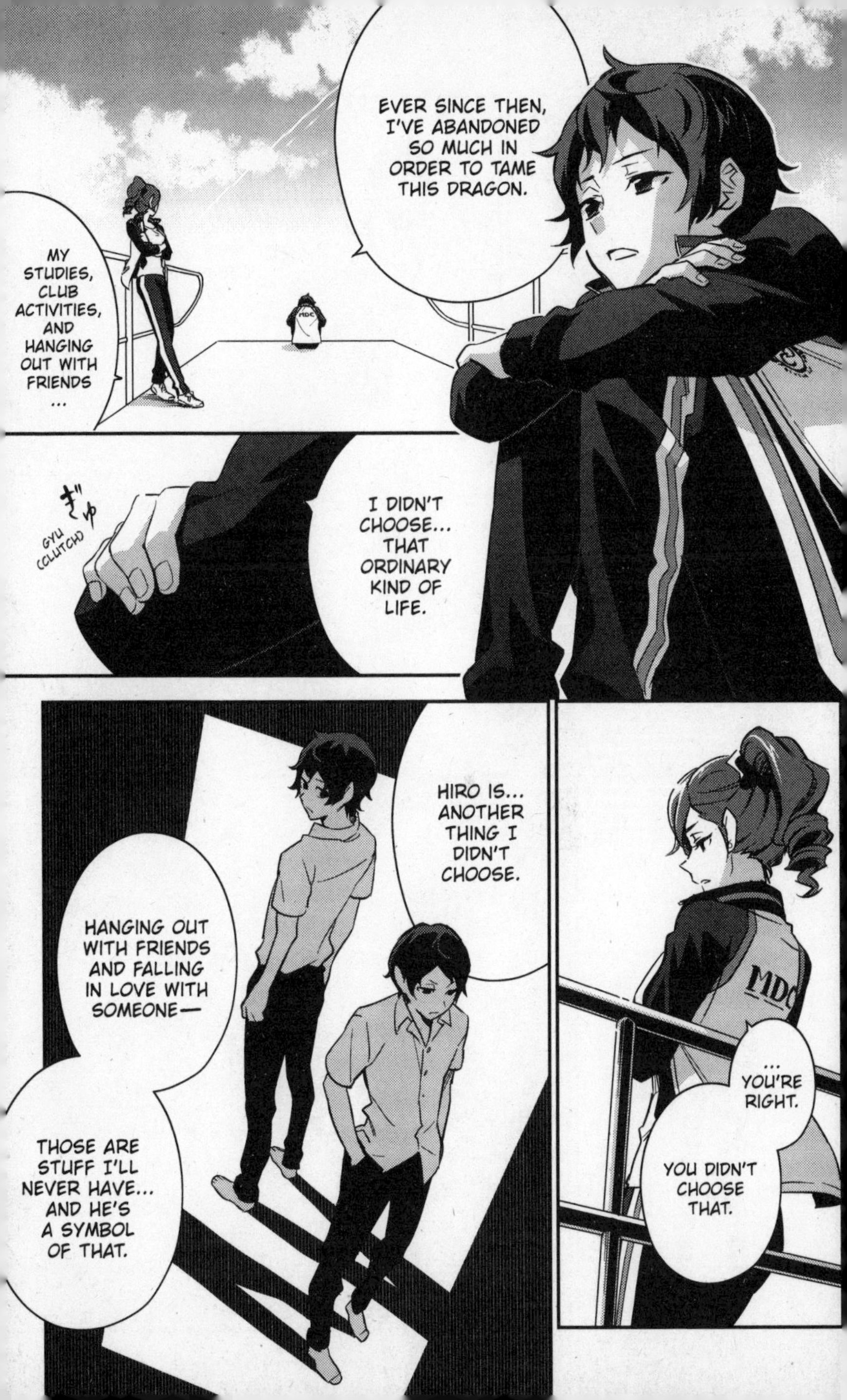
EVER SINCE THEN, I'VE ABANDONED SO MUCH IN ORDER TO TAME THIS DRAGON.
MY STUDIES, CLUB ACTIVITIES, AND HANGING OUT WITH FRIENDS ...
I DIDN'T CHOOSE... THAT ORDINARY KIND OF LIFE.
ぎゅ
GYU (CLUTCH)
... YOU'RE RIGHT.
YOU DIDN'T CHOOSE THAT.
HIRO IS... ANOTHER THING I DIDN'T CHOOSE.
HANGING OUT WITH FRIENDS AND FALLING IN LOVE WITH SOMEONE—
THOSE ARE STUFF I'LL NEVER HAVE... AND HE'S A SYMBOL OF THAT.

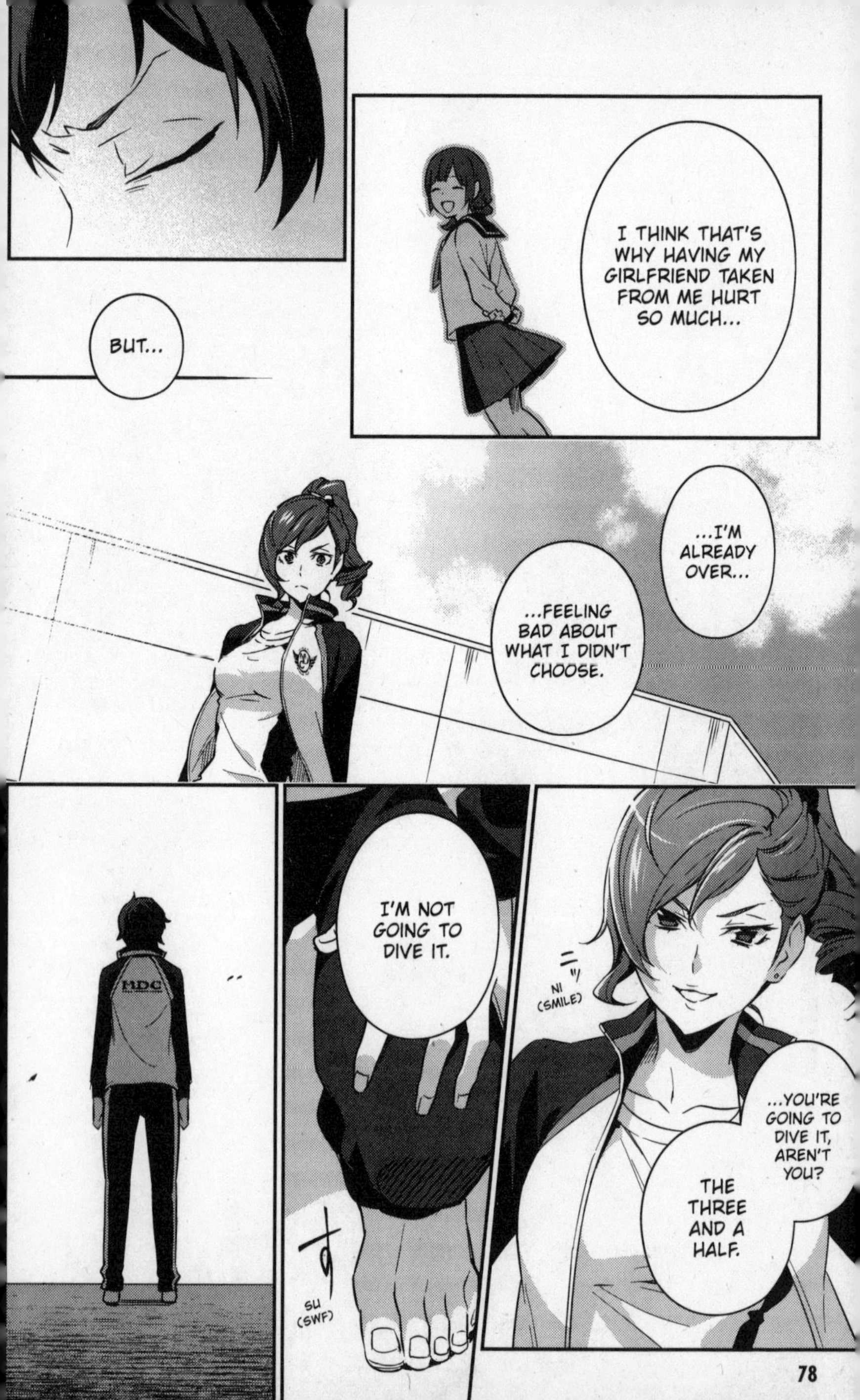
I THINK THAT'S WHY HAVING MY GIRLFRIEND TAKEN FROM ME HURT SO MUCH...
BUT...
...I'M ALREADY OVER...
...FEELING BAD ABOUT WHAT I DIDN'T CHOOSE.
NI (SMILE)
...YOU'RE GOING TO DIVE IT, AREN'T YOU?
THE THREE AND A HALF.
I'M NOT GOING TO DIVE IT.
SU (SWF)
MDC

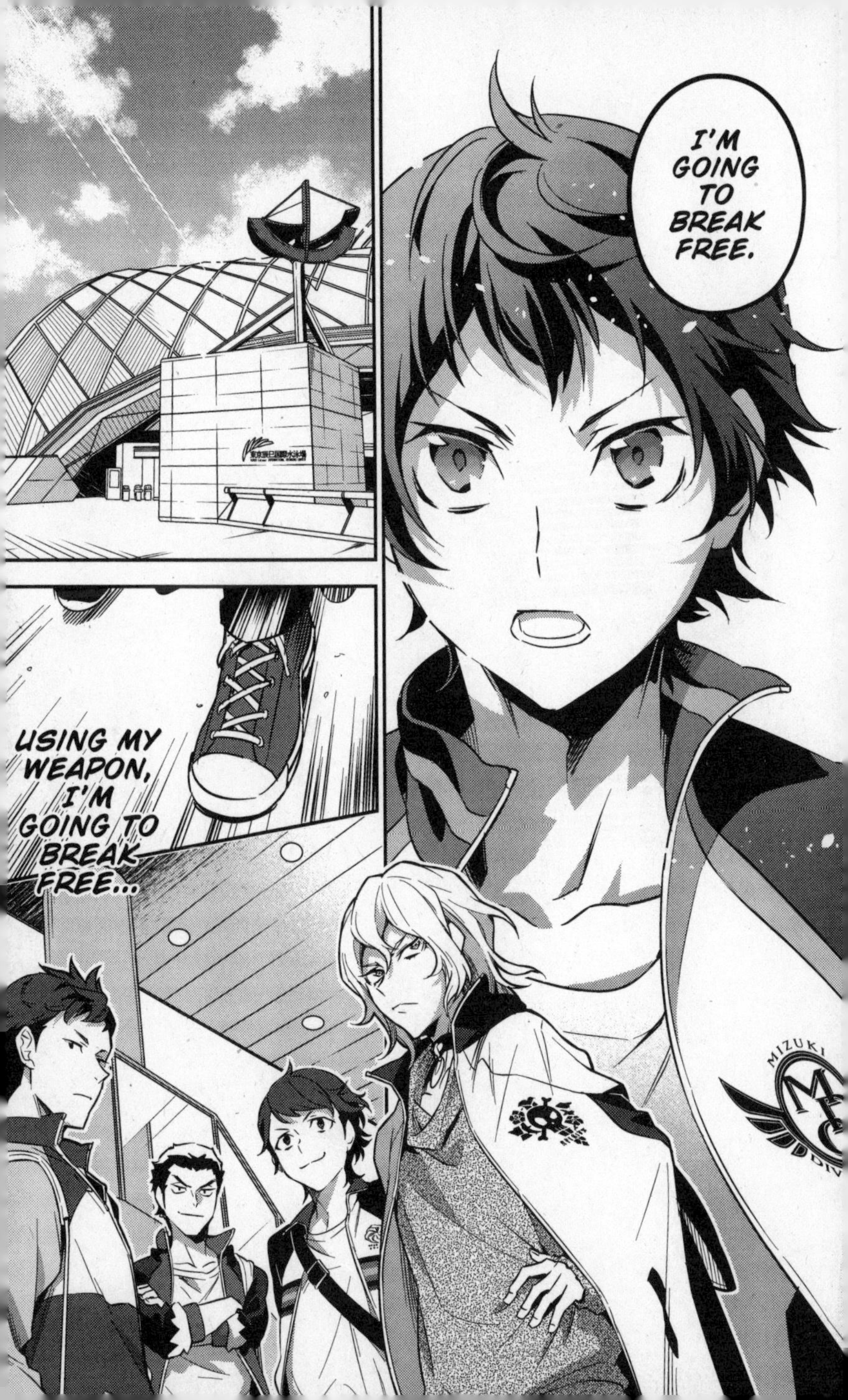
I'M GOING TO BREAK FREE.
USING MY WEAPON, I'M GOING TO BREAK FREE...
MIZUKI

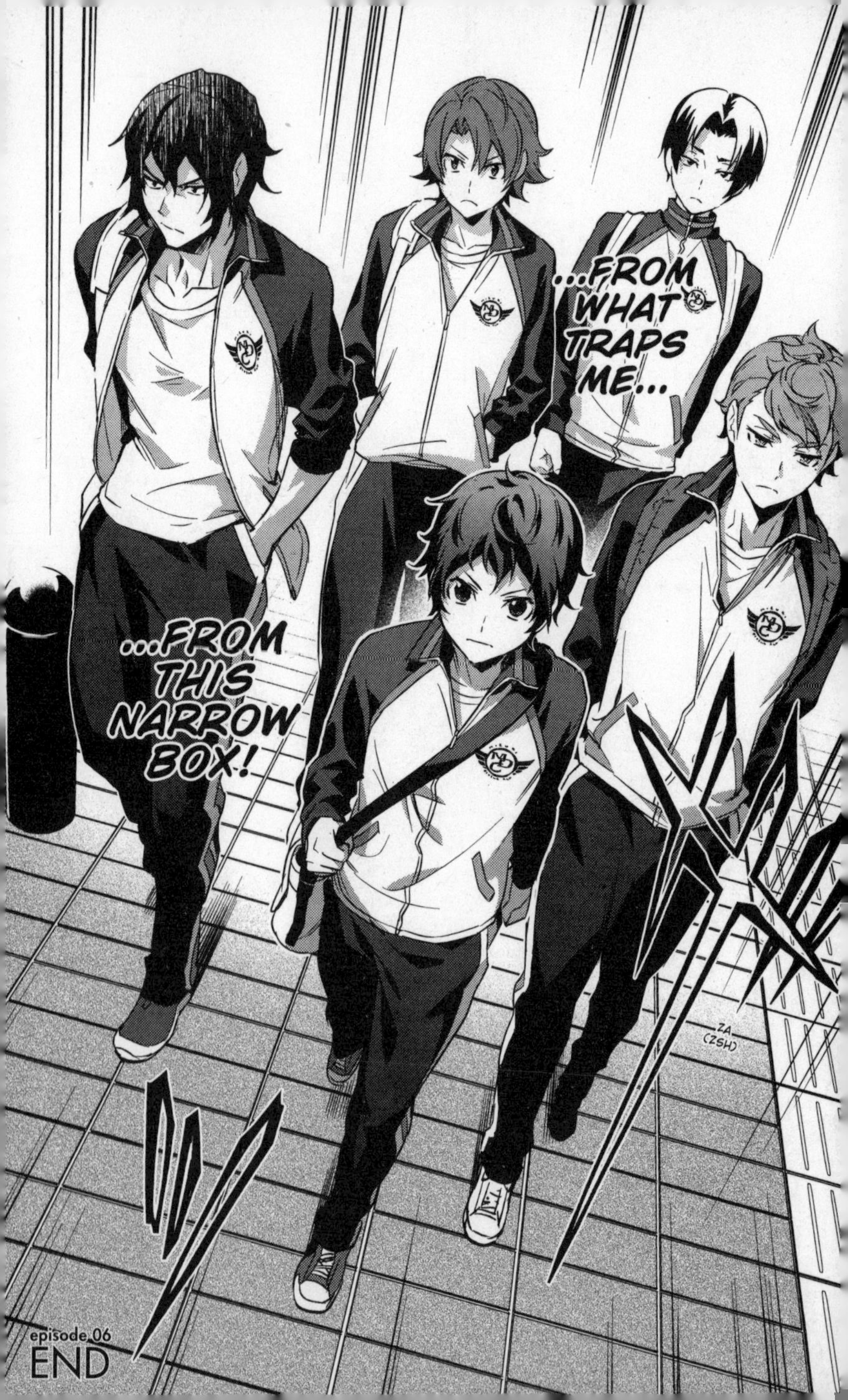
...FROM WHAT TRAPS ME...
...FROM THIS NARROW BOX!
ZA (ZSH)
episode 06 END

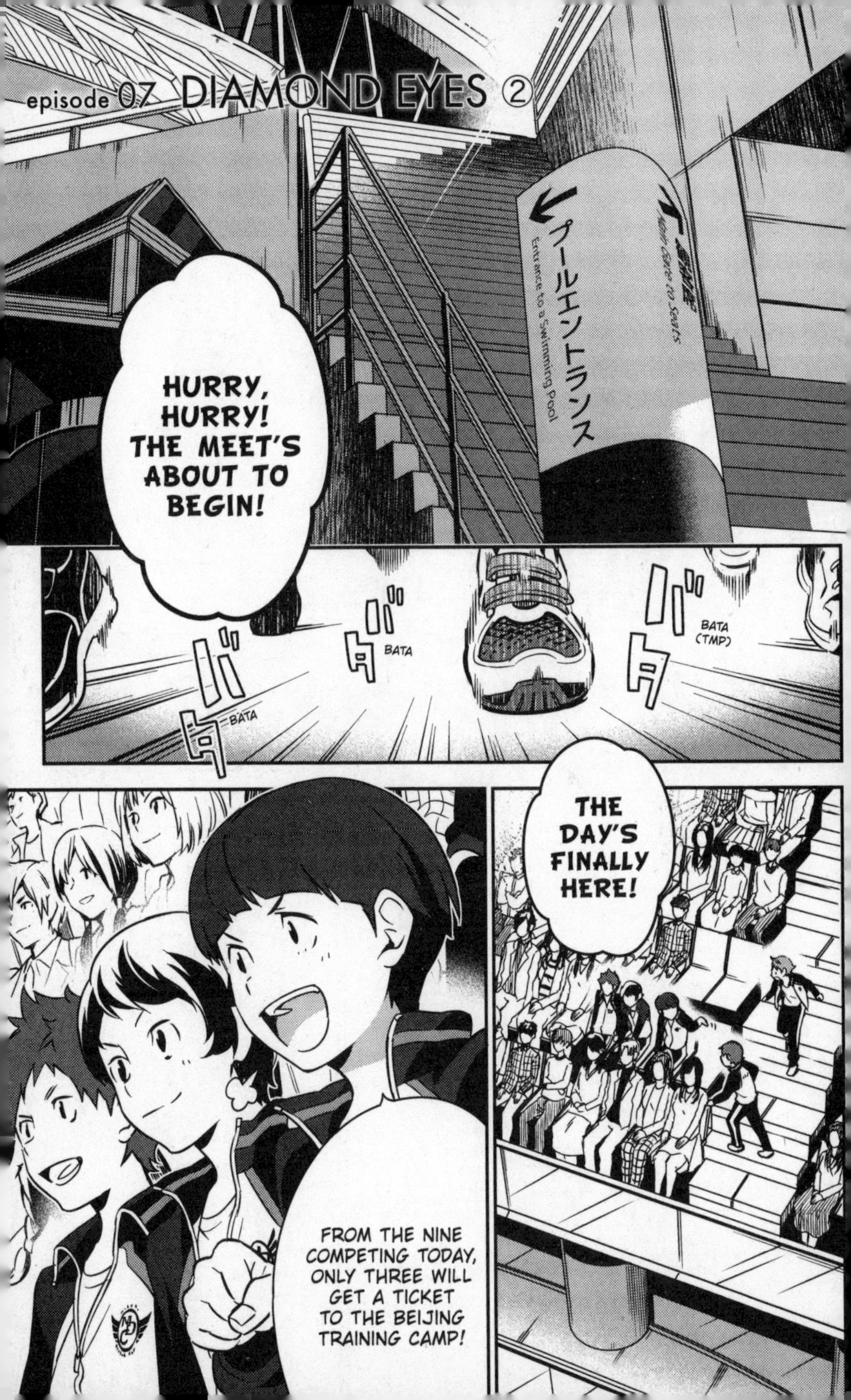
episode 07 DIAMOND EYES ②
プールエントランス
Entrance to a Swimming Pool
HURRY, HURRY! THE MEET'S ABOUT TO BEGIN!
バタ
BATA (TMP)
バタ
BATA
バタ
BATA
THE DAY'S FINALLY HERE!
FROM THE NINE COMPETING TODAY, ONLY THREE WILL GET A TICKET TO THE BEIJING TRAINING CAMP!

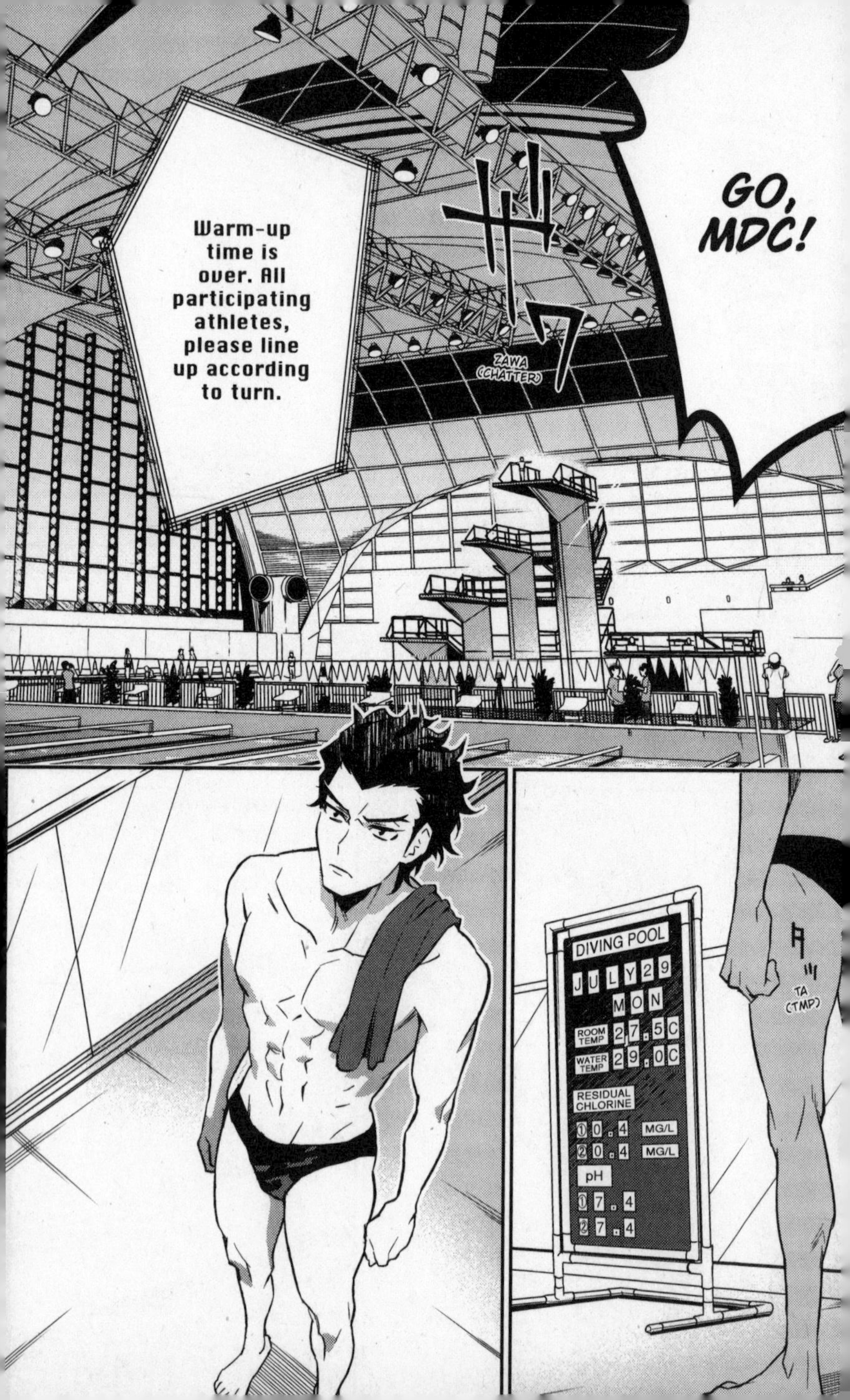
GO, MDC!
ZAWA (CHATTER)
Warm-up time is over. All participating athletes, please line up according to turn.
TA (TMP)
DIVING POOL
JULY 29
MON
ROOM TEMP 27.5C
WATER TEMP 29.0C
RESIDUAL CHLORINE
① 0.4 MG/L
② 0.4 MG/L
pH
① 7.4
② 7.4

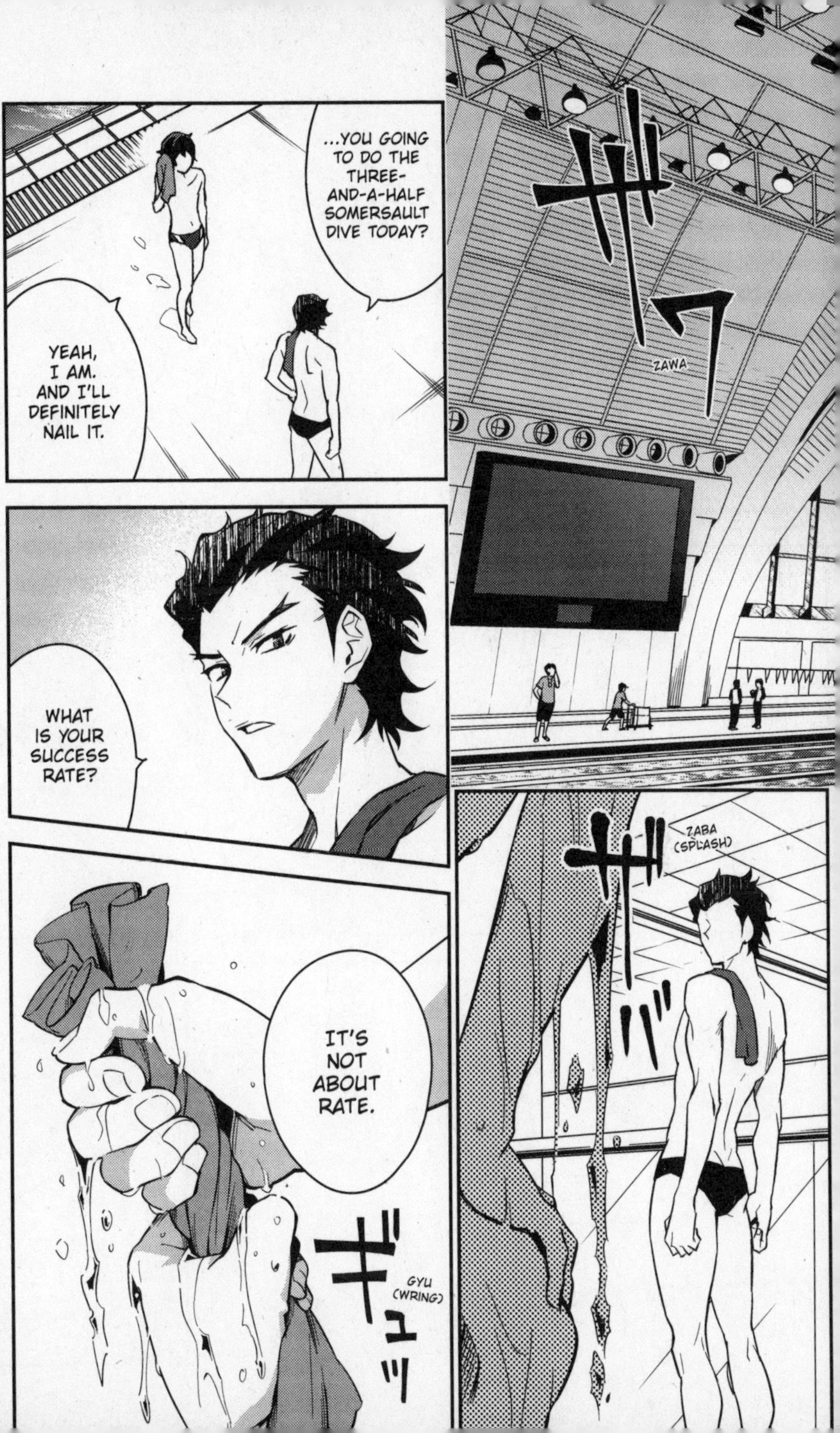

ザワ
ZAWA
ザバ
ZABA (SPLASH)
...YOU GOING TO DO THE THREE-AND-A-HALF SOMERSAULT DIVE TODAY?
YEAH, I AM. AND I'LL DEFINITELY NAIL IT.
WHAT IS YOUR SUCCESS RATE?
IT'S NOT ABOUT RATE.
ギュッ
GYU (WRING)

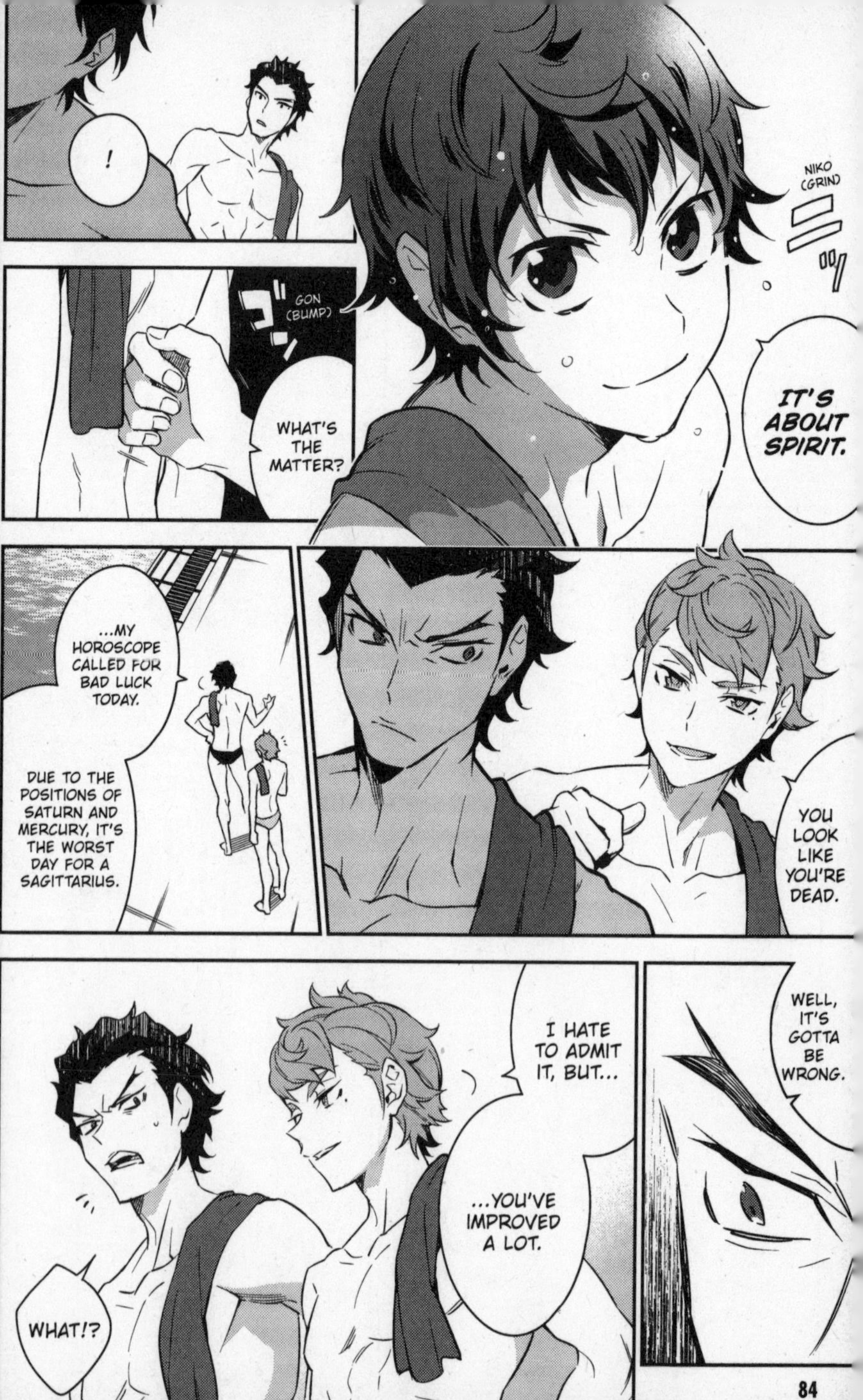
NIKO (GRIN)
IT'S ABOUT SPIRIT.
!
GON (BUMP)
WHAT'S THE MATTER?
YOU LOOK LIKE YOU'RE DEAD.
...MY HOROSCOPE CALLED FOR BAD LUCK TODAY.
DUE TO THE POSITIONS OF SATURN AND MERCURY, IT'S THE WORST DAY FOR A SAGITTARIUS.
WELL, IT'S GOTTA BE WRONG.
I HATE TO ADMIT IT, BUT...
...YOU'VE IMPROVED A LOT.
WHAT!?

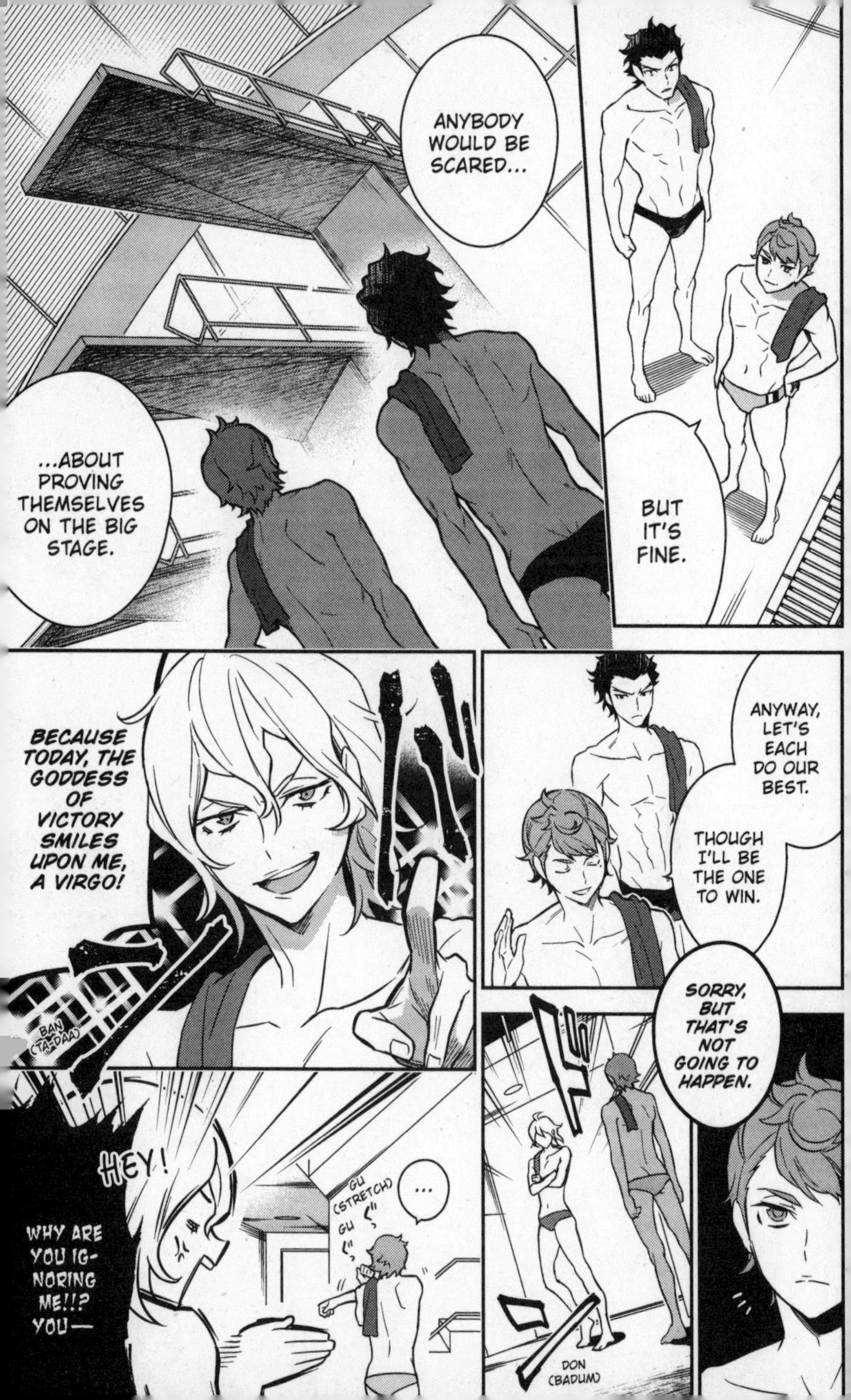
BUT IT'S FINE.
ANYBODY WOULD BE SCARED...
...ABOUT PROVING THEMSELVES ON THE BIG STAGE.
ANYWAY, LET'S EACH DO OUR BEST.
THOUGH I'LL BE THE ONE TO WIN.
BECAUSE TODAY, THE GODDESS OF VICTORY SMILES UPON ME, A VIRGO!
BAN (TA-DAA)
SORRY, BUT THAT'S NOT GOING TO HAPPEN.
DON (BADUM)
...
GU (STRETCH) GU
HEY!
WHY ARE YOU IG-NORING ME!!? YOU—

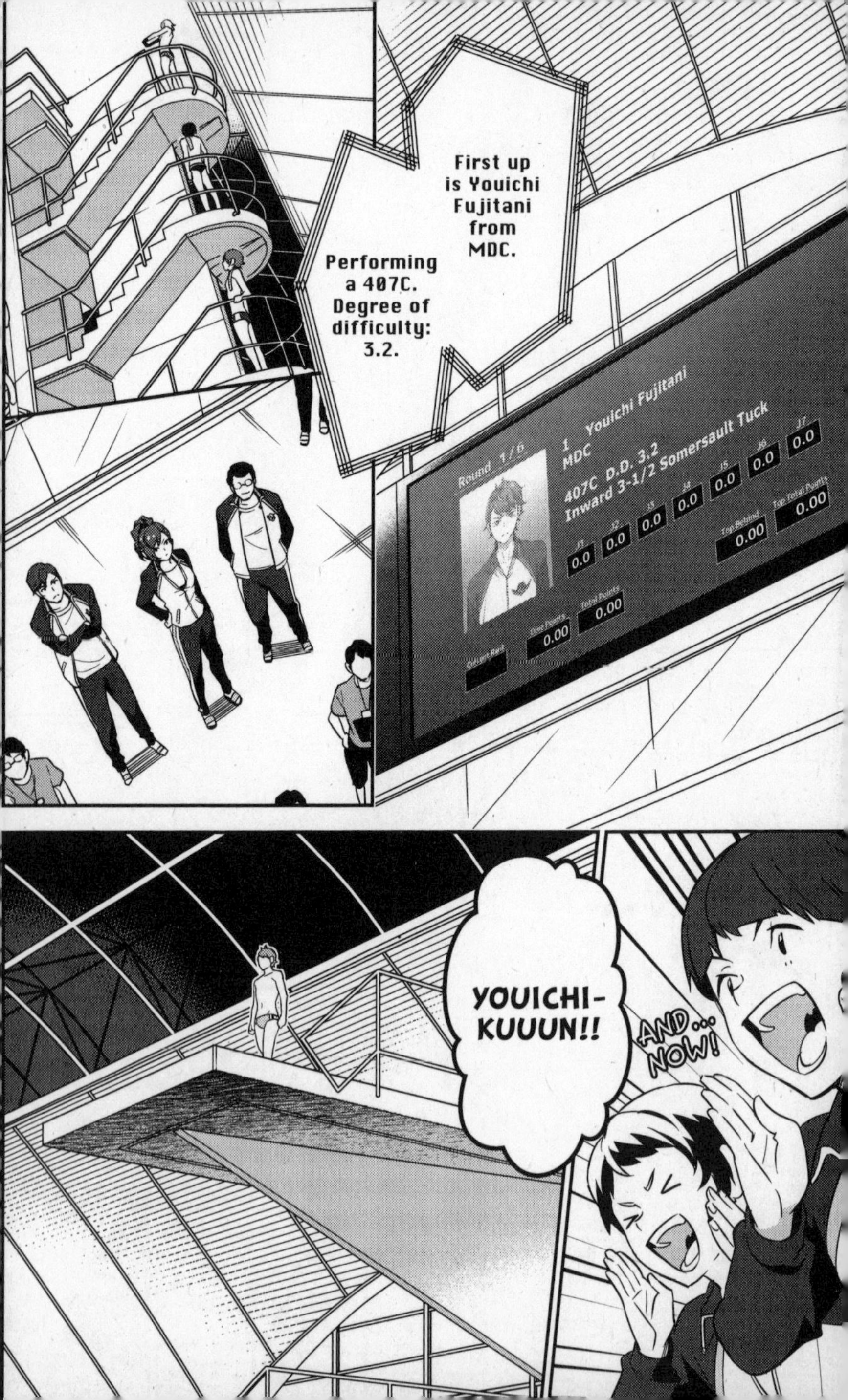

First up is Youichi Fujitani from MDC.
Performing a 407C. Degree of difficulty: 3.2.
Round 1/6
1 Youichi Fujitani
MDC
407C D.D. 3.2
Inward 3-1/2 Somersault Tuck
AND... NOW!
YOUICHI-KUUUN!!

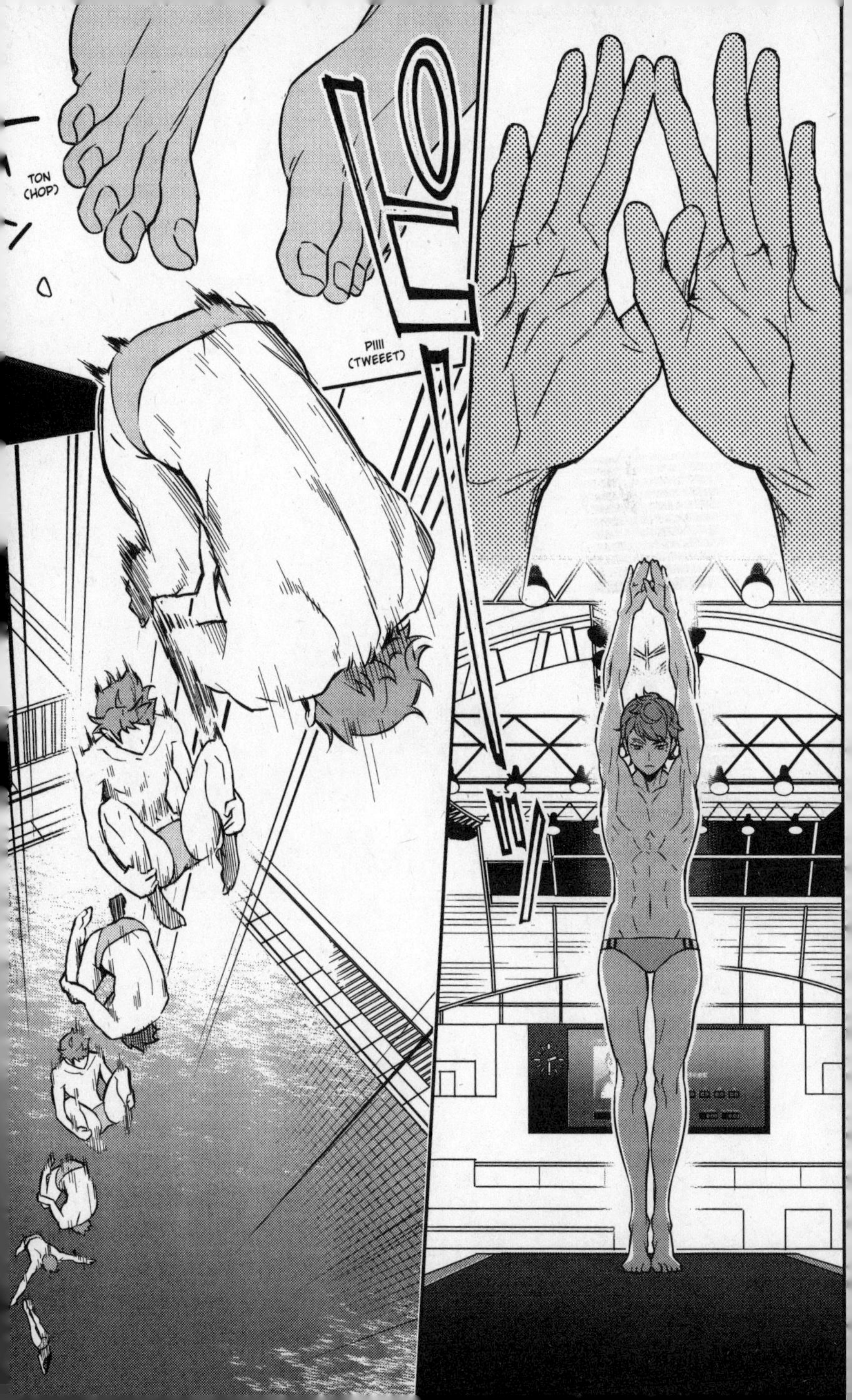
PIIII
(TWEEET)
TON
(HOP)

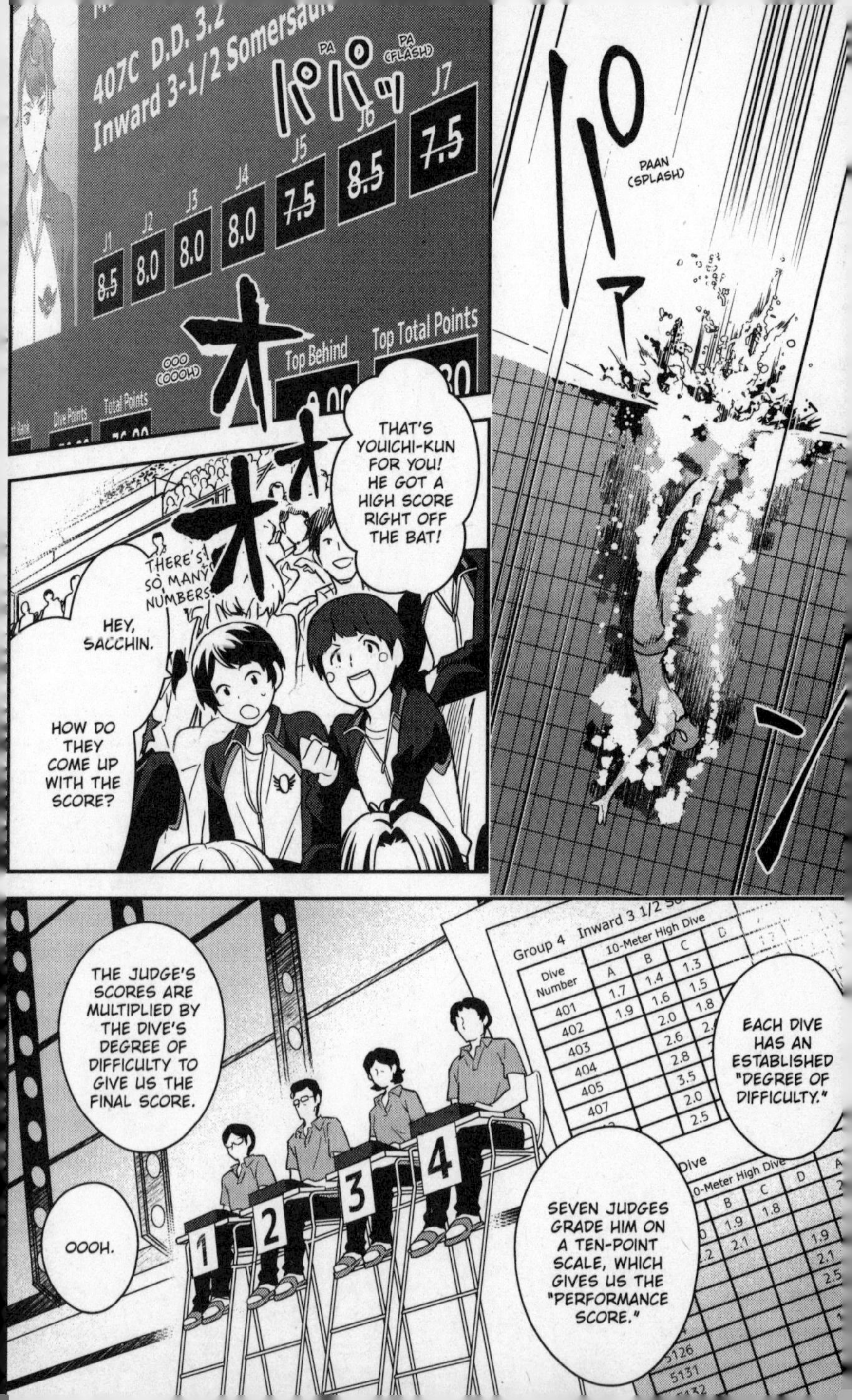
パァーン
PAAN (SPLASH)
407C D.D. 3.2
Inward 3-1/2 Somersault
パパッ
PA PA (FLASH)
J1 8.5
J2 8.0
J3 8.0
J4 8.0
J5 7.5
J6 8.5
J7 7.5
Top Total Points
Top Behind
Total Points
Dive Points
オオオ
OOO (OOOH)
THAT'S YOUICHI-KUN FOR YOU! HE GOT A HIGH SCORE RIGHT OFF THE BAT!
THERE'S SO MANY NUMBERS.
HEY, SACCHIN.
HOW DO THEY COME UP WITH THE SCORE?
Group 4 Inward 3 1/2
10-Meter High Dive
Dive Number
EACH DIVE HAS AN ESTABLISHED "DEGREE OF DIFFICULTY."
SEVEN JUDGES GRADE HIM ON A TEN-POINT SCALE, WHICH GIVES US THE "PERFORMANCE SCORE."
THE JUDGE'S SCORES ARE MULTIPLIED BY THE DIVE'S DEGREE OF DIFFICULTY TO GIVE US THE FINAL SCORE.
OOOH.

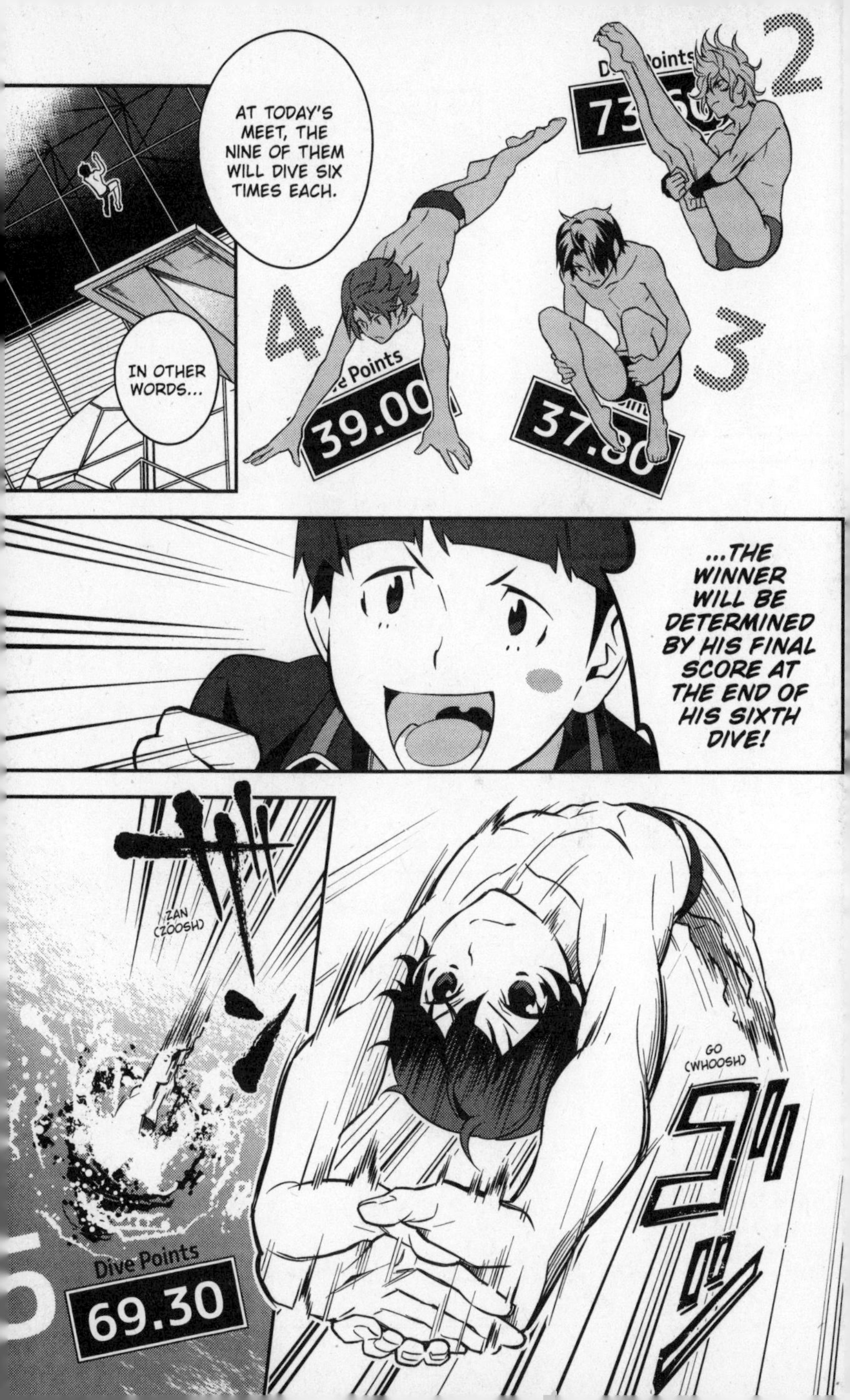

AT TODAY'S MEET, THE NINE OF THEM WILL DIVE SIX TIMES EACH.
39.00
IN OTHER WORDS...
...THE WINNER WILL BE DETERMINED BY HIS FINAL SCORE AT THE END OF HIS SIXTH DIVE!
GO (WHOOSH)
ZAN (ZOOSH)
Dive Points
69.30

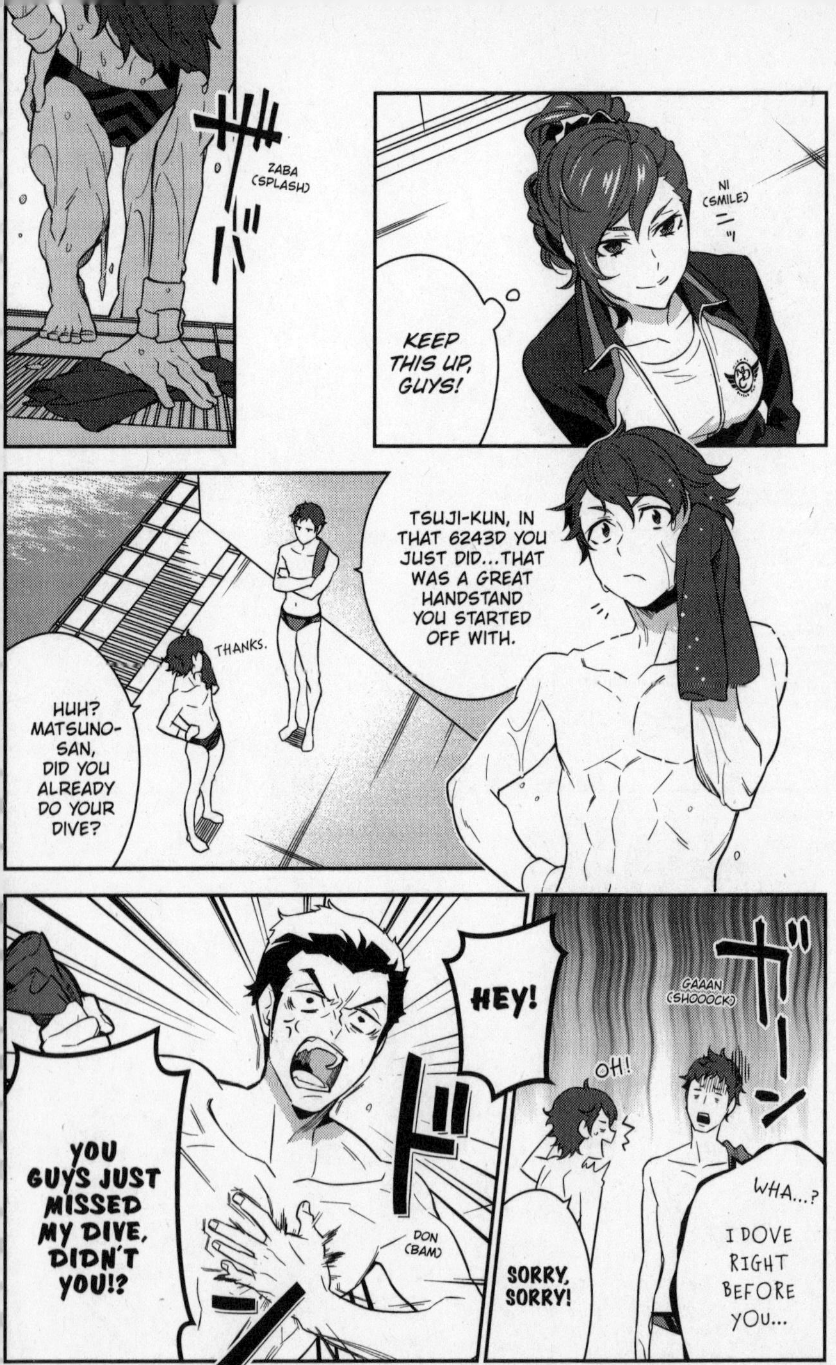
NI (SMILE)
KEEP THIS UP, GUYS!
ZABA (SPLASH)
TSUJI-KUN, IN THAT 6243D YOU JUST DID...THAT WAS A GREAT HANDSTAND YOU STARTED OFF WITH.
THANKS.
HUH? MATSUNO-SAN, DID YOU ALREADY DO YOUR DIVE?
GAAAN (SHOOOCK)
OH!
WHA...?
I DOVE RIGHT BEFORE YOU...
SORRY, SORRY!
HEY!
DON (BAM)
YOU GUYS JUST MISSED MY DIVE, DIDN'T YOU!?

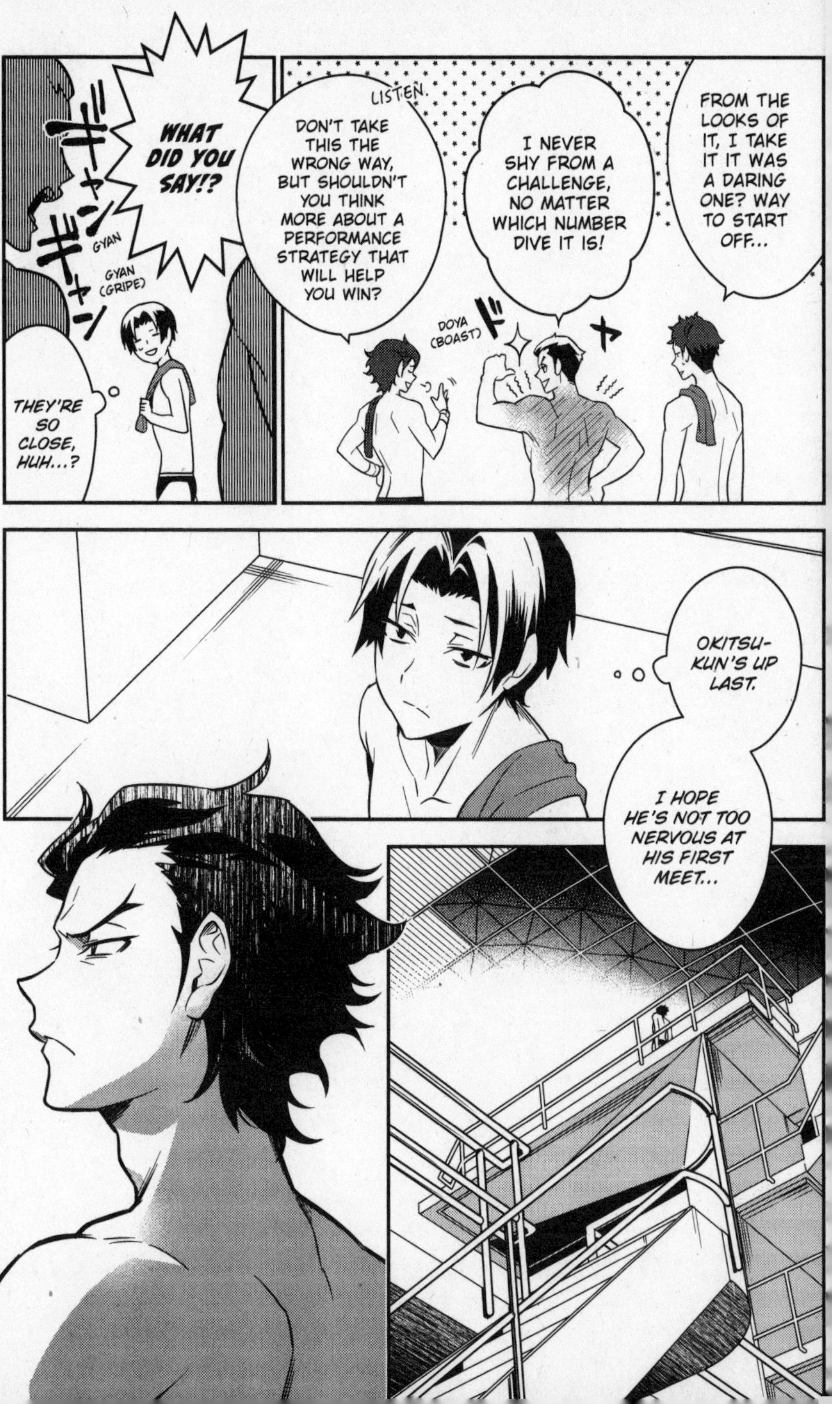
FROM THE LOOKS OF IT, I TAKE IT IT WAS A DARING ONE? WAY TO START OFF...
I NEVER SHY FROM A CHALLENGE, NO MATTER WHICH NUMBER DIVE IT IS!
DOYA (BOAST)
LISTEN.
DON'T TAKE THIS THE WRONG WAY, BUT SHOULDN'T YOU THINK MORE ABOUT A PERFORMANCE STRATEGY THAT WILL HELP YOU WIN?
WHAT DID YOU SAY!?
GYAN
GYAN (GRIPE)
THEY'RE SO CLOSE, HUH...?
OKITSU-KUN'S UP LAST.
I HOPE HE'S NOT TOO NERVOUS AT HIS FIRST MEET...

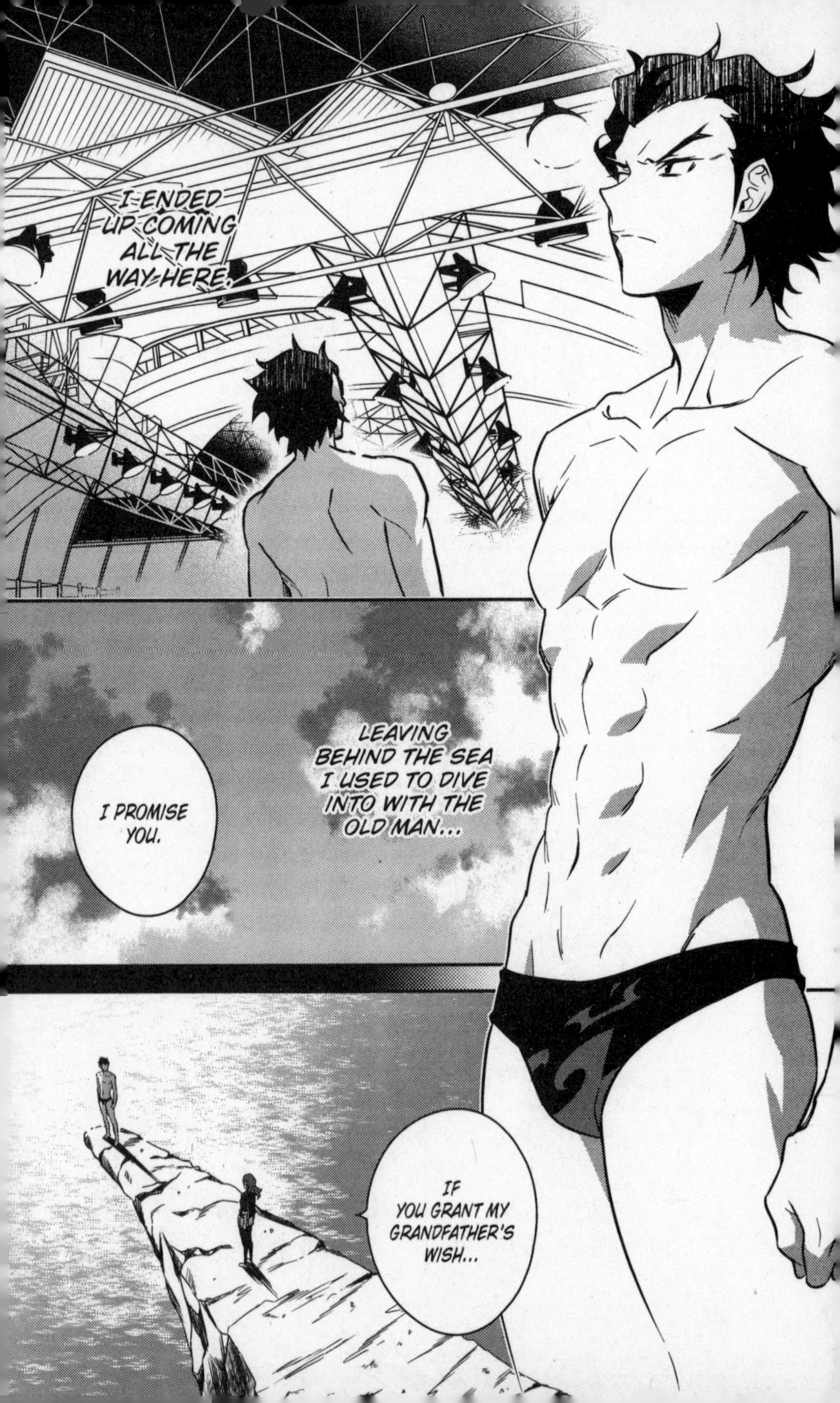
I ENDED UP COMING ALL THE WAY HERE.
LEAVING BEHIND THE SEA I USED TO DIVE INTO WITH THE OLD MAN...
I PROMISE YOU.
IF YOU GRANT MY GRANDFATHER'S WISH...

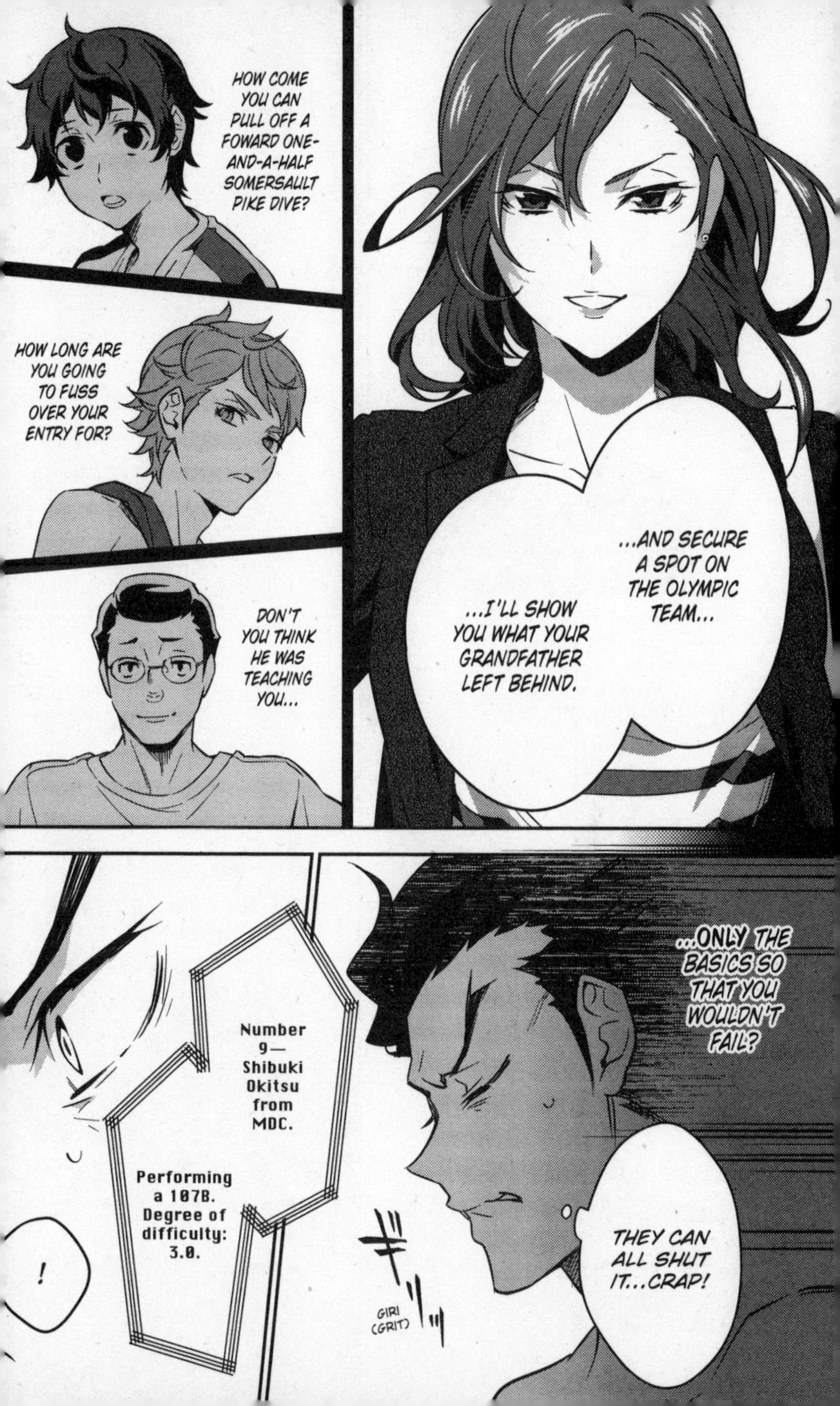
...AND SECURE A SPOT ON THE OLYMPIC TEAM...
...I'LL SHOW YOU WHAT YOUR GRANDFATHER LEFT BEHIND.
HOW COME YOU CAN PULL OFF A FOWARD ONE-AND-A-HALF SOMERSAULT PIKE DIVE?
HOW LONG ARE YOU GOING TO FUSS OVER YOUR ENTRY FOR?
DON'T YOU THINK HE WAS TEACHING YOU...
...ONLY THE BASICS SO THAT YOU WOULDN'T FAIL?
THEY CAN ALL SHUT IT...CRAP!
GIRI (GRIT)
Number 9—Shibuki Okitsu from MDC.
Performing a 107B. Degree of difficulty: 3.0.
!

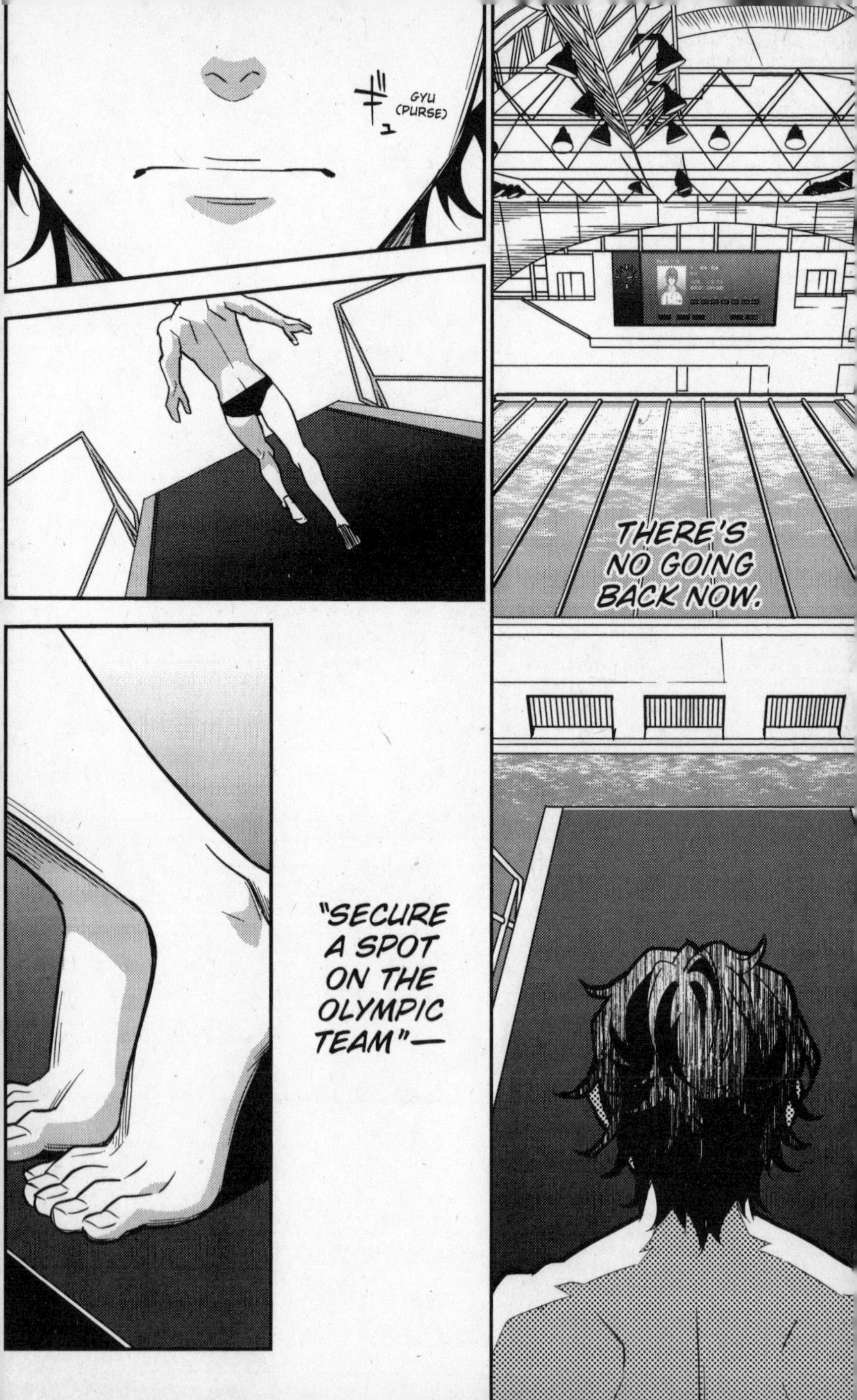
THERE'S NO GOING BACK NOW.
ギュ
GYU (PURSE)
"SECURE A SPOT ON THE OLYMPIC TEAM"—

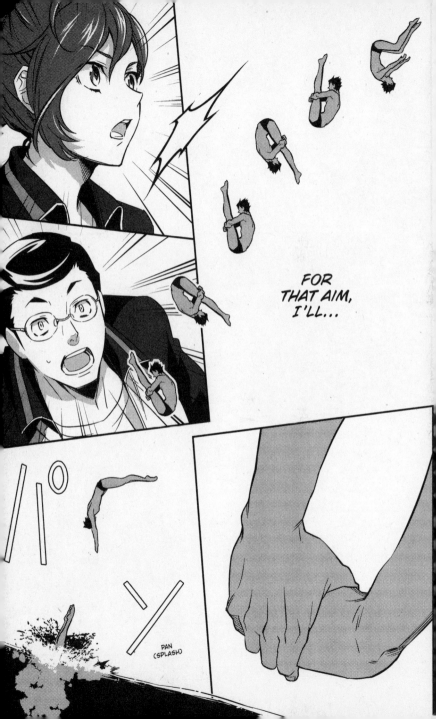

FOR
THAT AIM,
I'LL...

PAN
(SPLASH)

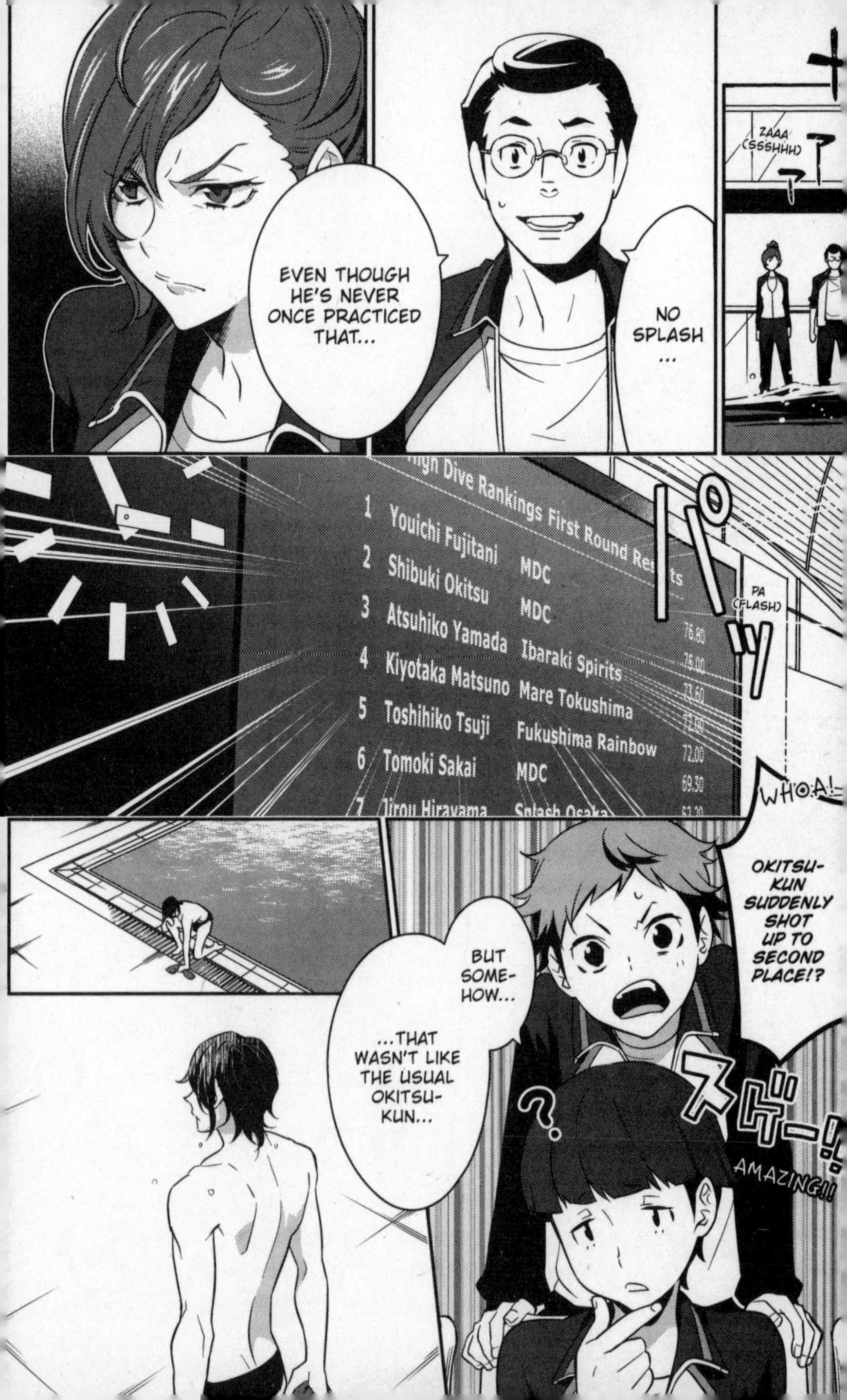
ZAAA (SSSHHH)
NO SPLASH...
EVEN THOUGH HE'S NEVER ONCE PRACTICED THAT...
High Dive Rankings First Round Results
1 Youichi Fujitani MDC
2 Shibuki Okitsu MDC
3 Atsuhiko Yamada Ibaraki Spirits 76.80
4 Kiyotaka Matsuno Mare Tokushima 76.00
5 Toshihiko Tsuji Fukushima Rainbow 73.60
6 Tomoki Sakai MDC 72.00
7 Jirou Hirayama Splash Osaka 69.30
PA (FLASH)
WHOA!
OKITSU-KUN SUDDENLY SHOT UP TO SECOND PLACE!?
AMAZING!!
BUT SOMEHOW...
...THAT WASN'T LIKE THE USUAL OKITSU-KUN...

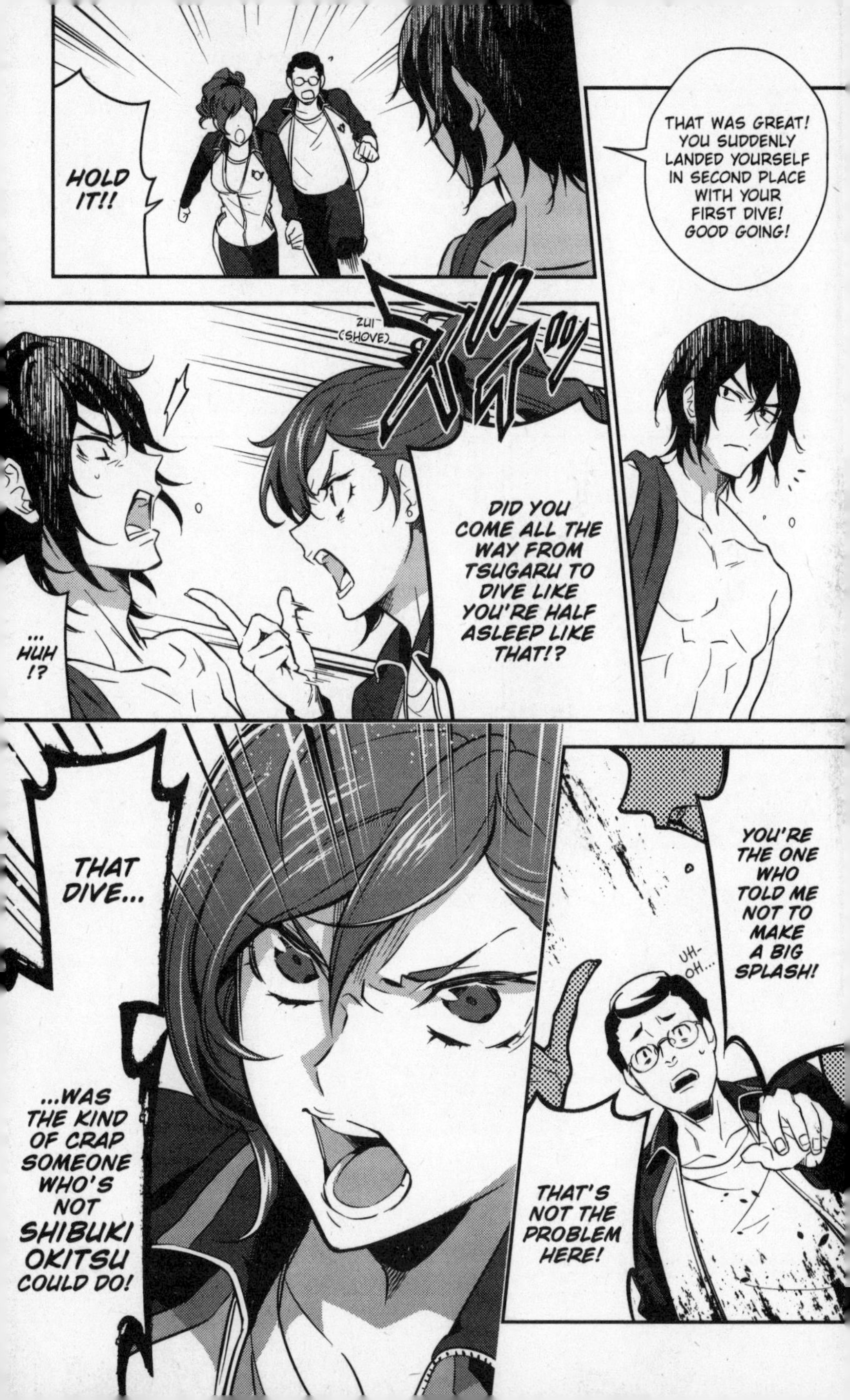
THAT WAS GREAT! YOU SUDDENLY LANDED YOURSELF IN SECOND PLACE WITH YOUR FIRST DIVE! GOOD GOING!
HOLD IT!!
ZUI (SHOVE)
DID YOU COME ALL THE WAY FROM TSUGARU TO DIVE LIKE YOU'RE HALF ASLEEP LIKE THAT!?
...HUH!?
YOU'RE THE ONE WHO TOLD ME NOT TO MAKE A BIG SPLASH!
UH-OH...
THAT'S NOT THE PROBLEM HERE!
THAT DIVE...
...WAS THE KIND OF CRAP SOMEONE WHO'S NOT SHIBUKI OKITSU COULD DO!

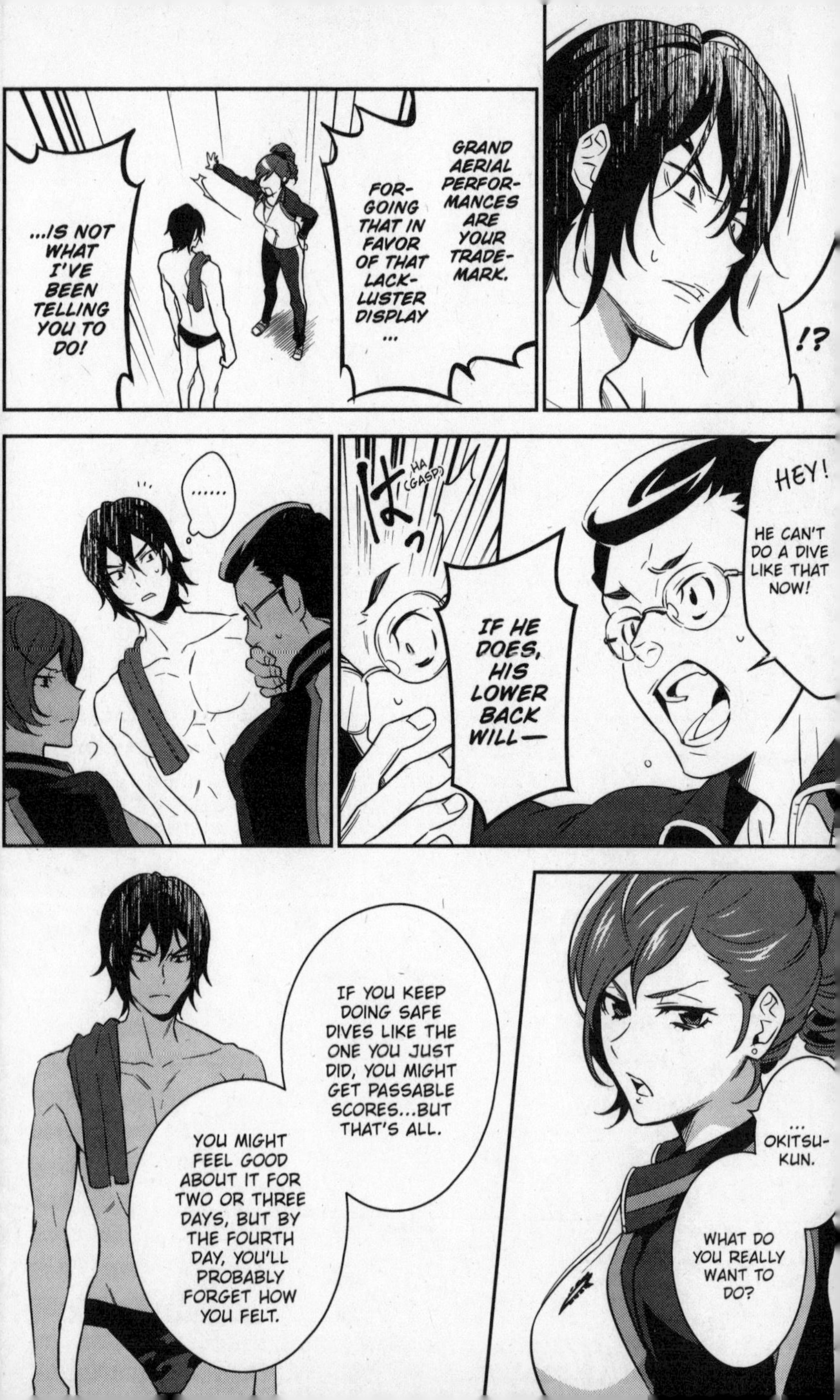
!?
GRAND AERIAL PERFORMANCES ARE YOUR TRADEMARK.
FORGOING THAT IN FAVOR OF THAT LACKLUSTER DISPLAY...
...IS NOT WHAT I'VE BEEN TELLING YOU TO DO!
HEY!
HE CAN'T DO A DIVE LIKE THAT NOW!
はっ
HA (GASP)
IF HE DOES, HIS LOWER BACK WILL—
......
...OKITSU-KUN.
WHAT DO YOU REALLY WANT TO DO?
IF YOU KEEP DOING SAFE DIVES LIKE THE ONE YOU JUST DID, YOU MIGHT GET PASSABLE SCORES...BUT THAT'S ALL.
YOU MIGHT FEEL GOOD ABOUT IT FOR TWO OR THREE DAYS, BUT BY THE FOURTH DAY, YOU'LL PROBABLY FORGET HOW YOU FELT.

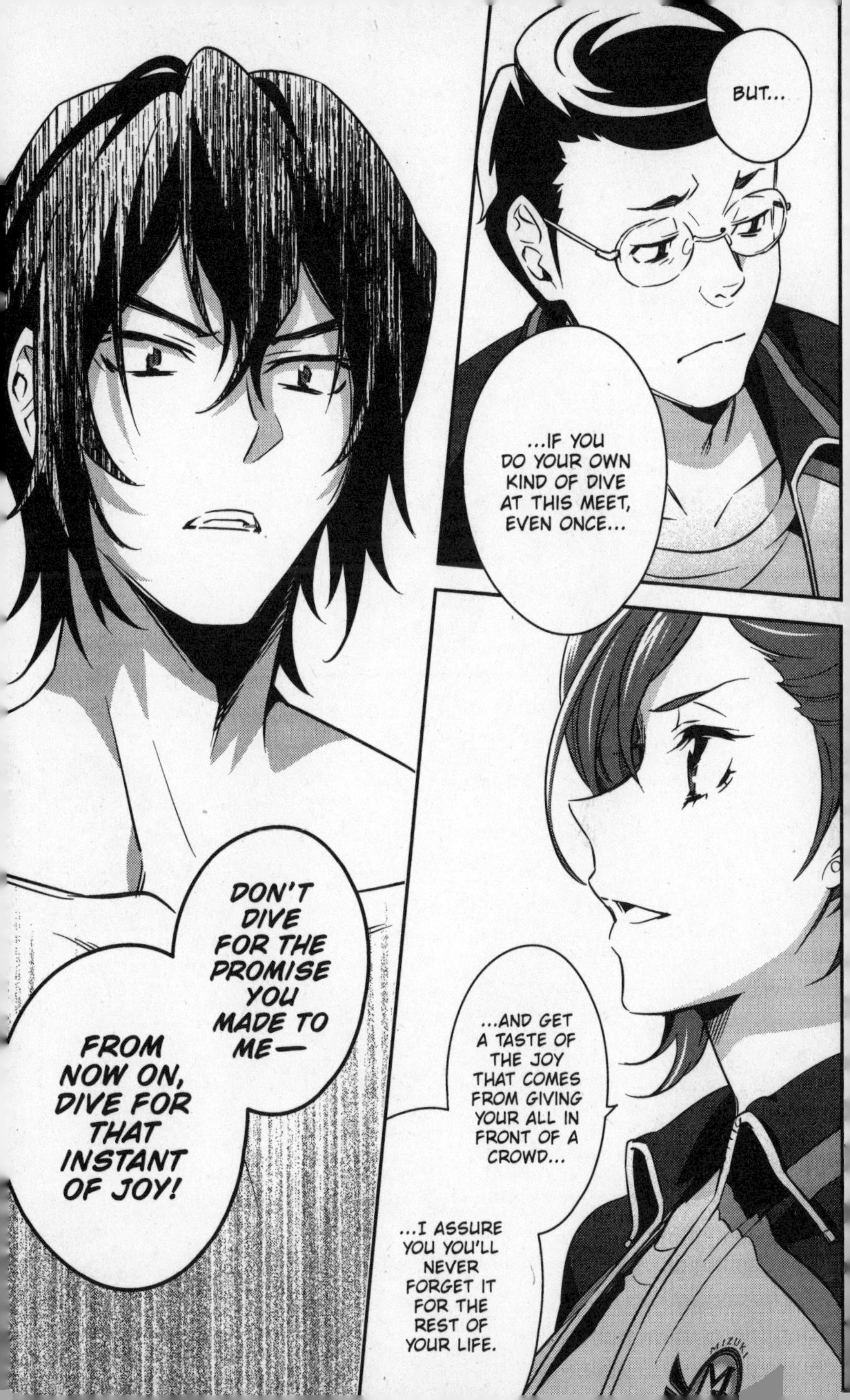
BUT...
...IF YOU DO YOUR OWN KIND OF DIVE AT THIS MEET, EVEN ONCE...
...AND GET A TASTE OF THE JOY THAT COMES FROM GIVING YOUR ALL IN FRONT OF A CROWD...
...I ASSURE YOU YOU'LL NEVER FORGET IT FOR THE REST OF YOUR LIFE.
DON'T DIVE FOR THE PROMISE YOU MADE TO ME—
FROM NOW ON, DIVE FOR THAT INSTANT OF JOY!

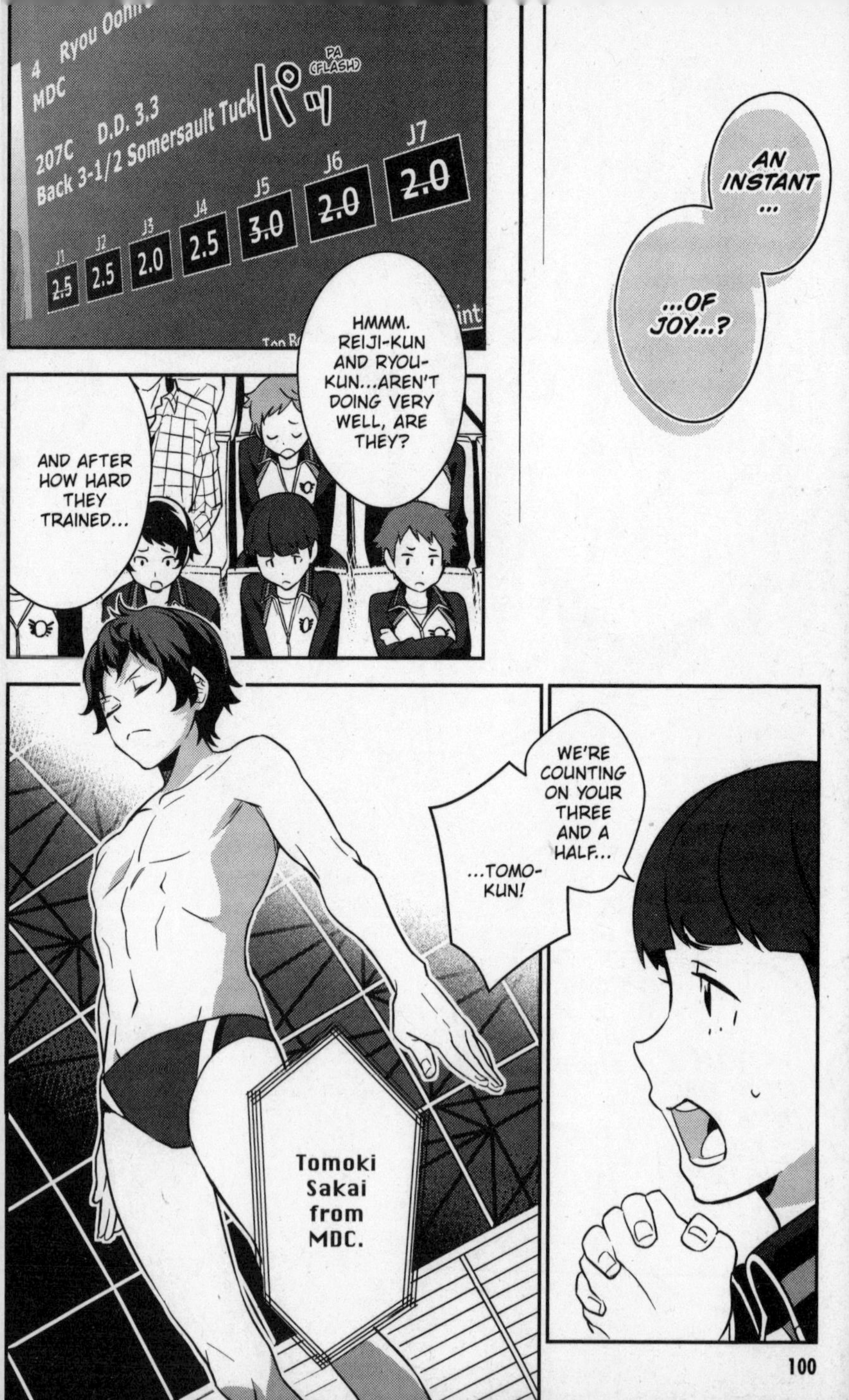
AN INSTANT...
...OF JOY...?
4
MDC
207C D.D. 3.3
Back 3-1/2 Somersault Tuck
J1 2.5 J2 2.5 J3 2.0 J4 2.5 J5 3.0 J6 2.0 J7 2.0
PA (FLASH)
HMMM. REIJI-KUN AND RYOU-KUN...AREN'T DOING VERY WELL, ARE THEY?
AND AFTER HOW HARD THEY TRAINED...
WE'RE COUNTING ON YOUR THREE AND A HALF...
...TOMO-KUN!
Tomoki Sakai from MDC.

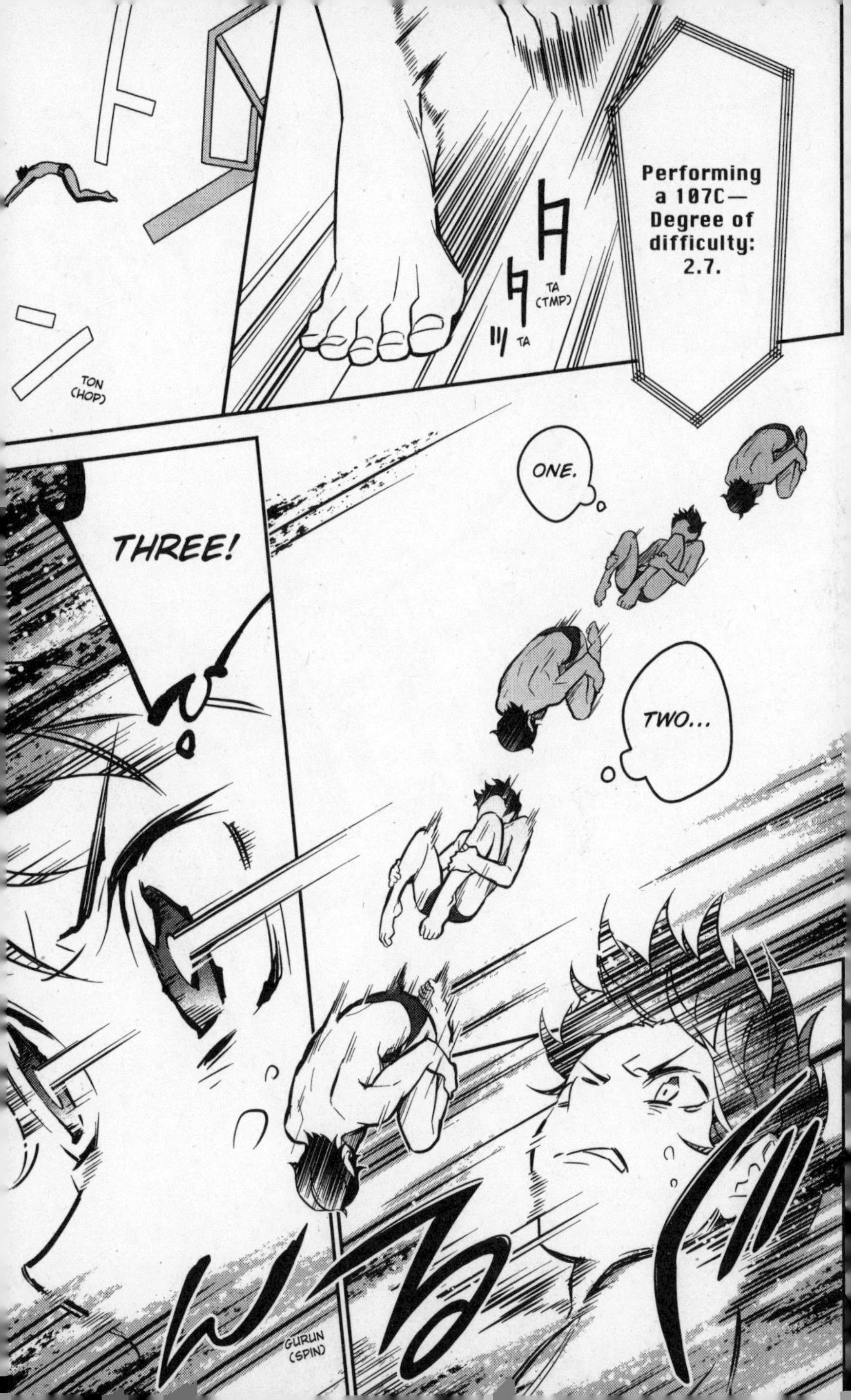
Performing a 107C—Degree of difficulty: 2.7.
TA (TMP)
TA
TON (HOP)
ONE.
TWO...
GURUN (SPIN)
THREE!

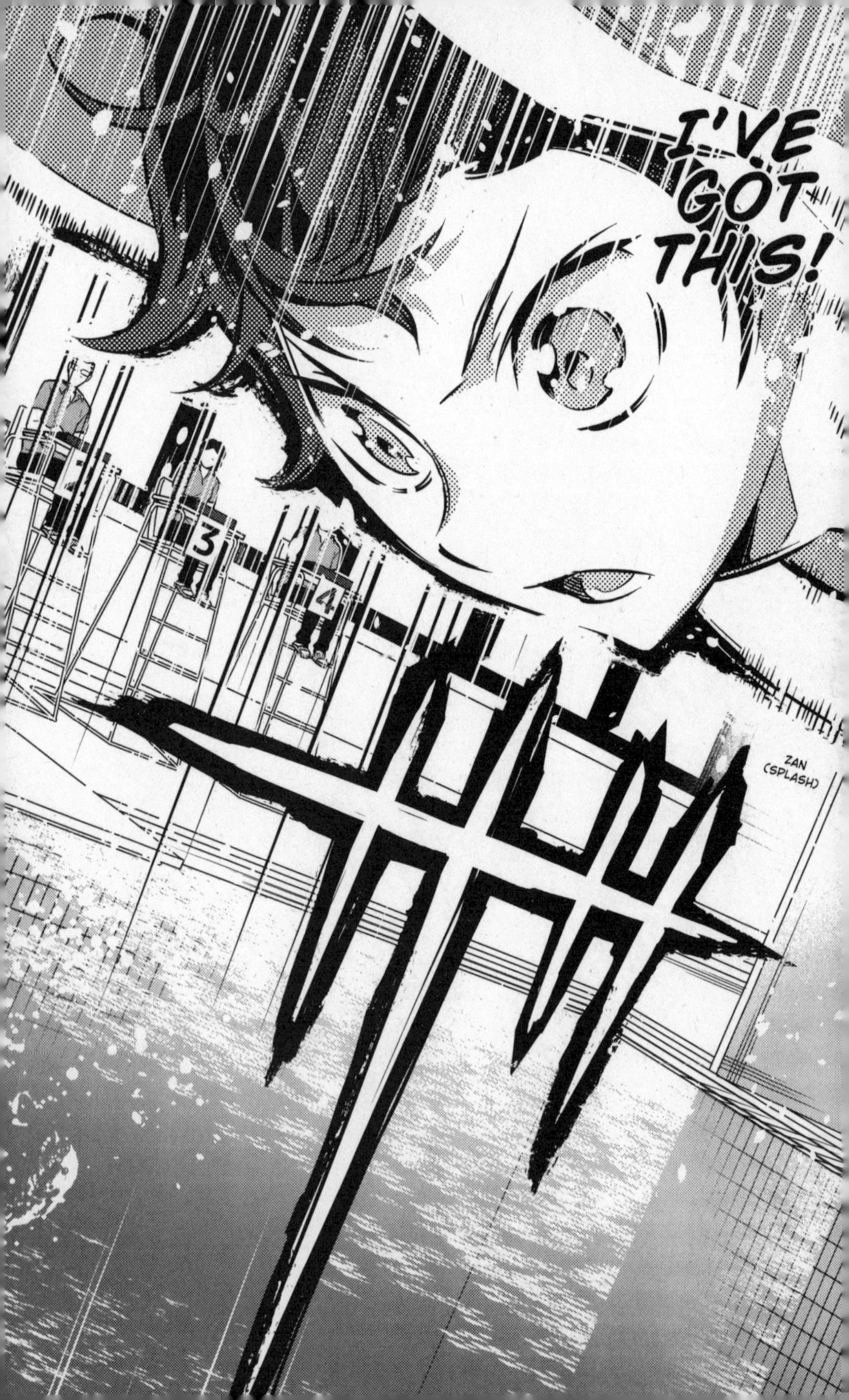
I'VE GOT THIS!
ザン
ZAN (SPLASH)

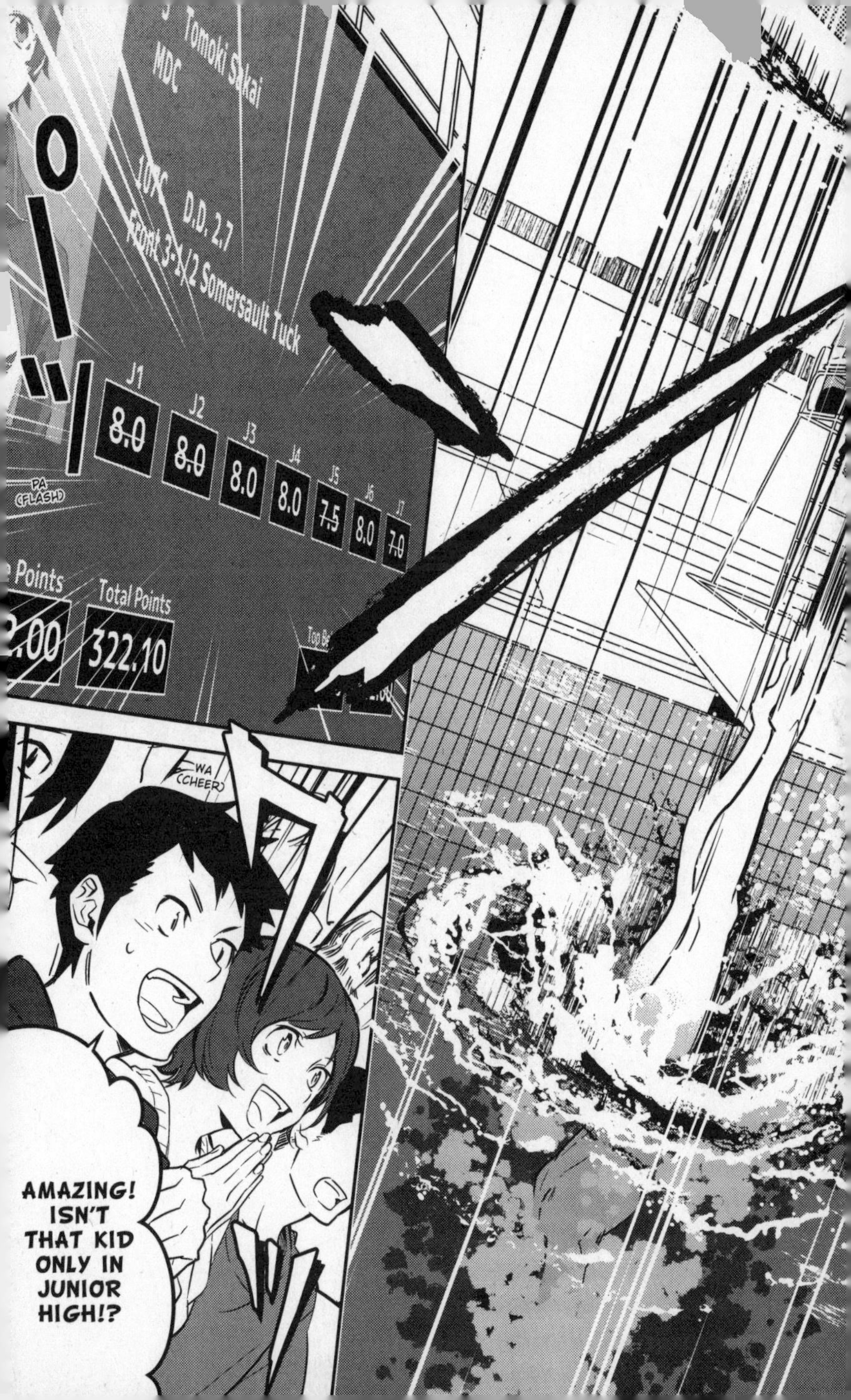

Tomoki Sakai
MDC
107C D.D. 2.7
Front 3-1/2 Somersault Tuck
J1 8.0 J2 8.0 J3 8.0 J4 8.0 J5 7.5 J6 8.0 J7 7.0
Total Points
322.10
PA (FLASH)
WA (CHEER)
AMAZING! ISN'T THAT KID ONLY IN JUNIOR HIGH!?

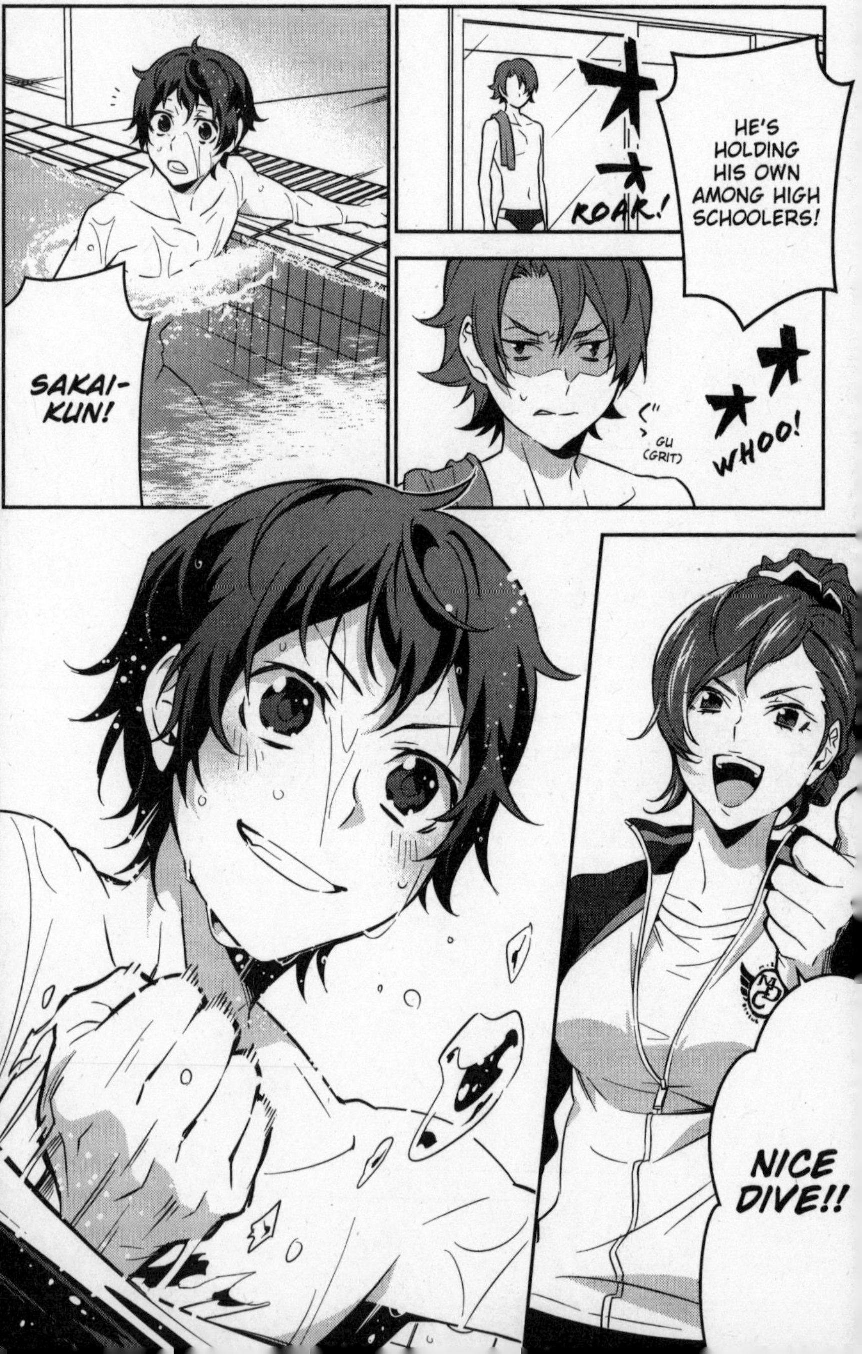
ROAR!
HE'S HOLDING HIS OWN AMONG HIGH SCHOOLERS!
WHOO!
GU (GRIT)
SAKAI-KUN!
NICE DIVE!!

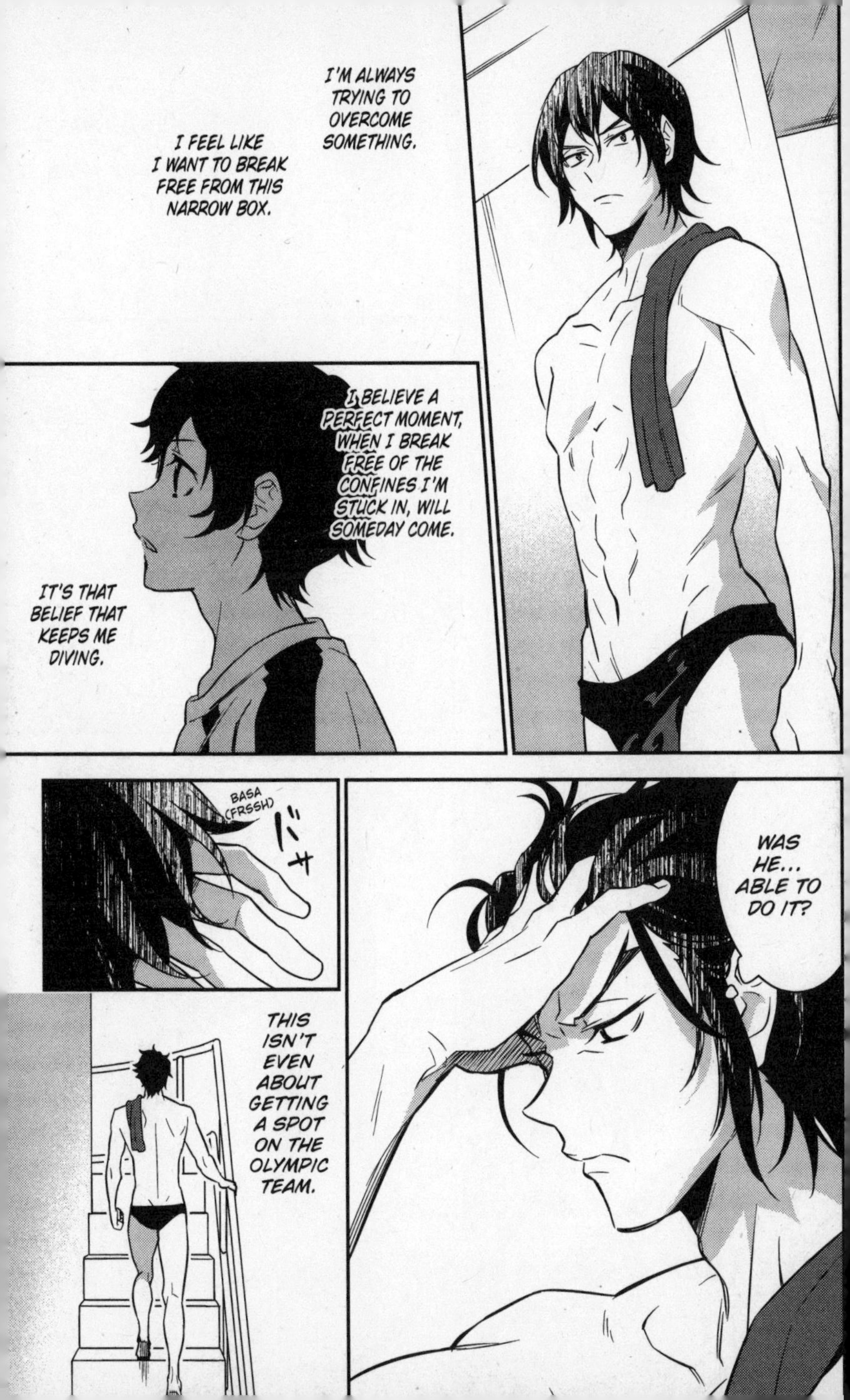
I'M ALWAYS TRYING TO OVERCOME SOMETHING.
I FEEL LIKE I WANT TO BREAK FREE FROM THIS NARROW BOX.
I BELIEVE A PERFECT MOMENT, WHEN I BREAK FREE OF THE CONFINES I'M STUCK IN, WILL SOMEDAY COME.
IT'S THAT BELIEF THAT KEEPS ME DIVING.
WAS HE... ABLE TO DO IT?
バサ
BASA (FRSSH)
THIS ISN'T EVEN ABOUT GETTING A SPOT ON THE OLYMPIC TEAM.

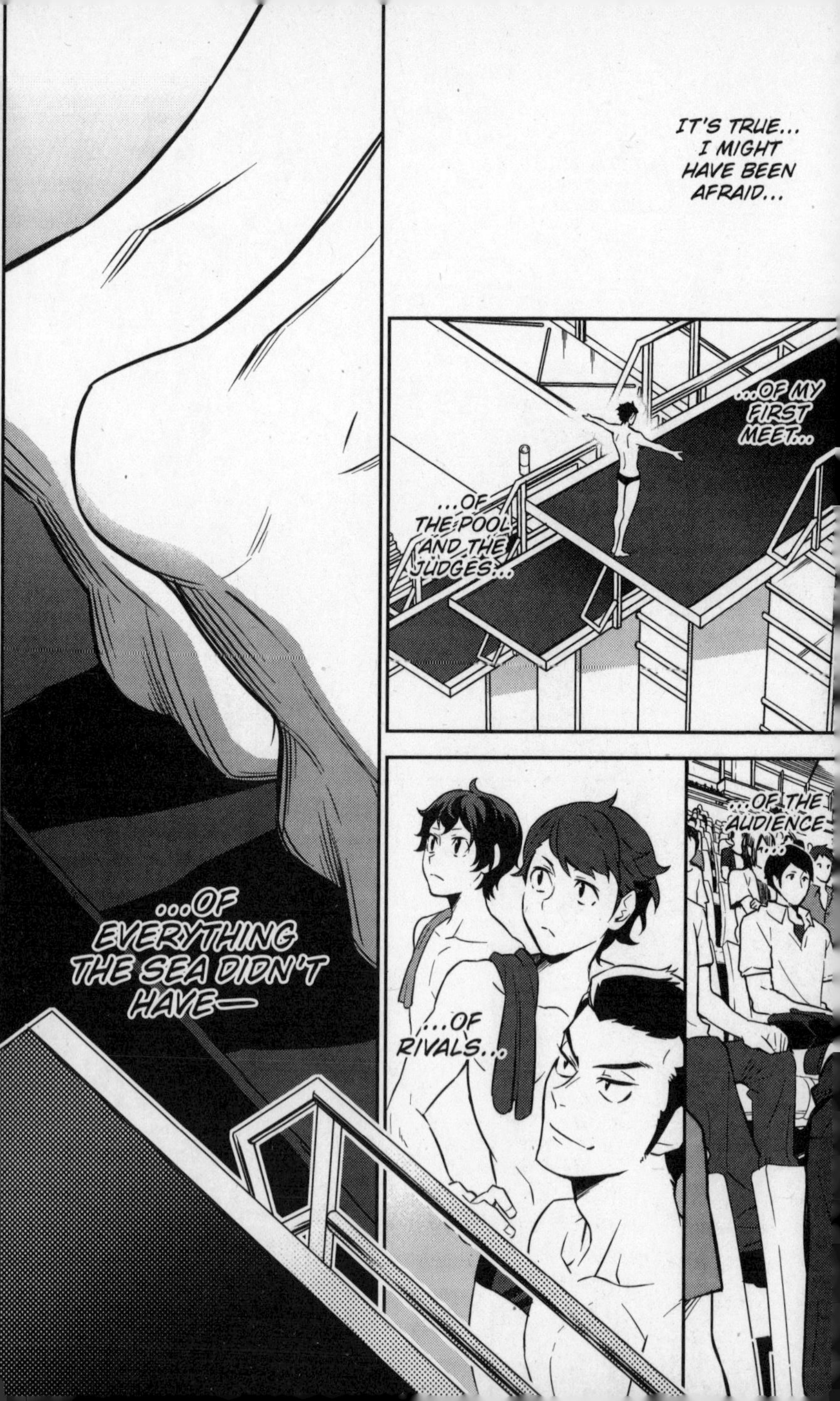
IT'S TRUE... I MIGHT HAVE BEEN AFRAID...
...OF MY FIRST MEET...
...OF THE POOL AND THE JUDGES...
...OF THE AUDIENCE...
...OF RIVALS...
...OF EVERYTHING THE SEA DIDN'T HAVE—

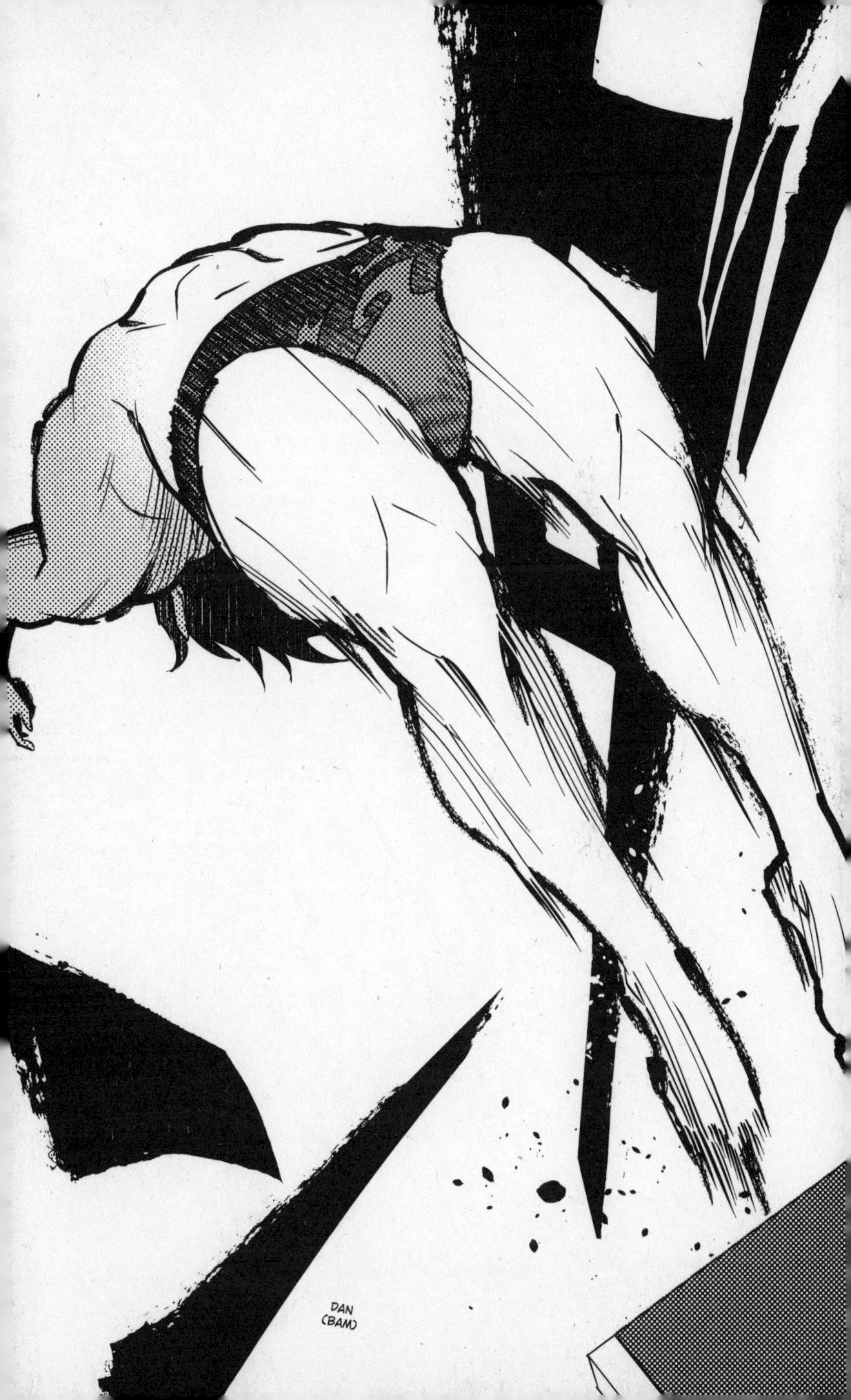
DAN
(BAM)

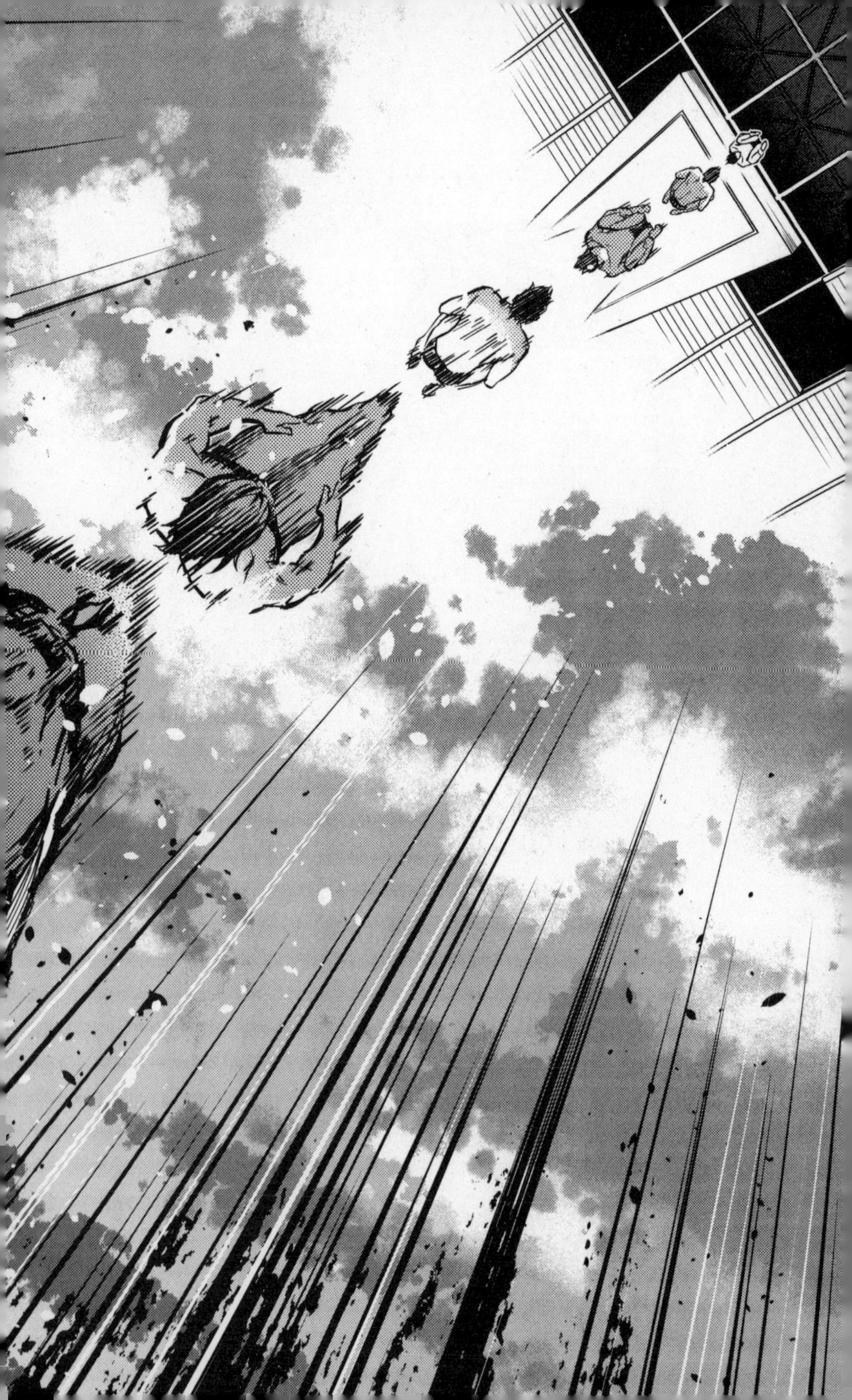

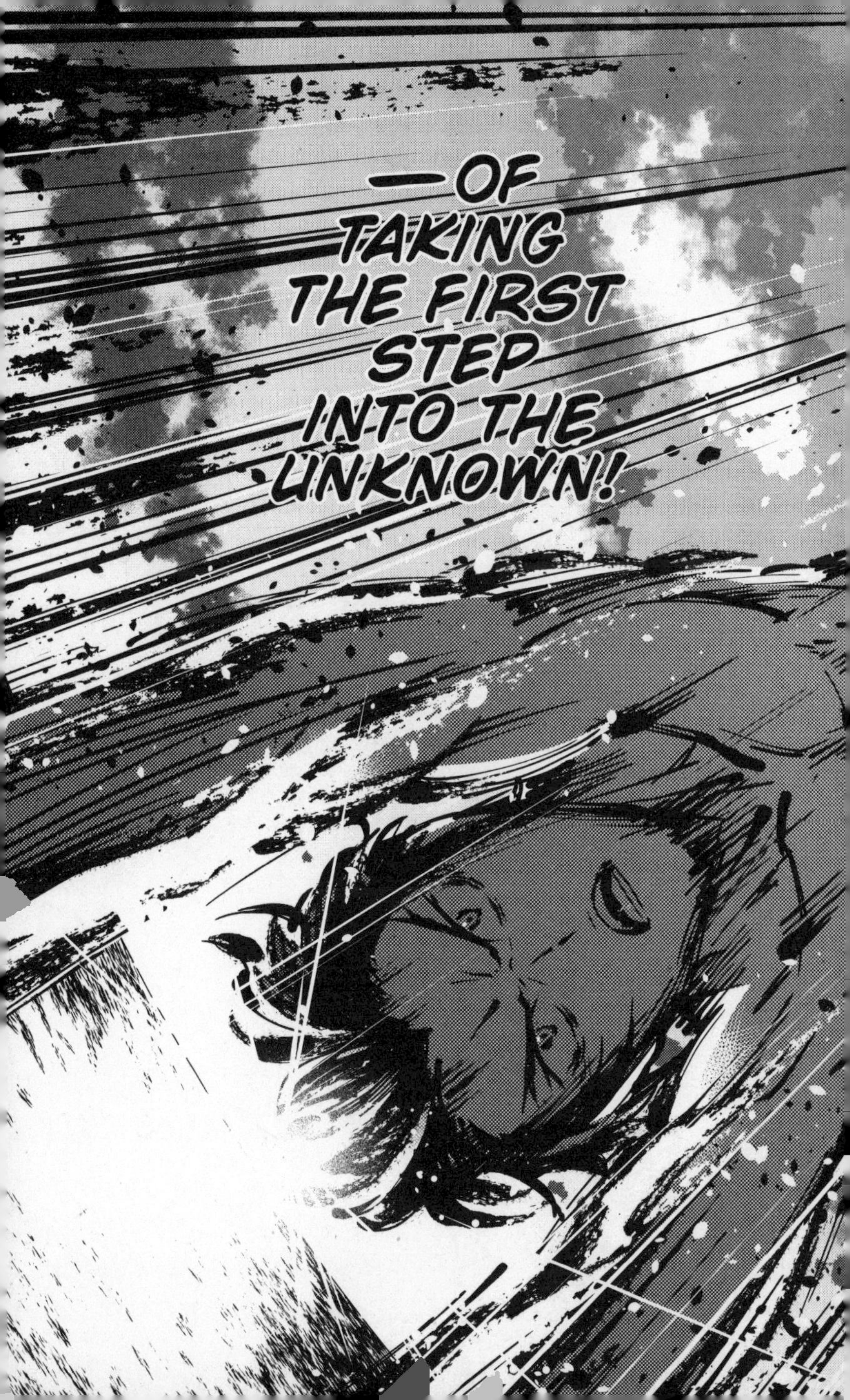
—OF TAKING THE FIRST STEP INTO THE UNKNOWN!

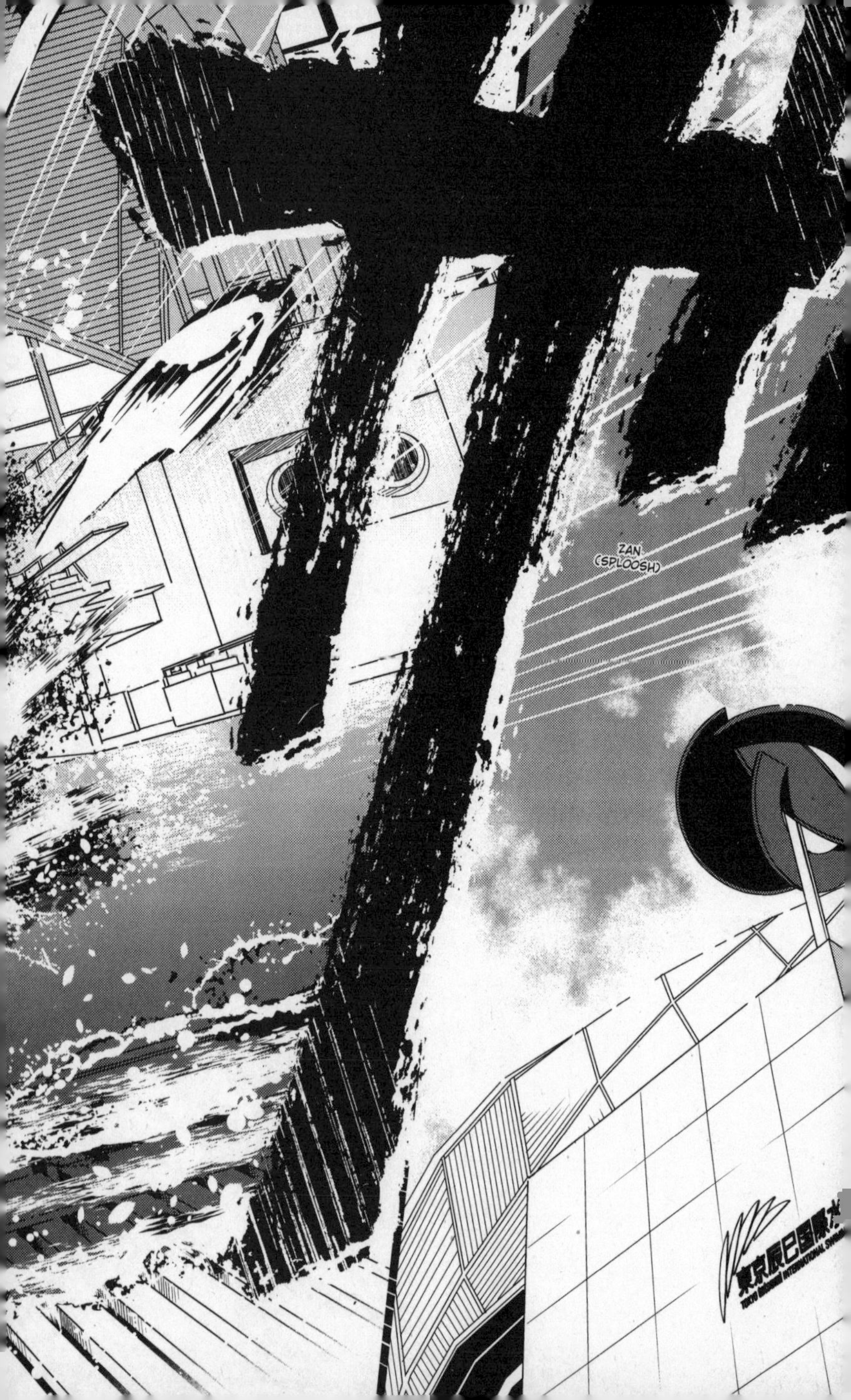
ZAN
(SPLOOSH)
東京辰巳国際水

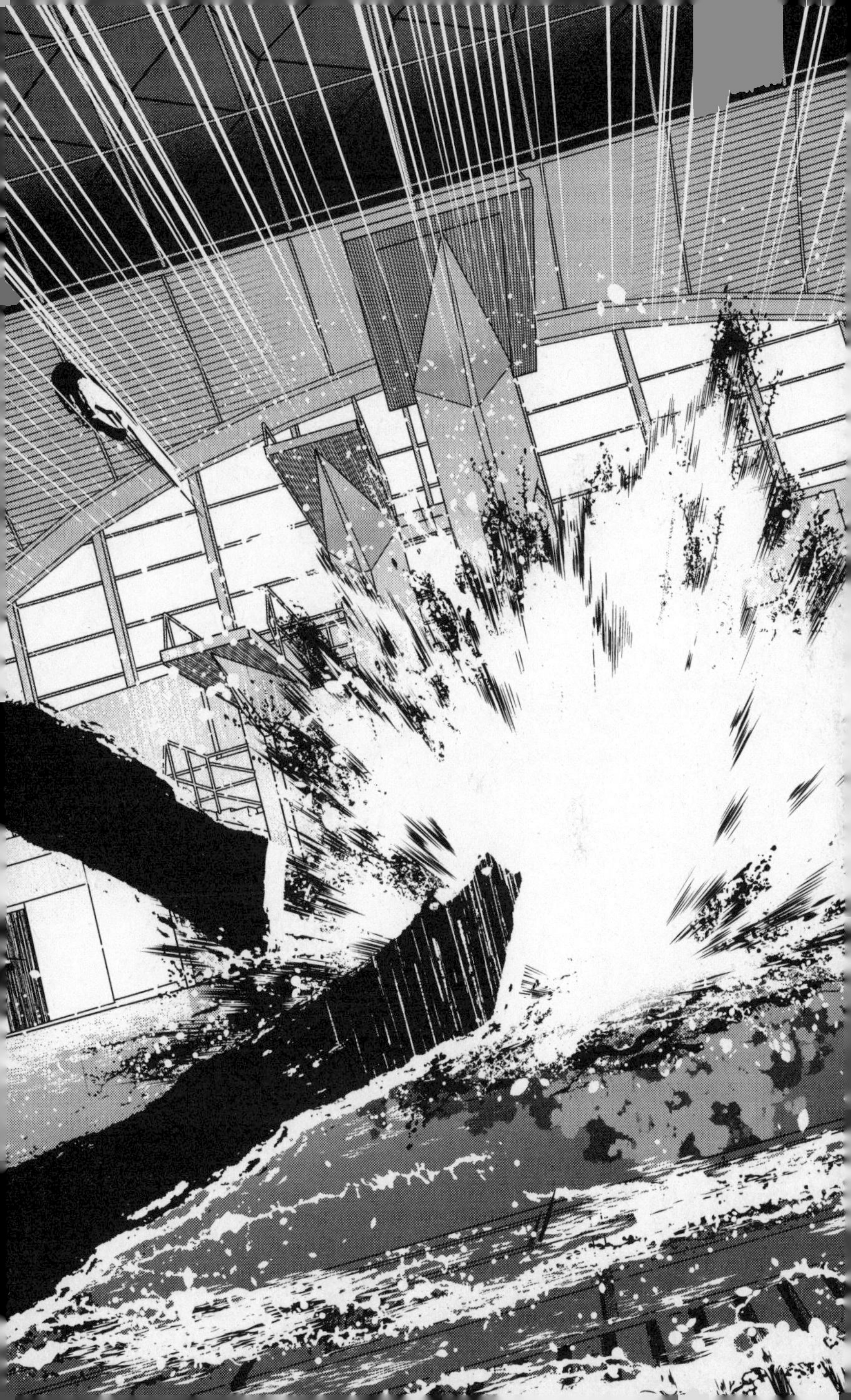

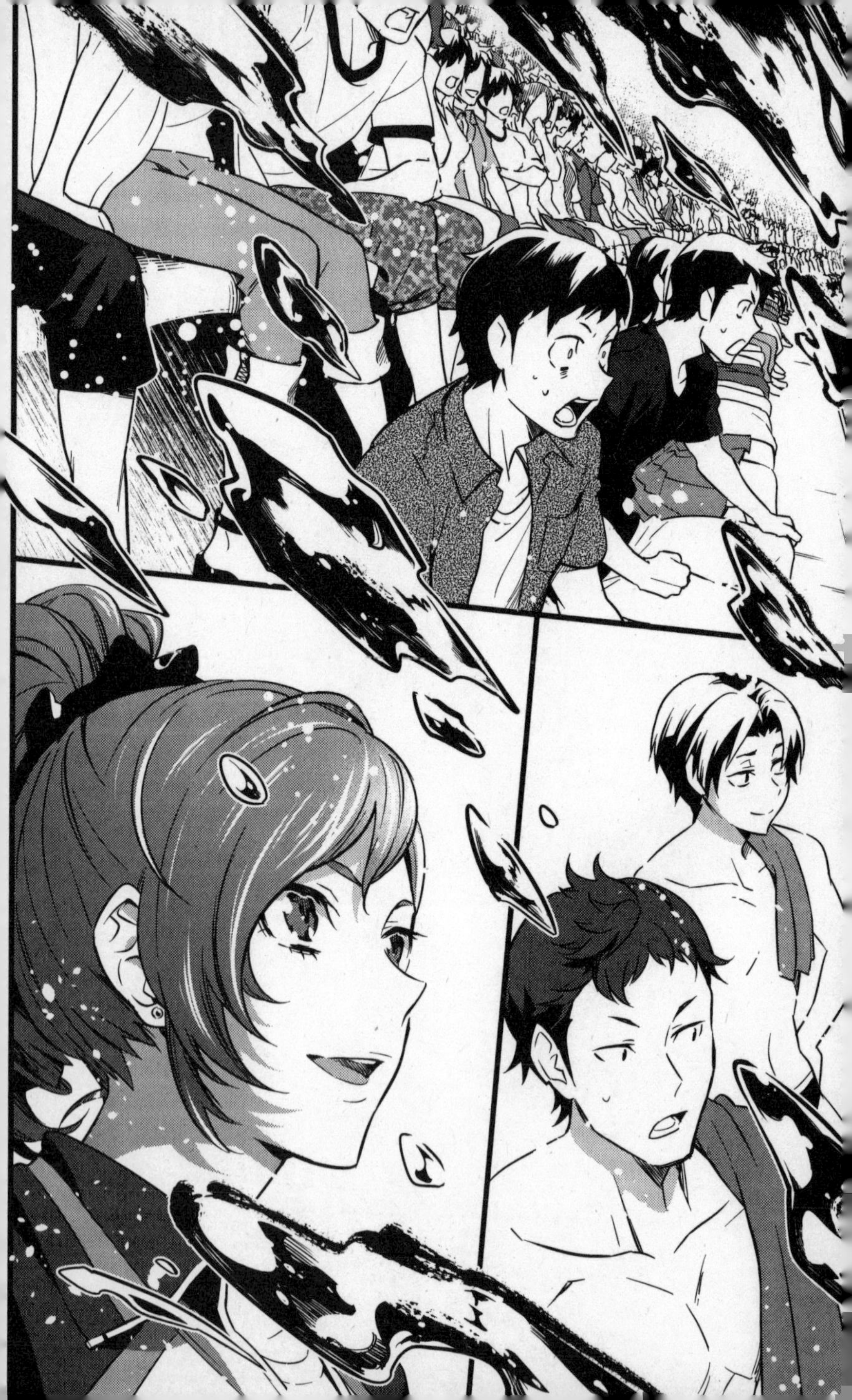

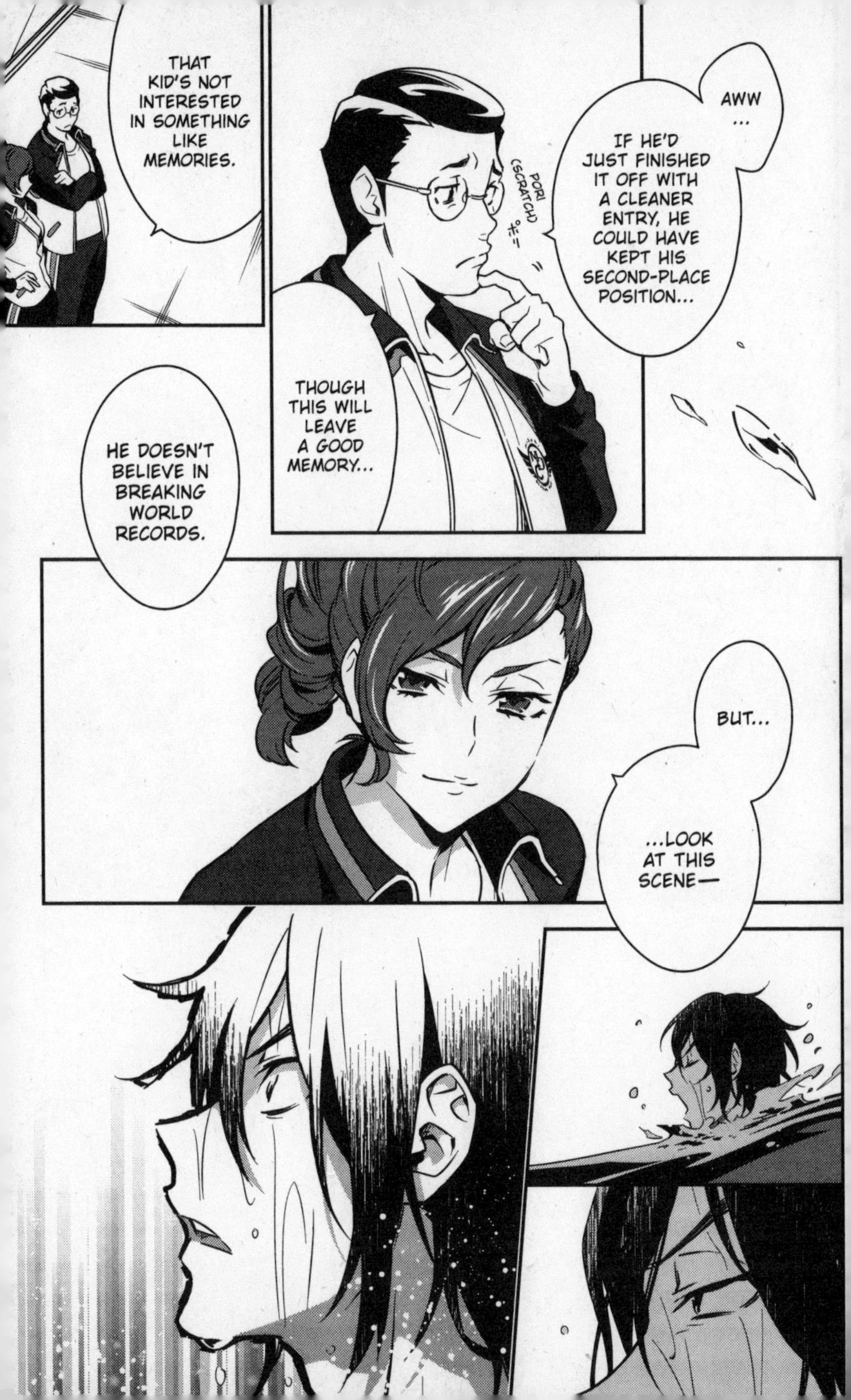
AWW...
IF HE'D JUST FINISHED IT OFF WITH A CLEANER ENTRY, HE COULD HAVE KEPT HIS SECOND-PLACE POSITION...
PORI (SCRATCH)
THOUGH THIS WILL LEAVE A GOOD MEMORY...
THAT KID'S NOT INTERESTED IN SOMETHING LIKE MEMORIES.
HE DOESN'T BELIEVE IN BREAKING WORLD RECORDS.
BUT...
...LOOK AT THIS SCENE—

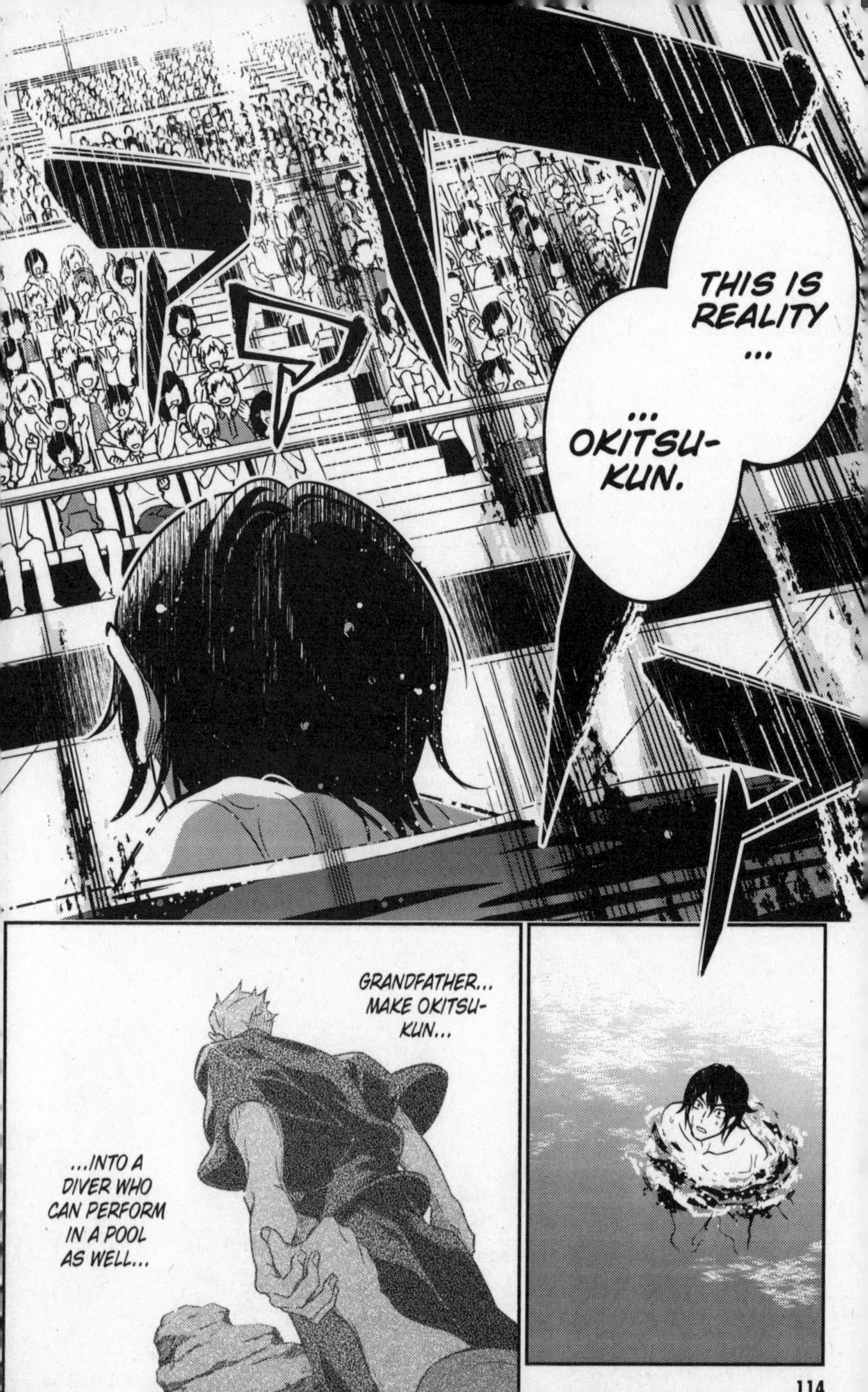
THIS IS REALITY ...
... OKITSU-KUN.
GRANDFATHER... MAKE OKITSU-KUN...
...INTO A DIVER WHO CAN PERFORM IN A POOL AS WELL...

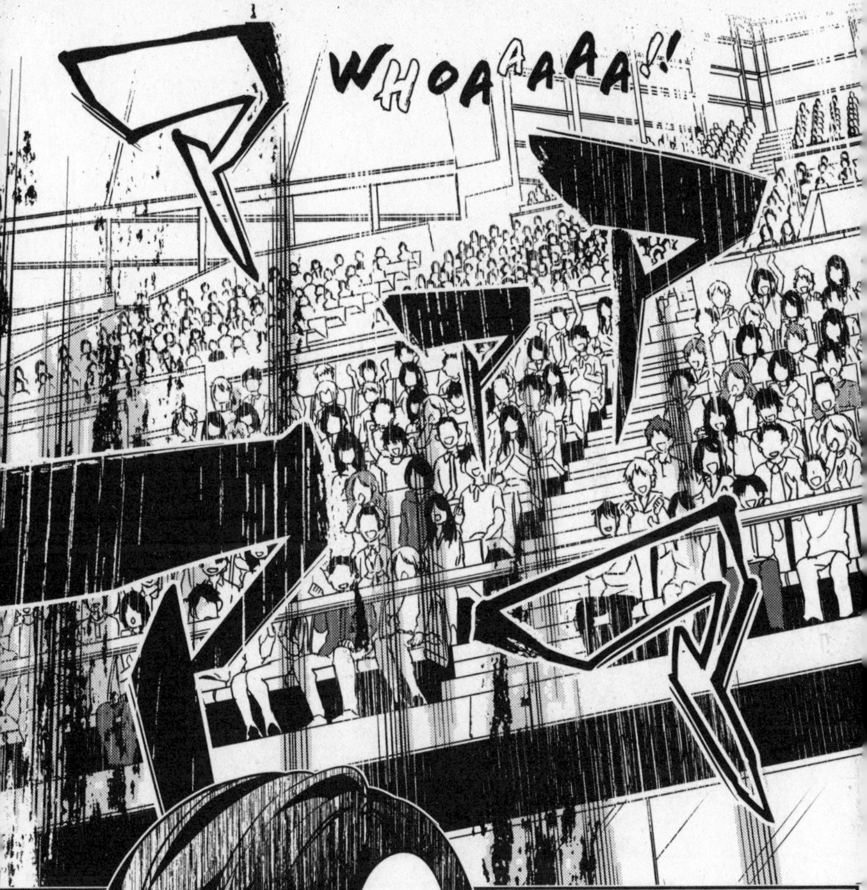
WHOAAAAA!!

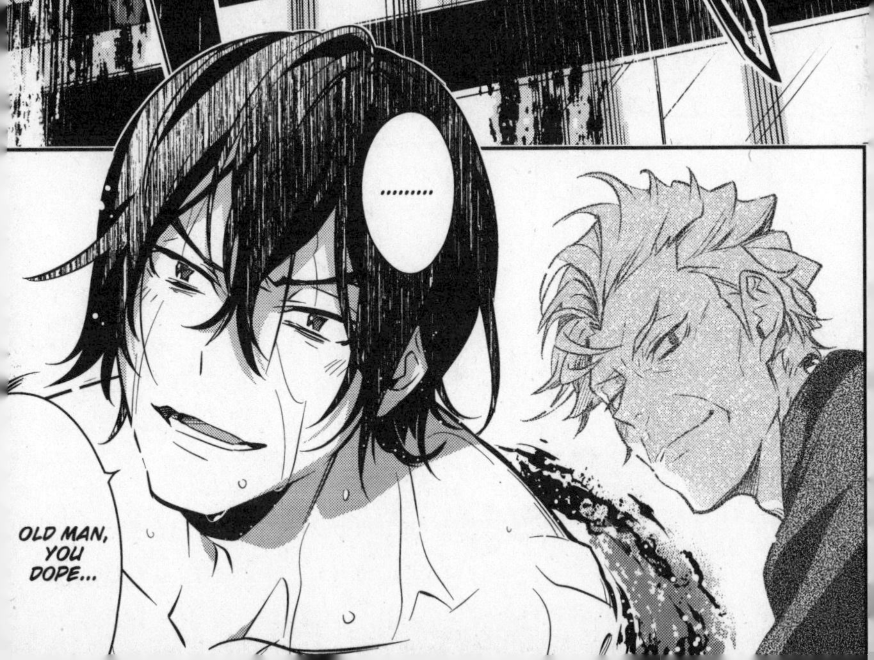
....
OLD MAN, YOU DOPE...

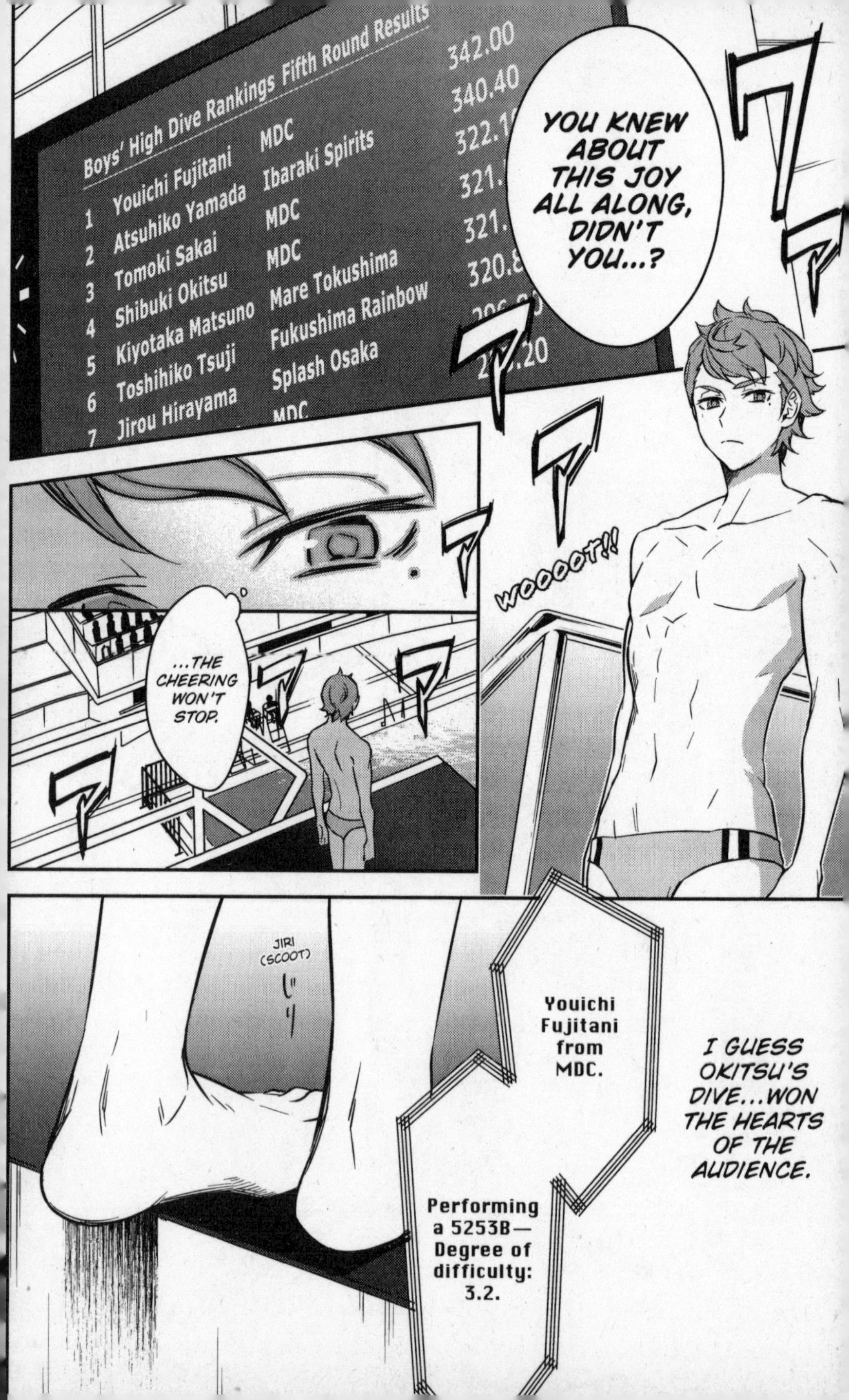
YOU KNEW ABOUT THIS JOY ALL ALONG, DIDN'T YOU...?
Boys' High Dive Rankings Fifth Round Results
1 Youichi Fujitani MDC 342.00
2 Atsuhiko Yamada Ibaraki Spirits 340.40
3 Tomoki Sakai MDC
4 Shibuki Okitsu MDC
5 Kiyotaka Matsuno Mare Tokushima
6 Toshihiko Tsuji Fukushima Rainbow
7 Jirou Hirayama Splash Osaka
WOOOOT!!
...THE CHEERING WON'T STOP.
I GUESS OKITSU'S DIVE...WON THE HEARTS OF THE AUDIENCE.
Youichi Fujitani from MDC.
Performing a 5253B—Degree of difficulty: 3.2.
JIRI (SCOOT)
じり

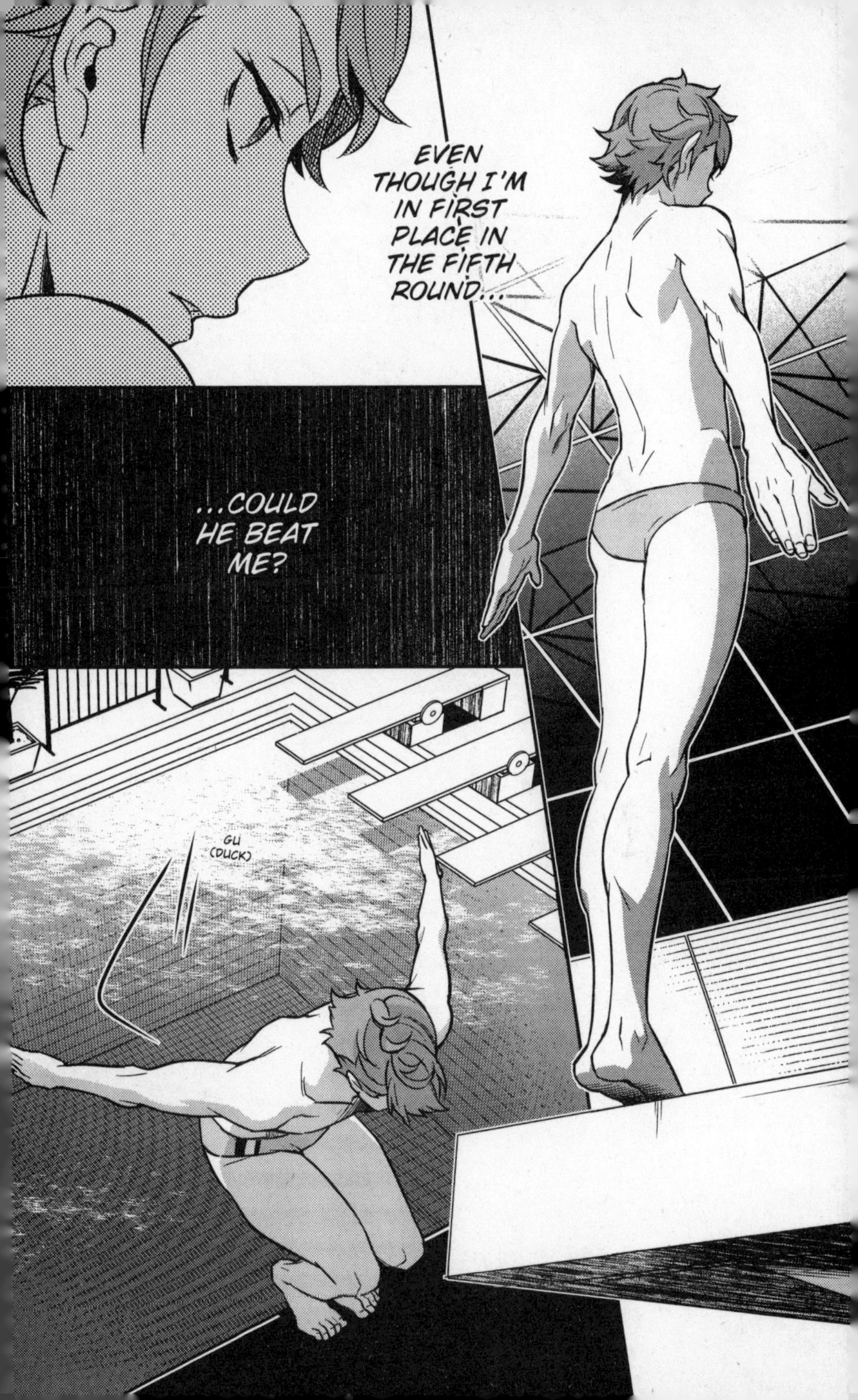
EVEN THOUGH I'M IN FIRST PLACE IN THE FIFTH ROUND...
...COULD HE BEAT ME?
GU (DUCK)

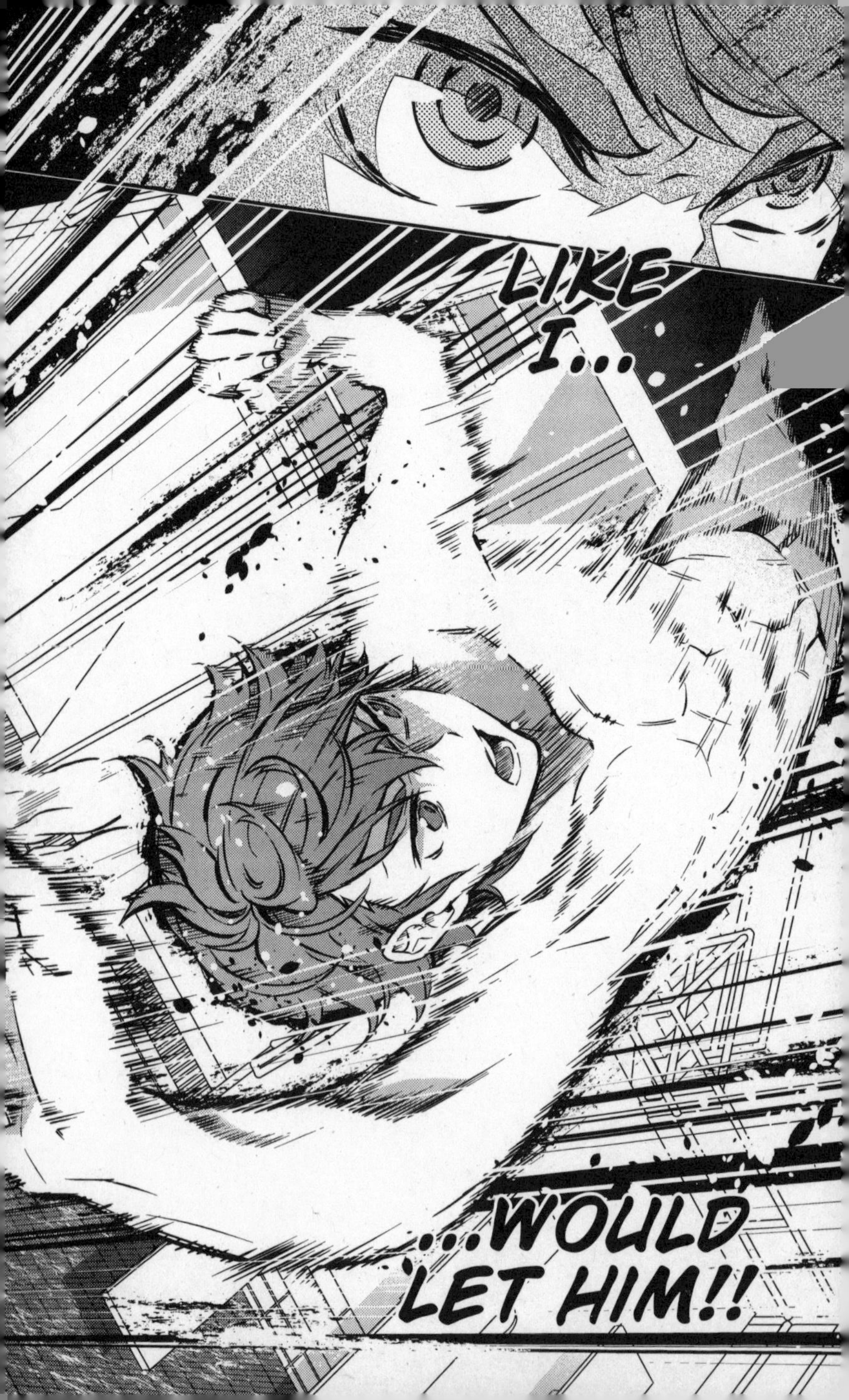
LIKE I...
...WOULD LET HIM!!

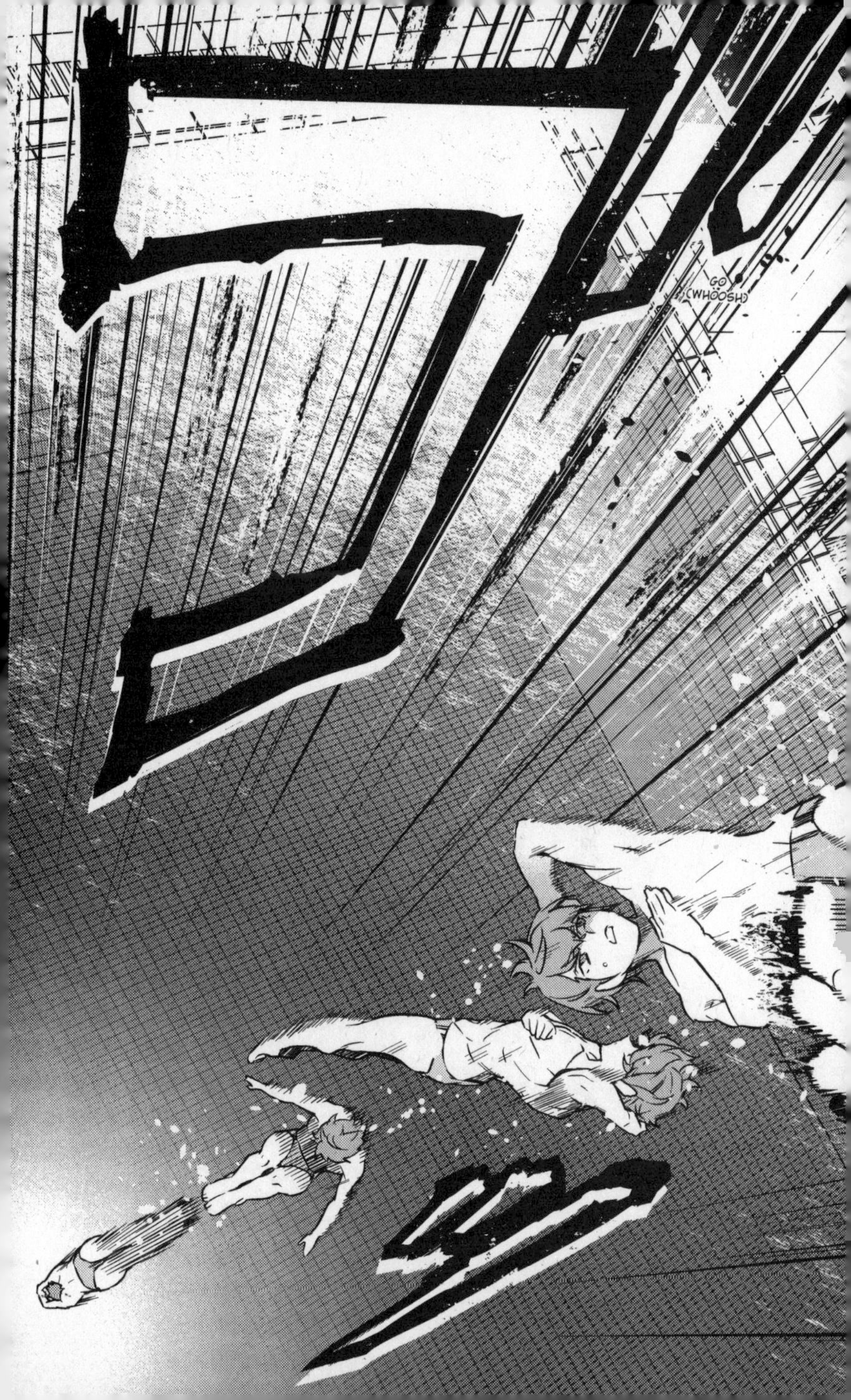
GO
(WHOOSH)

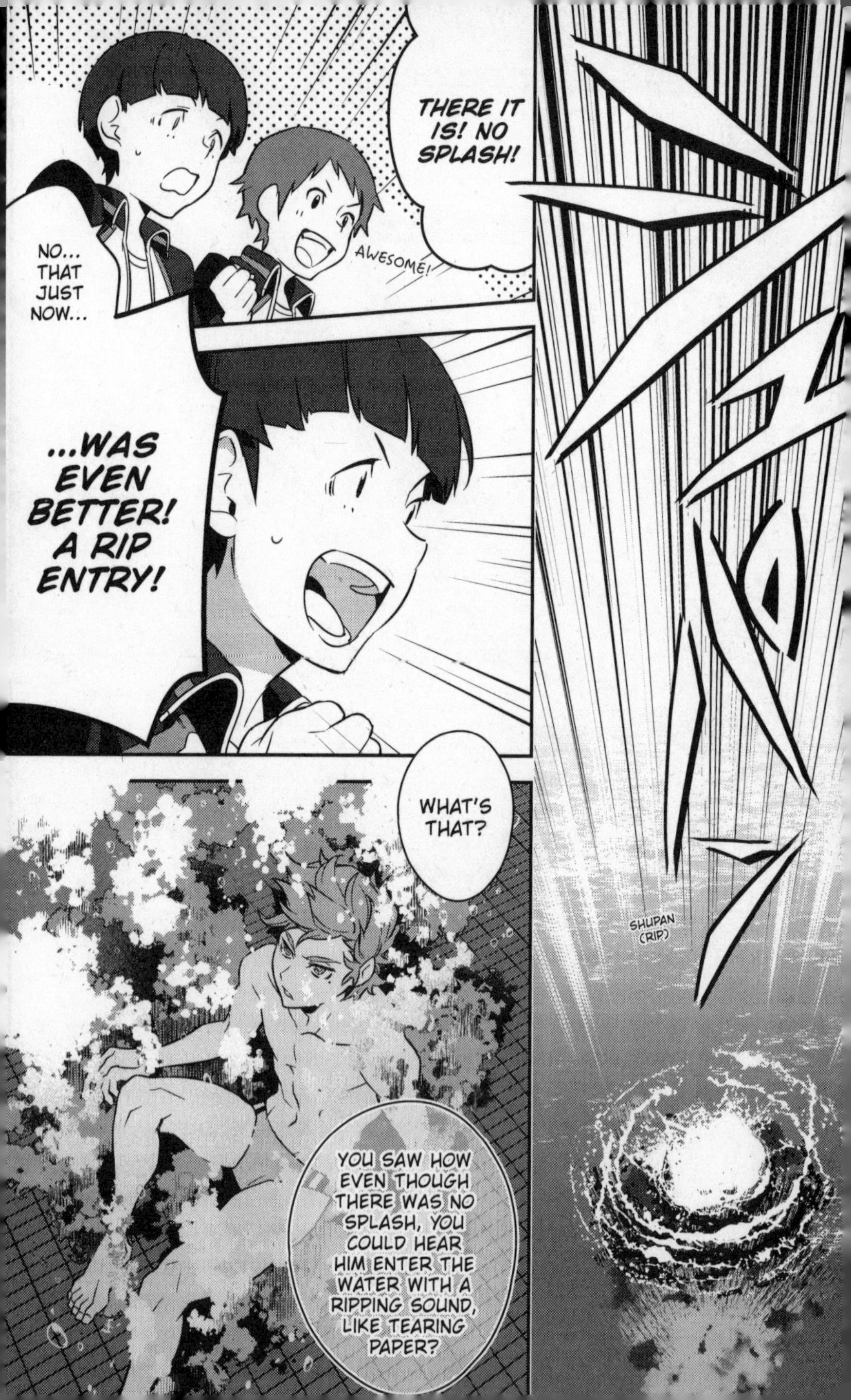
SHUPAN (RIP)
THERE IT IS! NO SPLASH!
AWESOME!
NO... THAT JUST NOW...
...WAS EVEN BETTER! A RIP ENTRY!
WHAT'S THAT?
YOU SAW HOW EVEN THOUGH THERE WAS NO SPLASH, YOU COULD HEAR HIM ENTER THE WATER WITH A RIPPING SOUND, LIKE TEARING PAPER?

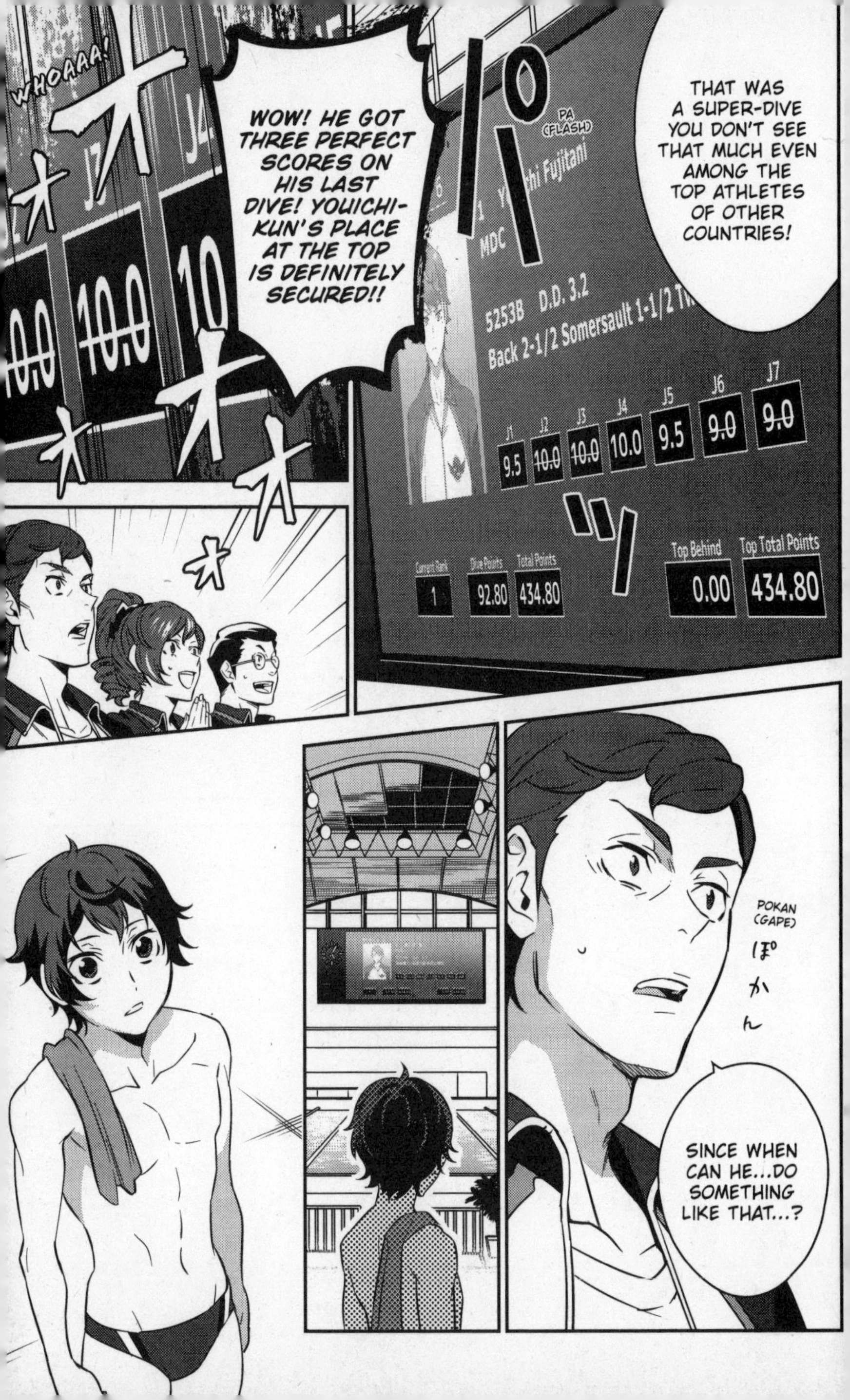
THAT WAS A SUPER-DIVE YOU DON'T SEE THAT MUCH EVEN AMONG THE TOP ATHLETES OF OTHER COUNTRIES!
PA (FLASH)
MDC
5253B D.D. 3.2
J1 J2 J3 J4 J5 J6 J7
9.5 10.0 10.0 10.0 9.5 9.0 9.0
Current Rank 1
Dive Points 92.80
Total Points 434.80
Top Behind 0.00
Top Total Points 434.80
WHOAAA!
WOW! HE GOT THREE PERFECT SCORES ON HIS LAST DIVE! YOUICHI-KUN'S PLACE AT THE TOP IS DEFINITELY SECURED!!
POKAN (GAPE)
ぽかん
SINCE WHEN CAN HE...DO SOMETHING LIKE THAT...?

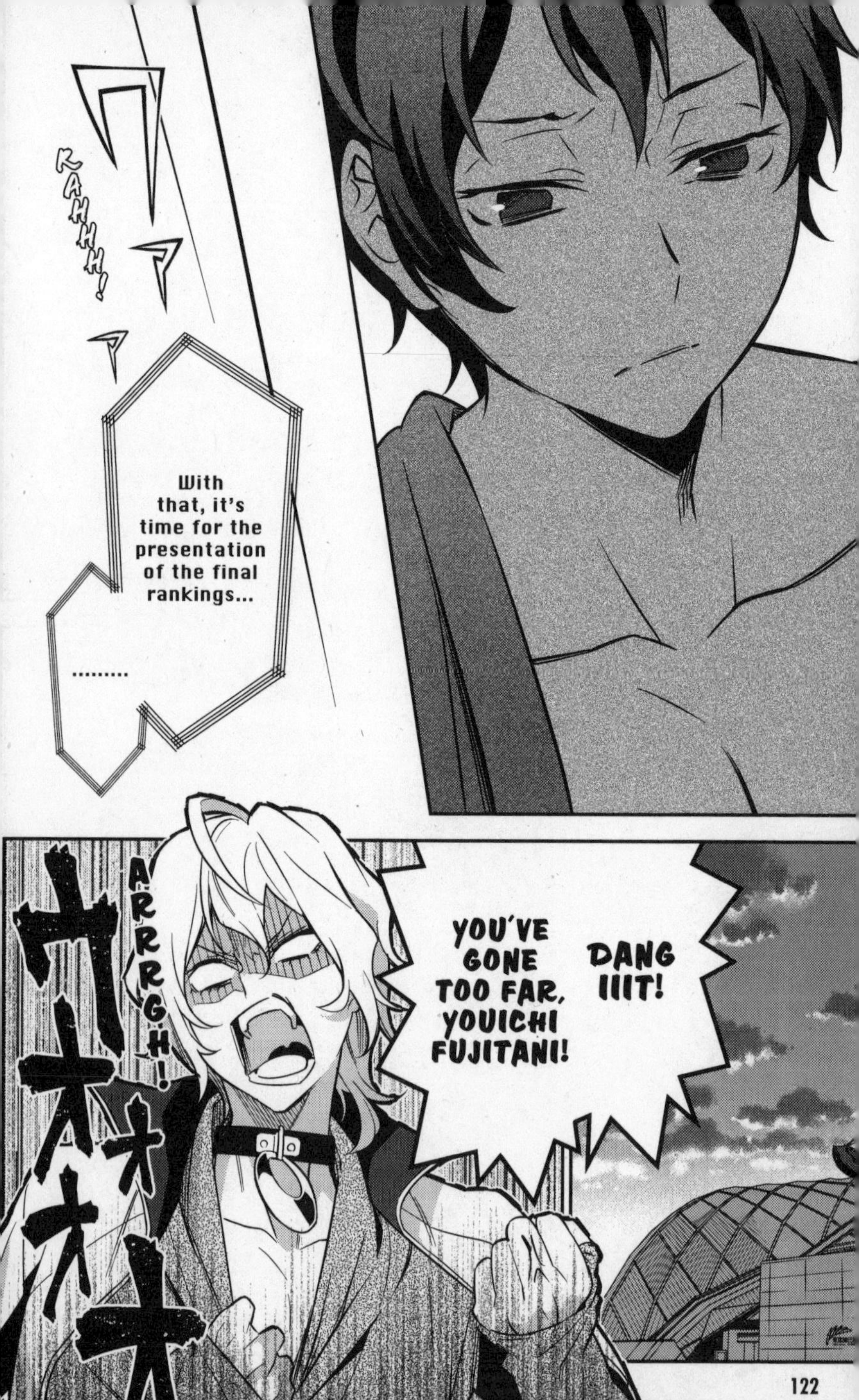

RAHHHH!
With that, it's time for the presentation of the final rankings...
....
DANG IIIT!
YOU'VE GONE TOO FAR, YOUICHI FUJITANI!
ARRRGH!

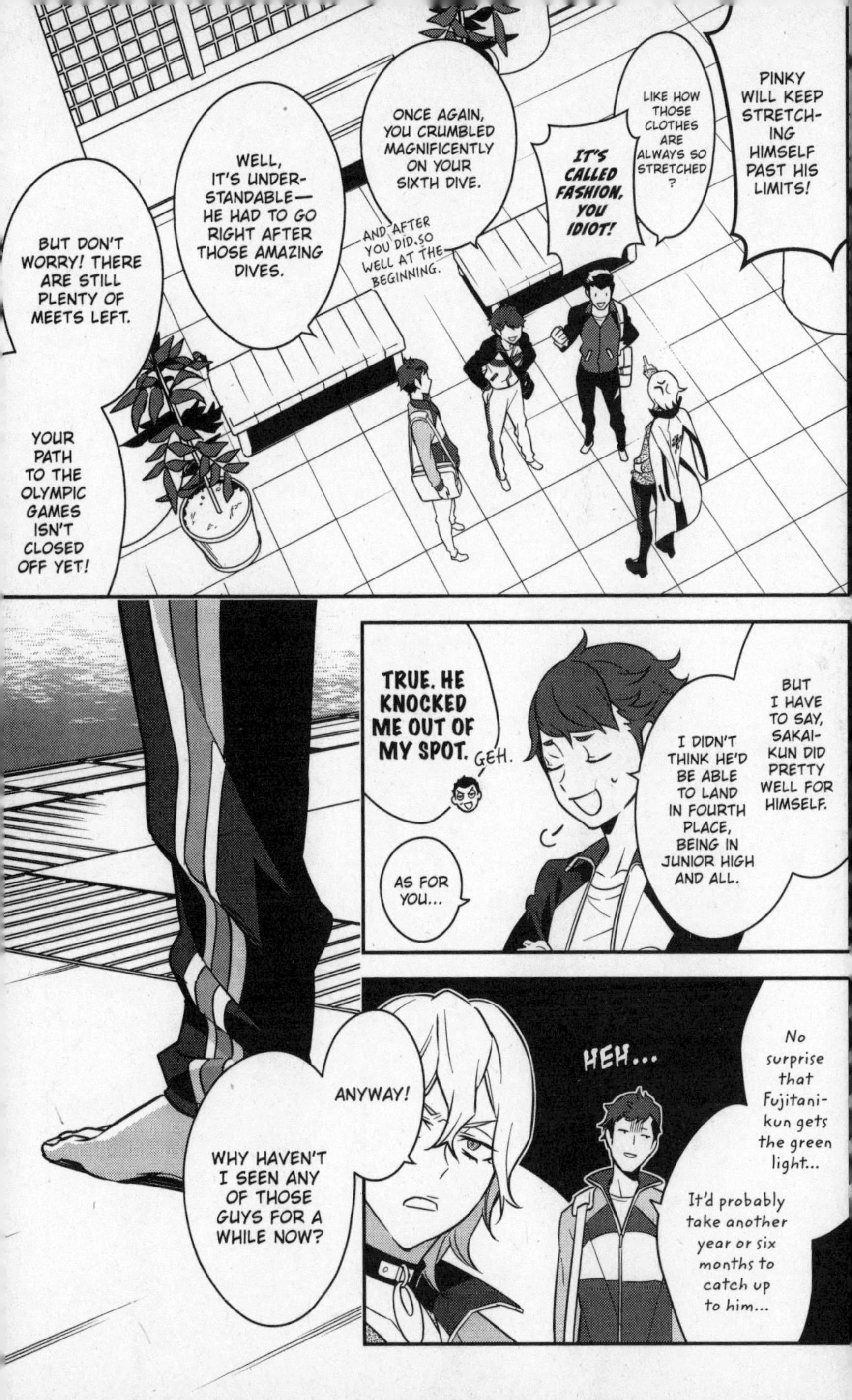
PINKY WILL KEEP STRETCHING HIMSELF PAST HIS LIMITS!
LIKE HOW THOSE CLOTHES ARE ALWAYS SO STRETCHED?
IT'S CALLED FASHION, YOU IDIOT!
ONCE AGAIN, YOU CRUMBLED MAGNIFICENTLY ON YOUR SIXTH DIVE.
AND AFTER YOU DID SO WELL AT THE BEGINNING.
WELL, IT'S UNDERSTANDABLE—HE HAD TO GO RIGHT AFTER THOSE AMAZING DIVES.
BUT DON'T WORRY! THERE ARE STILL PLENTY OF MEETS LEFT.
YOUR PATH TO THE OLYMPIC GAMES ISN'T CLOSED OFF YET!
BUT I HAVE TO SAY, SAKAI-KUN DID PRETTY WELL FOR HIMSELF.
I DIDN'T THINK HE'D BE ABLE TO LAND IN FOURTH PLACE, BEING IN JUNIOR HIGH AND ALL.
TRUE. HE KNOCKED ME OUT OF MY SPOT.
GEH.
AS FOR YOU...
No surprise that Fujitani-kun gets the green light...
It'd probably take another year or six months to catch up to him...
HEH...
ANYWAY!
WHY HAVEN'T I SEEN ANY OF THOSE GUYS FOR A WHILE NOW?

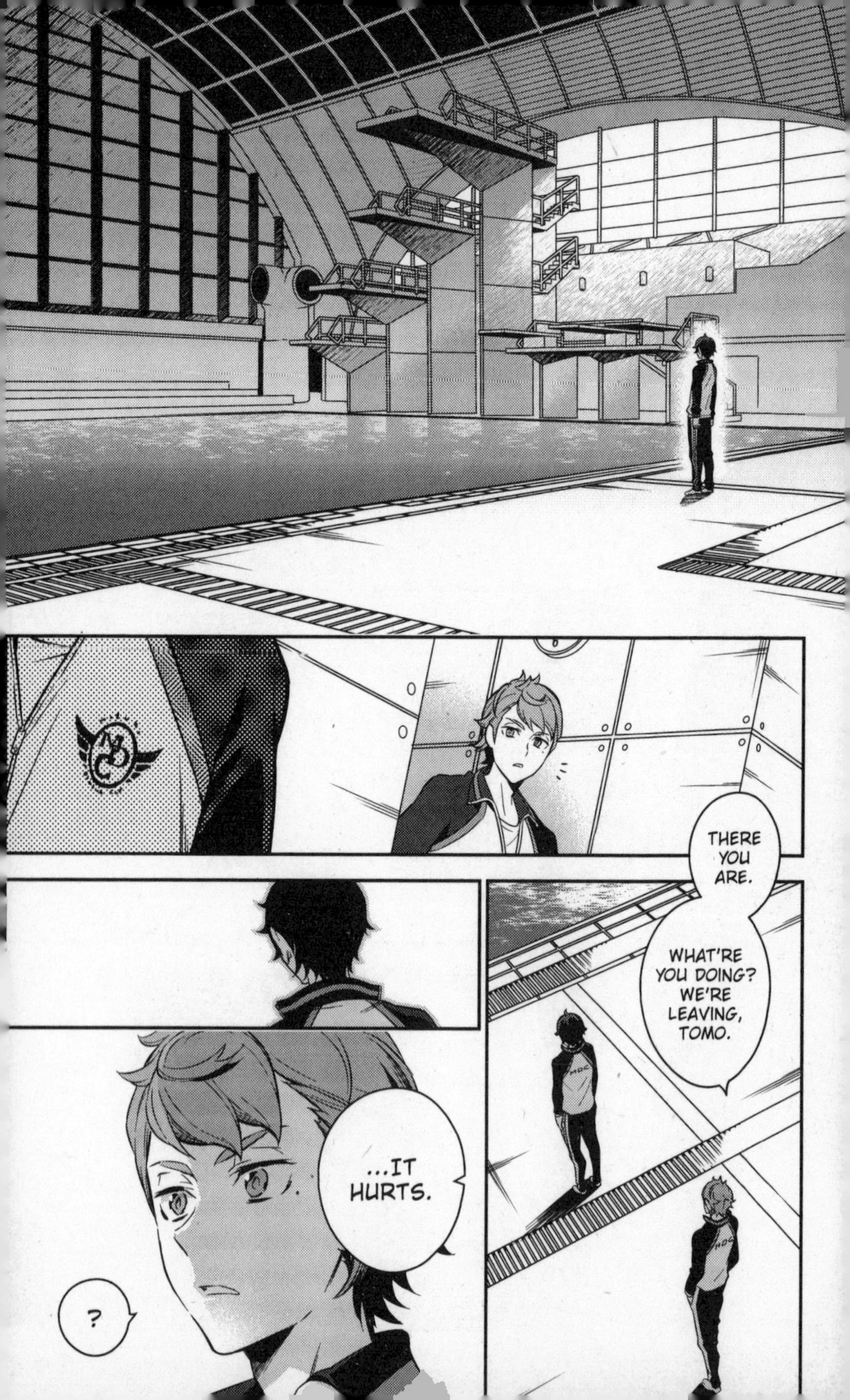
THERE YOU ARE.
WHAT'RE YOU DOING? WE'RE LEAVING, TOMO.
...IT HURTS.
?

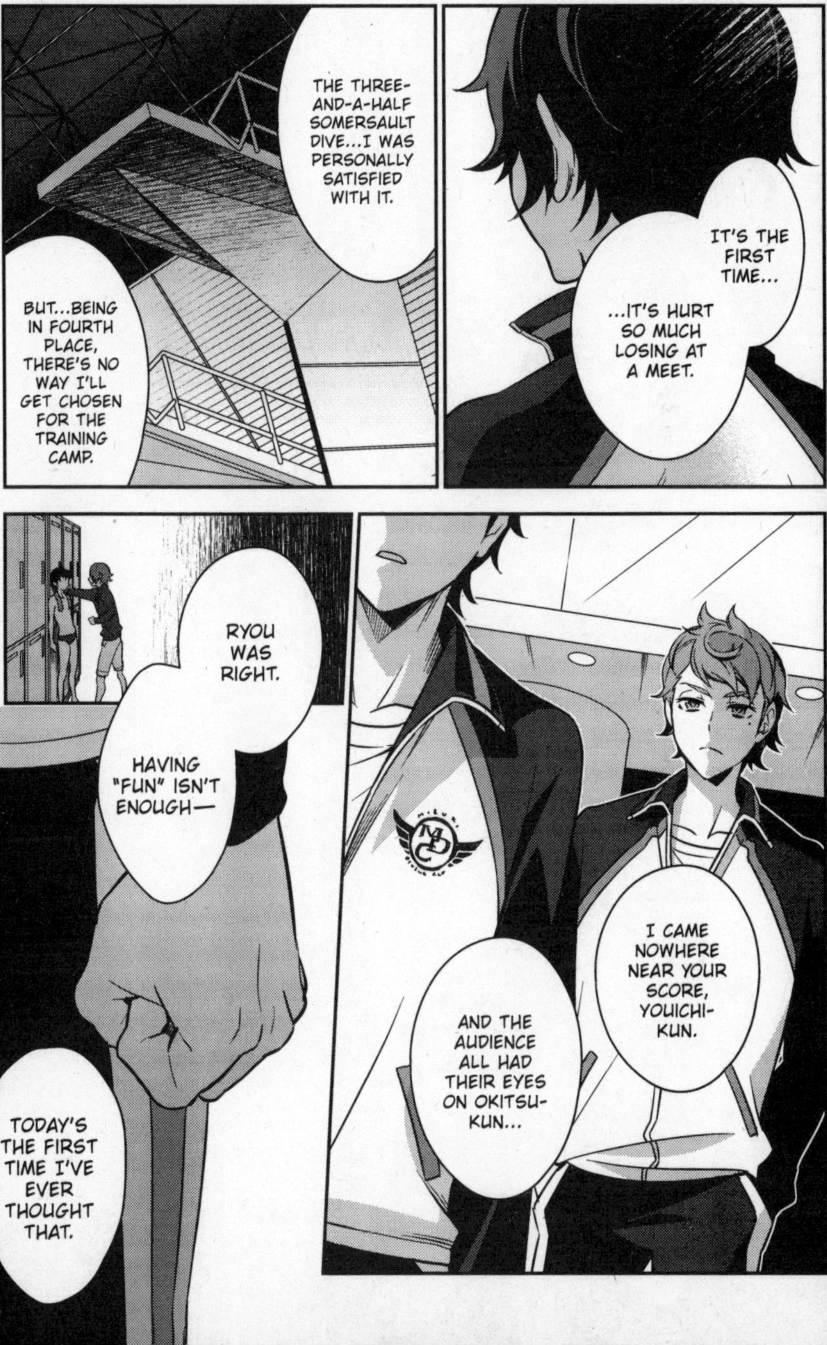
IT'S THE FIRST TIME...
...IT'S HURT SO MUCH LOSING AT A MEET.
THE THREE-AND-A-HALF SOMERSAULT DIVE...I WAS PERSONALLY SATISFIED WITH IT.
BUT...BEING IN FOURTH PLACE, THERE'S NO WAY I'LL GET CHOSEN FOR THE TRAINING CAMP.
I CAME NOWHERE NEAR YOUR SCORE, YOUICHI-KUN.
AND THE AUDIENCE ALL HAD THEIR EYES ON OKITSU-KUN...
RYOU WAS RIGHT.
HAVING "FUN" ISN'T ENOUGH—
TODAY'S THE FIRST TIME I'VE EVER THOUGHT THAT.

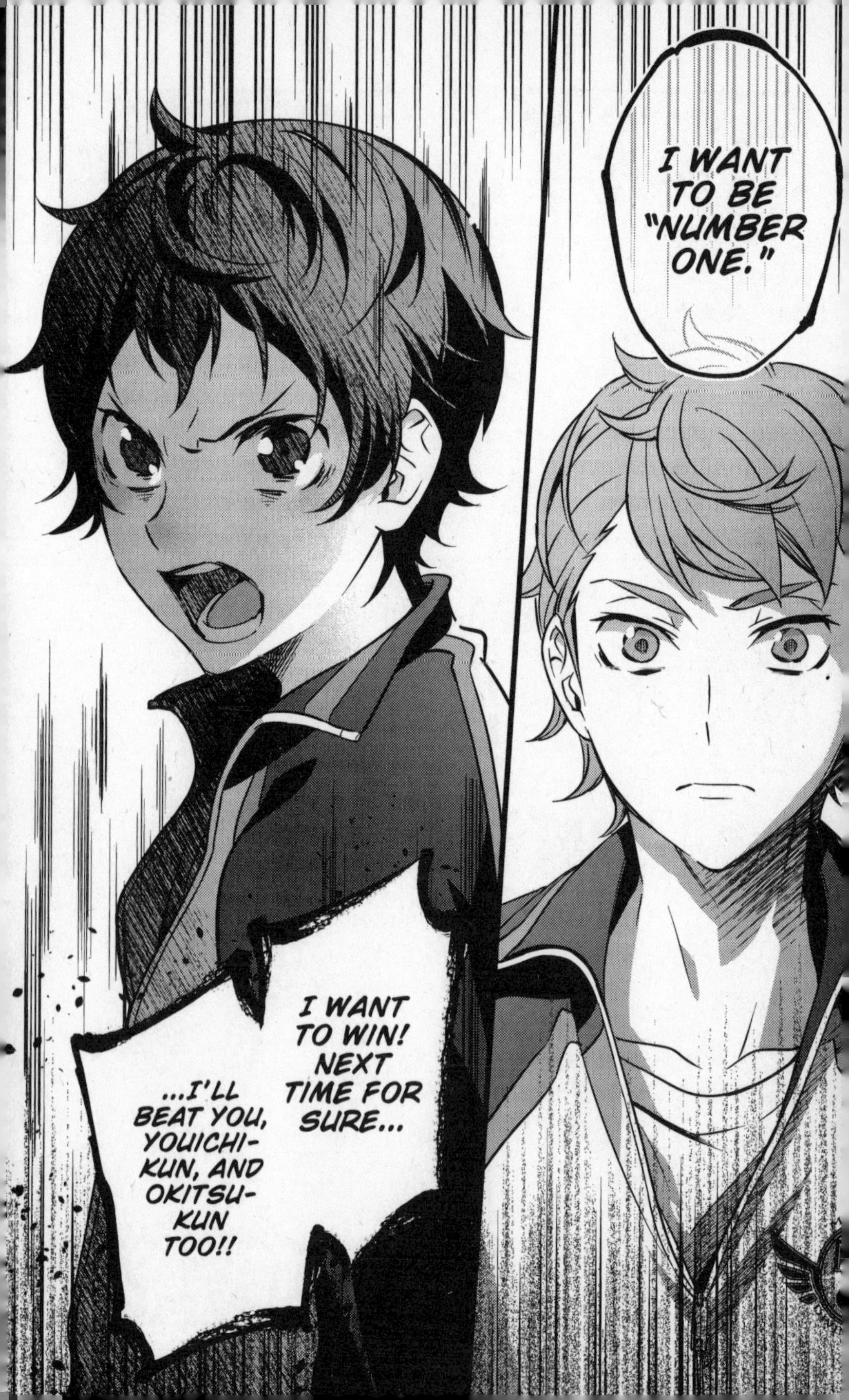
I WANT TO BE "NUMBER ONE."
I WANT TO WIN! NEXT TIME FOR SURE...
...I'LL BEAT YOU, YOUICHI-KUN, AND OKITSU-KUN TOO!!

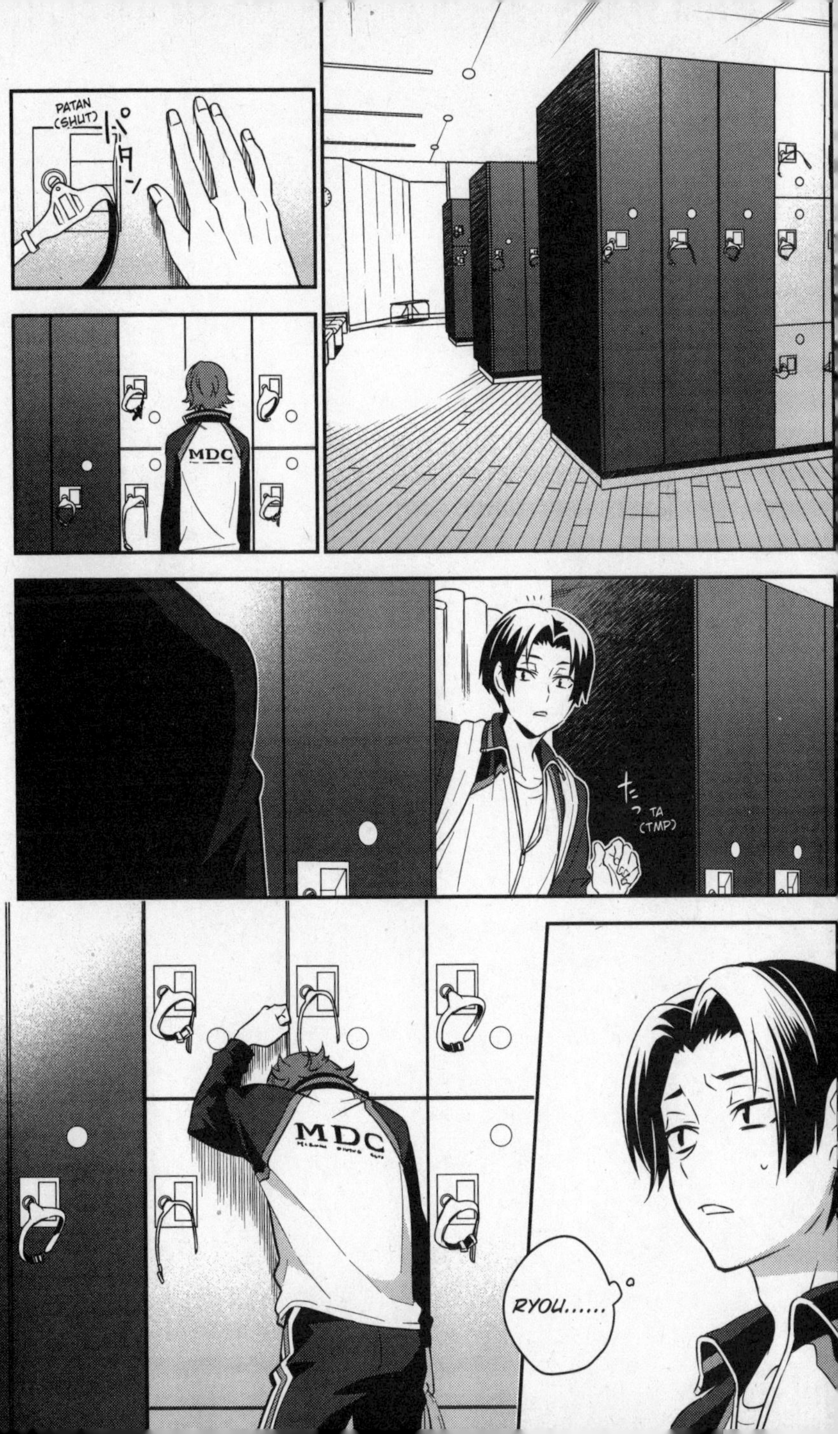
パタン
PATAN (SHUT)
MDC
たっ
TA (TMP)
MDC
RYOU......

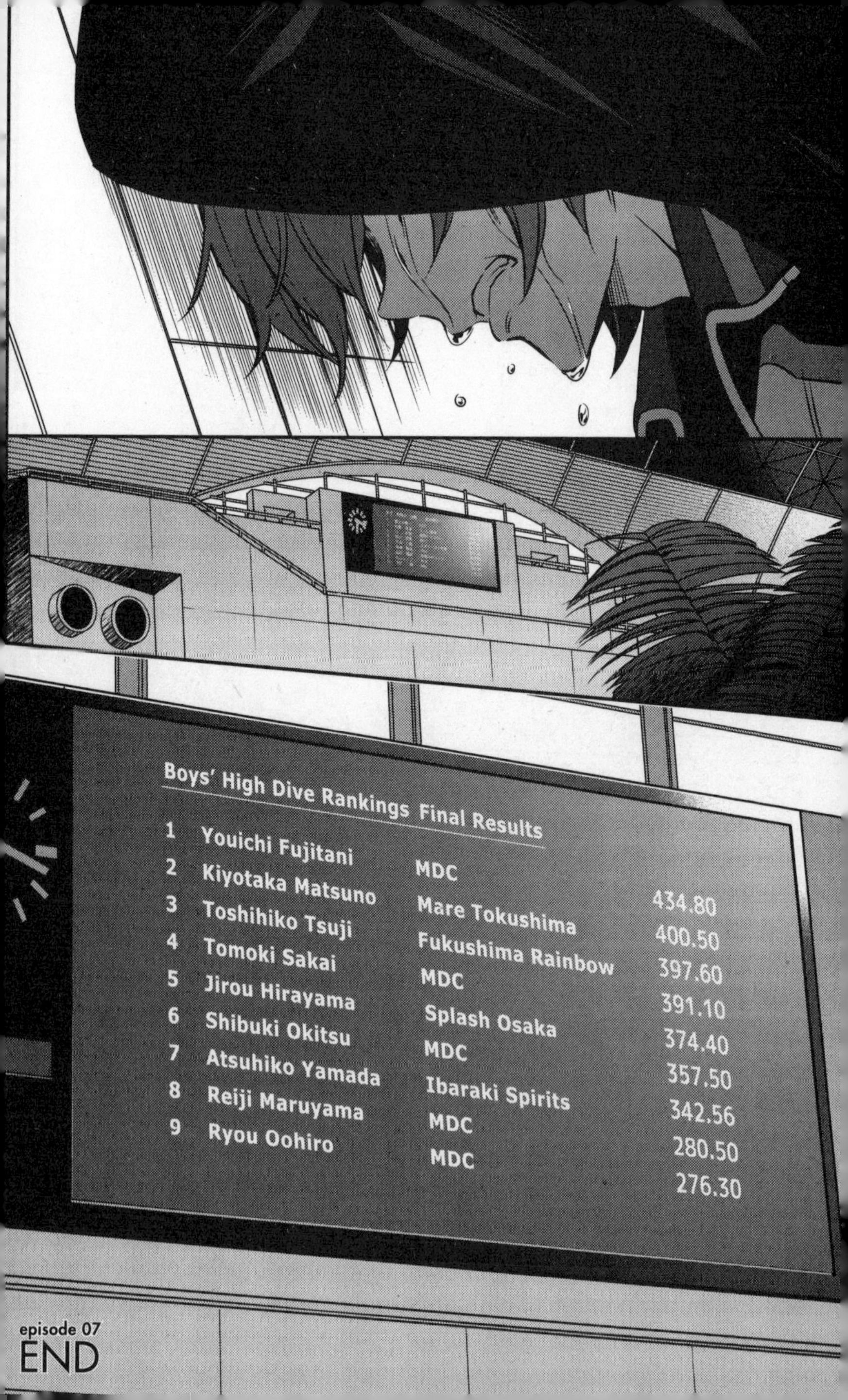

Boys' High Dive Rankings Final Results
1 Youichi Fujitani MDC 434.80
2 Kiyotaka Matsuno Mare Tokushima 400.50
3 Toshihiko Tsuji Fukushima Rainbow 397.60
4 Tomoki Sakai MDC 391.10
5 Jirou Hirayama Splash Osaka 374.40
6 Shibuki Okitsu MDC 357.50
7 Atsuhiko Yamada Ibaraki Spirits 342.56
8 Reiji Maruyama MDC 280.50
9 Ryou Oohiro MDC 276.30
episode 07
END

episode 08

DEAR FRIENDS

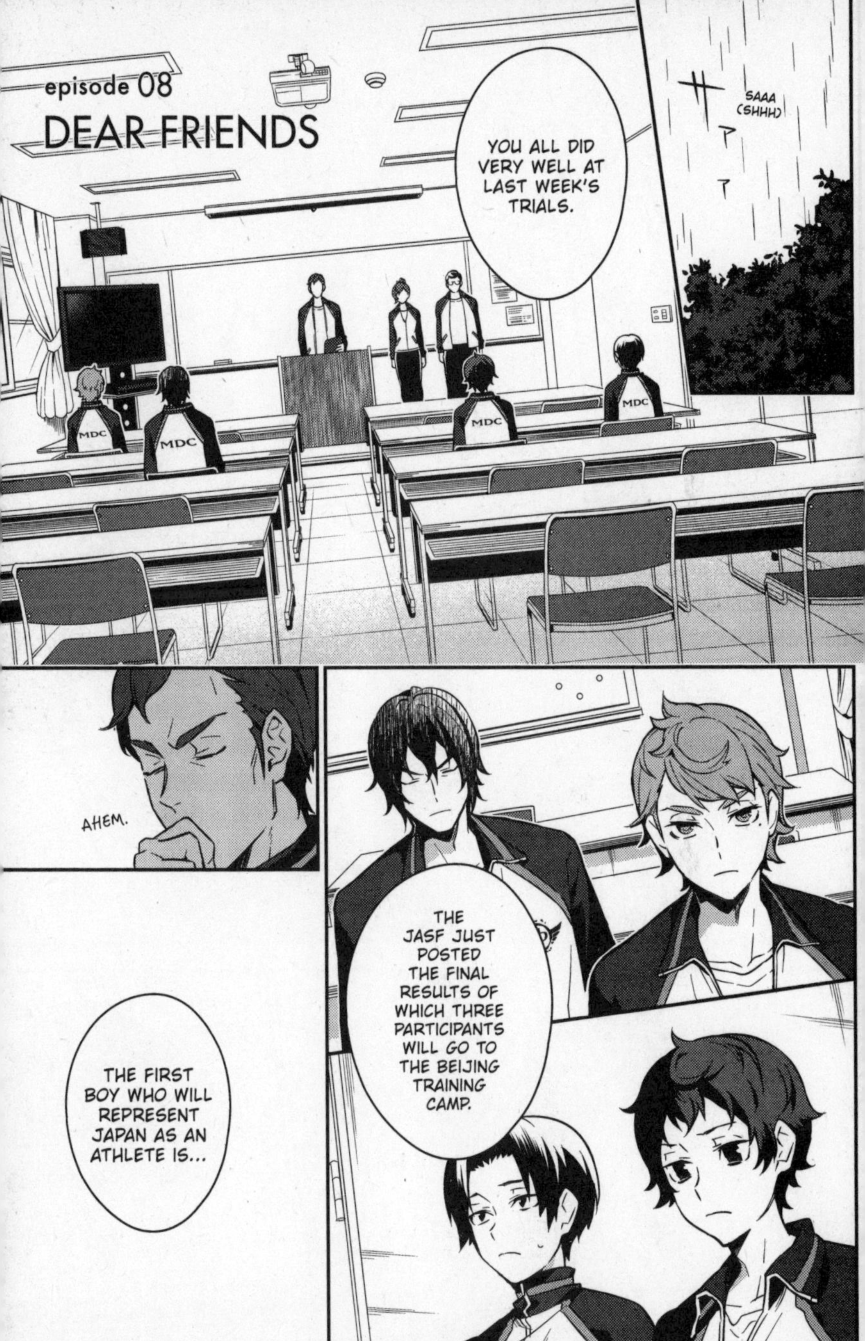
SAAA (SHHH)
YOU ALL DID VERY WELL AT LAST WEEK'S TRIALS.
MDC
AHEM.
THE JASF JUST POSTED THE FINAL RESULTS OF WHICH THREE PARTICIPANTS WILL GO TO THE BEIJING TRAINING CAMP.
THE FIRST BOY WHO WILL REPRESENT JAPAN AS AN ATHLETE IS...

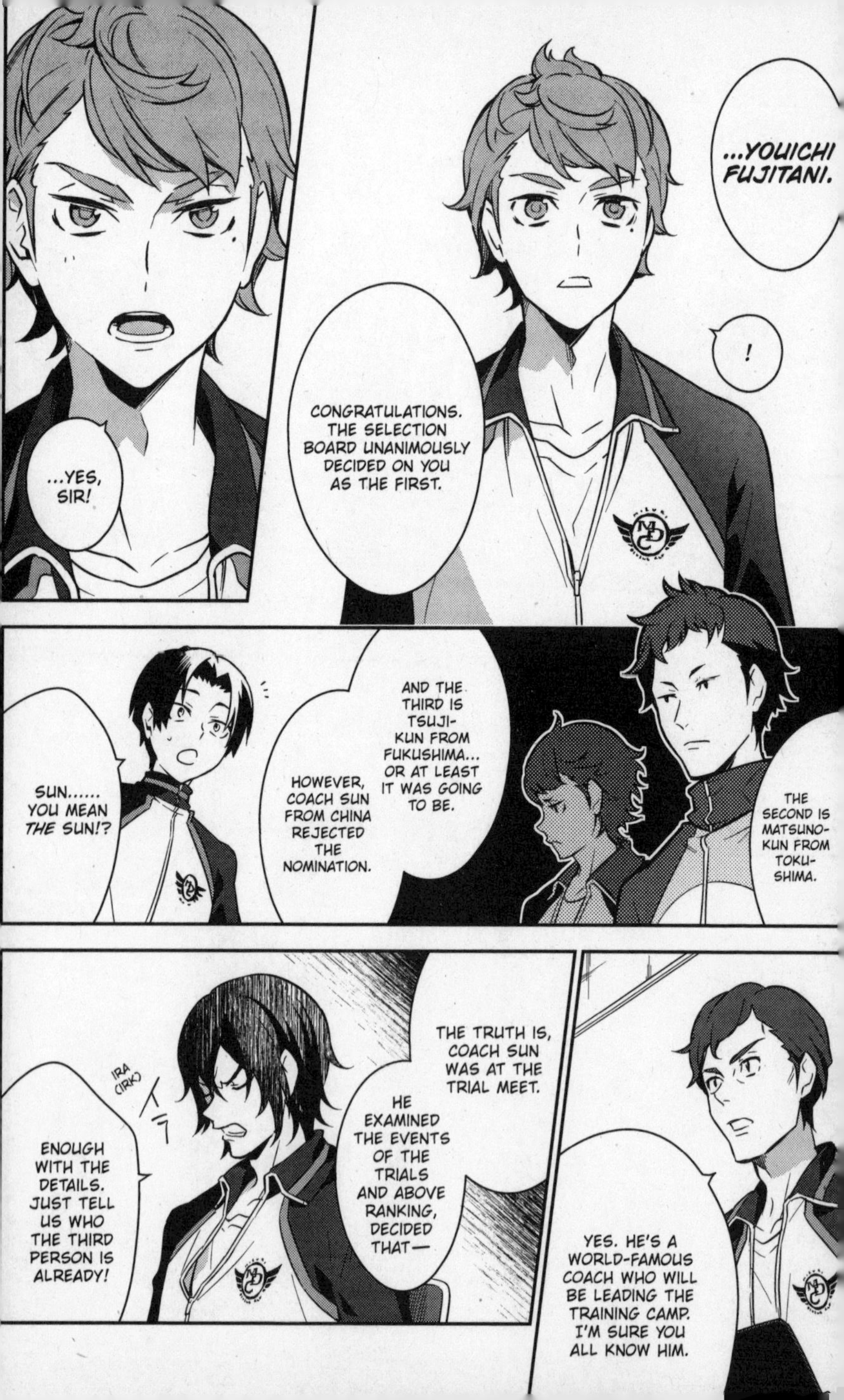
...YOUICHI FUJITANI.
!
CONGRATULATIONS. THE SELECTION BOARD UNANIMOUSLY DECIDED ON YOU AS THE FIRST.
...YES, SIR!
THE SECOND IS MATSUNO-KUN FROM TOKU-SHIMA.
AND THE THIRD IS TSUJI-KUN FROM FUKUSHIMA... OR AT LEAST IT WAS GOING TO BE.
HOWEVER, COACH SUN FROM CHINA REJECTED THE NOMINATION.
SUN...... YOU MEAN *THE* SUN!?
YES. HE'S A WORLD-FAMOUS COACH WHO WILL BE LEADING THE TRAINING CAMP. I'M SURE YOU ALL KNOW HIM.
THE TRUTH IS, COACH SUN WAS AT THE TRIAL MEET.
HE EXAMINED THE EVENTS OF THE TRIALS AND ABOVE RANKING, DECIDED THAT—
IRA (IRK)
ENOUGH WITH THE DETAILS. JUST TELL US WHO THE THIRD PERSON IS ALREADY!

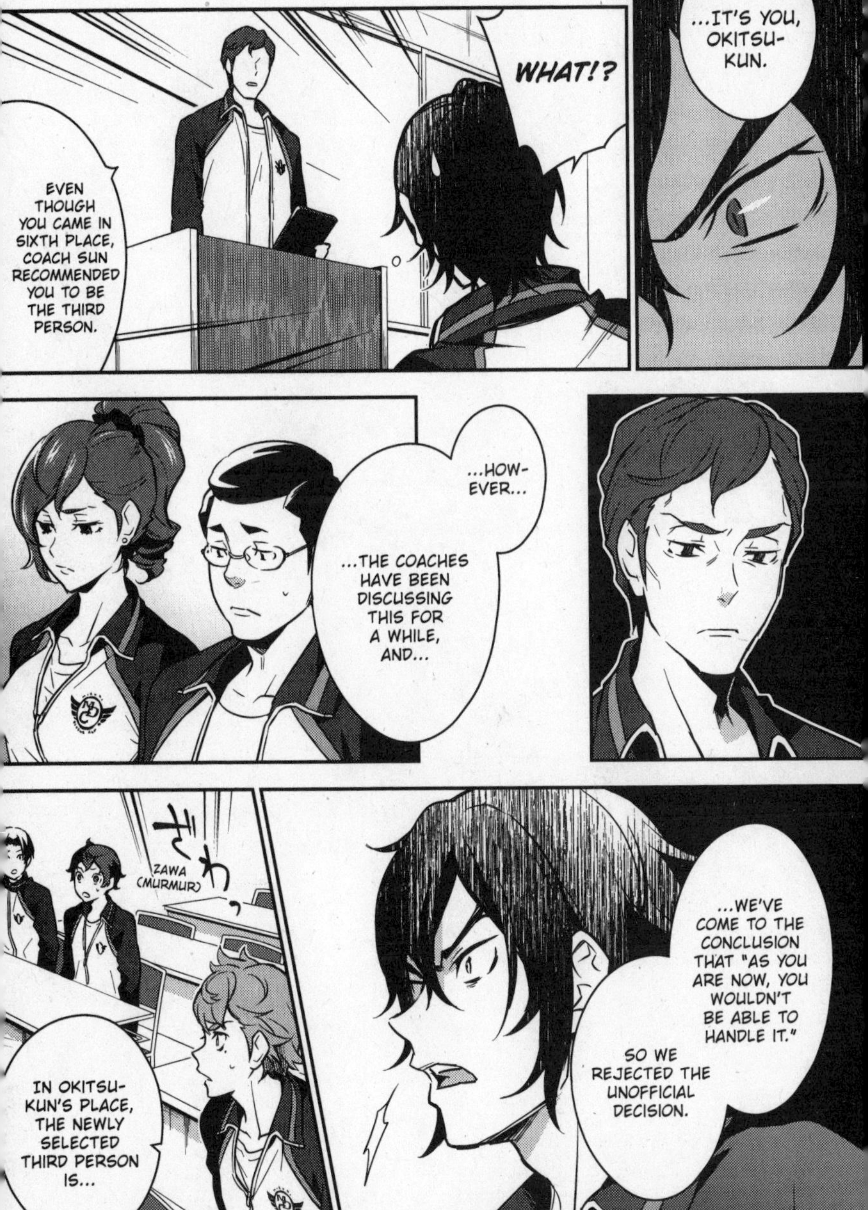
...IT'S YOU, OKITSU-KUN.
WHAT!?
EVEN THOUGH YOU CAME IN SIXTH PLACE, COACH SUN RECOMMENDED YOU TO BE THE THIRD PERSON.
...HOW-EVER...
...THE COACHES HAVE BEEN DISCUSSING THIS FOR A WHILE, AND...
...WE'VE COME TO THE CONCLUSION THAT "AS YOU ARE NOW, YOU WOULDN'T BE ABLE TO HANDLE IT."
SO WE REJECTED THE UNOFFICIAL DECISION.
ざわ
ZAWA (MURMUR)
IN OKITSU-KUN'S PLACE, THE NEWLY SELECTED THIRD PERSON IS...

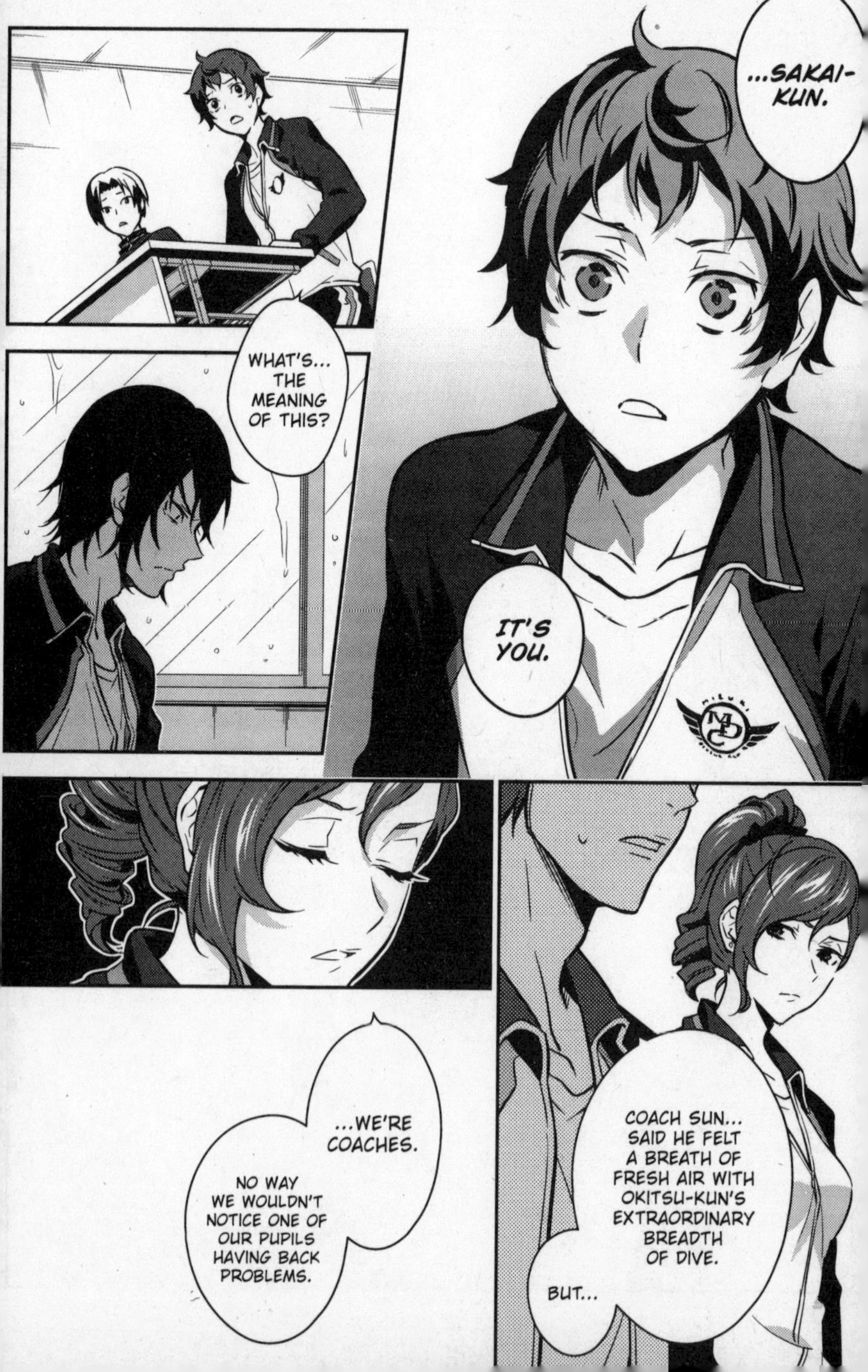
...SAKAI-KUN.
IT'S YOU.
WHAT'S... THE MEANING OF THIS?
...WE'RE COACHES.
NO WAY WE WOULDN'T NOTICE ONE OF OUR PUPILS HAVING BACK PROBLEMS.
COACH SUN... SAID HE FELT A BREATH OF FRESH AIR WITH OKITSU-KUN'S EXTRAORDINARY BREADTH OF DIVE.
BUT...

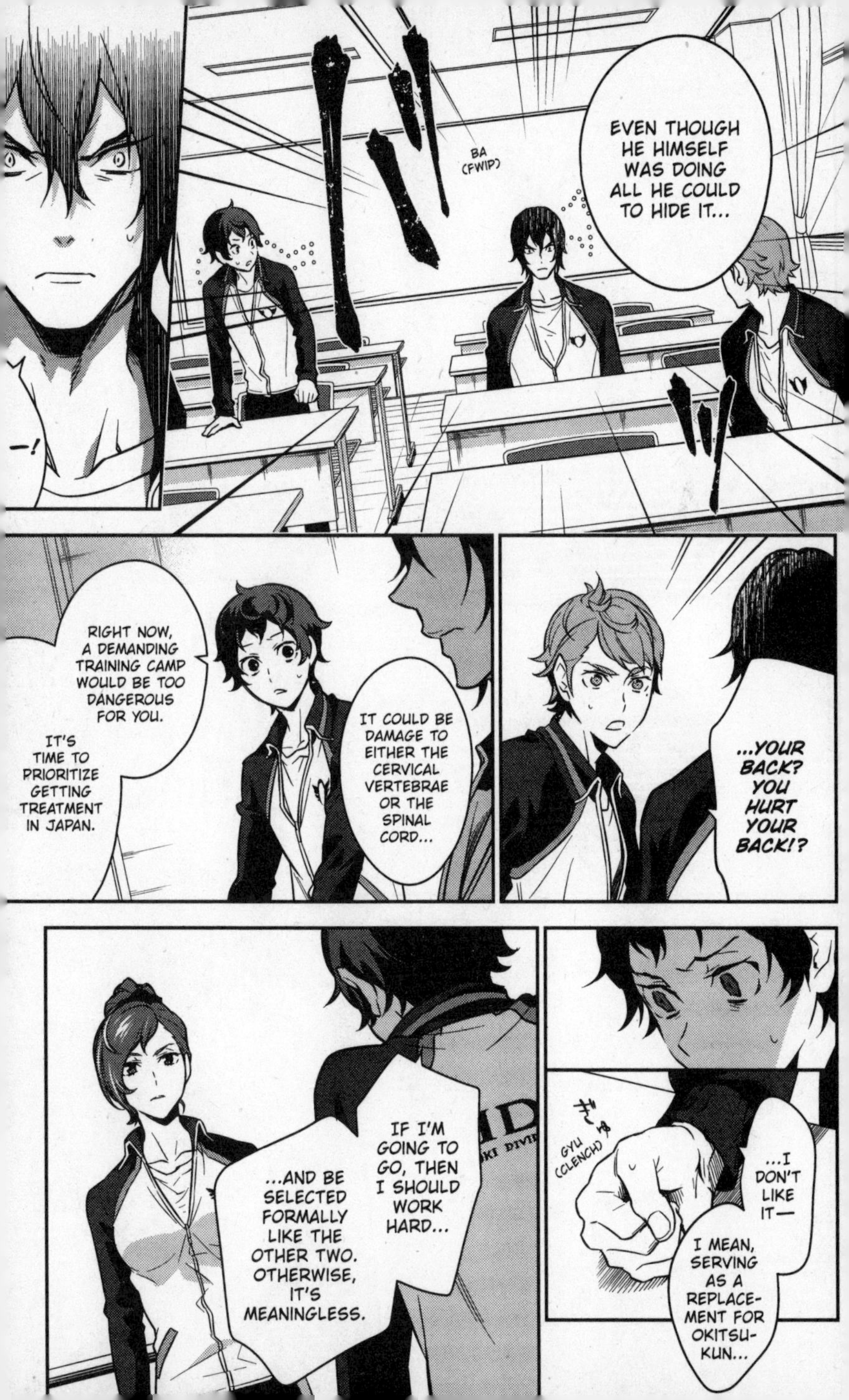
EVEN THOUGH HE HIMSELF WAS DOING ALL HE COULD TO HIDE IT...
BA (FWIP)
—!
...YOUR BACK? YOU HURT YOUR BACK!?
IT COULD BE DAMAGE TO EITHER THE CERVICAL VERTEBRAE OR THE SPINAL CORD...
RIGHT NOW, A DEMANDING TRAINING CAMP WOULD BE TOO DANGEROUS FOR YOU.
IT'S TIME TO PRIORITIZE GETTING TREATMENT IN JAPAN.
GYU (CLENCH)
...I DON'T LIKE IT—
I MEAN, SERVING AS A REPLACEMENT FOR OKITSU-KUN...
IF I'M GOING TO GO, THEN I SHOULD WORK HARD...
...AND BE SELECTED FORMALLY LIKE THE OTHER TWO. OTHERWISE, IT'S MEANINGLESS.

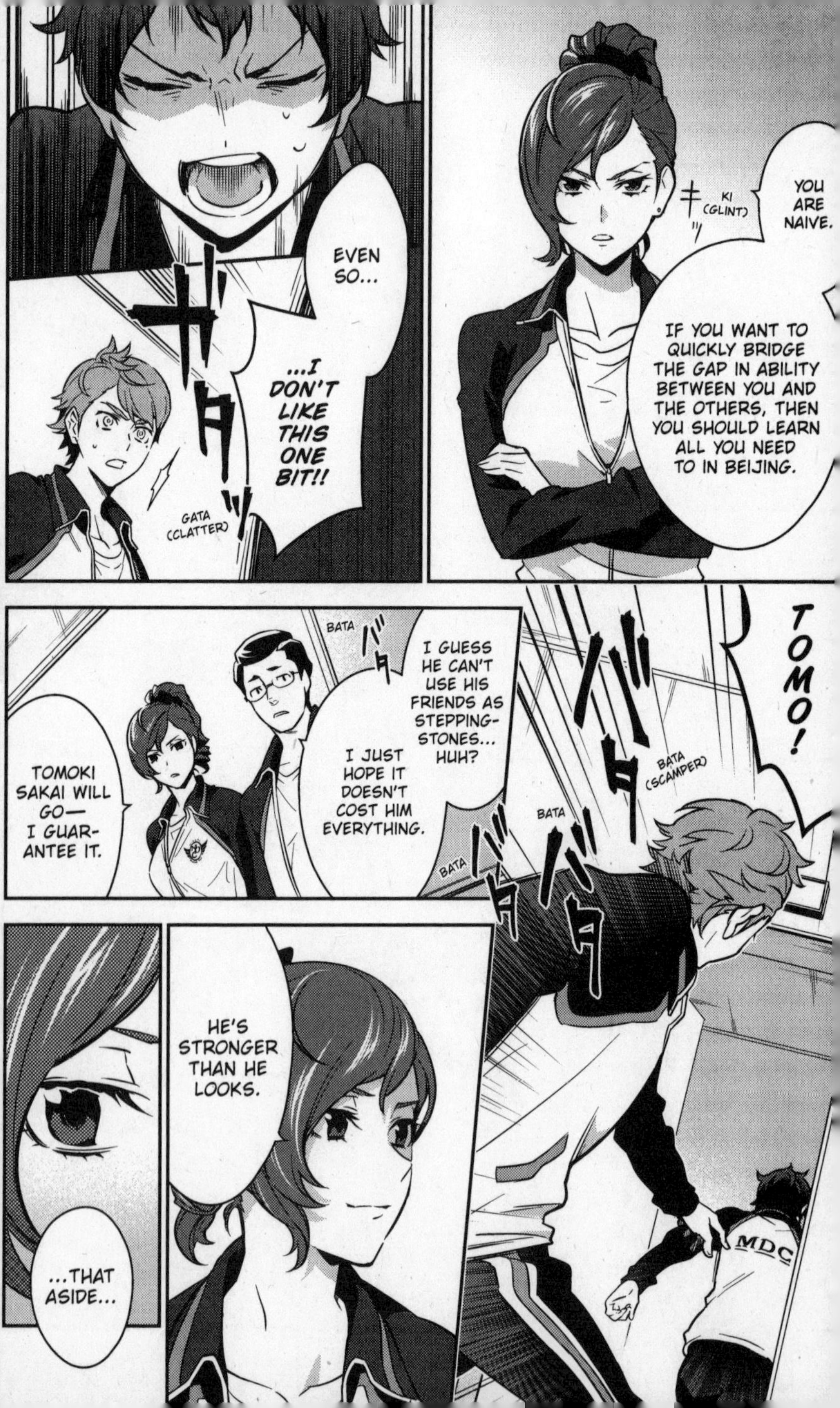
KI (GLINT)
YOU ARE NAIVE.
IF YOU WANT TO QUICKLY BRIDGE THE GAP IN ABILITY BETWEEN YOU AND THE OTHERS, THEN YOU SHOULD LEARN ALL YOU NEED TO IN BEIJING.
EVEN SO...
...I DON'T LIKE THIS ONE BIT!!
GATA (CLATTER)
TOMO!
BATA (SCAMPER)
BATA
BATA
BATA
I GUESS HE CAN'T USE HIS FRIENDS AS STEPPING-STONES... HUH?
I JUST HOPE IT DOESN'T COST HIM EVERYTHING.
TOMOKI SAKAI WILL GO— I GUARANTEE IT.
HE'S STRONGER THAN HE LOOKS.
...THAT ASIDE...

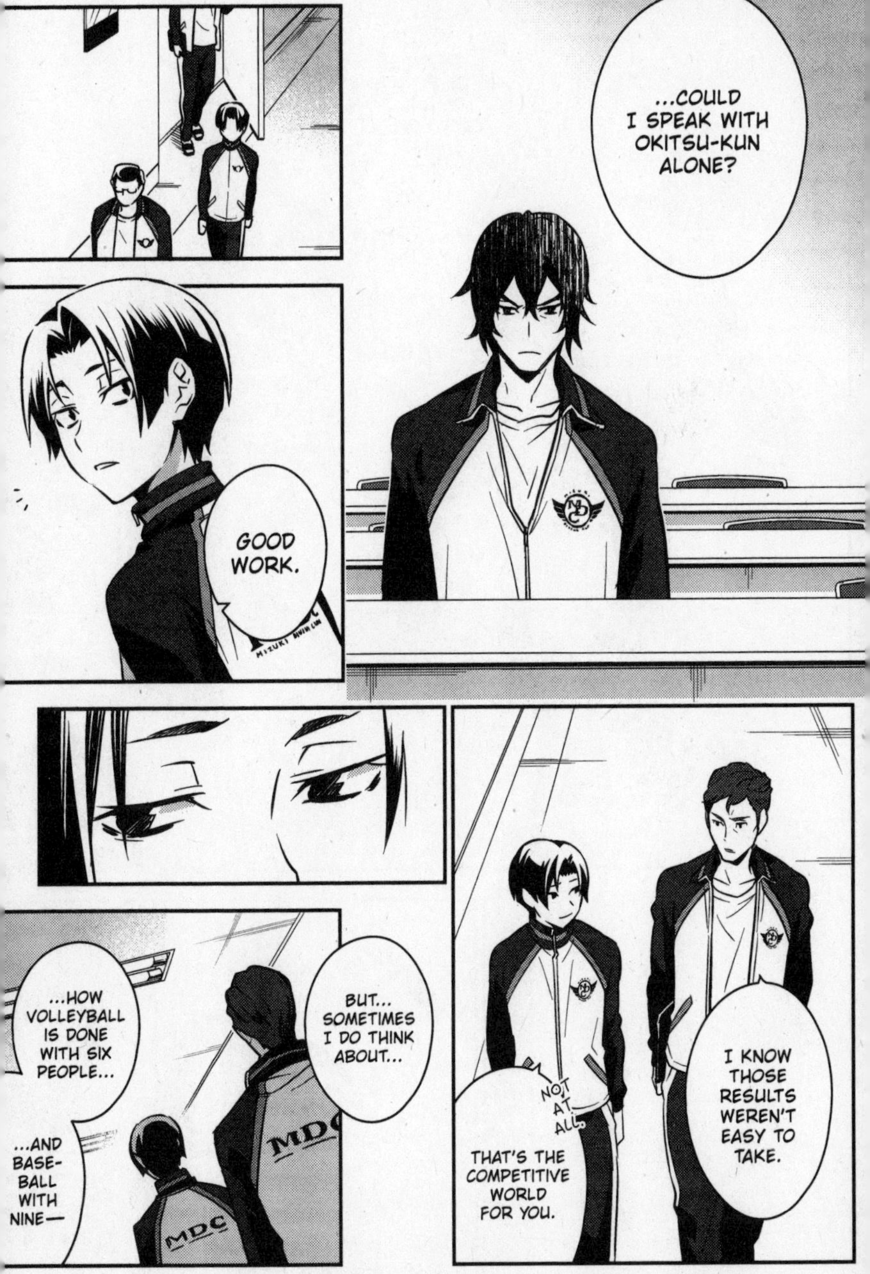
...COULD I SPEAK WITH OKITSU-KUN ALONE?
GOOD WORK.
I KNOW THOSE RESULTS WEREN'T EASY TO TAKE.
NOT AT ALL.
THAT'S THE COMPETITIVE WORLD FOR YOU.
BUT... SOMETIMES I DO THINK ABOUT...
...HOW VOLLEYBALL IS DONE WITH SIX PEOPLE...
...AND BASE-BALL WITH NINE—

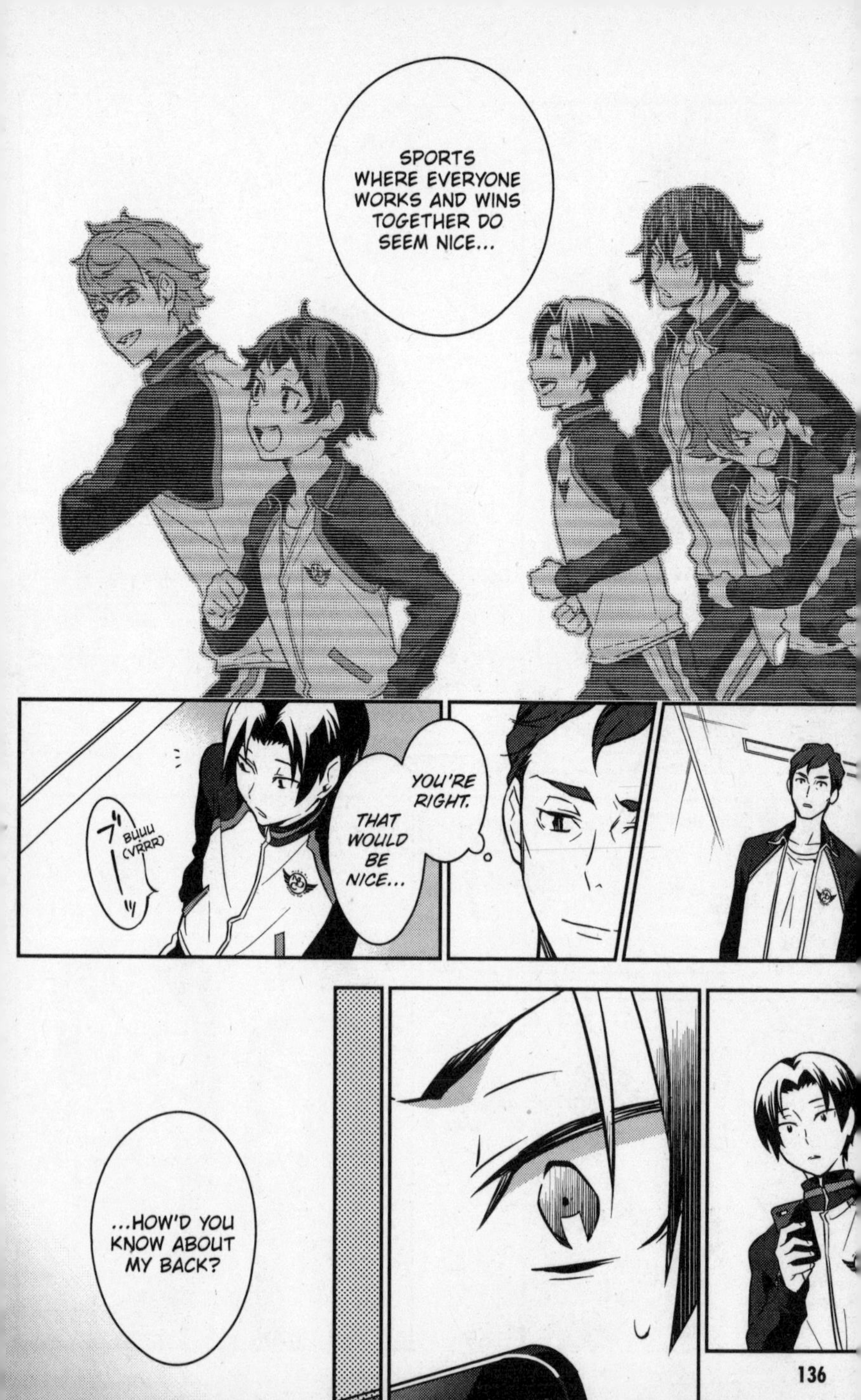
SPORTS WHERE EVERYONE WORKS AND WINS TOGETHER DO SEEM NICE...
YOU'RE RIGHT.
THAT WOULD BE NICE...
ブーッ
BUUU (VRRR)
...HOW'D YOU KNOW ABOUT MY BACK?

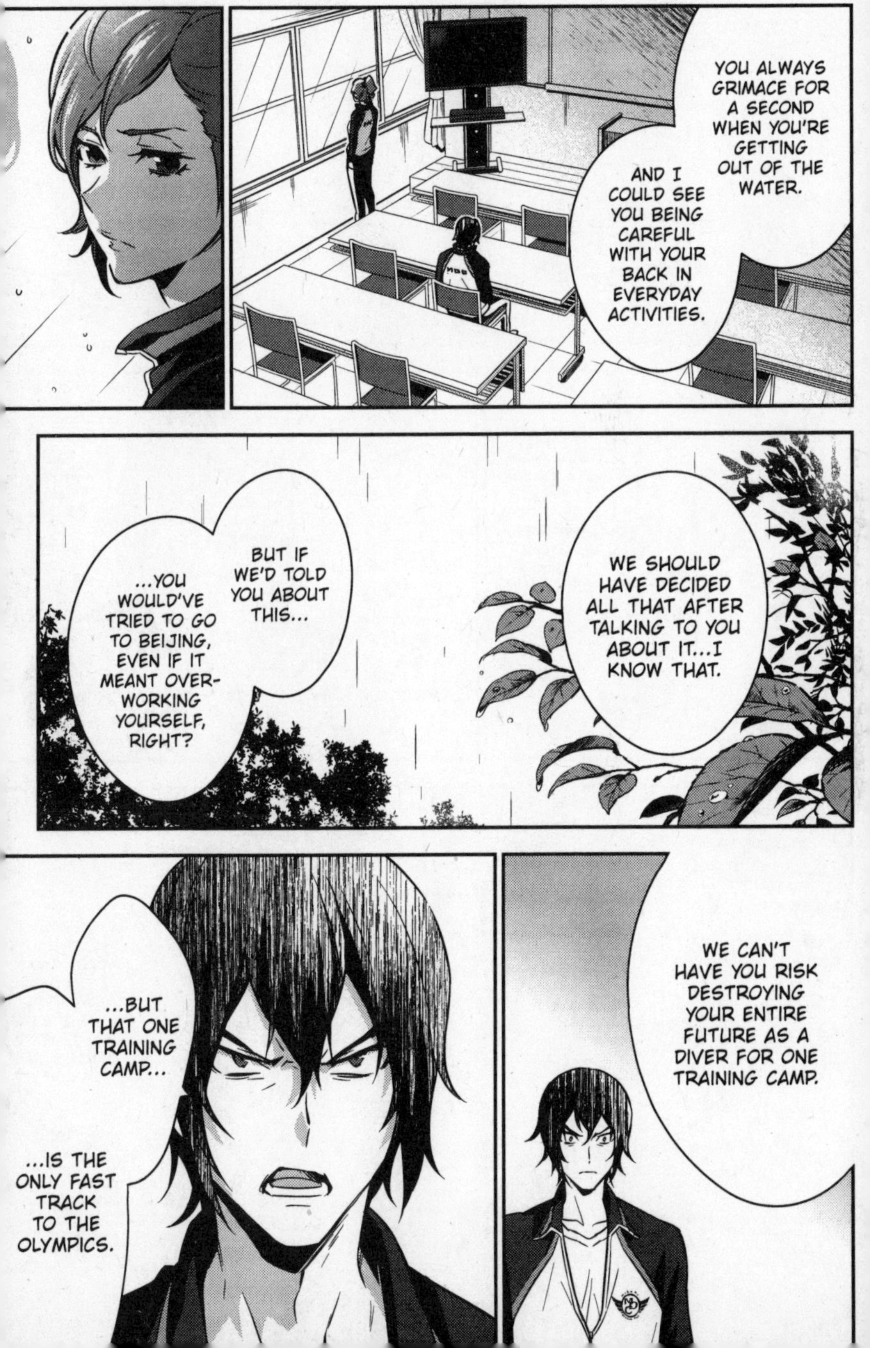
YOU ALWAYS GRIMACE FOR A SECOND WHEN YOU'RE GETTING OUT OF THE WATER.
AND I COULD SEE YOU BEING CAREFUL WITH YOUR BACK IN EVERYDAY ACTIVITIES.
WE SHOULD HAVE DECIDED ALL THAT AFTER TALKING TO YOU ABOUT IT...I KNOW THAT.
BUT IF WE'D TOLD YOU ABOUT THIS...
...YOU WOULD'VE TRIED TO GO TO BEIJING, EVEN IF IT MEANT OVER-WORKING YOURSELF, RIGHT?
WE CAN'T HAVE YOU RISK DESTROYING YOUR ENTIRE FUTURE AS A DIVER FOR ONE TRAINING CAMP.
...BUT THAT ONE TRAINING CAMP...
...IS THE ONLY FAST TRACK TO THE OLYMPICS.

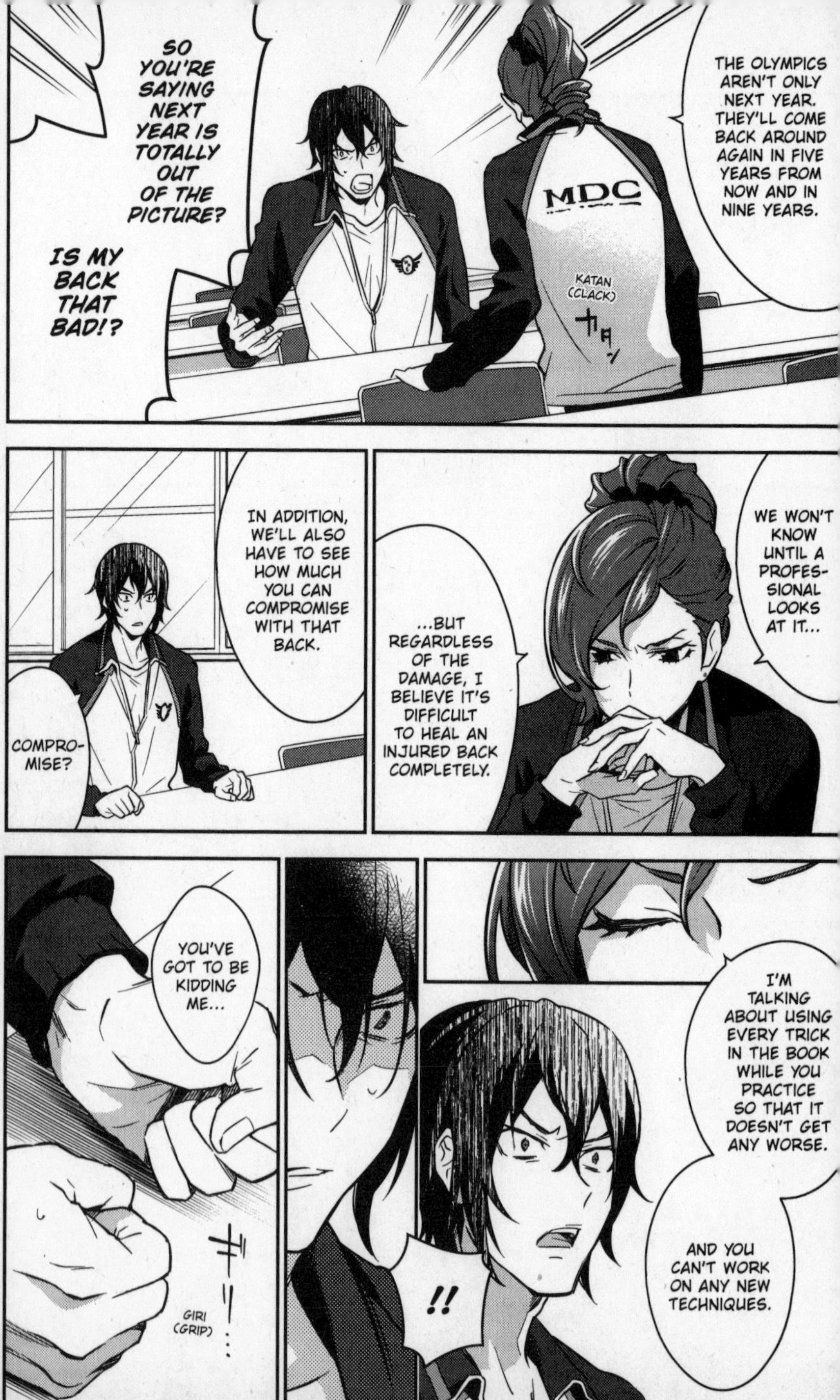
THE OLYMPICS AREN'T ONLY NEXT YEAR. THEY'LL COME BACK AROUND AGAIN IN FIVE YEARS FROM NOW AND IN NINE YEARS.
KATAN (CLACK)
SO YOU'RE SAYING NEXT YEAR IS TOTALLY OUT OF THE PICTURE?
IS MY BACK THAT BAD!?
WE WON'T KNOW UNTIL A PROFES- SIONAL LOOKS AT IT...
...BUT REGARDLESS OF THE DAMAGE, I BELIEVE IT'S DIFFICULT TO HEAL AN INJURED BACK COMPLETELY.
IN ADDITION, WE'LL ALSO HAVE TO SEE HOW MUCH YOU CAN COMPROMISE WITH THAT BACK.
COMPRO- MISE?
I'M TALKING ABOUT USING EVERY TRICK IN THE BOOK WHILE YOU PRACTICE SO THAT IT DOESN'T GET ANY WORSE.
AND YOU CAN'T WORK ON ANY NEW TECHNIQUES.
!!
YOU'VE GOT TO BE KIDDING ME...
GIRI (GRIP)

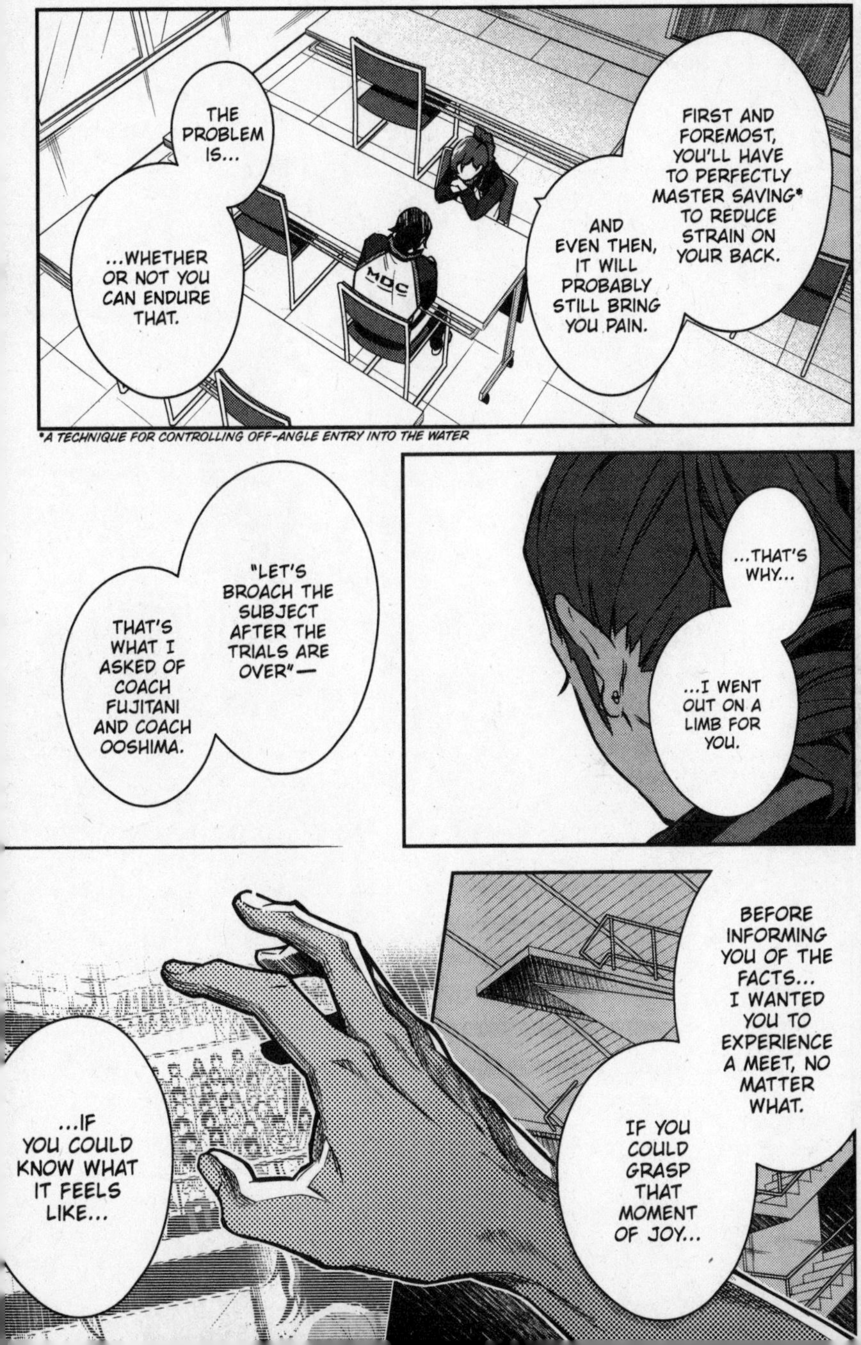
FIRST AND FOREMOST, YOU'LL HAVE TO PERFECTLY MASTER SAVING* TO REDUCE STRAIN ON YOUR BACK.
AND EVEN THEN, IT WILL PROBABLY STILL BRING YOU PAIN.
THE PROBLEM IS...
...WHETHER OR NOT YOU CAN ENDURE THAT.
...THAT'S WHY...
...I WENT OUT ON A LIMB FOR YOU.
"LET'S BROACH THE SUBJECT AFTER THE TRIALS ARE OVER"—
THAT'S WHAT I ASKED OF COACH FUJITANI AND COACH OOSHIMA.
BEFORE INFORMING YOU OF THE FACTS... I WANTED YOU TO EXPERIENCE A MEET, NO MATTER WHAT.
IF YOU COULD GRASP THAT MOMENT OF JOY...
...IF YOU COULD KNOW WHAT IT FEELS LIKE...

*A TECHNIQUE FOR CONTROLLING OFF-ANGLE ENTRY INTO THE WATER

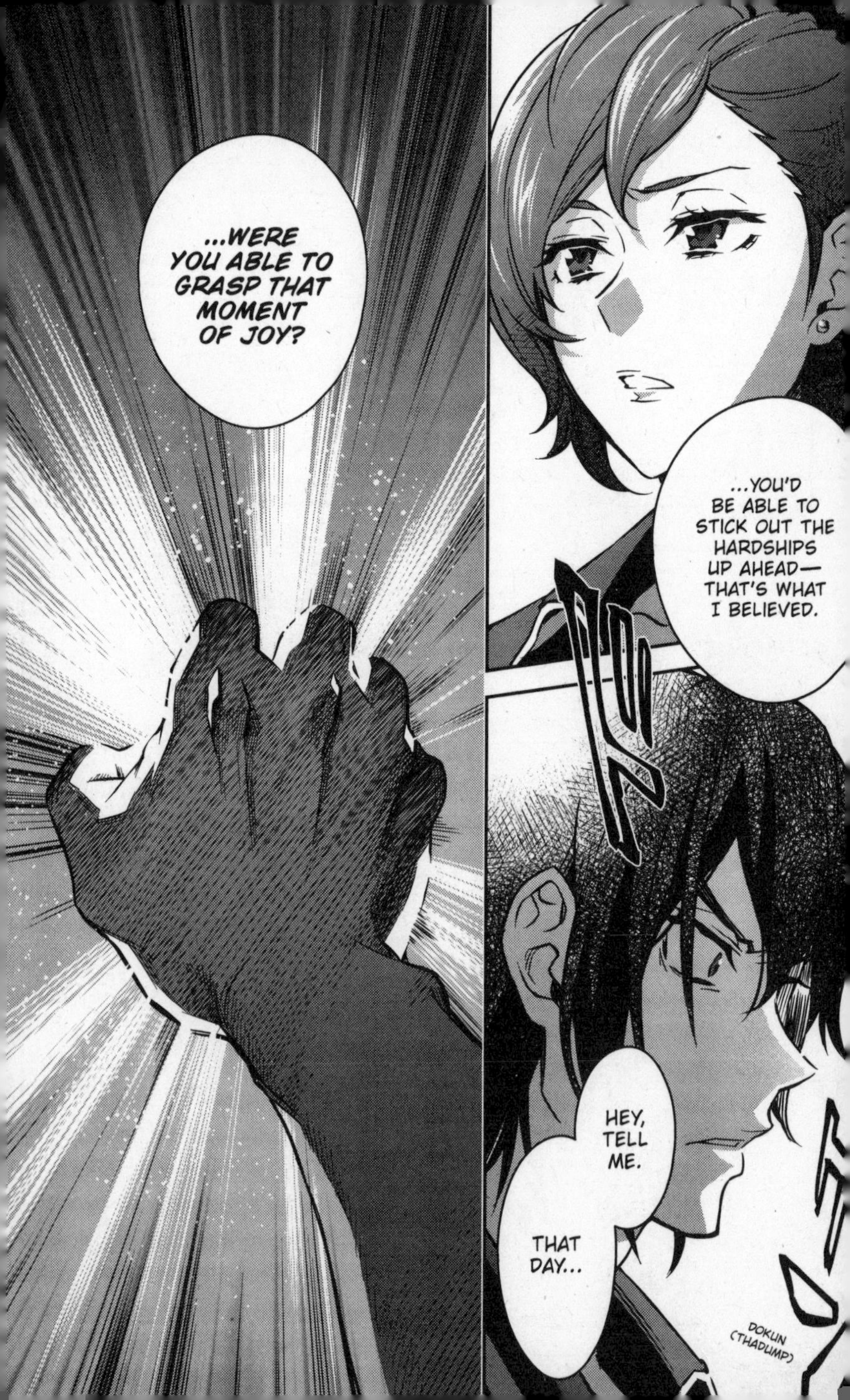
...YOU'D BE ABLE TO STICK OUT THE HARDSHIPS UP AHEAD— THAT'S WHAT I BELIEVED.
HEY, TELL ME.
THAT DAY...
DOKUN (THADUMP)
...WERE YOU ABLE TO GRASP THAT MOMENT OF JOY?

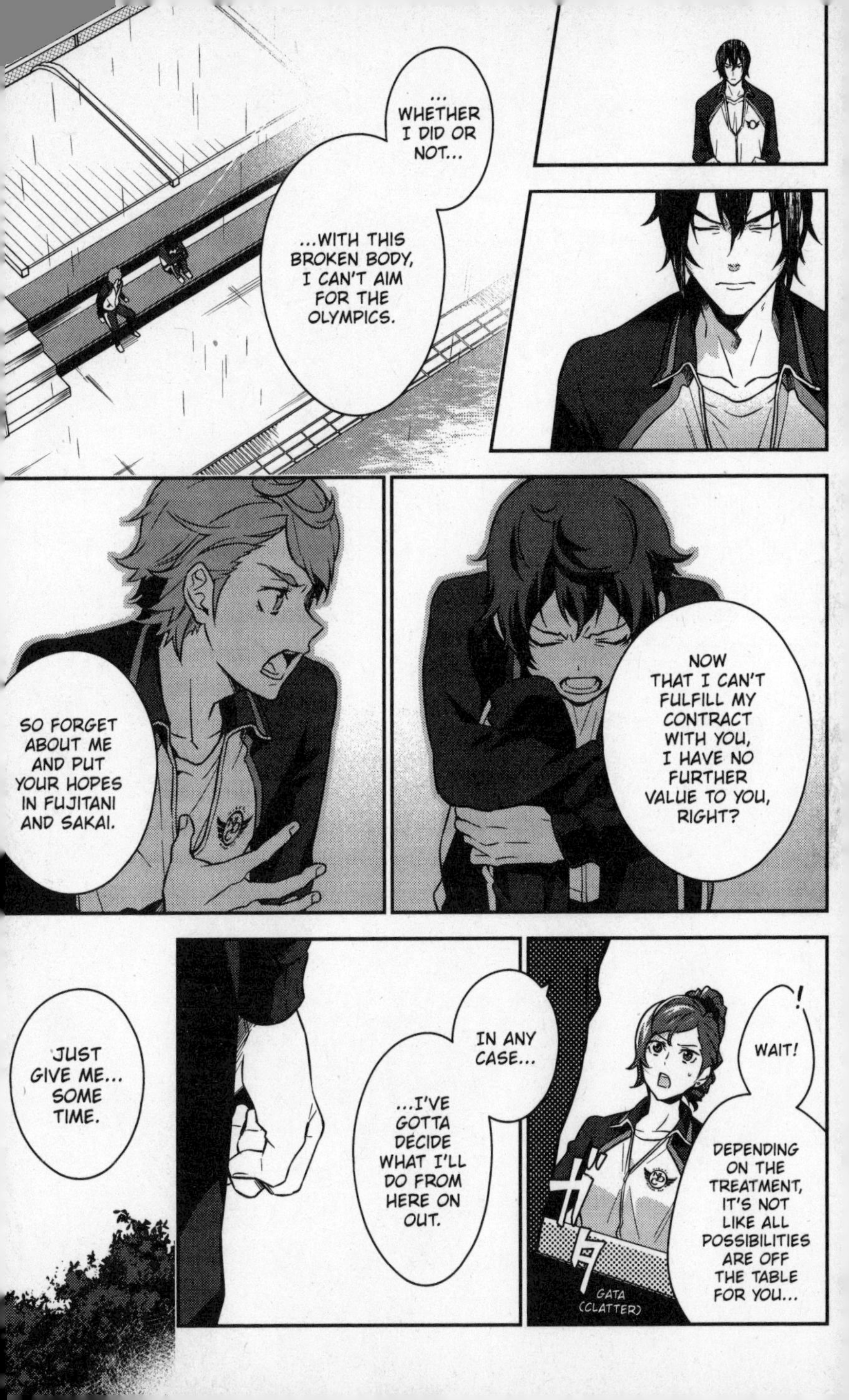
...WHETHER I DID OR NOT...
...WITH THIS BROKEN BODY, I CAN'T AIM FOR THE OLYMPICS.
NOW THAT I CAN'T FULFILL MY CONTRACT WITH YOU, I HAVE NO FURTHER VALUE TO YOU, RIGHT?
SO FORGET ABOUT ME AND PUT YOUR HOPES IN FUJITANI AND SAKAI.
!
WAIT!
DEPENDING ON THE TREATMENT, IT'S NOT LIKE ALL POSSIBILITIES ARE OFF THE TABLE FOR YOU...
GATA (CLATTER)
IN ANY CASE...
...I'VE GOTTA DECIDE WHAT I'LL DO FROM HERE ON OUT.
JUST GIVE ME... SOME TIME.

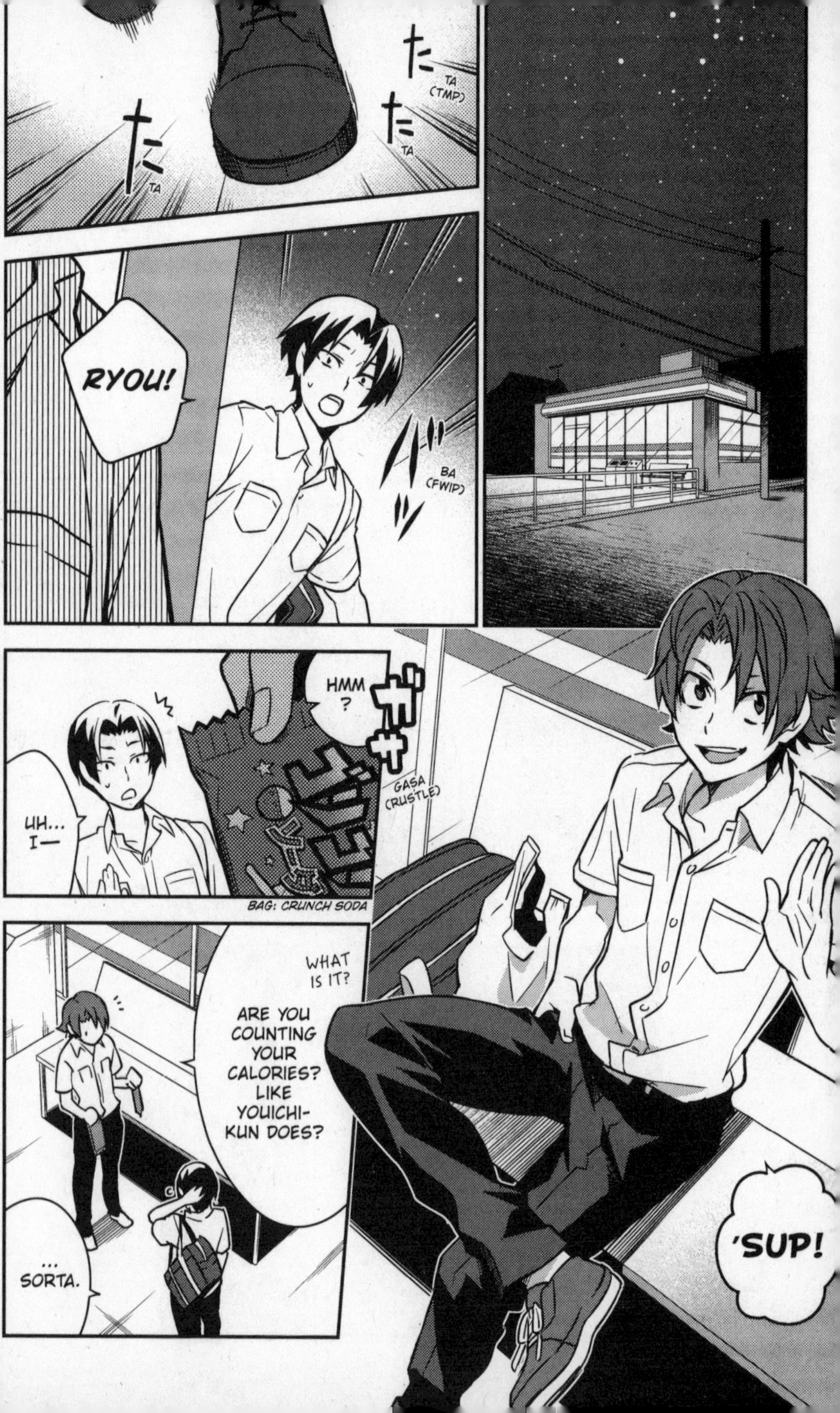
TA (TMP)
TA
TA
BA (FWIP)
RYOU!
'SUP!
HMM?
GASA (RUSTLE)
UH... I—
BAG: CRUNCH SODA
WHAT IS IT?
ARE YOU COUNTING YOUR CALORIES? LIKE YOUICHI-KUN DOES?
... SORTA.

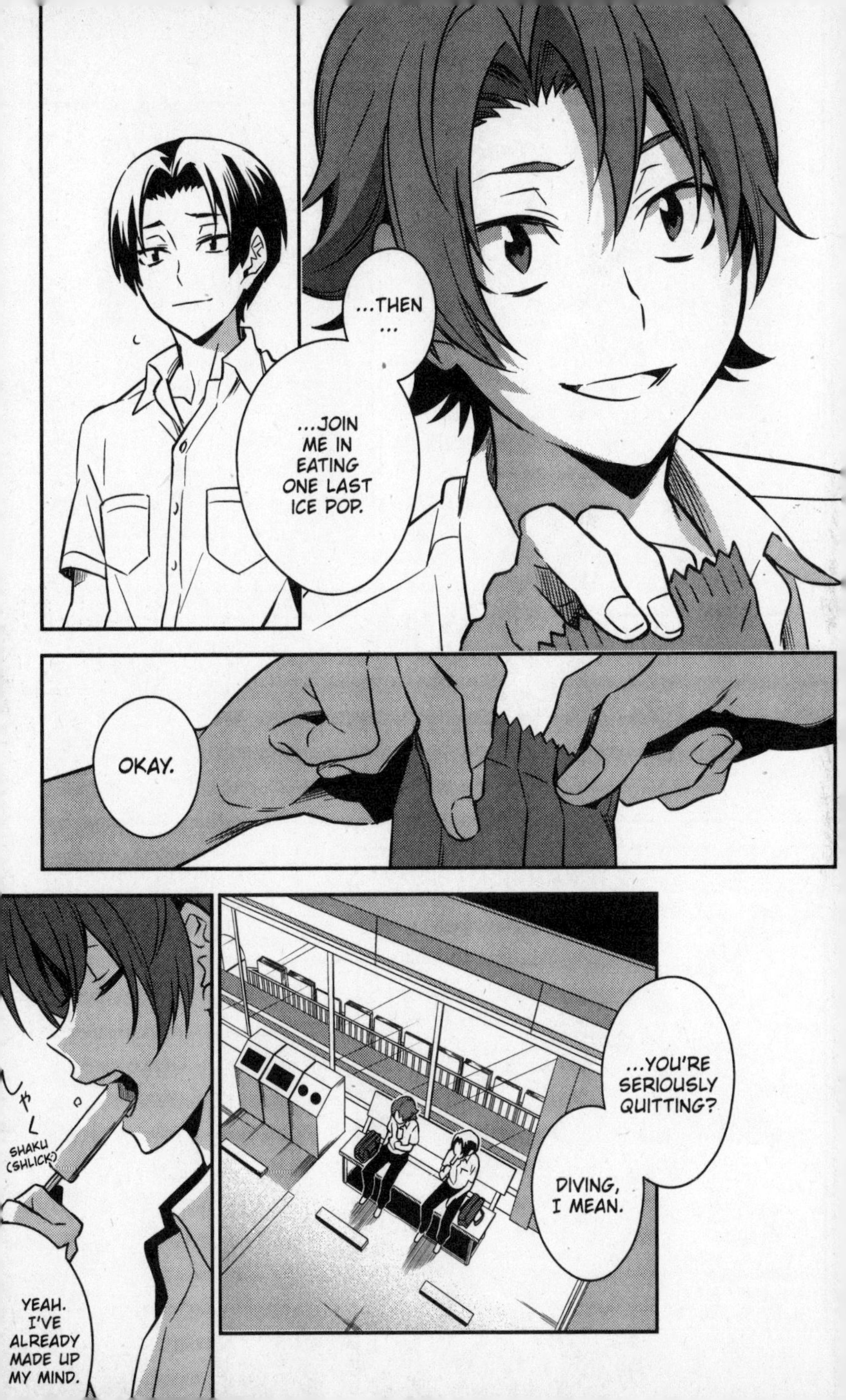
...THEN ...
...JOIN ME IN EATING ONE LAST ICE POP.
OKAY.
...YOU'RE SERIOUSLY QUITTING?
DIVING, I MEAN.
しゃく
SHAKU (SHLICK)
YEAH. I'VE ALREADY MADE UP MY MIND.

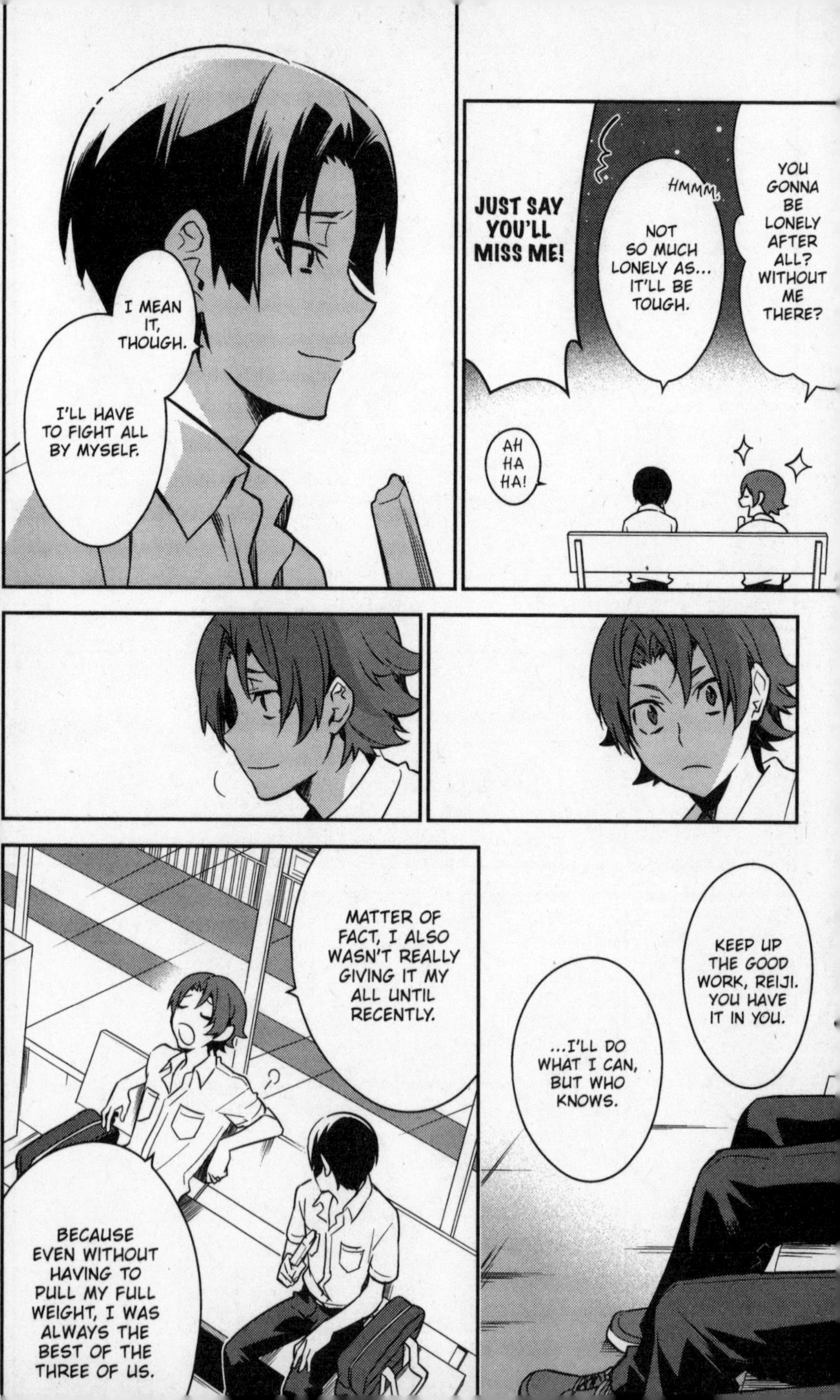
YOU GONNA BE LONELY AFTER ALL? WITHOUT ME THERE?
HMMM.
NOT SO MUCH LONELY AS... IT'LL BE TOUGH.
JUST SAY YOU'LL MISS ME!
AH HA HA!
I MEAN IT, THOUGH.
I'LL HAVE TO FIGHT ALL BY MYSELF.
KEEP UP THE GOOD WORK, REIJI. YOU HAVE IT IN YOU.
...I'LL DO WHAT I CAN, BUT WHO KNOWS.
MATTER OF FACT, I ALSO WASN'T REALLY GIVING IT MY ALL UNTIL RECENTLY.
BECAUSE EVEN WITHOUT HAVING TO PULL MY FULL WEIGHT, I WAS ALWAYS THE BEST OF THE THREE OF US.

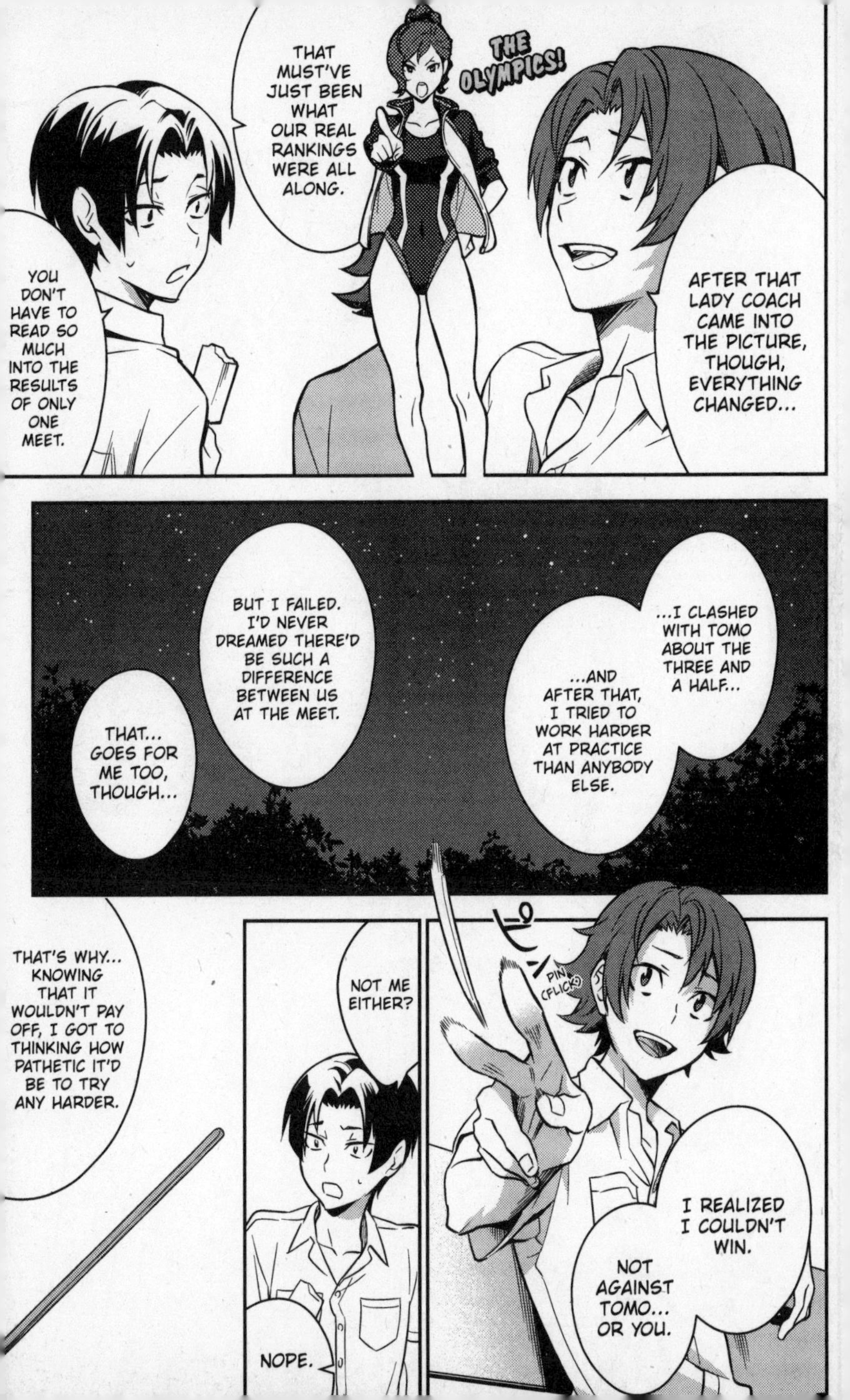
AFTER THAT LADY COACH CAME INTO THE PICTURE, THOUGH, EVERYTHING CHANGED...
THE OLYMPICS!
THAT MUST'VE JUST BEEN WHAT OUR REAL RANKINGS WERE ALL ALONG.
YOU DON'T HAVE TO READ SO MUCH INTO THE RESULTS OF ONLY ONE MEET.
...I CLASHED WITH TOMO ABOUT THE THREE AND A HALF...
...AND AFTER THAT, I TRIED TO WORK HARDER AT PRACTICE THAN ANYBODY ELSE.
BUT I FAILED. I'D NEVER DREAMED THERE'D BE SUCH A DIFFERENCE BETWEEN US AT THE MEET.
THAT... GOES FOR ME TOO, THOUGH...
PIN (FLICK)
I REALIZED I COULDN'T WIN.
NOT AGAINST TOMO... OR YOU.
NOT ME EITHER?
NOPE.
THAT'S WHY... KNOWING THAT IT WOULDN'T PAY OFF, I GOT TO THINKING HOW PATHETIC IT'D BE TO TRY ANY HARDER.

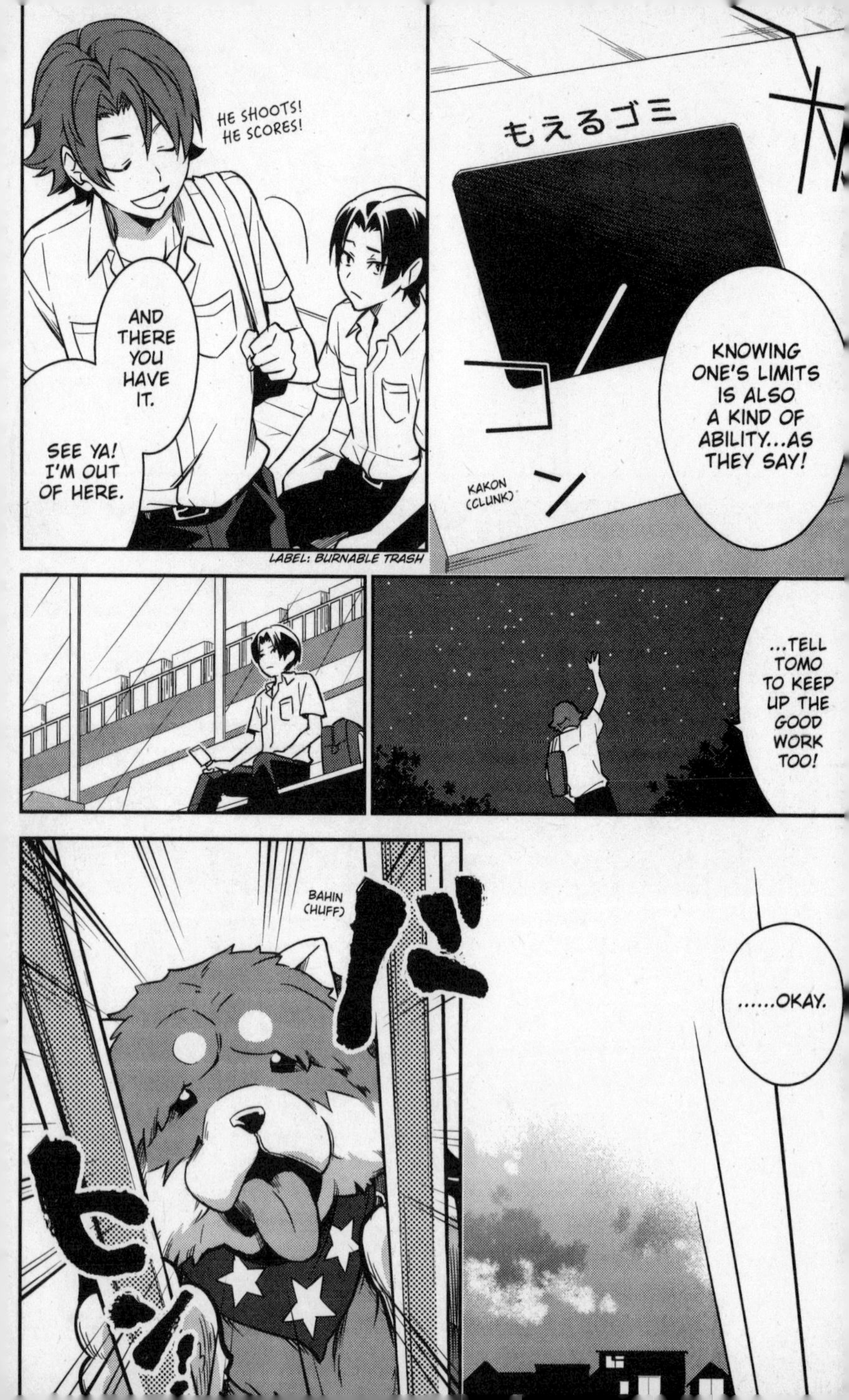
もえるゴミ
KNOWING ONE'S LIMITS IS ALSO A KIND OF ABILITY...AS THEY SAY!
KAKON (CLUNK)
HE SHOOTS! HE SCORES!
AND THERE YOU HAVE IT.
SEE YA! I'M OUT OF HERE.
LABEL: BURNABLE TRASH
...TELL TOMO TO KEEP UP THE GOOD WORK TOO!
......OKAY.
BAHIN (HUFF)

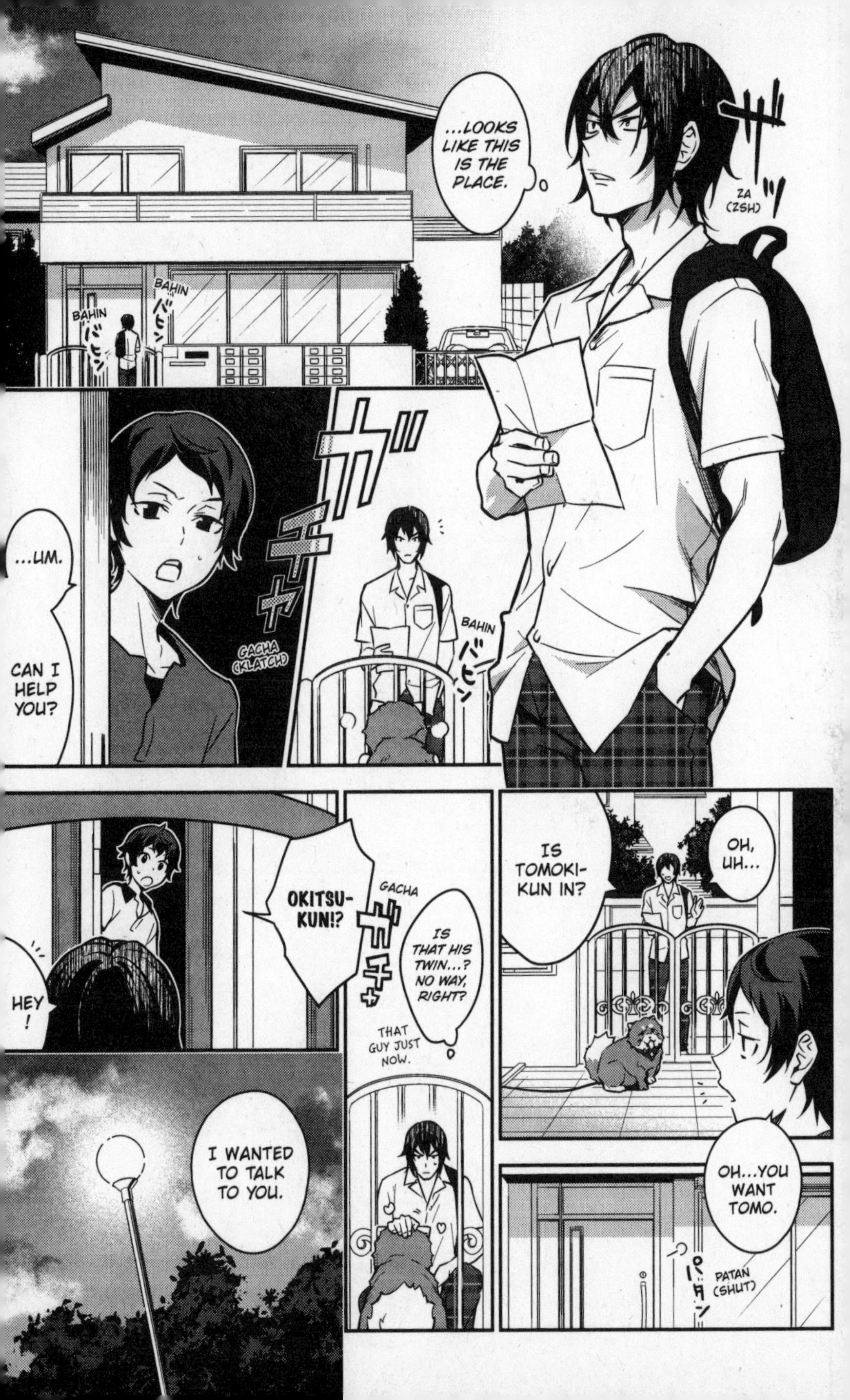

...LOOKS LIKE THIS IS THE PLACE.
ZA (ZSH)
BAHIN
BAHIN
GACHA (KLATCH)
BAHIN
...UM.
CAN I HELP YOU?
IS TOMOKI-KUN IN?
OH, UH...
OH...YOU WANT TOMO.
PATAN (SHUT)
GACHA
IS THAT HIS TWIN...? NO WAY, RIGHT?
THAT GUY JUST NOW.
OKITSU-KUN!?
HEY!
I WANTED TO TALK TO YOU.

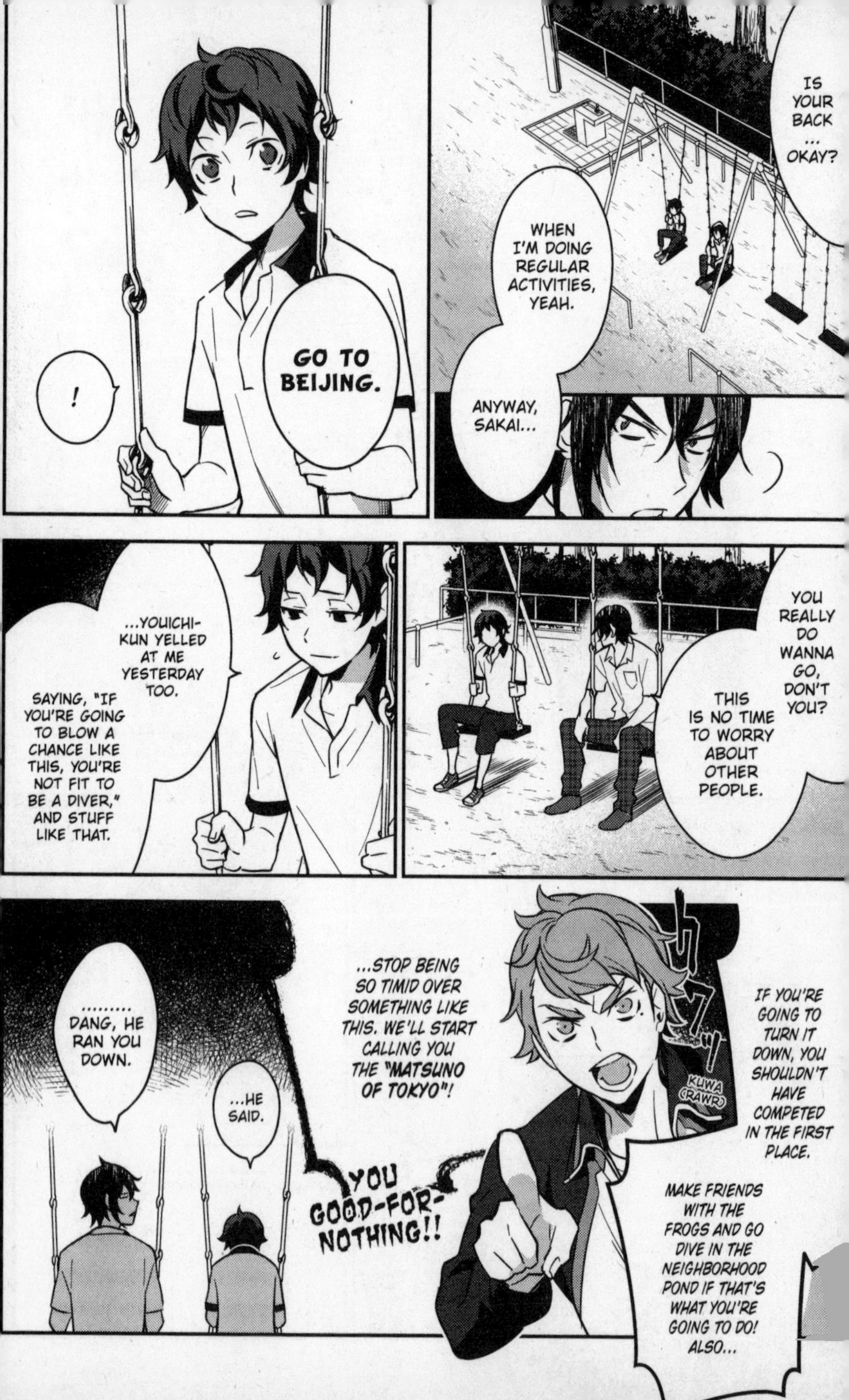
IS YOUR BACK ... OKAY?
WHEN I'M DOING REGULAR ACTIVITIES, YEAH.
ANYWAY, SAKAI...
GO TO BEIJING.
!
YOU REALLY DO WANNA GO, DON'T YOU?
THIS IS NO TIME TO WORRY ABOUT OTHER PEOPLE.
...YOUICHI-KUN YELLED AT ME YESTERDAY TOO.
SAYING, "IF YOU'RE GOING TO BLOW A CHANCE LIKE THIS, YOU'RE NOT FIT TO BE A DIVER," AND STUFF LIKE THAT.
IF YOU'RE GOING TO TURN IT DOWN, YOU SHOULDN'T HAVE COMPETED IN THE FIRST PLACE.
KUWA (RAWR)
...STOP BEING SO TIMID OVER SOMETHING LIKE THIS. WE'LL START CALLING YOU THE "MATSUNO OF TOKYO"!
MAKE FRIENDS WITH THE FROGS AND GO DIVE IN THE NEIGHBORHOOD POND IF THAT'S WHAT YOU'RE GOING TO DO! ALSO...
YOU GOOD-FOR-NOTHING!!
...HE SAID.
.... DANG, HE RAN YOU DOWN.

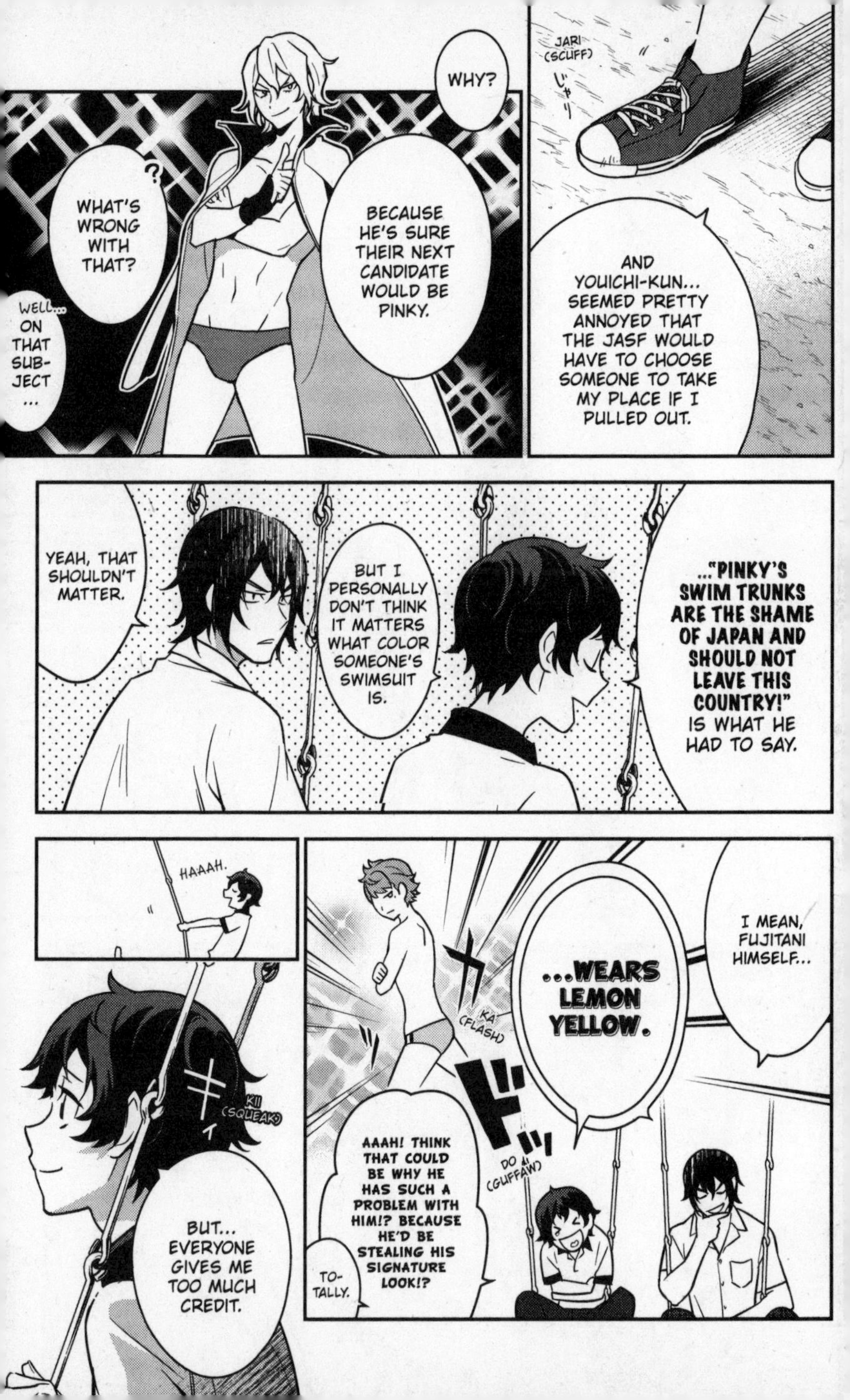
JARI (SCUFF)
じゃり
AND YOUICHI-KUN... SEEMED PRETTY ANNOYED THAT THE JASF WOULD HAVE TO CHOOSE SOMEONE TO TAKE MY PLACE IF I PULLED OUT.
WHY?
BECAUSE HE'S SURE THEIR NEXT CANDIDATE WOULD BE PINKY.
?
WHAT'S WRONG WITH THAT?
WELL... ON THAT SUB-JECT...
..."PINKY'S SWIM TRUNKS ARE THE SHAME OF JAPAN AND SHOULD NOT LEAVE THIS COUNTRY!" IS WHAT HE HAD TO SAY.
BUT I PERSONALLY DON'T THINK IT MATTERS WHAT COLOR SOMEONE'S SWIMSUIT IS.
YEAH, THAT SHOULDN'T MATTER.
I MEAN, FUJITANI HIMSELF...
KA (FLASH)
...WEARS LEMON YELLOW.
DO (GUFFAW)
AAAH! THINK THAT COULD BE WHY HE HAS SUCH A PROBLEM WITH HIM!? BECAUSE HE'D BE STEALING HIS SIGNATURE LOOK!?
TO-TALLY.
HAAAH.
KII (SQUEAK)
BUT... EVERYONE GIVES ME TOO MUCH CREDIT.

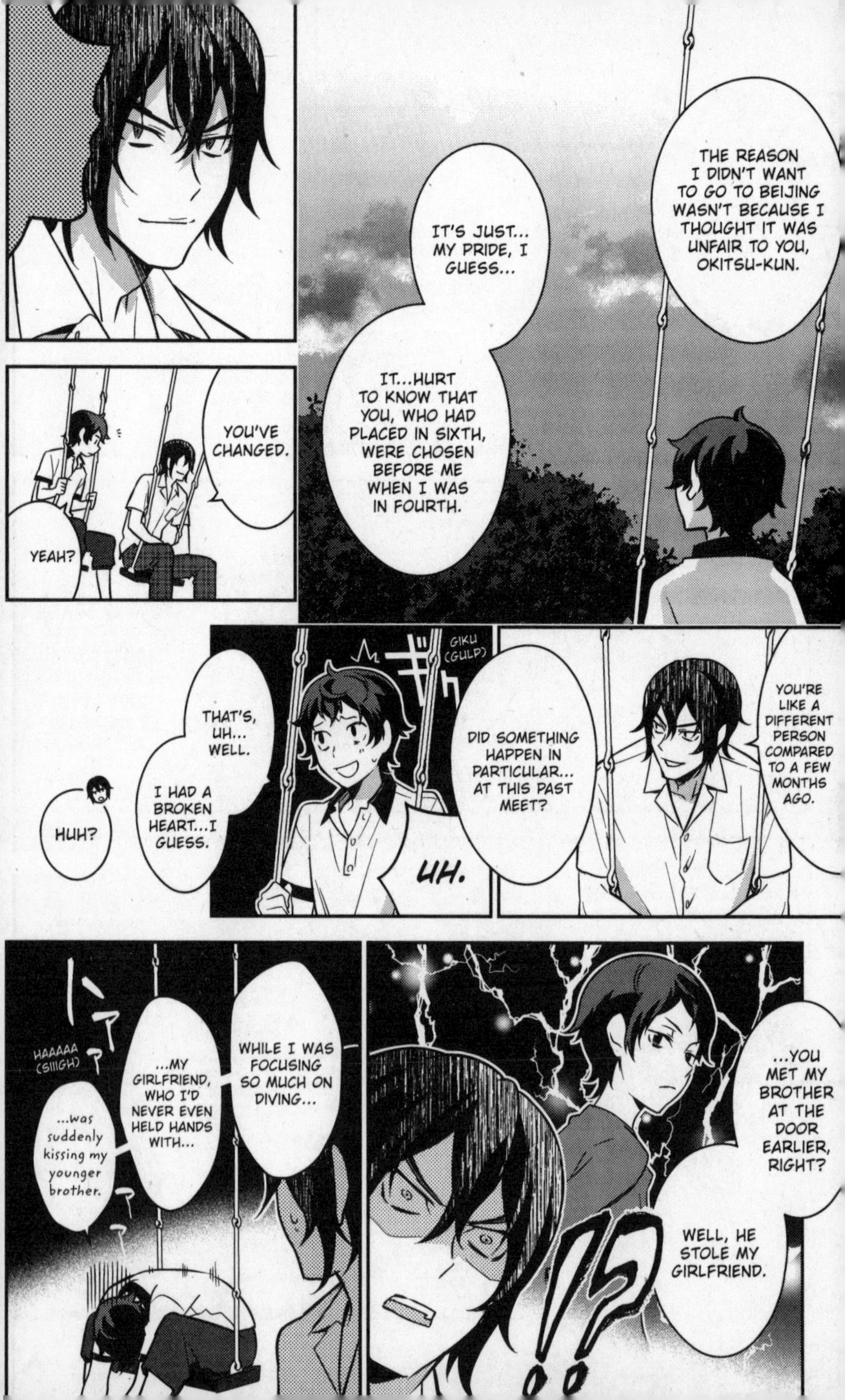
THE REASON I DIDN'T WANT TO GO TO BEIJING WASN'T BECAUSE I THOUGHT IT WAS UNFAIR TO YOU, OKITSU-KUN.
IT'S JUST... MY PRIDE, I GUESS...
IT...HURT TO KNOW THAT YOU, WHO HAD PLACED IN SIXTH, WERE CHOSEN BEFORE ME WHEN I WAS IN FOURTH.
YOU'VE CHANGED.
YEAH?
YOU'RE LIKE A DIFFERENT PERSON COMPARED TO A FEW MONTHS AGO.
DID SOMETHING HAPPEN IN PARTICULAR... AT THIS PAST MEET?
GIKU (GULP)
UH.
THAT'S, UH... WELL.
I HAD A BROKEN HEART...I GUESS.
HUH?
...YOU MET MY BROTHER AT THE DOOR EARLIER, RIGHT?
WELL, HE STOLE MY GIRLFRIEND.
!?
WHILE I WAS FOCUSING SO MUCH ON DIVING...
...MY GIRLFRIEND, WHO I'D NEVER EVEN HELD HANDS WITH...
...was suddenly kissing my younger brother.
HAAAAA (SIIIGH)

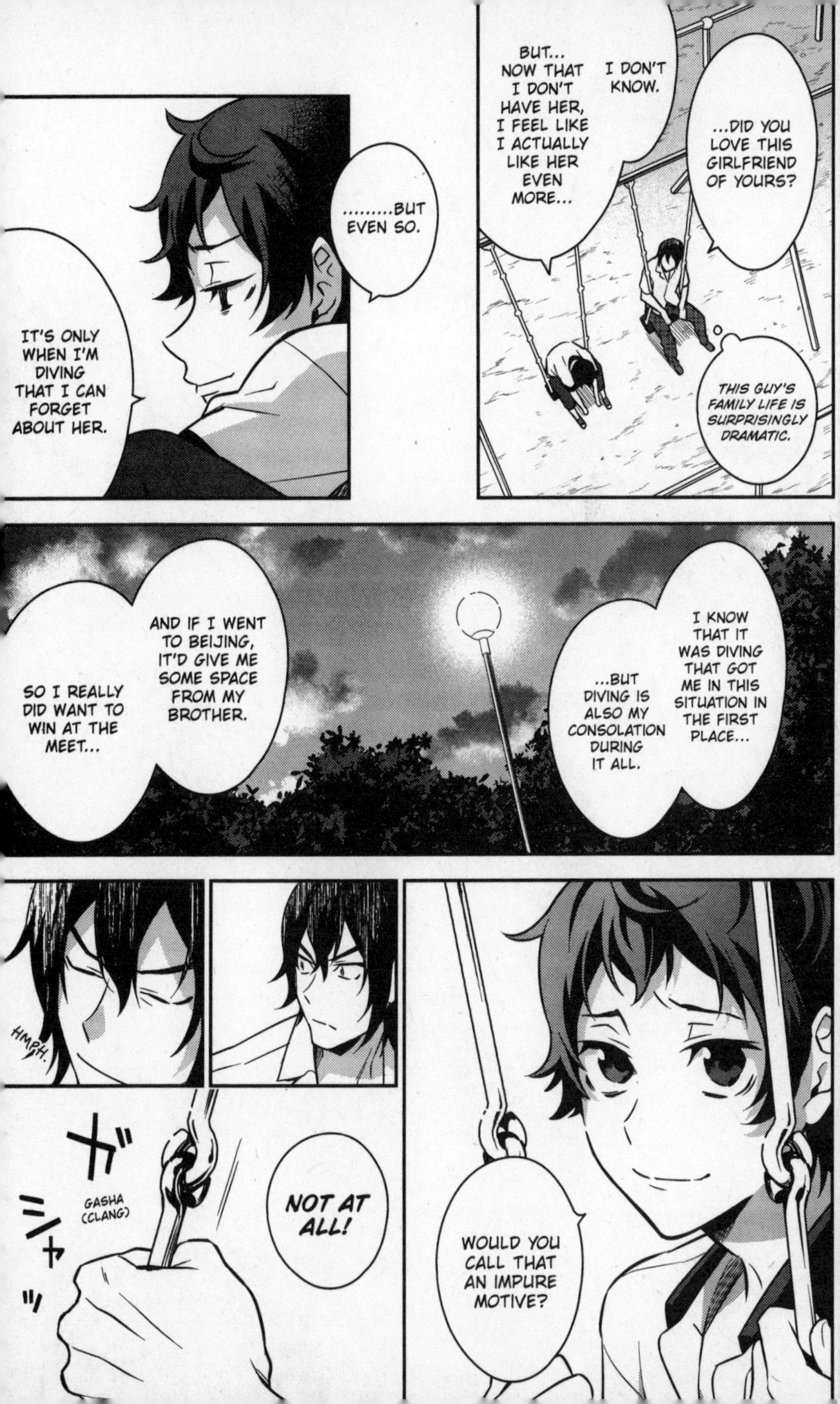
...DID YOU LOVE THIS GIRLFRIEND OF YOURS?
I DON'T KNOW.
BUT... NOW THAT I DON'T HAVE HER, I FEEL LIKE I ACTUALLY LIKE HER EVEN MORE...
THIS GUY'S FAMILY LIFE IS SURPRISINGLY DRAMATIC.
.........BUT EVEN SO.
IT'S ONLY WHEN I'M DIVING THAT I CAN FORGET ABOUT HER.
I KNOW THAT IT WAS DIVING THAT GOT ME IN THIS SITUATION IN THE FIRST PLACE...
...BUT DIVING IS ALSO MY CONSOLATION DURING IT ALL.
AND IF I WENT TO BEIJING, IT'D GIVE ME SOME SPACE FROM MY BROTHER.
SO I REALLY DID WANT TO WIN AT THE MEET...
WOULD YOU CALL THAT AN IMPURE MOTIVE?
HMPH.
NOT AT ALL!
ガシャッ
GASHA (CLANG)

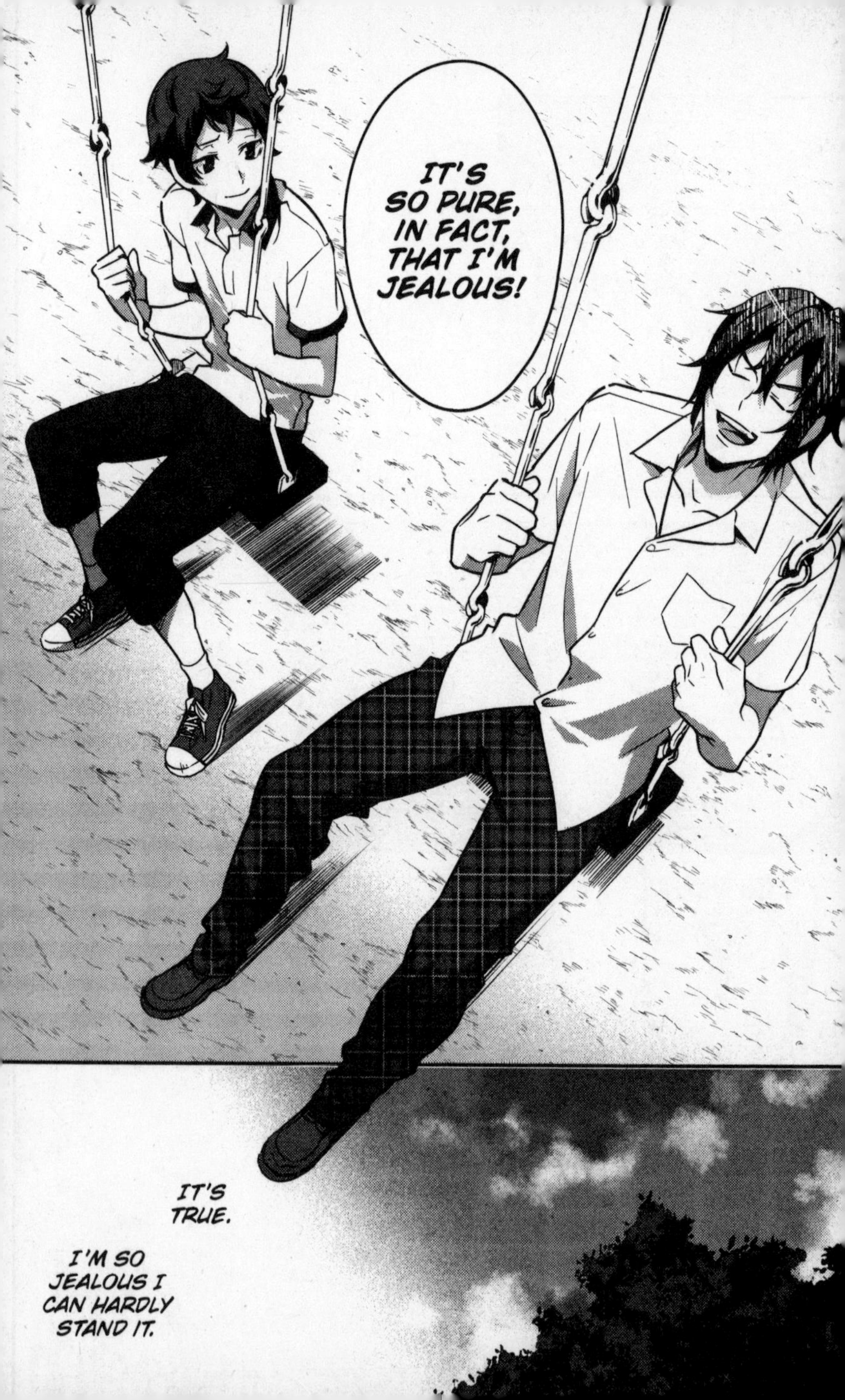
IT'S SO PURE, IN FACT, THAT I'M JEALOUS!
IT'S TRUE.
I'M SO JEALOUS I CAN HARDLY STAND IT.

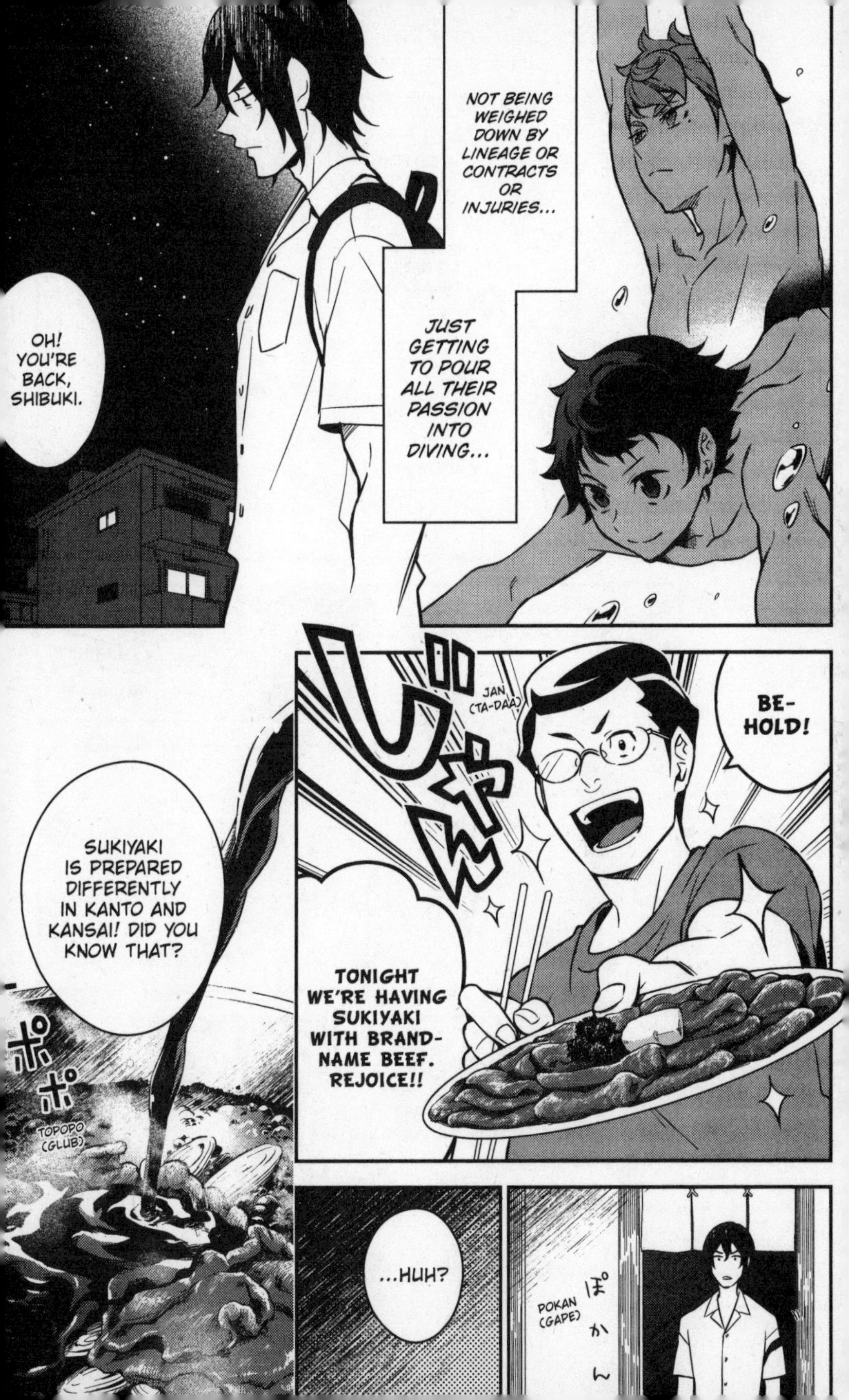
NOT BEING WEIGHED DOWN BY LINEAGE OR CONTRACTS OR INJURIES...
JUST GETTING TO POUR ALL THEIR PASSION INTO DIVING...
OH! YOU'RE BACK, SHIBUKI.
BE-HOLD!
じゃん
JAN (TA-DAA)
TONIGHT WE'RE HAVING SUKIYAKI WITH BRAND-NAME BEEF. REJOICE!!
ぽかん
POKAN (GAPE)
...HUH?
SUKIYAKI IS PREPARED DIFFERENTLY IN KANTO AND KANSAI! DID YOU KNOW THAT?
ポポ
TOPOPO (GLUB)

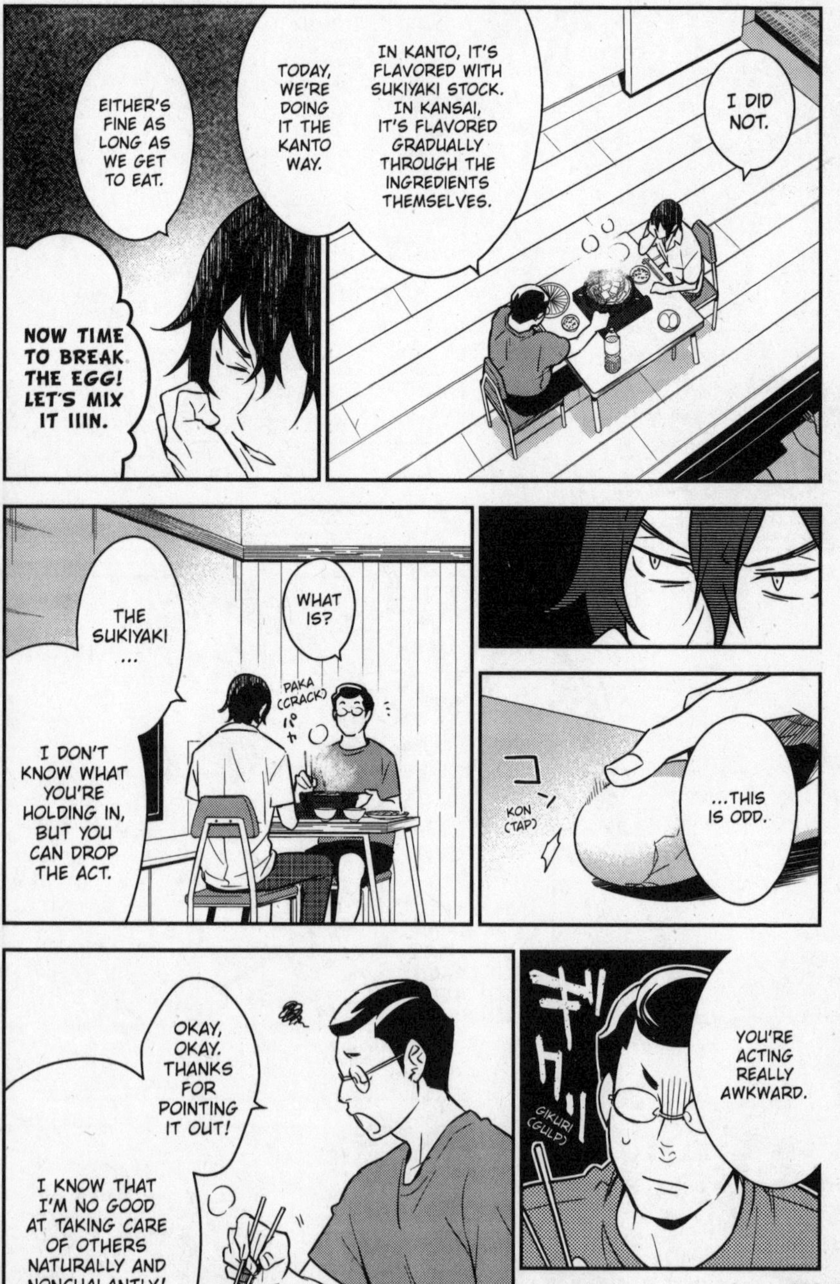
I DID NOT.
TODAY, WE'RE DOING IT THE KANTO WAY. IN KANTO, IT'S FLAVORED WITH SUKIYAKI STOCK. IN KANSAI, IT'S FLAVORED GRADUALLY THROUGH THE INGREDIENTS THEMSELVES.
EITHER'S FINE AS LONG AS WE GET TO EAT.
NOW TIME TO BREAK THE EGG! LET'S MIX IT IIIN.
KON (TAP)
...THIS IS ODD.
WHAT IS?
PAKA (CRACK)
THE SUKIYAKI ...
I DON'T KNOW WHAT YOU'RE HOLDING IN, BUT YOU CAN DROP THE ACT.
YOU'RE ACTING REALLY AWKWARD.
GIKURI (GULP)
OKAY, OKAY. THANKS FOR POINTING IT OUT!
I KNOW THAT I'M NO GOOD AT TAKING CARE OF OTHERS NATURALLY AND NONCHALANTLY!

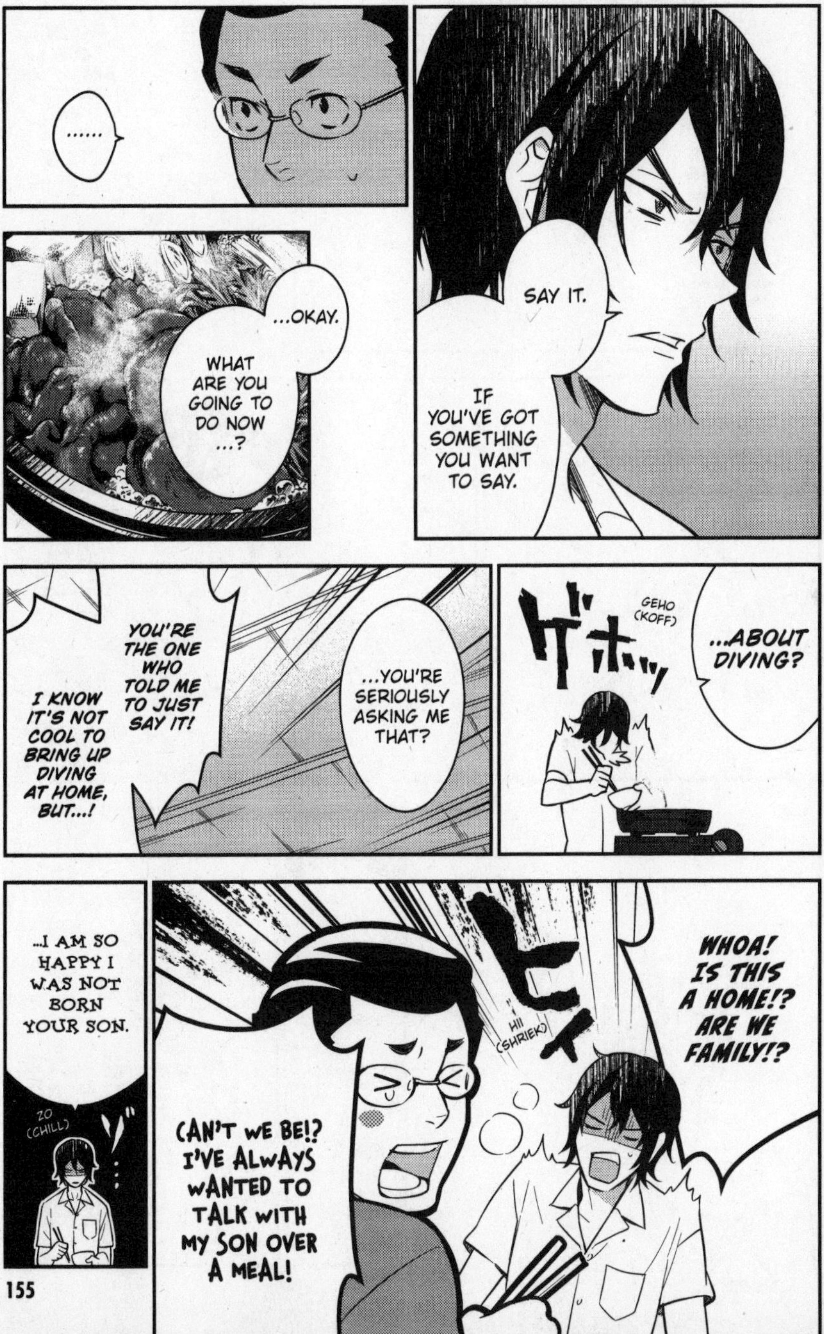
SAY IT.
IF YOU'VE GOT SOMETHING YOU WANT TO SAY.
......
...OKAY.
WHAT ARE YOU GOING TO DO NOW ...?
...ABOUT DIVING?
ゲホッ
GEHO (KOFF)
...YOU'RE SERIOUSLY ASKING ME THAT?
YOU'RE THE ONE WHO TOLD ME TO JUST SAY IT!
I KNOW IT'S NOT COOL TO BRING UP DIVING AT HOME, BUT...!
WHOA! IS THIS A HOME!? ARE WE FAMILY!?
HII (SHRIEK)
CAN'T WE BE!? I'VE ALWAYS WANTED TO TALK WITH MY SON OVER A MEAL!
...I AM SO HAPPY I WAS NOT BORN YOUR SON.
ZO (CHILL)

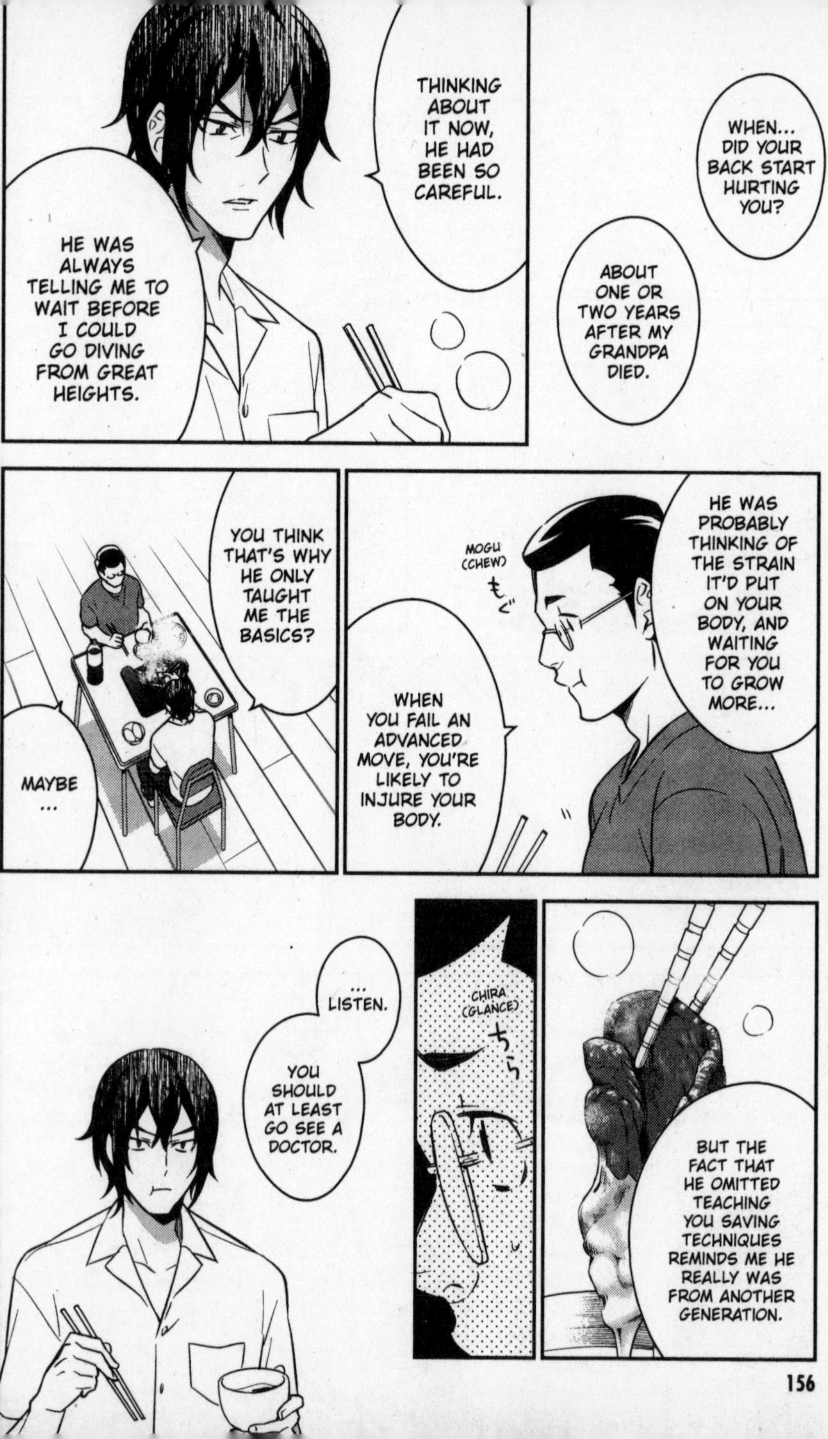
WHEN... DID YOUR BACK START HURTING YOU?
ABOUT ONE OR TWO YEARS AFTER MY GRANDPA DIED.
THINKING ABOUT IT NOW, HE HAD BEEN SO CAREFUL.
HE WAS ALWAYS TELLING ME TO WAIT BEFORE I COULD GO DIVING FROM GREAT HEIGHTS.
HE WAS PROBABLY THINKING OF THE STRAIN IT'D PUT ON YOUR BODY, AND WAITING FOR YOU TO GROW MORE...
MOGU (CHEW)
WHEN YOU FAIL AN ADVANCED MOVE, YOU'RE LIKELY TO INJURE YOUR BODY.
YOU THINK THAT'S WHY HE ONLY TAUGHT ME THE BASICS?
MAYBE...
BUT THE FACT THAT HE OMITTED TEACHING YOU SAVING TECHNIQUES REMINDS ME HE REALLY WAS FROM ANOTHER GENERATION.
CHIRA (GLANCE)
... LISTEN.
YOU SHOULD AT LEAST GO SEE A DOCTOR.

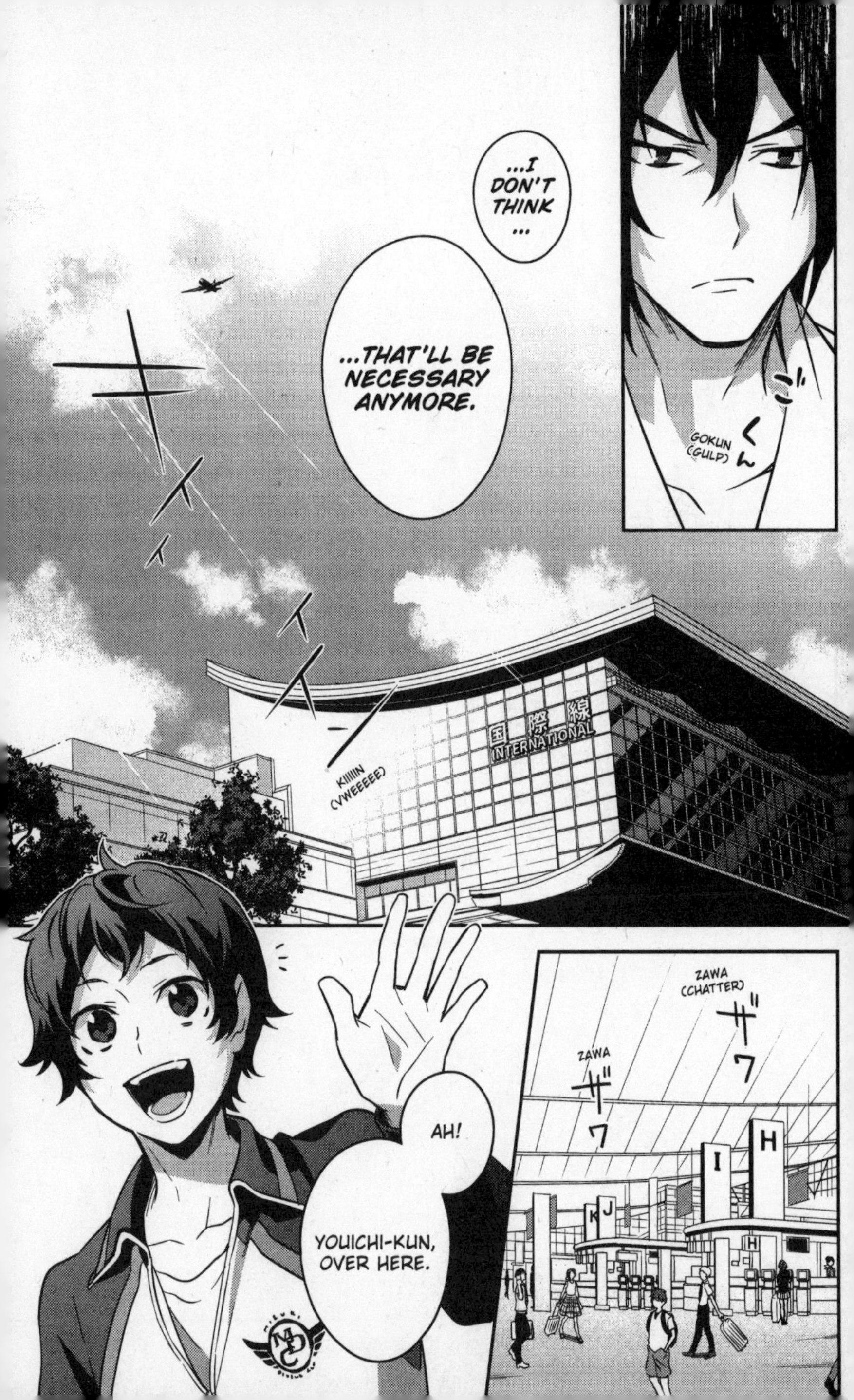
...I DON'T THINK...
GOKUN (GULP)
...THAT'LL BE NECESSARY ANYMORE.
国際線
INTERNATIONAL
KIIIIIN (VWEEEEE)
ZAWA (CHATTER)
ZAWA
H
I
K
J
H
AH!
YOUICHI-KUN, OVER HERE.

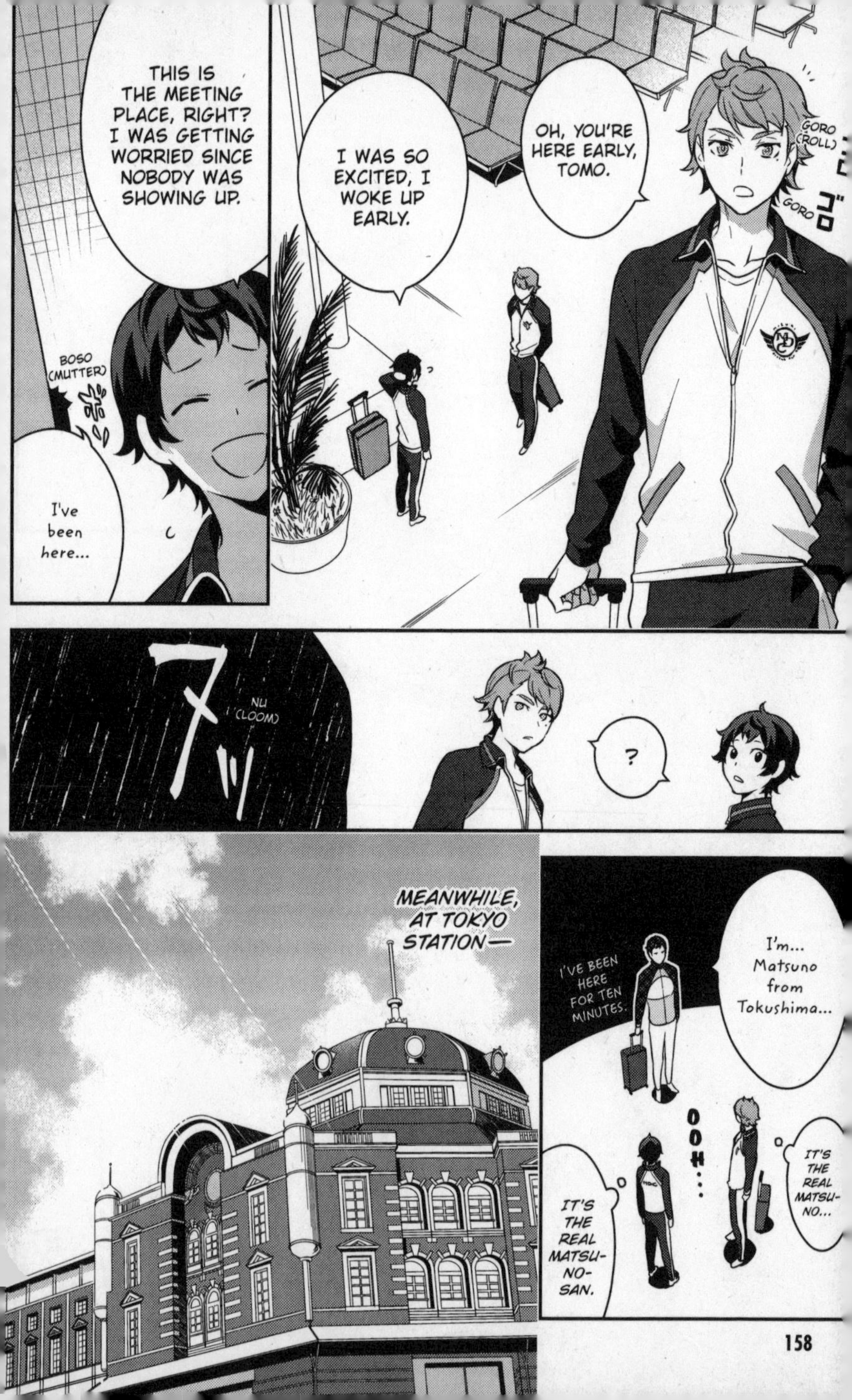
GORO (ROLL)
GORO
OH, YOU'RE HERE EARLY, TOMO.
I WAS SO EXCITED, I WOKE UP EARLY.
THIS IS THE MEETING PLACE, RIGHT? I WAS GETTING WORRIED SINCE NOBODY WAS SHOWING UP.
BOSO (MUTTER)
I've been here...
?
NU (LOOM)
I'm... Matsuno from Tokushima...
I'VE BEEN HERE FOR TEN MINUTES.
OOH...
IT'S THE REAL MATSUNO...
IT'S THE REAL MATSUNO-SAN.
MEANWHILE, AT TOKYO STATION—

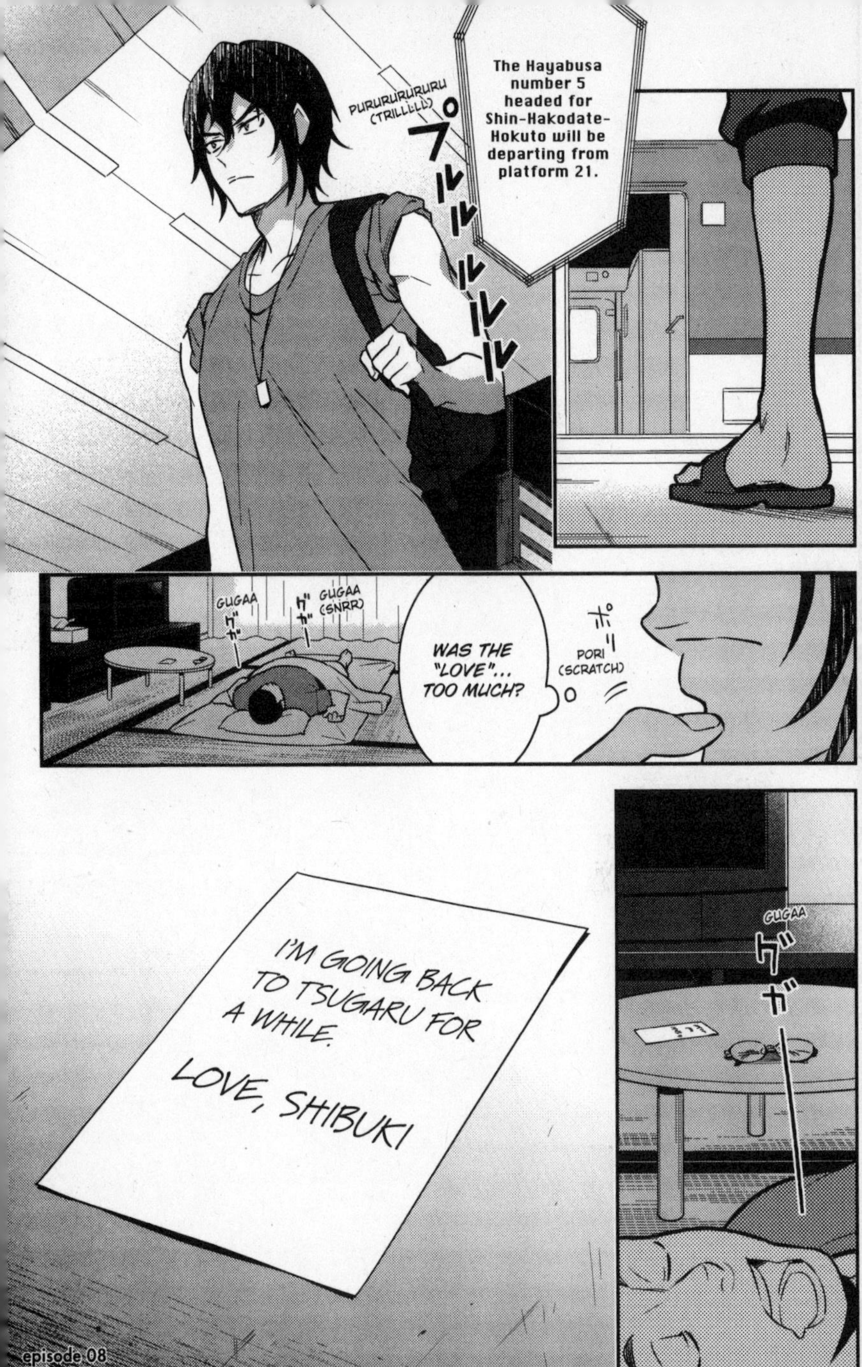

The Hayabusa number 5 headed for Shin-Hakodate-Hokuto will be departing from platform 21.
PURURURURURU (TRILLLLL)
PORI (SCRATCH)
WAS THE "LOVE"... TOO MUCH?
GUGAA (SNRR)
GUGAA
GUGAA
I'M GOING BACK TO TSUGARU FOR A WHILE.
LOVE, SHIBUKI
episode 08 END

DIVE!!

Dear Coach Asaki,
How are you doing? It's me, Sakai. Tomorrow's the last day of the training camp. I've been working so hard to keep up with the others that before I knew it, two weeks had flown by!

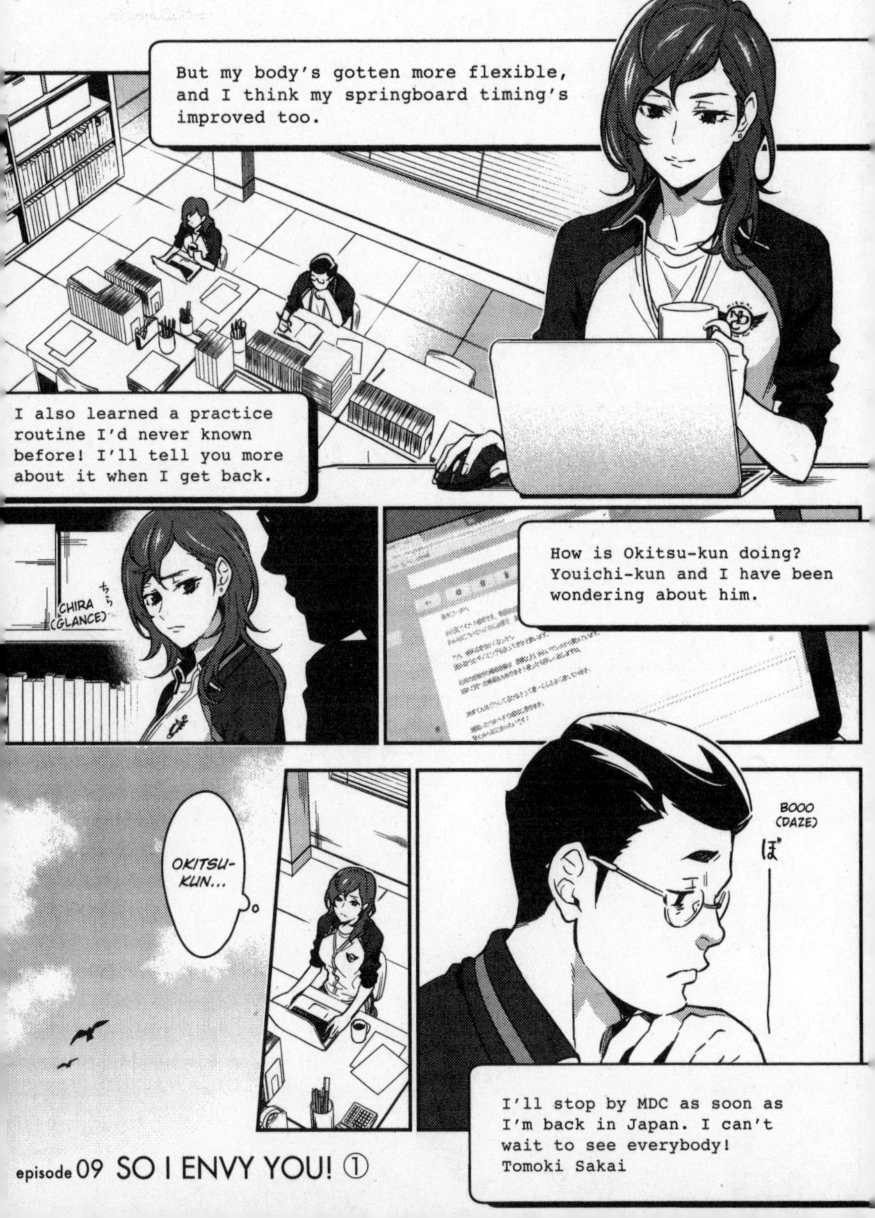
But my body's gotten more flexible, and I think my springboard timing's improved too.
I also learned a practice routine I'd never known before! I'll tell you more about it when I get back.
How is Okitsu-kun doing? Youichi-kun and I have been wondering about him.
ちら
CHIRA (GLANCE)
ぼ
BOOO (DAZE)
I'll stop by MDC as soon as I'm back in Japan. I can't wait to see everybody!
Tomoki Sakai
OKITSU-KUN...

episode 09 SO I ENVY YOU! ①

episode 09 SO I ENVY YOU! ①

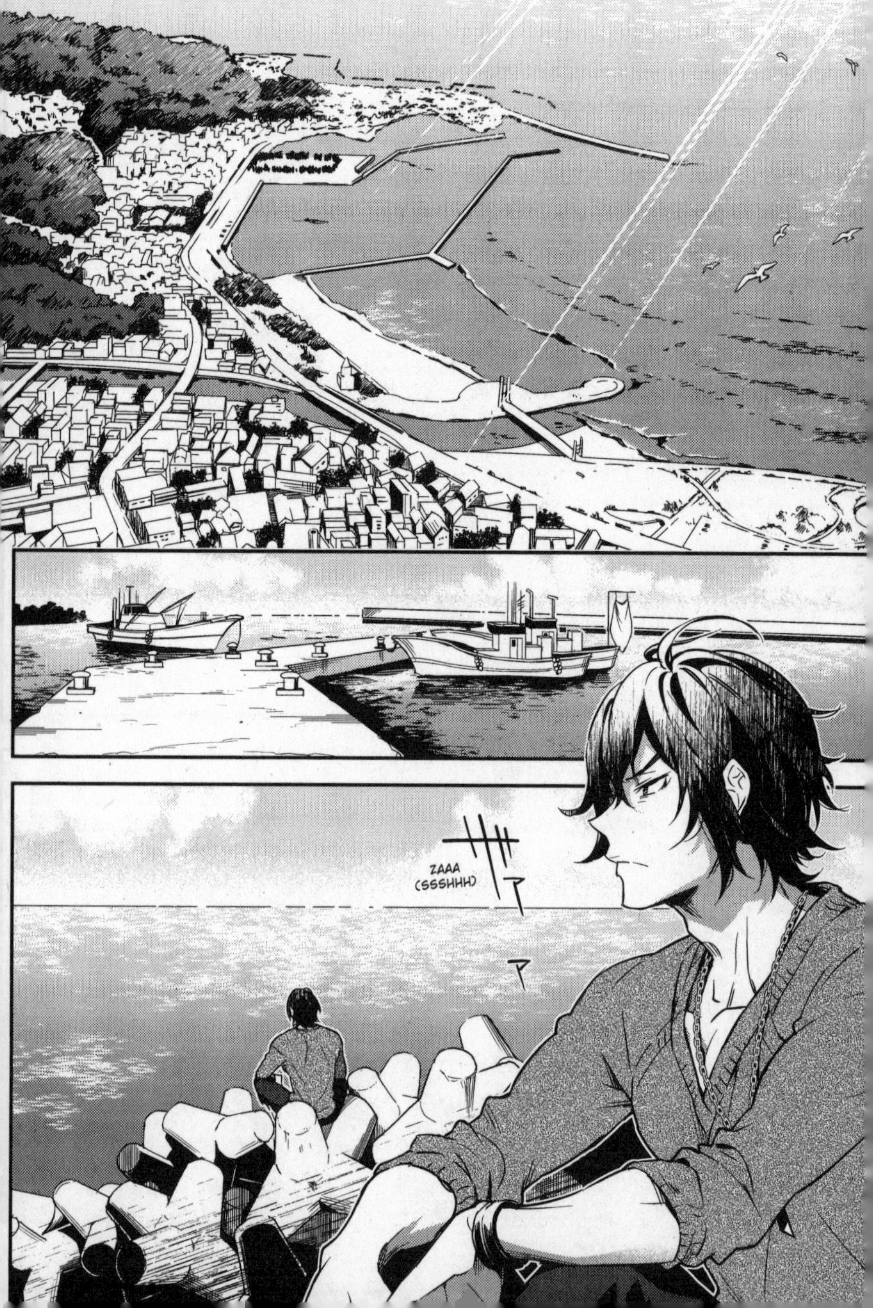
ZAAA
(SSSHHH)

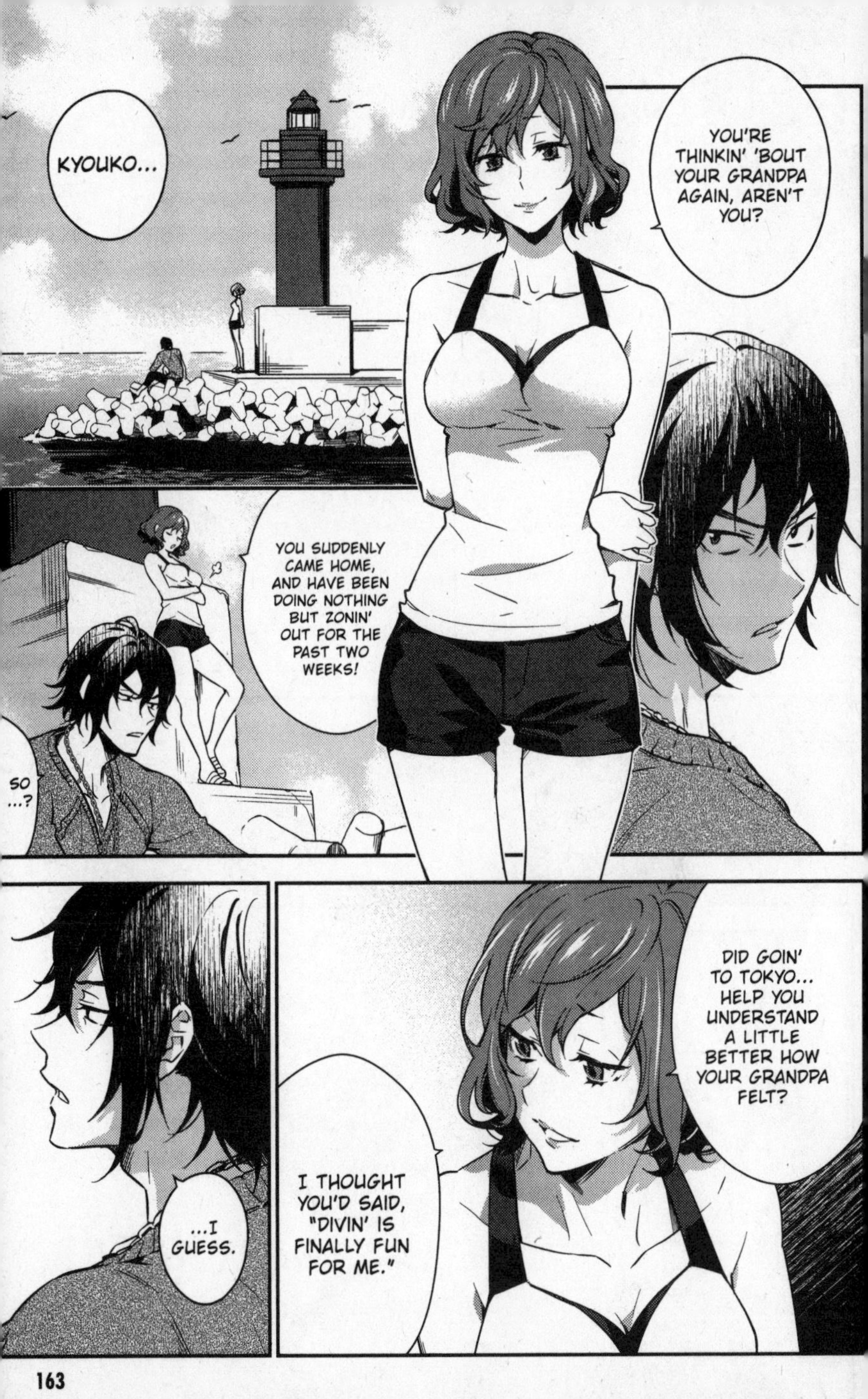
YOU'RE THINKIN' 'BOUT YOUR GRANDPA AGAIN, AREN'T YOU?
KYOUKO...
YOU SUDDENLY CAME HOME, AND HAVE BEEN DOING NOTHING BUT ZONIN' OUT FOR THE PAST TWO WEEKS!
SO ...?
DID GOIN' TO TOKYO... HELP YOU UNDERSTAND A LITTLE BETTER HOW YOUR GRANDPA FELT?
I THOUGHT YOU'D SAID, "DIVIN' IS FINALLY FUN FOR ME."
...I GUESS.

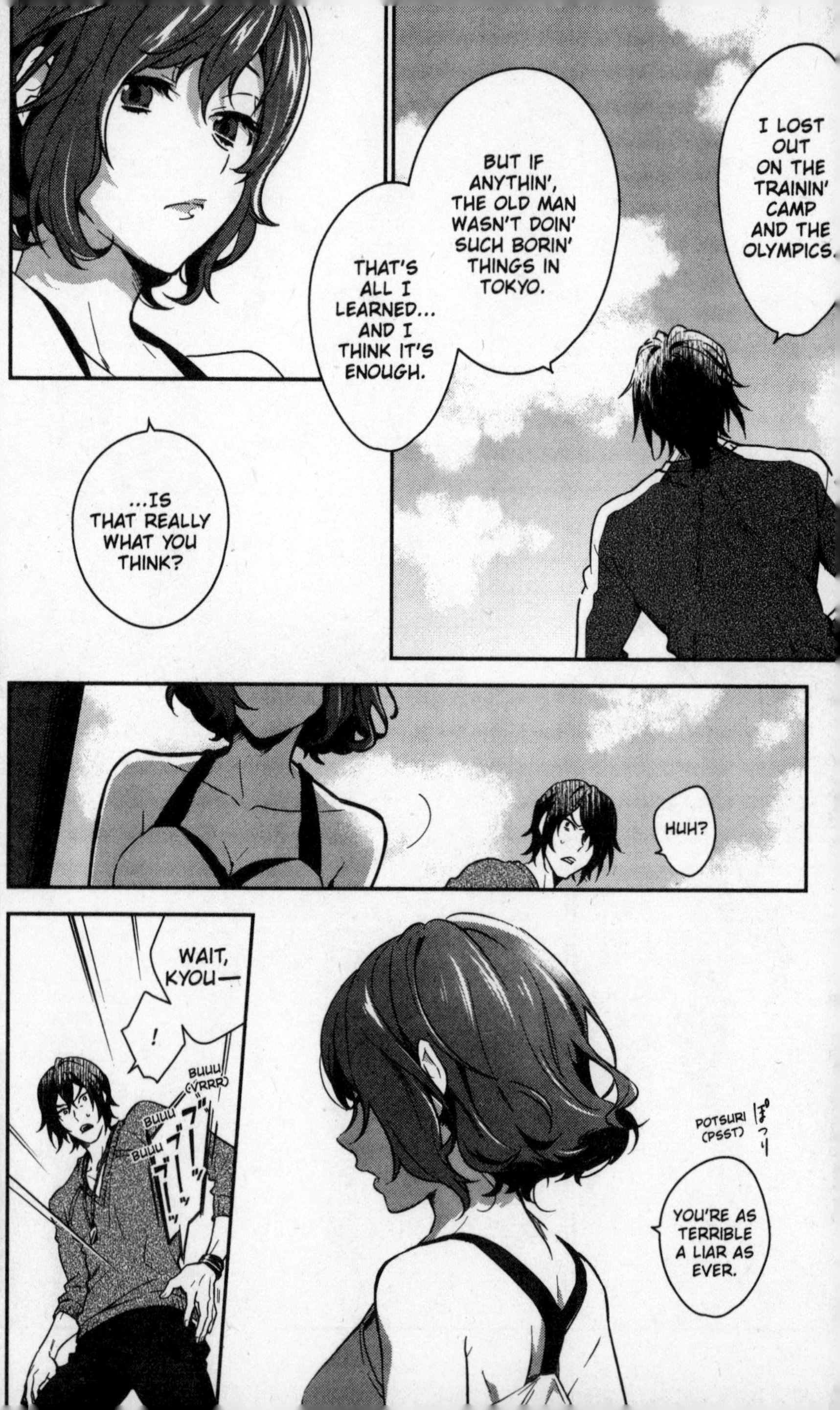
I LOST OUT ON THE TRAININ' CAMP AND THE OLYMPICS.
BUT IF ANYTHIN', THE OLD MAN WASN'T DOIN' SUCH BORIN' THINGS IN TOKYO.
THAT'S ALL I LEARNED... AND I THINK IT'S ENOUGH.
...IS THAT REALLY WHAT YOU THINK?
HUH?
POTSURI (PSST) ぽつり
YOU'RE AS TERRIBLE A LIAR AS EVER.
WAIT, KYOU—
!
BUUU (VRRR)
BUUU
BUUU

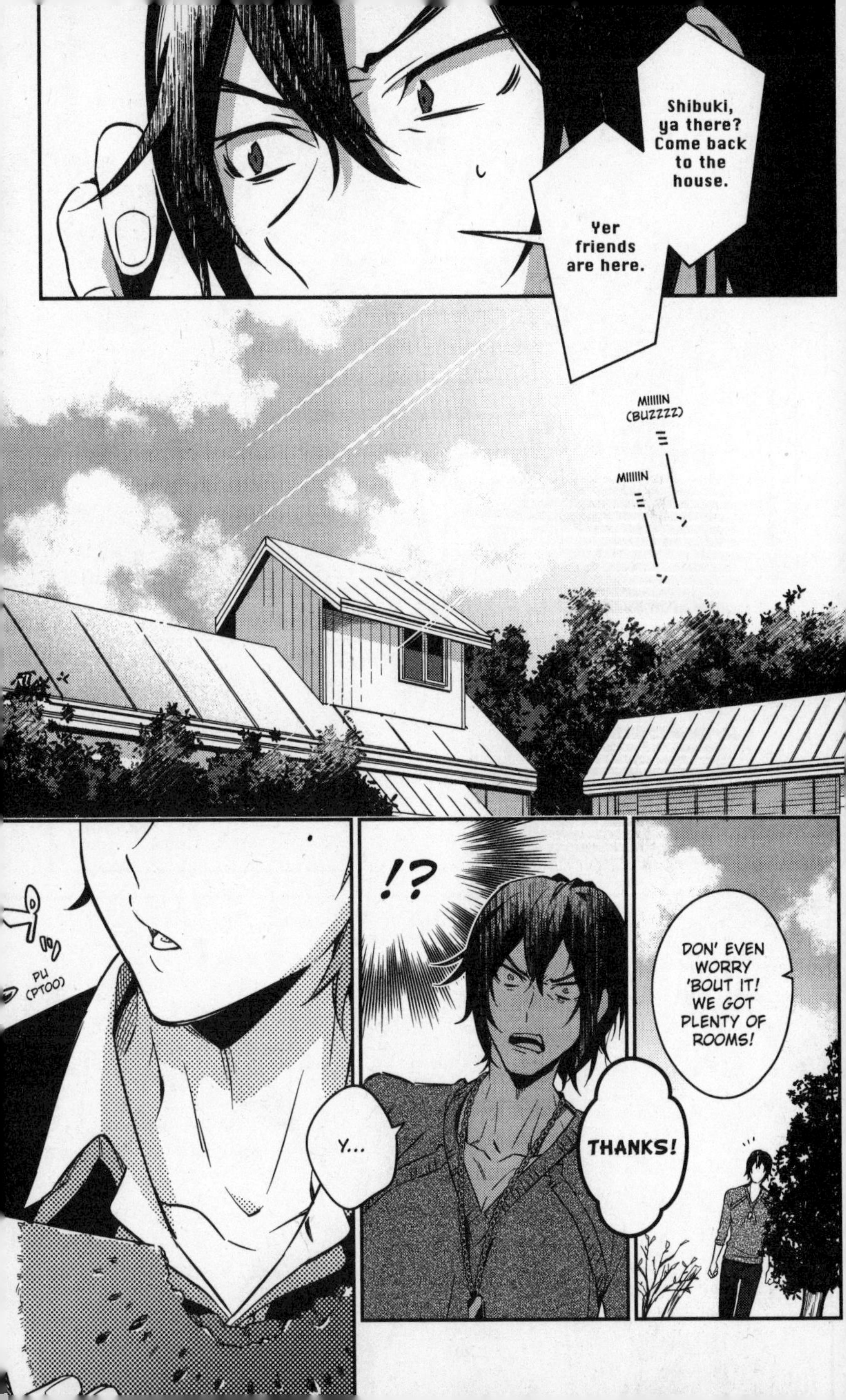
Shibuki, ya there? Come back to the house.
Yer friends are here.
MIIIIN (BUZZZZ)
MIIIIN
DON' EVEN WORRY 'BOUT IT! WE GOT PLENTY OF ROOMS!
!?
THANKS!
Y...
PU (PTOO)

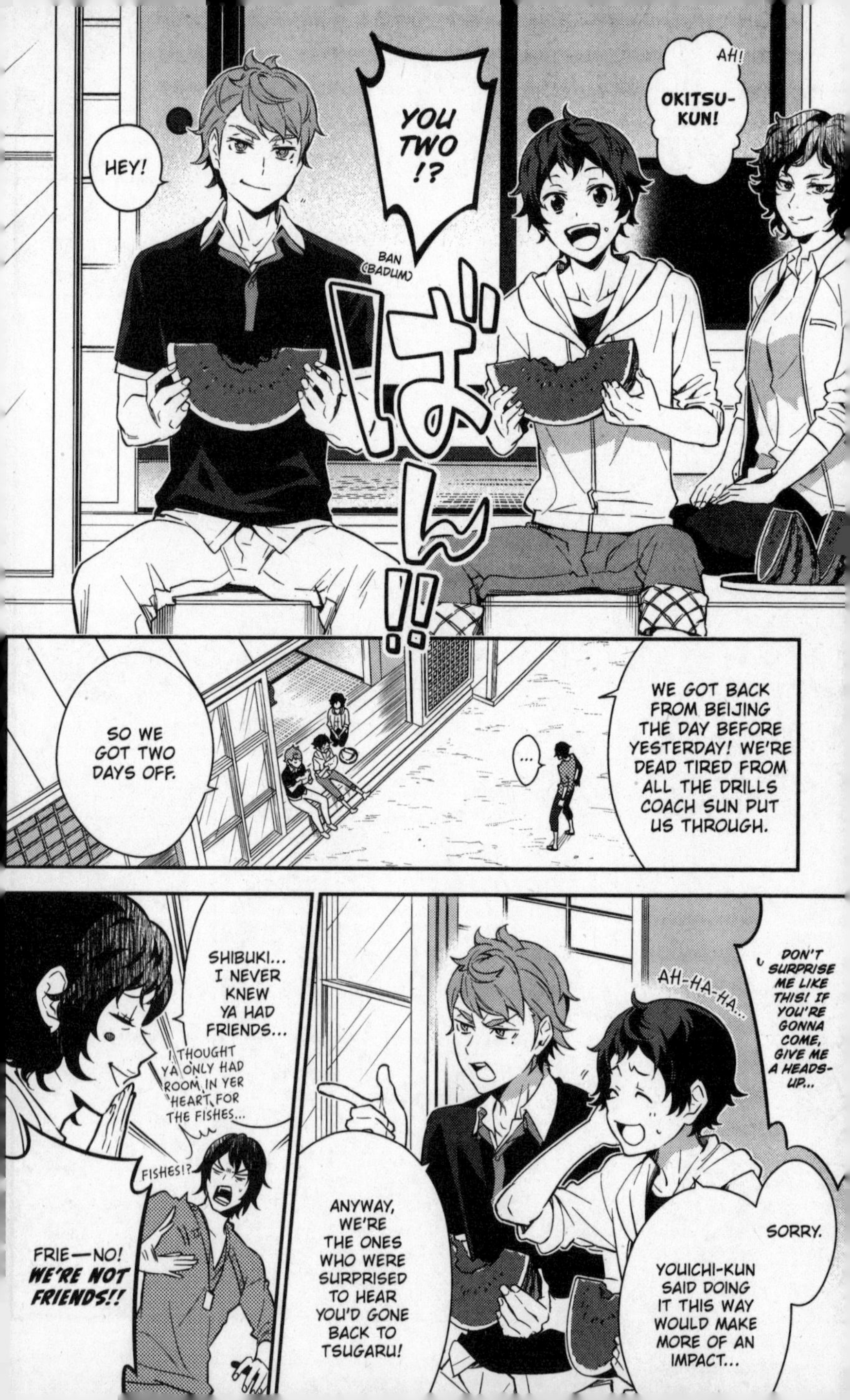
AH!
OKITSU-KUN!
YOU TWO !?
HEY!
BAN (BADUM)
ばん!!
WE GOT BACK FROM BEIJING THE DAY BEFORE YESTERDAY! WE'RE DEAD TIRED FROM ALL THE DRILLS COACH SUN PUT US THROUGH.
...
SO WE GOT TWO DAYS OFF.
DON'T SURPRISE ME LIKE THIS! IF YOU'RE GONNA COME, GIVE ME A HEADS-UP...
AH-HA-HA...
SORRY.
YOUICHI-KUN SAID DOING IT THIS WAY WOULD MAKE MORE OF AN IMPACT...
ANYWAY, WE'RE THE ONES WHO WERE SURPRISED TO HEAR YOU'D GONE BACK TO TSUGARU!
SHIBUKI... I NEVER KNEW YA HAD FRIENDS...
I THOUGHT YA ONLY HAD ROOM IN YER HEART FOR THE FISHES...
FISHES!?
FRIE—NO! ***WE'RE NOT FRIENDS!!***

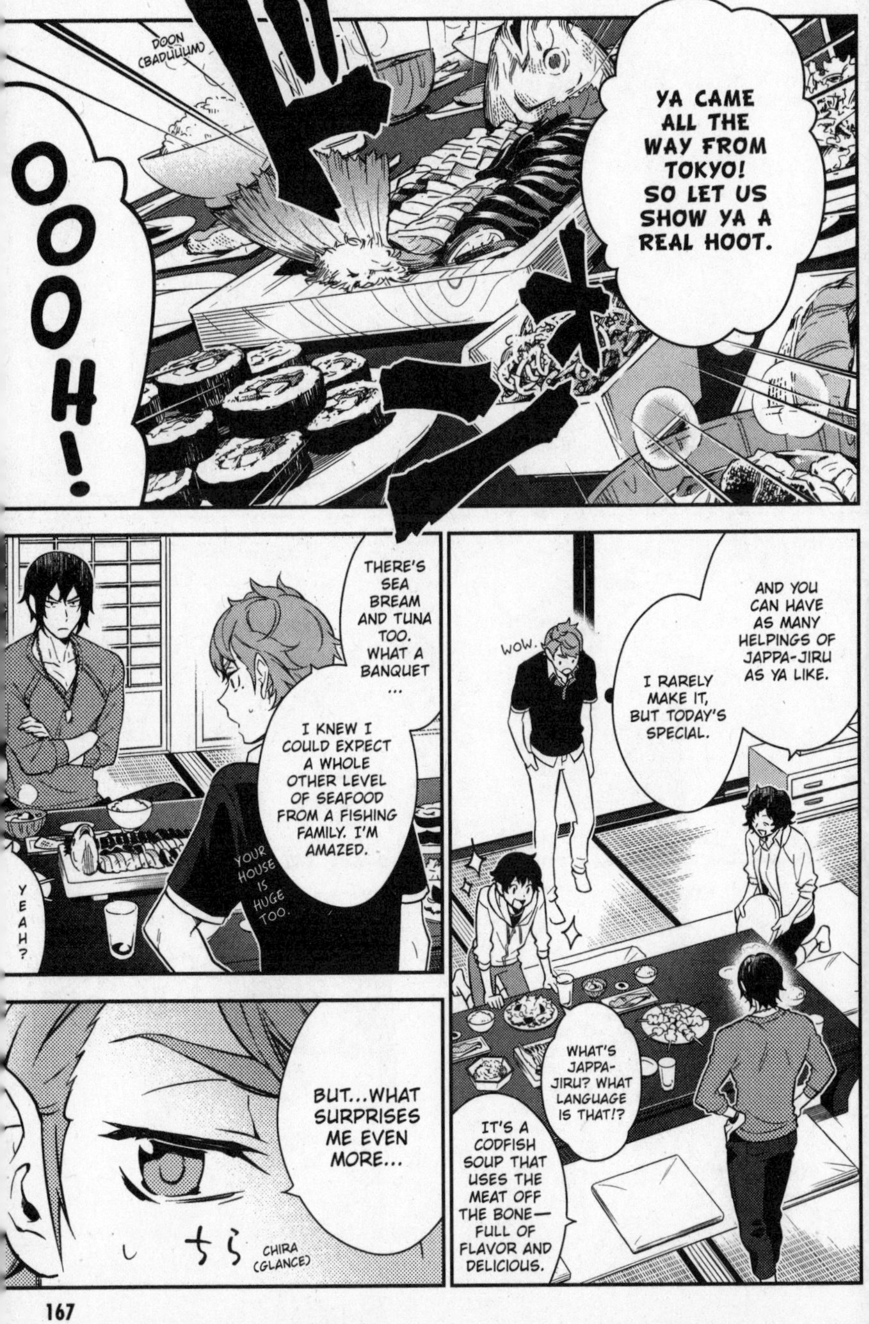
YA CAME ALL THE WAY FROM TOKYO! SO LET US SHOW YA A REAL HOOT.
DOON (BADUUUM)
OOOH!
AND YOU CAN HAVE AS MANY HELPINGS OF JAPPA-JIRU AS YA LIKE.
I RARELY MAKE IT, BUT TODAY'S SPECIAL.
WOW.
WHAT'S JAPPA-JIRU? WHAT LANGUAGE IS THAT!?
IT'S A CODFISH SOUP THAT USES THE MEAT OFF THE BONE—FULL OF FLAVOR AND DELICIOUS.
THERE'S SEA BREAM AND TUNA TOO. WHAT A BANQUET...
I KNEW I COULD EXPECT A WHOLE OTHER LEVEL OF SEAFOOD FROM A FISHING FAMILY. I'M AMAZED.
YOUR HOUSE IS HUGE TOO.
YEAH?
BUT...WHAT SURPRISES ME EVEN MORE...
ちら CHIRA (GLANCE)

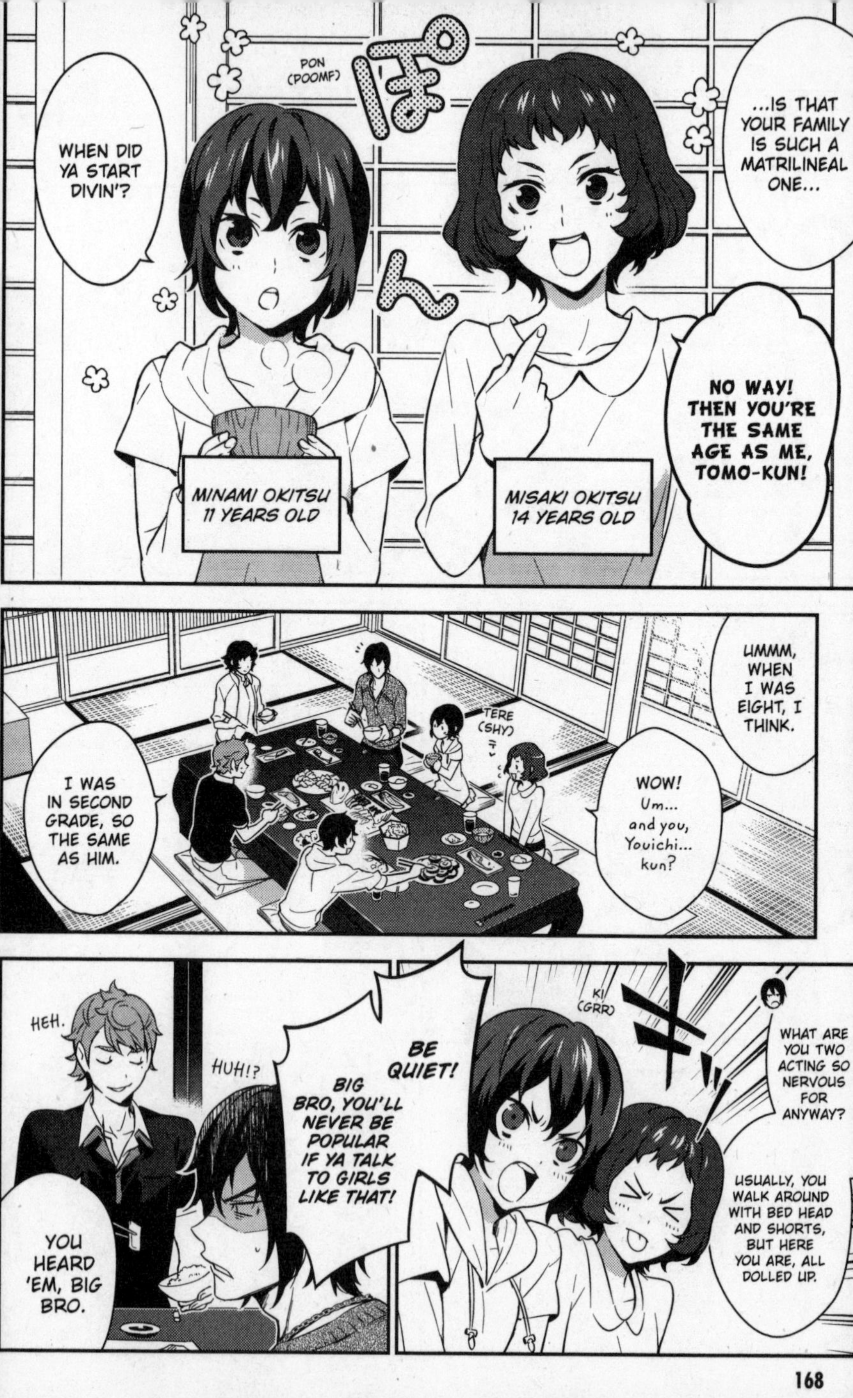

...IS THAT YOUR FAMILY IS SUCH A MATRILINEAL ONE...
PON (POOMF)
NO WAY! THEN YOU'RE THE SAME AGE AS ME, TOMO-KUN!
MISAKI OKITSU 14 YEARS OLD
WHEN DID YA START DIVIN'?
MINAMI OKITSU 11 YEARS OLD
UMMM, WHEN I WAS EIGHT, I THINK.
TERE (SHY)
WOW! Um... and you, Youichi... kun?
I WAS IN SECOND GRADE, SO THE SAME AS HIM.
WHAT ARE YOU TWO ACTING SO NERVOUS FOR ANYWAY?
USUALLY, YOU WALK AROUND WITH BED HEAD AND SHORTS, BUT HERE YOU ARE, ALL DOLLED UP.
KI (GRR)
BE QUIET!
BIG BRO, YOU'LL NEVER BE POPULAR IF YA TALK TO GIRLS LIKE THAT!
HEH.
HUH!?
YOU HEARD 'EM, BIG BRO.

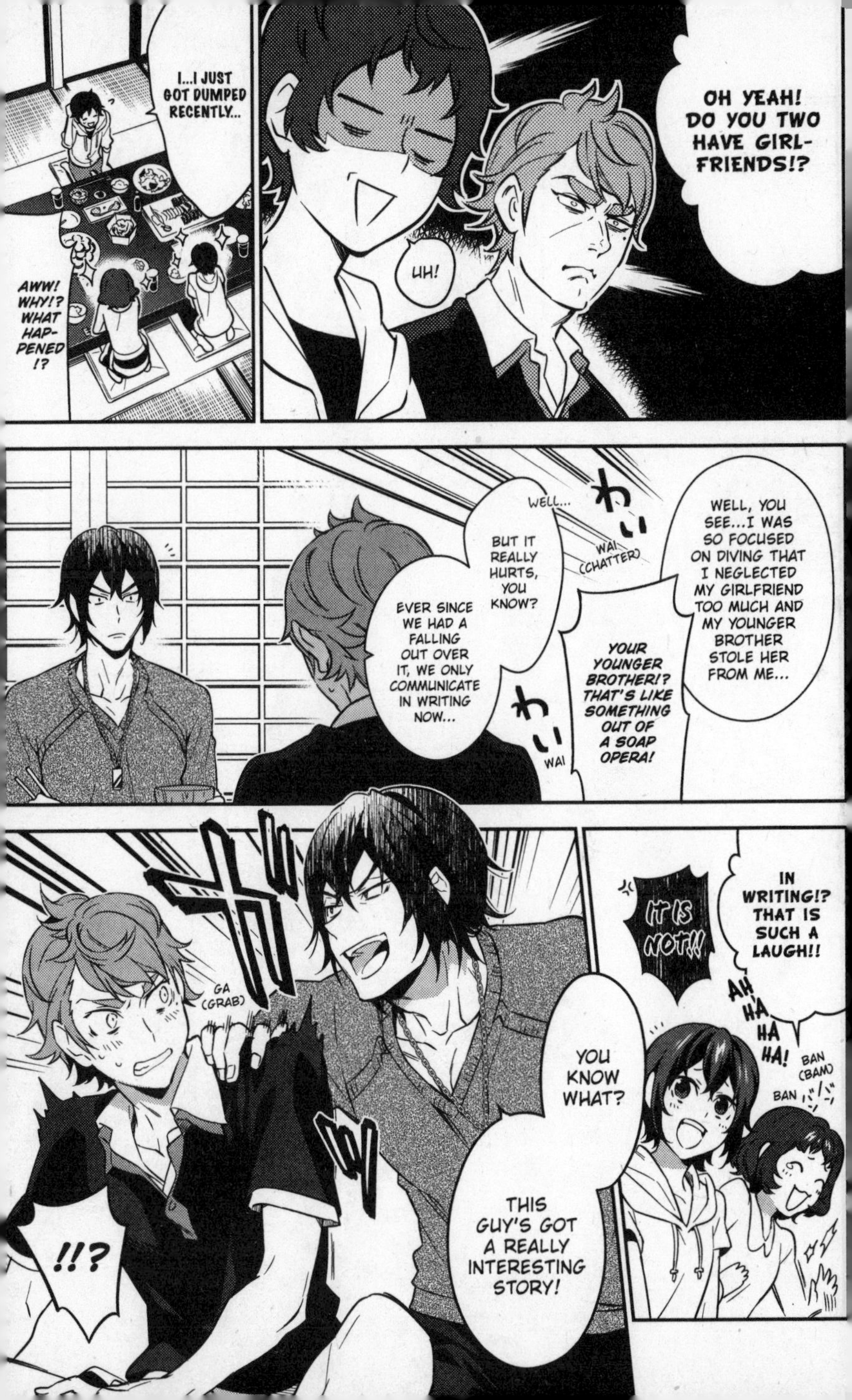
OH YEAH! DO YOU TWO HAVE GIRL-FRIENDS!?
UH!
I...I JUST GOT DUMPED RECENTLY...
AWW! WHY!? WHAT HAP-PENED!?
WELL, YOU SEE...I WAS SO FOCUSED ON DIVING THAT I NEGLECTED MY GIRLFRIEND TOO MUCH AND MY YOUNGER BROTHER STOLE HER FROM ME...
わい
WAI (CHATTER)
YOUR YOUNGER BROTHER!? THAT'S LIKE SOMETHING OUT OF A SOAP OPERA!
わい
WAI
WELL...
BUT IT REALLY HURTS, YOU KNOW?
EVER SINCE WE HAD A FALLING OUT OVER IT, WE ONLY COMMUNICATE IN WRITING NOW...
IN WRITING!? THAT IS SUCH A LAUGH!!
AH HA HA HA HA!
BAN (BAM)
BAN
IT IS NOT!!
GA (GRAB)
YOU KNOW WHAT?
THIS GUY'S GOT A REALLY INTERESTING STORY!
!!?

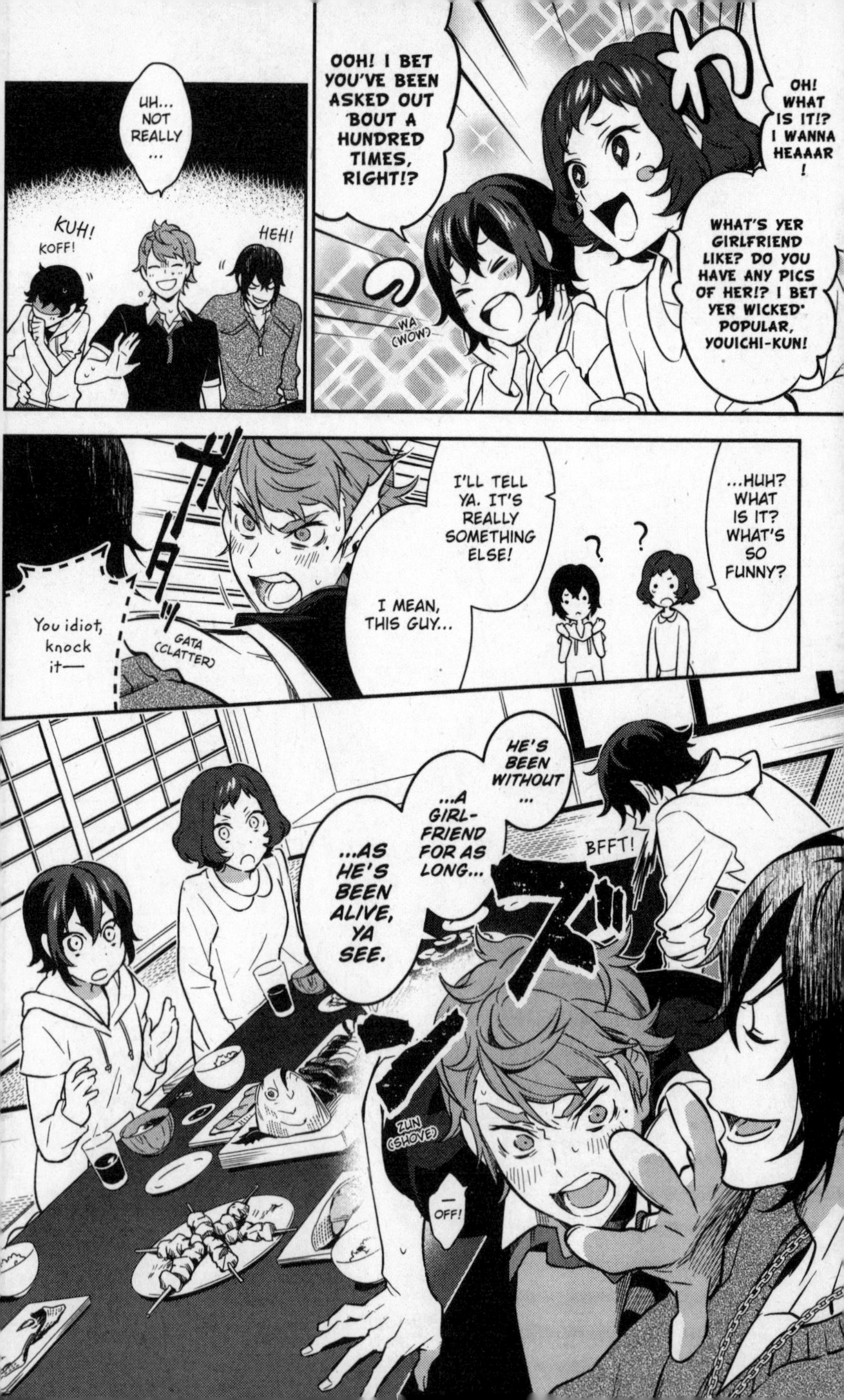
OH! WHAT IS IT!? I WANNA HEAAAR!
WHAT'S YER GIRLFRIEND LIKE? DO YOU HAVE ANY PICS OF HER!? I BET YER WICKED* POPULAR, YOUICHI-KUN!
OOH! I BET YOU'VE BEEN ASKED OUT 'BOUT A HUNDRED TIMES, RIGHT!?
WA (WOW)
UH... NOT REALLY...
HEH!
KUH! KOFF!
...HUH? WHAT IS IT? WHAT'S SO FUNNY?
I'LL TELL YA. IT'S REALLY SOMETHING ELSE!
I MEAN, THIS GUY...
GATA (CLATTER)
You idiot, knock it—
HE'S BEEN WITHOUT...
...A GIRLFRIEND FOR AS LONG...
...AS HE'S BEEN ALIVE, YA SEE.
BFFT!
ZUN (SHOVE)
—OFF!

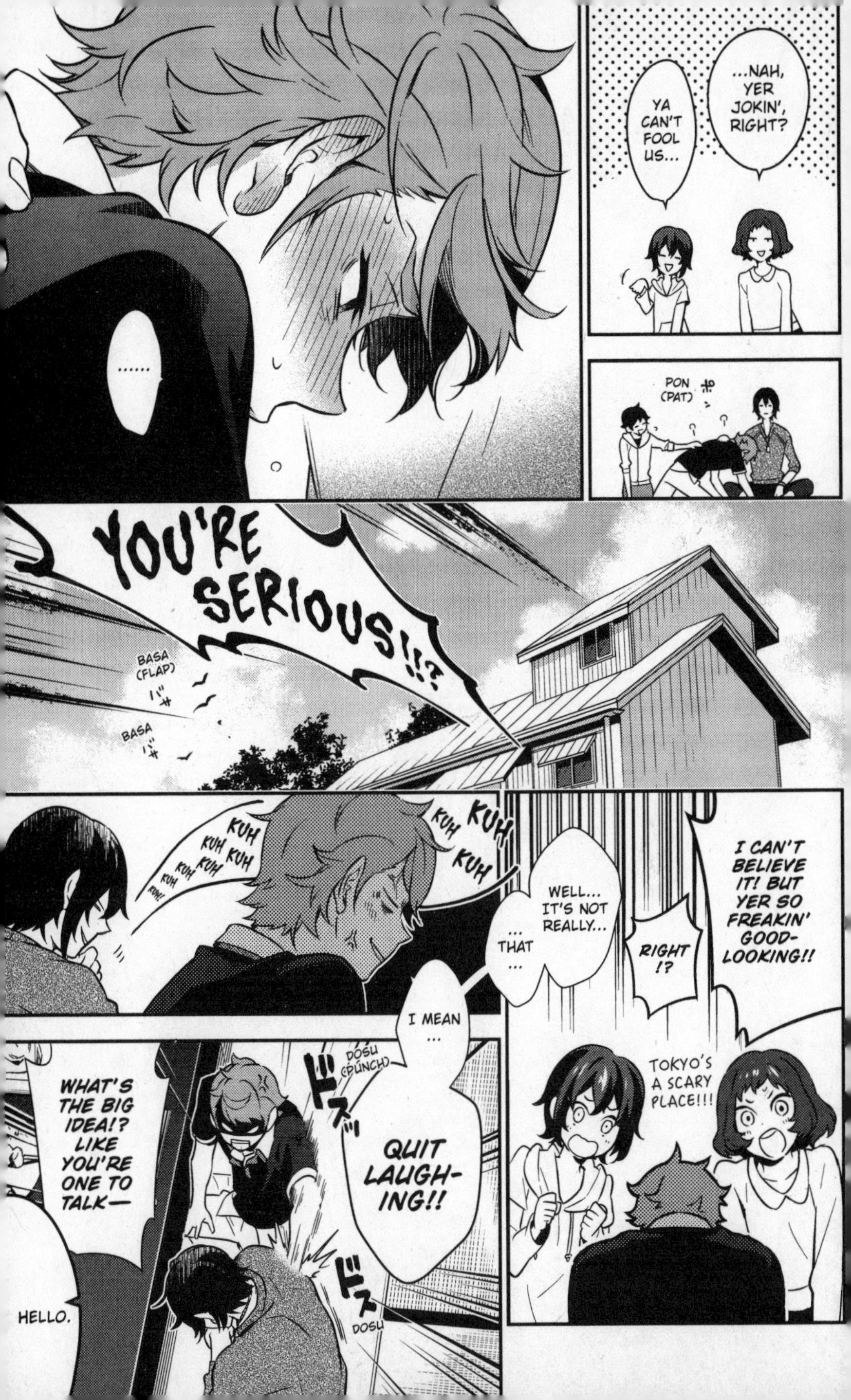
...NAH, YER JOKIN', RIGHT?
YA CAN'T FOOL US...
PON (PAT)
......
YOU'RE SERIOUS!!?
BASA (FLAP)
BASA
I CAN'T BELIEVE IT! BUT YER SO FREAKIN' GOOD-LOOKING!!
RIGHT!?
WELL... IT'S NOT REALLY...
...THAT...
KUH KUH KUH
KUH KUH KUH KUH KUH
I MEAN...
TOKYO'S A SCARY PLACE!!!
QUIT LAUGHING!!
DOSU (PUNCH)
DOSU
WHAT'S THE BIG IDEA!? LIKE YOU'RE ONE TO TALK—
HELLO.

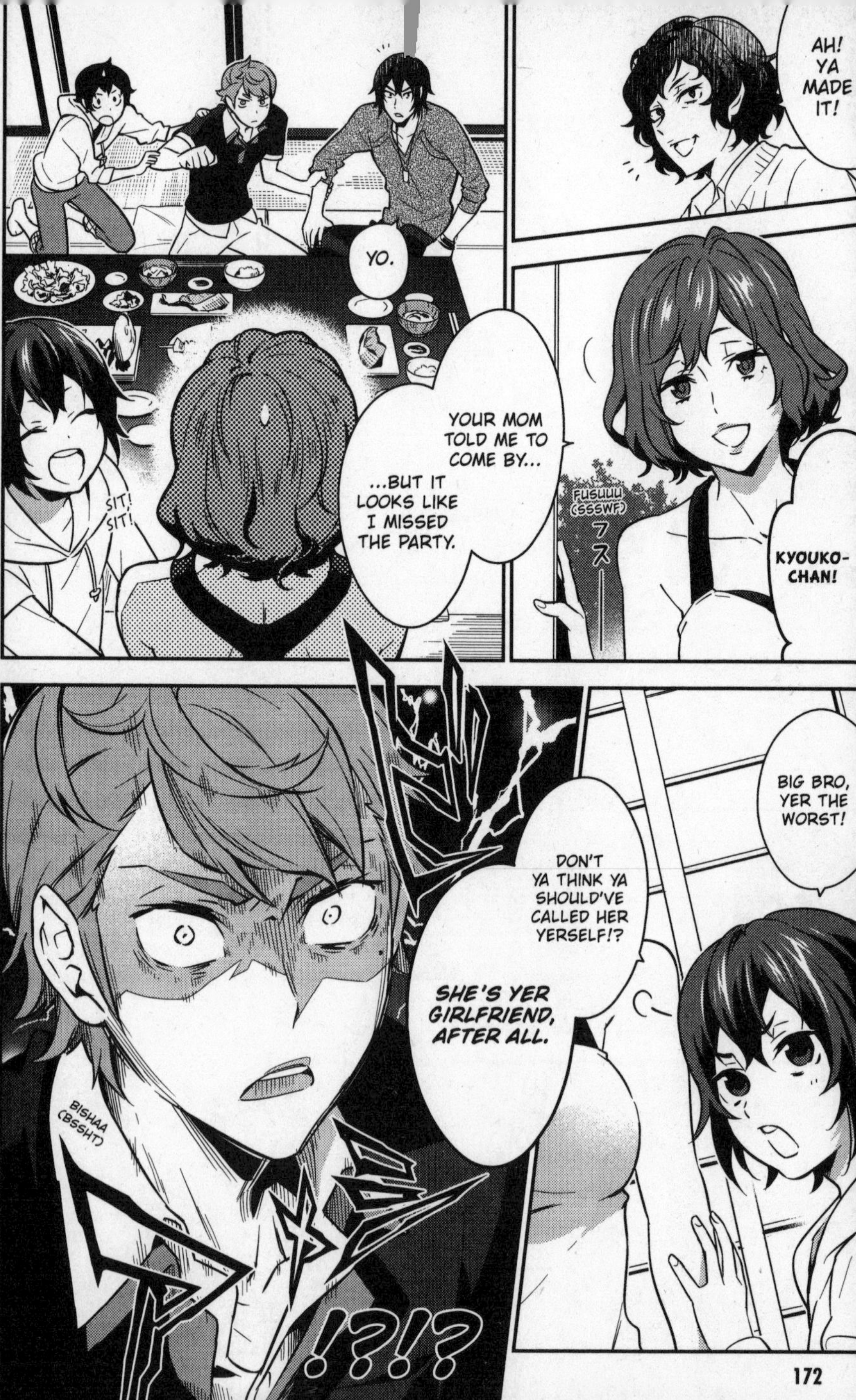
AH! YA MADE IT!
KYOUKO-CHAN!
FUSUUU (SSSWF)
フスー
YO.
YOUR MOM TOLD ME TO COME BY...
...BUT IT LOOKS LIKE I MISSED THE PARTY.
SIT! SIT!
BIG BRO, YER THE WORST!
DON'T YA THINK YA SHOULD'VE CALLED HER YERSELF!?
SHE'S YER GIRLFRIEND, AFTER ALL.
BISHAA (BSSHT)
!?!?

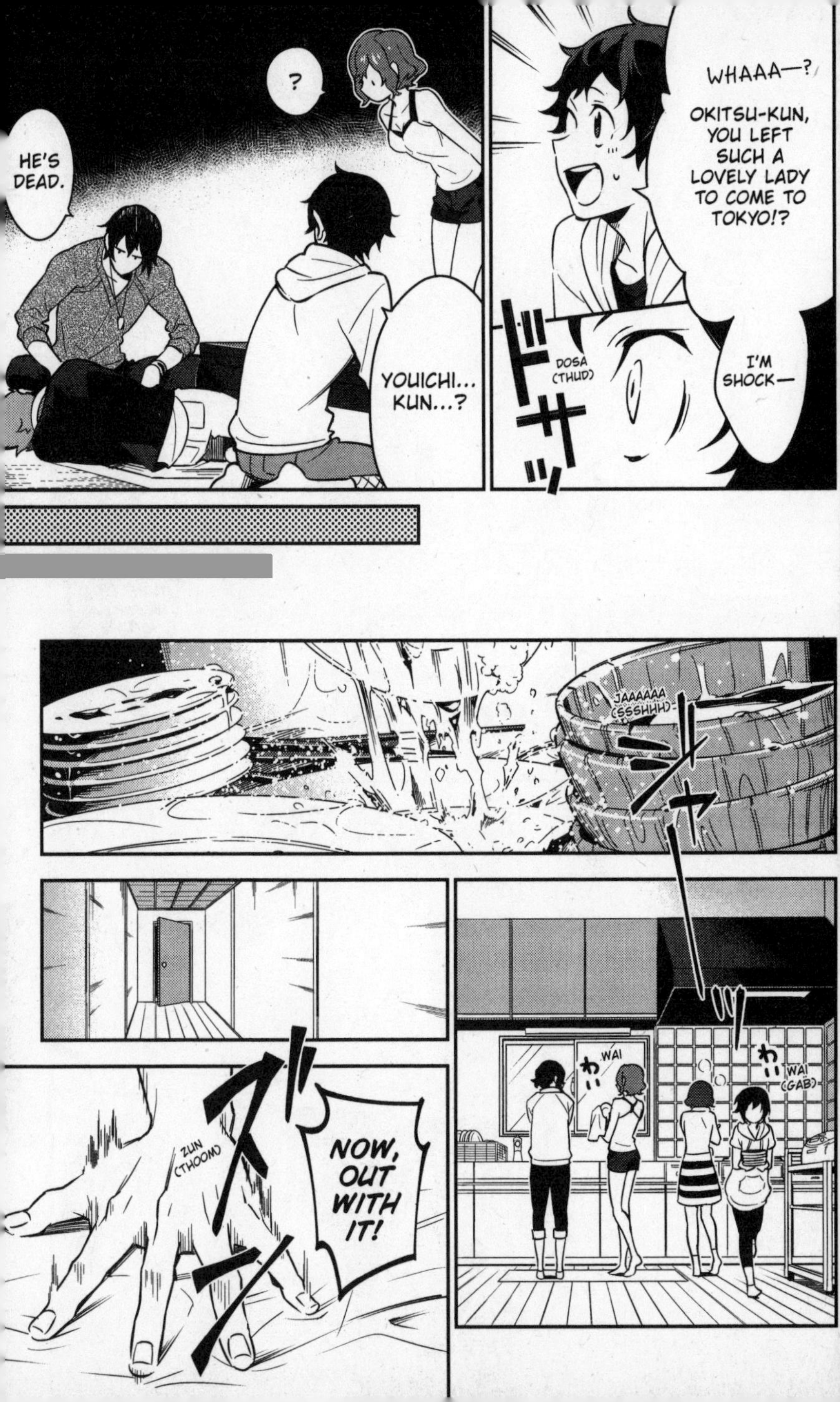
WHAAA—?
OKITSU-KUN, YOU LEFT SUCH A LOVELY LADY TO COME TO TOKYO!?
I'M SHOCK—
DOSA (THUD)
?
HE'S DEAD.
YOUICHI... KUN...?
JAAAAAA (SSSHHH)
WAI
WAI (GAB)
ZUN (THOOM)
NOW, OUT WITH IT!

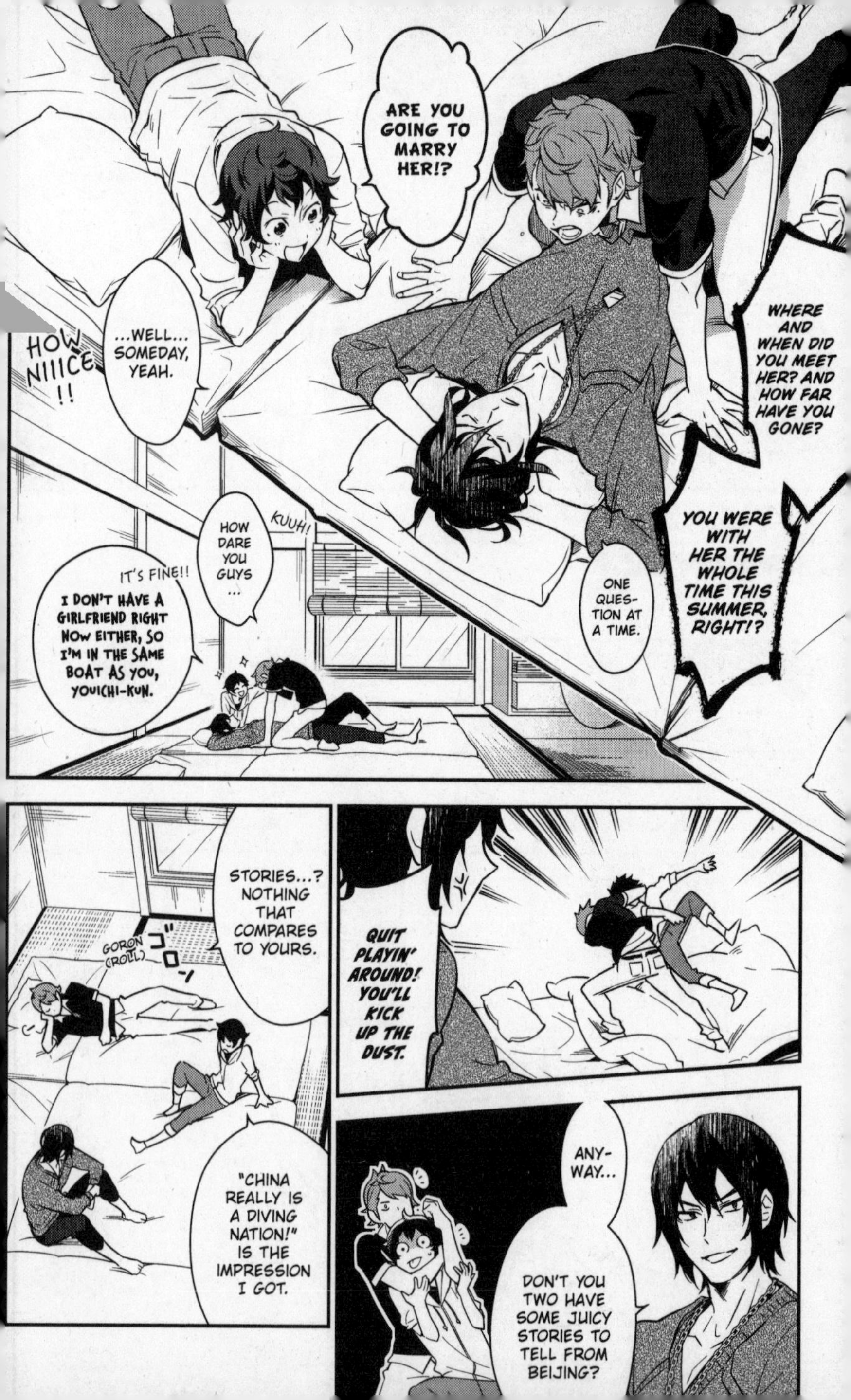
ARE YOU GOING TO MARRY HER!?
WHERE AND WHEN DID YOU MEET HER? AND HOW FAR HAVE YOU GONE?
YOU WERE WITH HER THE WHOLE TIME THIS SUMMER, RIGHT!?
...WELL... SOMEDAY, YEAH.
HOW NIIICE!!
ONE QUES-TION AT A TIME.
KUUH!
HOW DARE YOU GUYS...
IT'S FINE!!
I DON'T HAVE A GIRLFRIEND RIGHT NOW EITHER, SO I'M IN THE SAME BOAT AS YOU, YOUICHI-KUN.
QUIT PLAYIN' AROUND! YOU'LL KICK UP THE DUST.
ANY-WAY...
DON'T YOU TWO HAVE SOME JUICY STORIES TO TELL FROM BEIJING?
STORIES...? NOTHING THAT COMPARES TO YOURS.
GORON (ROLL)
"CHINA REALLY IS A DIVING NATION!" IS THE IMPRESSION I GOT.

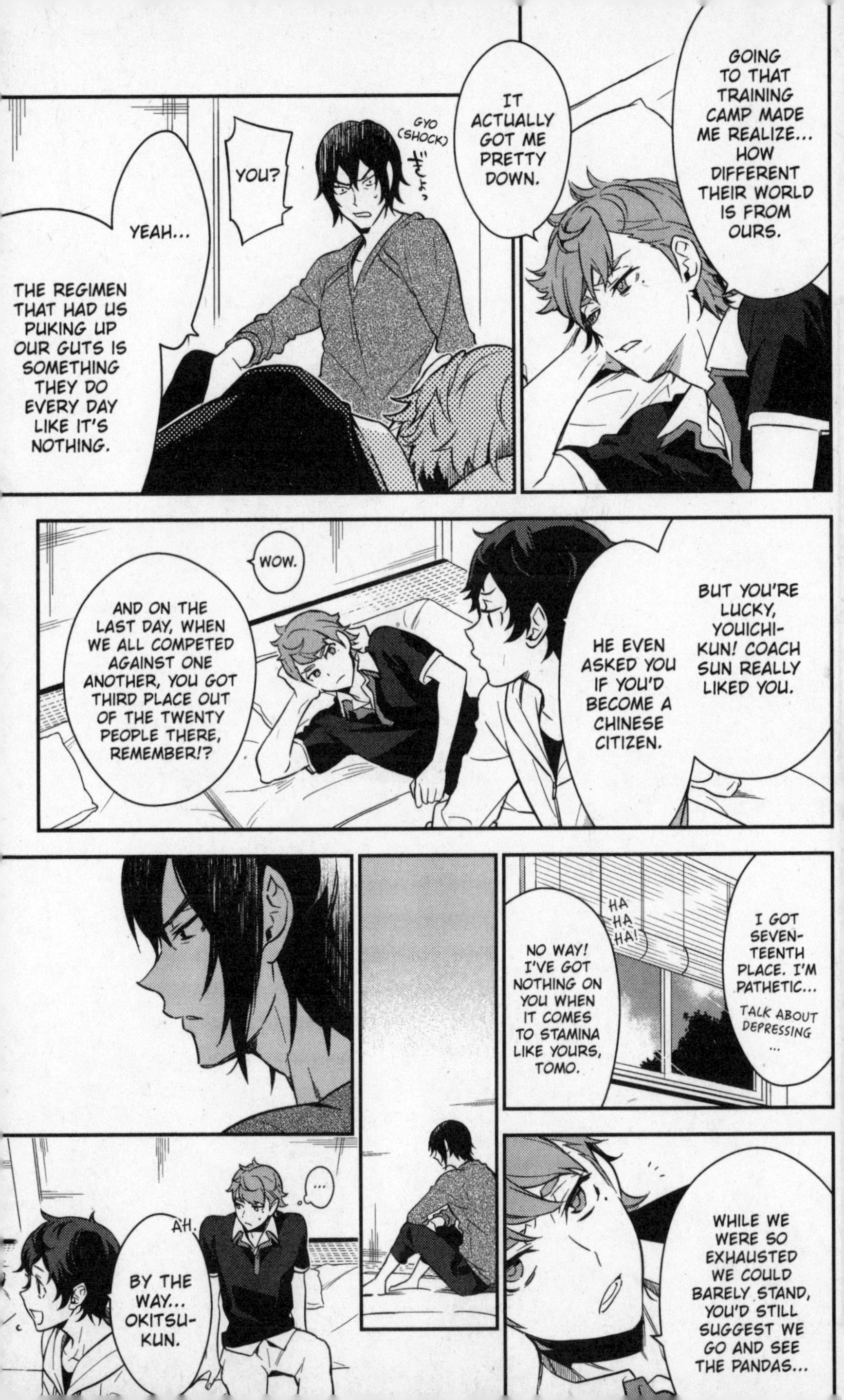
GOING TO THAT TRAINING CAMP MADE ME REALIZE... HOW DIFFERENT THEIR WORLD IS FROM OURS.
IT ACTUALLY GOT ME PRETTY DOWN.
GYO (SHOCK)
YOU?
YEAH...
THE REGIMEN THAT HAD US PUKING UP OUR GUTS IS SOMETHING THEY DO EVERY DAY LIKE IT'S NOTHING.
BUT YOU'RE LUCKY, YOUICHI-KUN! COACH SUN REALLY LIKED YOU.
HE EVEN ASKED YOU IF YOU'D BECOME A CHINESE CITIZEN.
AND ON THE LAST DAY, WHEN WE ALL COMPETED AGAINST ONE ANOTHER, YOU GOT THIRD PLACE OUT OF THE TWENTY PEOPLE THERE, REMEMBER!?
WOW.
I GOT SEVENTEENTH PLACE. I'M PATHETIC...
TALK ABOUT DEPRESSING...
HA HA HA!
NO WAY! I'VE GOT NOTHING ON YOU WHEN IT COMES TO STAMINA LIKE YOURS, TOMO.
WHILE WE WERE SO EXHAUSTED WE COULD BARELY STAND, YOU'D STILL SUGGEST WE GO AND SEE THE PANDAS...
...
AH.
BY THE WAY... OKITSU-KUN.

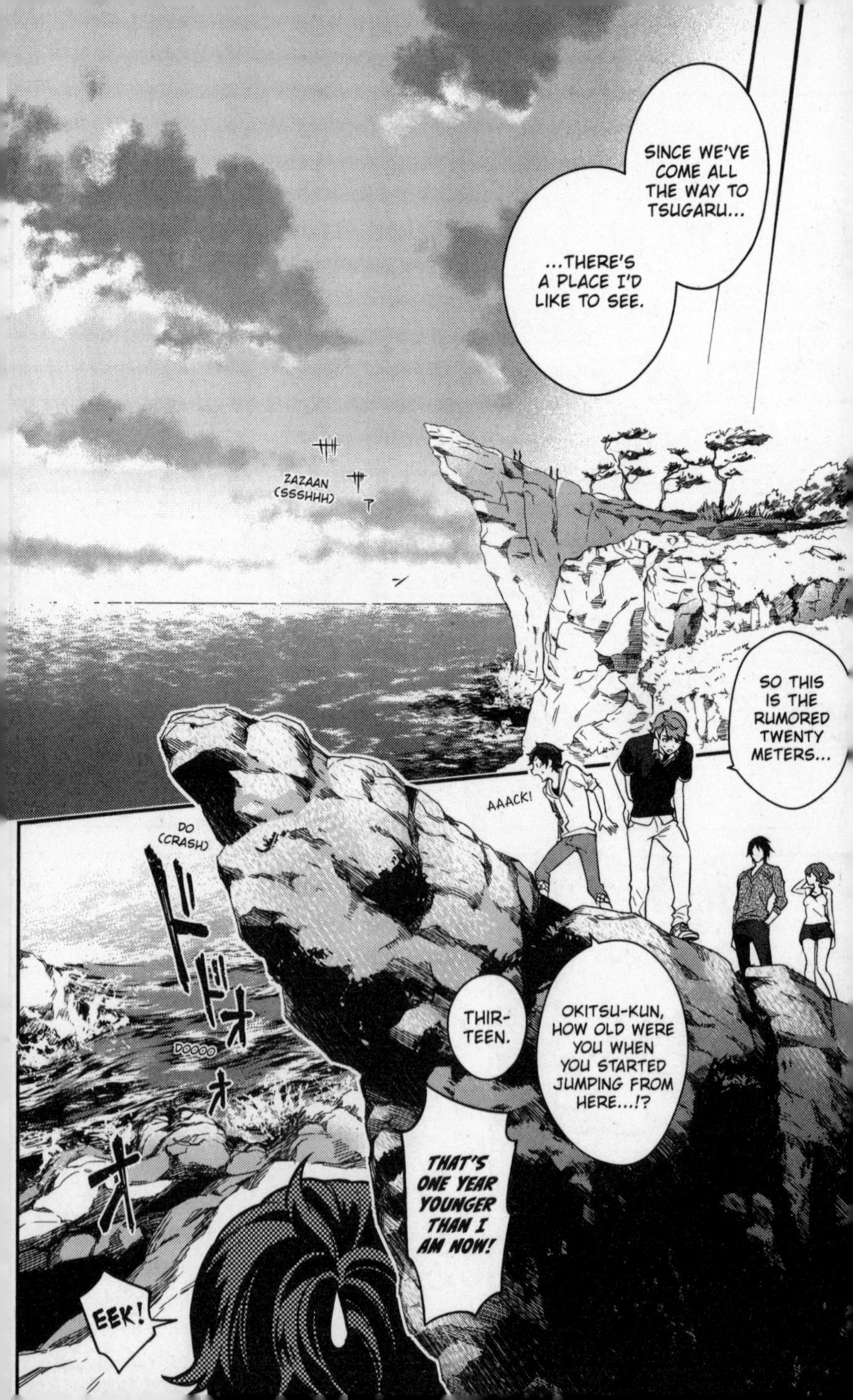
SINCE WE'VE COME ALL THE WAY TO TSUGARU...
...THERE'S A PLACE I'D LIKE TO SEE.
ZAZAAN (SSSHHH)
SO THIS IS THE RUMORED TWENTY METERS...
AAACK!
DO (CRASH)
DOOOO
OKITSU-KUN, HOW OLD WERE YOU WHEN YOU STARTED JUMPING FROM HERE...!?
THIR-TEEN.
THAT'S ONE YEAR YOUNGER THAN I AM NOW!
EEK!

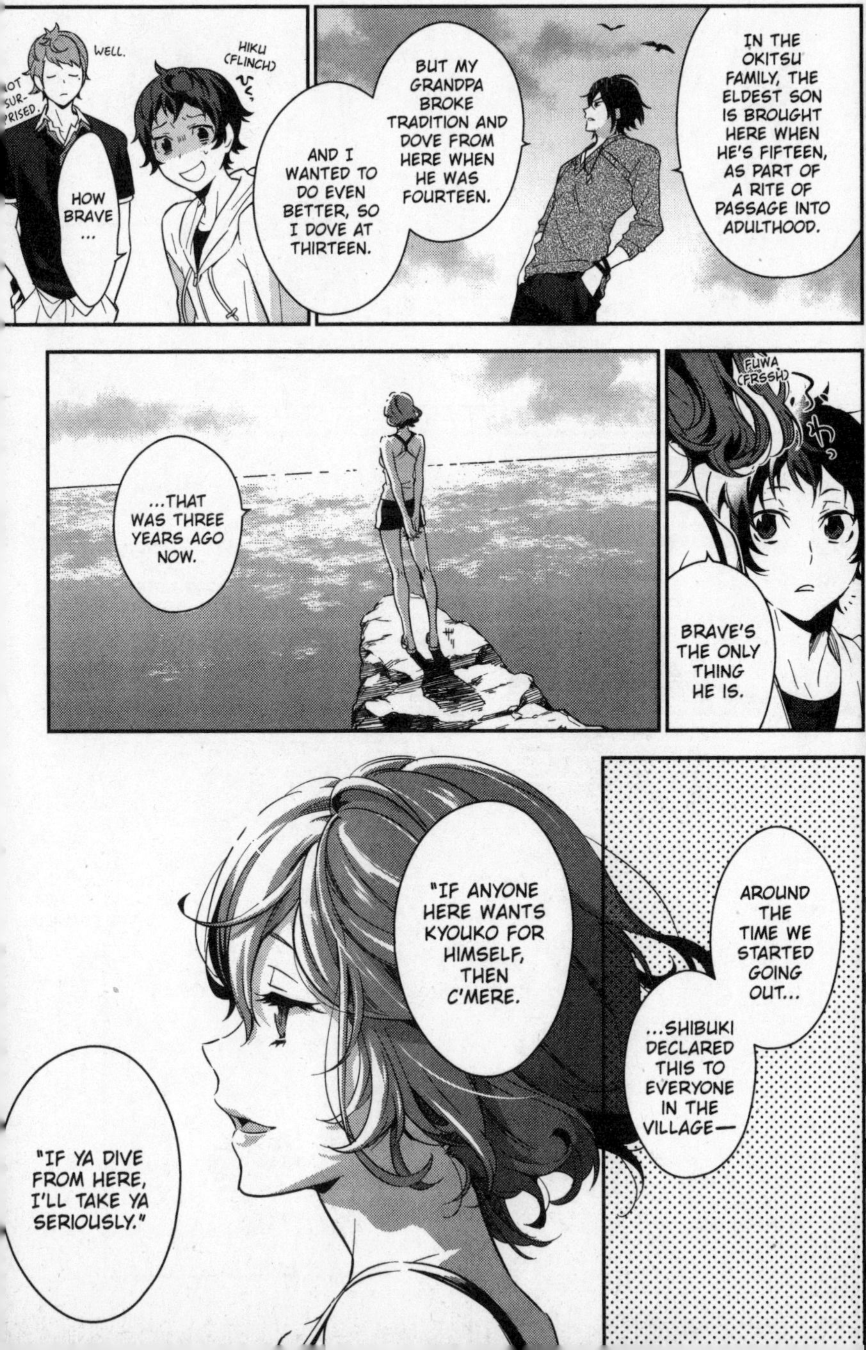
IN THE OKITSU FAMILY, THE ELDEST SON IS BROUGHT HERE WHEN HE'S FIFTEEN, AS PART OF A RITE OF PASSAGE INTO ADULTHOOD.
BUT MY GRANDPA BROKE TRADITION AND DOVE FROM HERE WHEN HE WAS FOURTEEN.
AND I WANTED TO DO EVEN BETTER, SO I DOVE AT THIRTEEN.
HIKU (FLINCH)
WELL.
NOT SURPRISED.
HOW BRAVE ...
FUWA (FRSSH)
BRAVE'S THE ONLY THING HE IS.
...THAT WAS THREE YEARS AGO NOW.
AROUND THE TIME WE STARTED GOING OUT...
...SHIBUKI DECLARED THIS TO EVERYONE IN THE VILLAGE—
"IF ANYONE HERE WANTS KYOUKO FOR HIMSELF, THEN C'MERE.
"IF YA DIVE FROM HERE, I'LL TAKE YA SERIOUSLY."

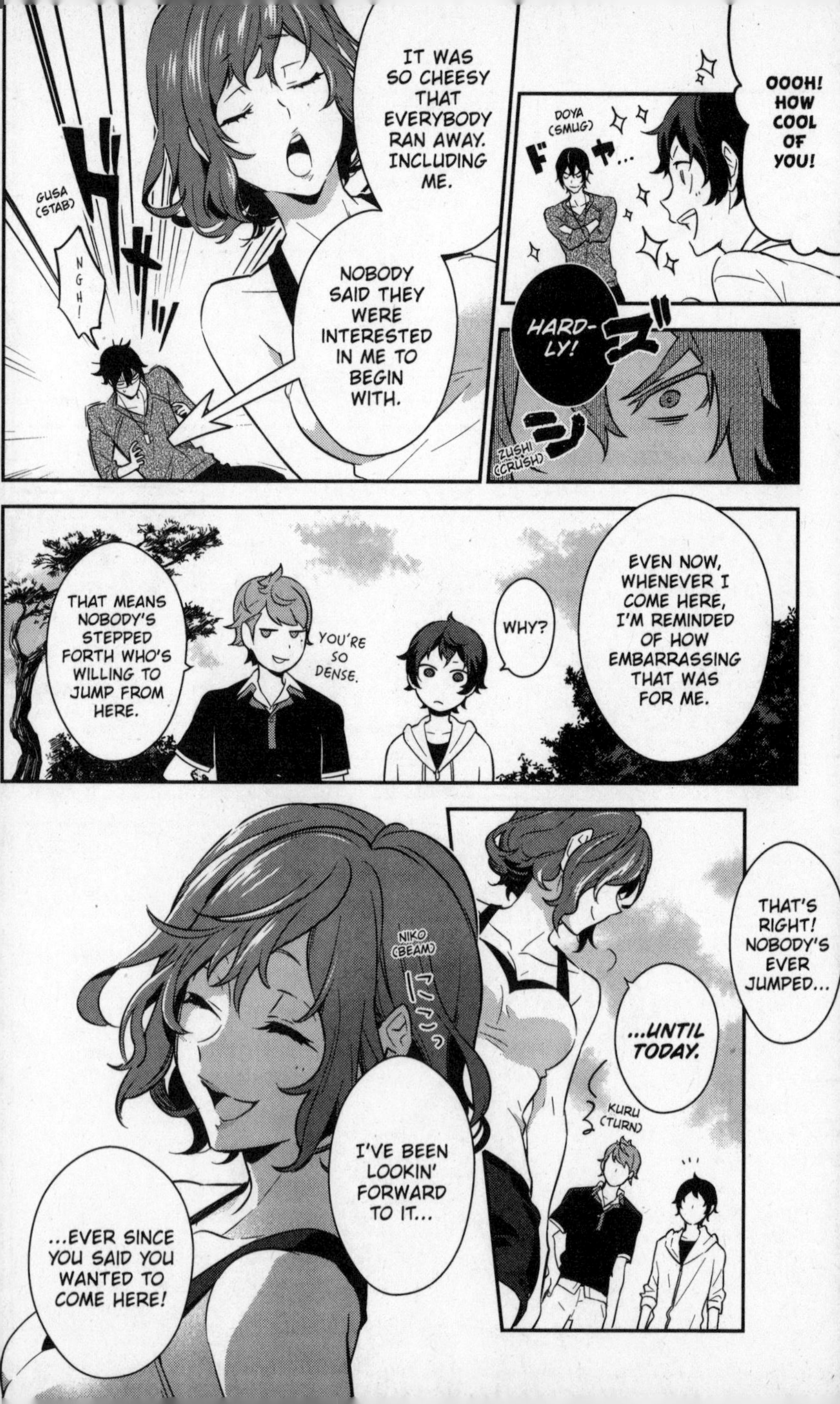

OOOH! HOW COOL OF YOU!
DOYA (SMUG)
HARD-LY!
ZUSHI (CRUSH)
IT WAS SO CHEESY THAT EVERYBODY RAN AWAY. INCLUDING ME.
NOBODY SAID THEY WERE INTERESTED IN ME TO BEGIN WITH.
GUSA (STAB)
NGH!
EVEN NOW, WHENEVER I COME HERE, I'M REMINDED OF HOW EMBARRASSING THAT WAS FOR ME.
WHY?
YOU'RE SO DENSE.
THAT MEANS NOBODY'S STEPPED FORTH WHO'S WILLING TO JUMP FROM HERE.
THAT'S RIGHT! NOBODY'S EVER JUMPED...
...UNTIL TODAY.
KURU (TURN)
NIKO (BEAM)
I'VE BEEN LOOKIN' FORWARD TO IT...
...EVER SINCE YOU SAID YOU WANTED TO COME HERE!

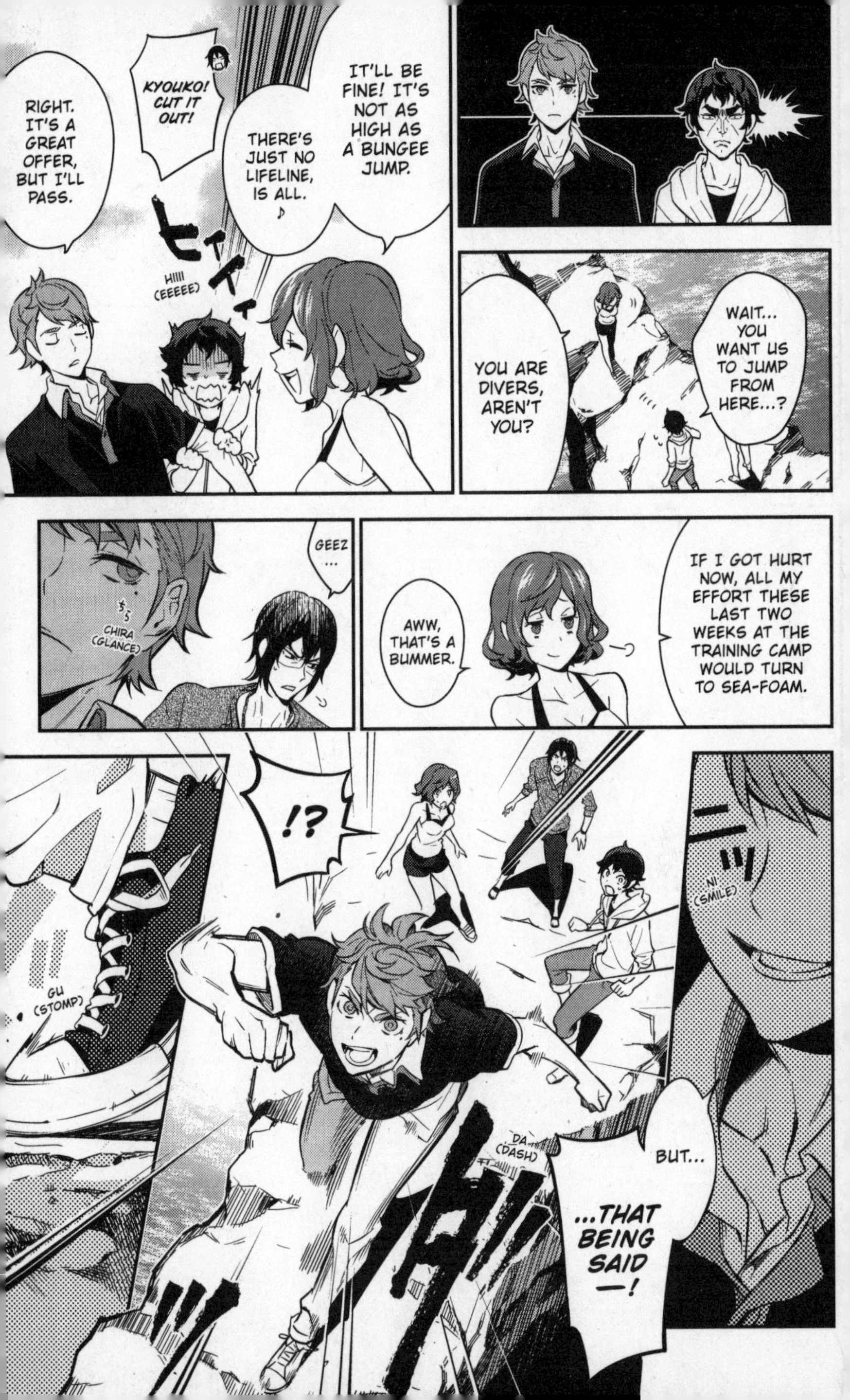
WAIT... YOU WANT US TO JUMP FROM HERE...?
YOU ARE DIVERS, AREN'T YOU?
IT'LL BE FINE! IT'S NOT AS HIGH AS A BUNGEE JUMP.
THERE'S JUST NO LIFELINE, IS ALL. ♪
KYOUKO! CUT IT OUT!
RIGHT. IT'S A GREAT OFFER, BUT I'LL PASS.
HIIII (EEEEE)
IF I GOT HURT NOW, ALL MY EFFORT THESE LAST TWO WEEKS AT THE TRAINING CAMP WOULD TURN TO SEA-FOAM.
AWW, THAT'S A BUMMER.
GEEZ...
CHIRA (GLANCE)
NI (SMILE)
BUT...
...THAT BEING SAID—!
!?
DA (DASH)
GU (STOMP)

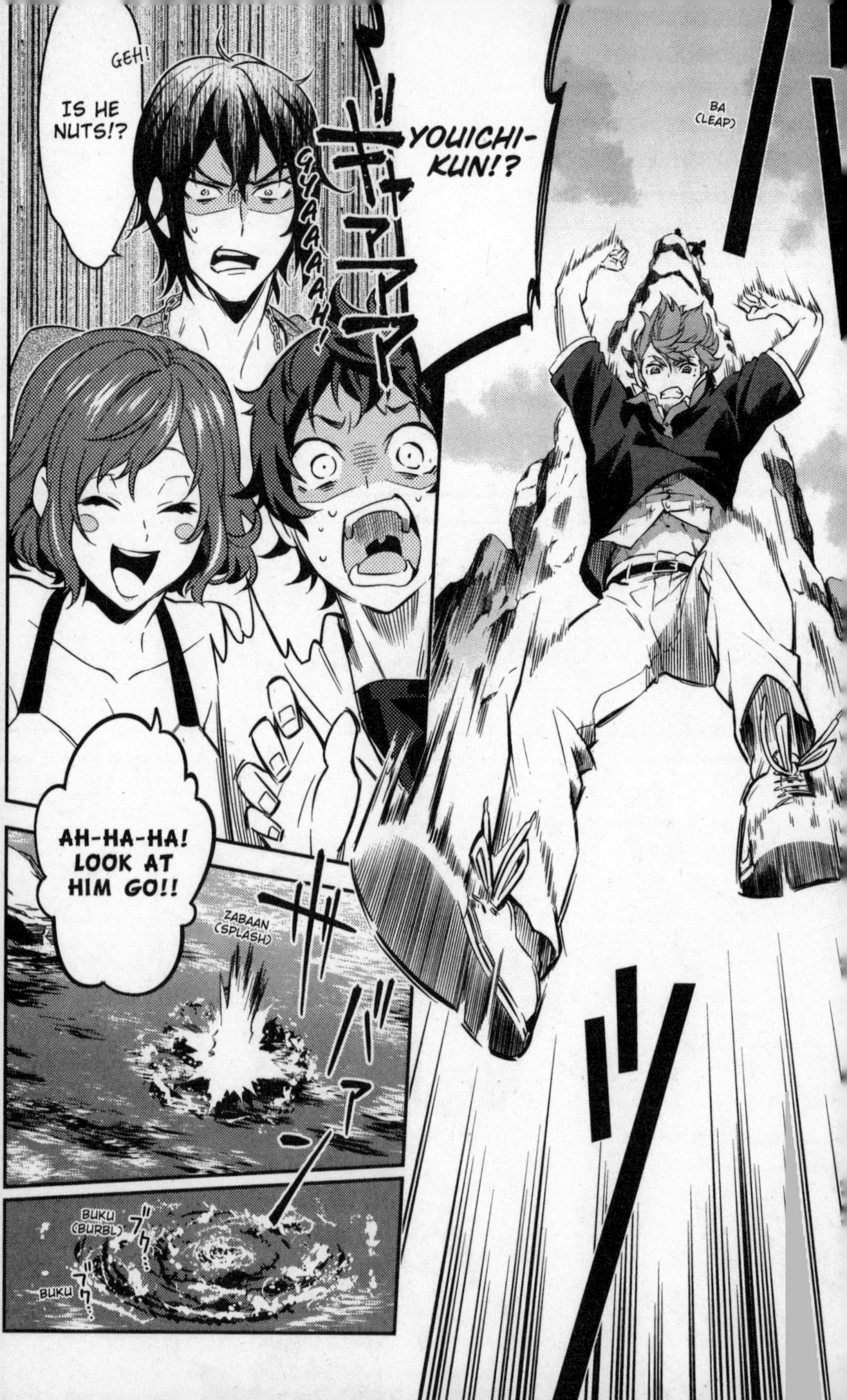
BA (LEAP)
YOUICHI-KUN!?
GYAAAAAAH!
GEH!
IS HE NUTS!?
AH-HA-HA! LOOK AT HIM GO!!
ZABAAN (SPLASH)
BUKU (BURBL)
BUKU

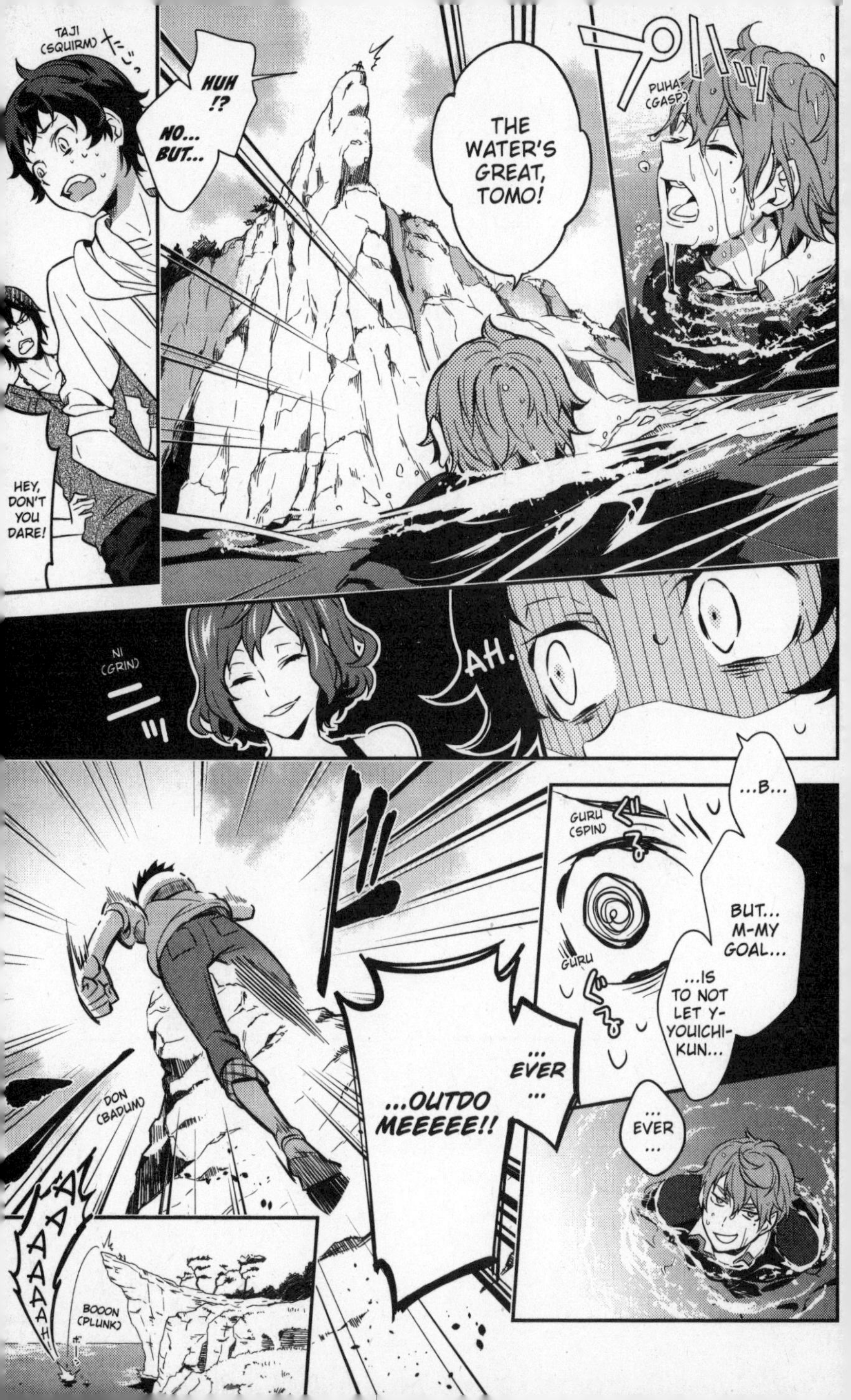
PUHA (GASP)
THE WATER'S GREAT, TOMO!
HUH!?
NO... BUT...
TAJI (SQUIRM)
HEY, DON'T YOU DARE!
AH.
NI (GRIN)
...B...
GURU (SPIN)
BUT... M-MY GOAL...
...IS TO NOT LET Y-YOUICHI-KUN...
GURU
...EVER...
...EVER...
...OUTDO MEEEEE!!
DON (BADUM)
BOOON (PLUNK)

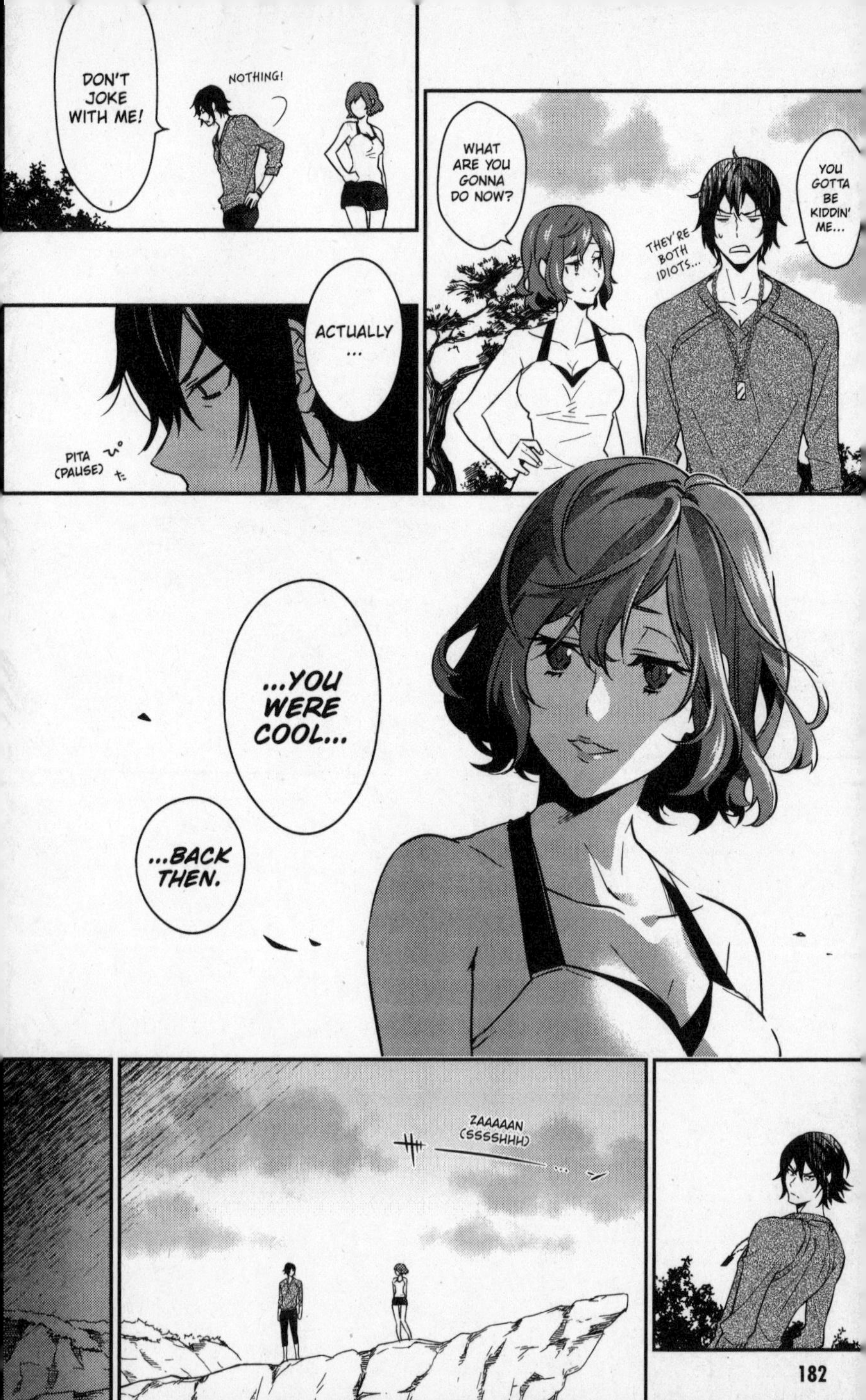
YOU GOTTA BE KIDDIN' ME...
THEY'RE BOTH IDIOTS...
WHAT ARE YOU GONNA DO NOW?
DON'T JOKE WITH ME!
NOTHING!
ACTUALLY...
PITA (PAUSE)
...YOU WERE COOL...
...BACK THEN.
ZAAAAAN (SSSSHHH)

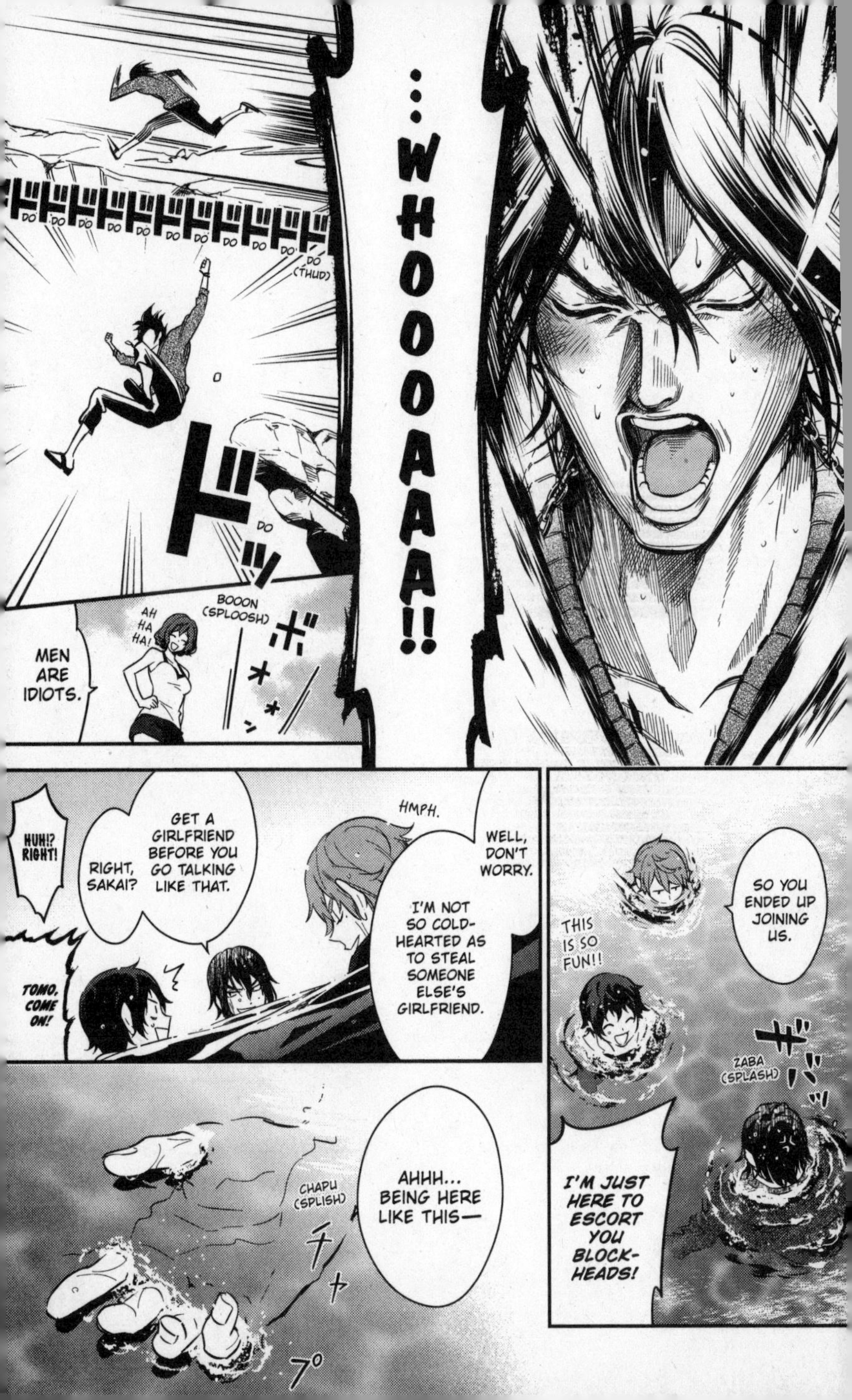

...WHOOOAAA!!
DO DO DO DO DO DO DO DO DO DO DO (THUD)
DO
BOOON (SPLOOSH)
AH HA HA!
MEN ARE IDIOTS.
SO YOU ENDED UP JOINING US.
THIS IS SO FUN!!
ZABA (SPLASH)
I'M JUST HERE TO ESCORT YOU BLOCK-HEADS!
HMPH.
WELL, DON'T WORRY.
I'M NOT SO COLD-HEARTED AS TO STEAL SOMEONE ELSE'S GIRLFRIEND.
GET A GIRLFRIEND BEFORE YOU GO TALKING LIKE THAT.
RIGHT, SAKAI?
HUH!? RIGHT!
TOMO, COME ON!
AHHH... BEING HERE LIKE THIS—
CHAPU (SPLISH)

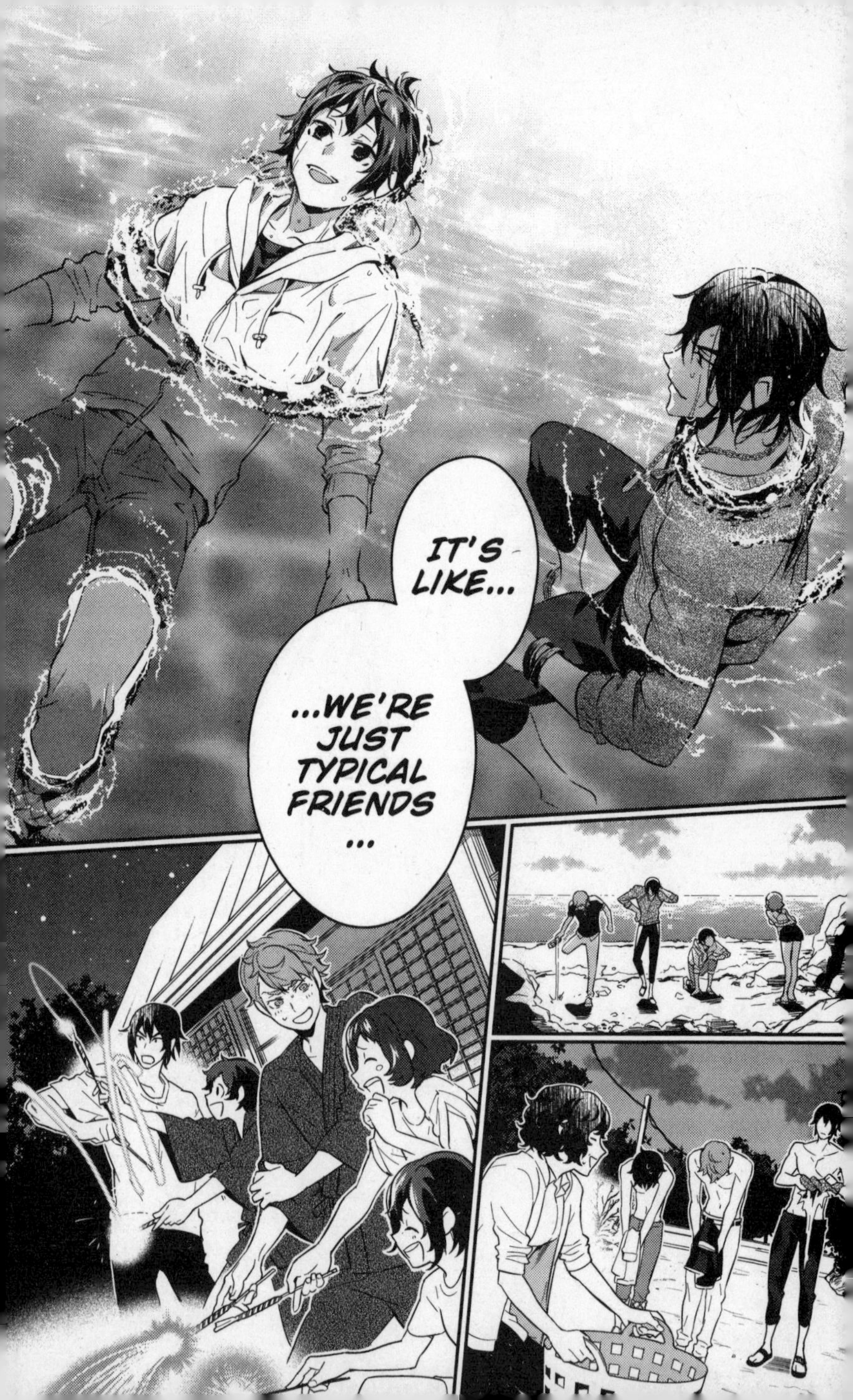
IT'S LIKE...
...WE'RE JUST TYPICAL FRIENDS ...

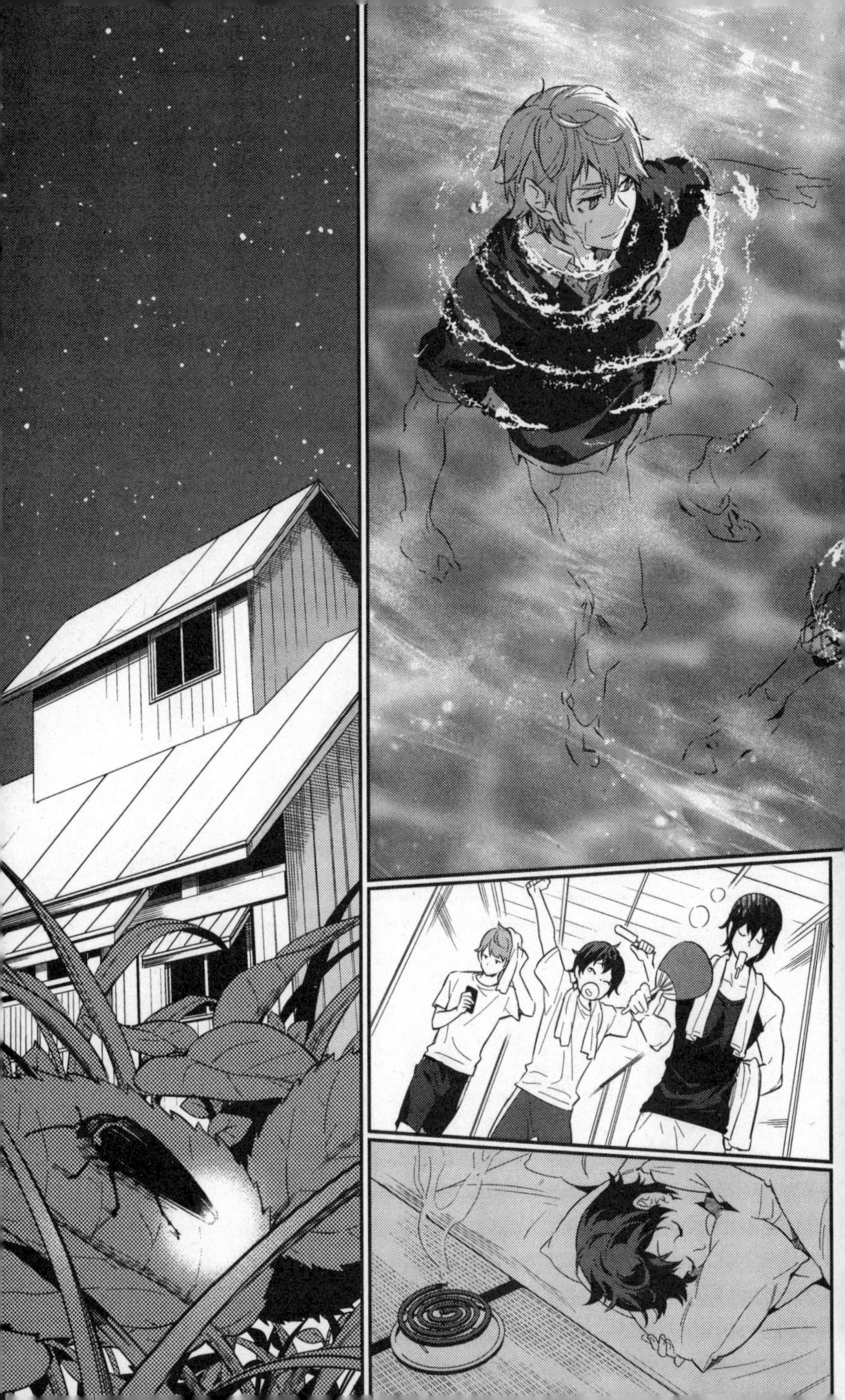

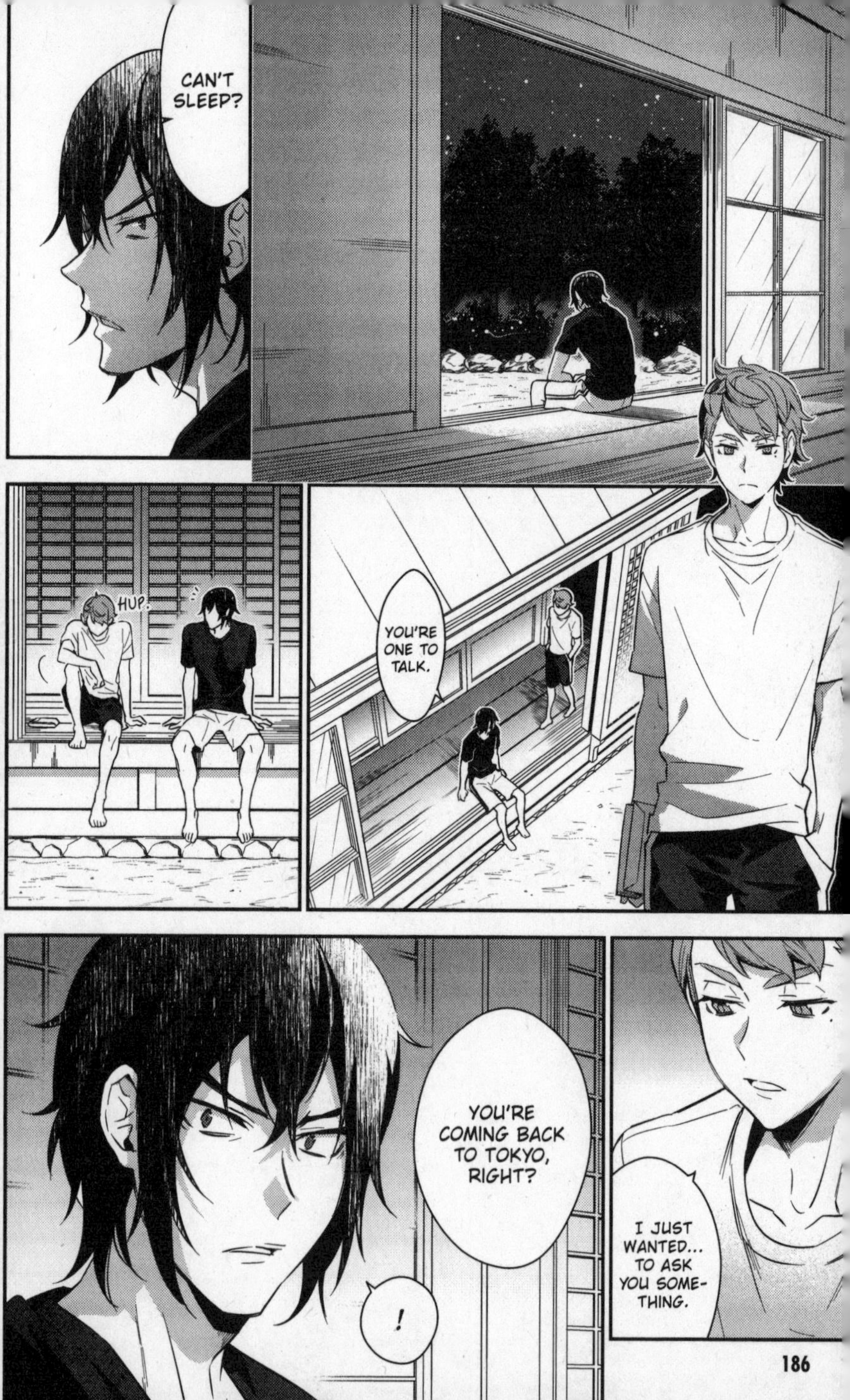
CAN'T SLEEP?
YOU'RE ONE TO TALK.
HUP.
I JUST WANTED... TO ASK YOU SOME-THING.
YOU'RE COMING BACK TO TOKYO, RIGHT?
!

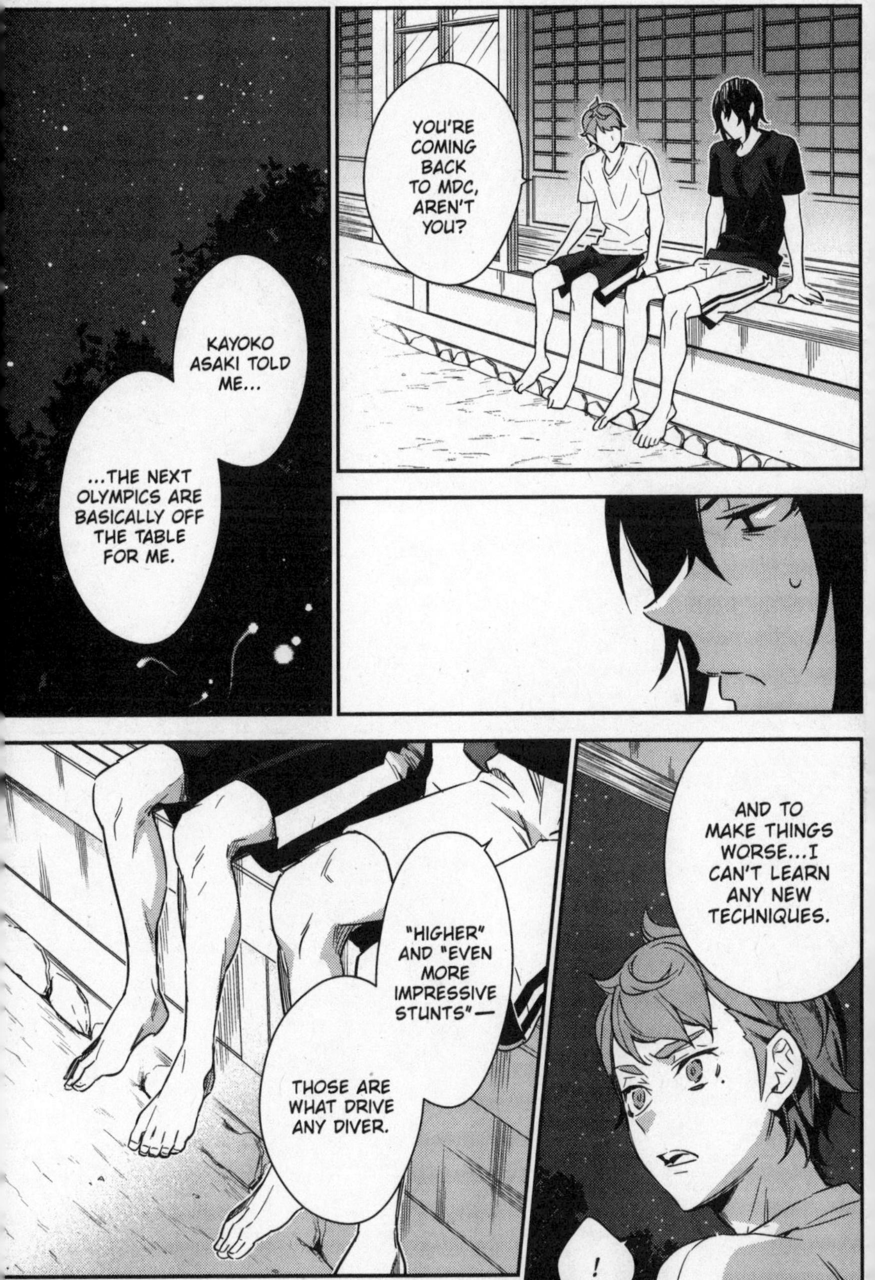
YOU'RE COMING BACK TO MDC, AREN'T YOU?
KAYOKO ASAKI TOLD ME...
...THE NEXT OLYMPICS ARE BASICALLY OFF THE TABLE FOR ME.
AND TO MAKE THINGS WORSE...I CAN'T LEARN ANY NEW TECHNIQUES.
!
"HIGHER" AND "EVEN MORE IMPRESSIVE STUNTS"—
THOSE ARE WHAT DRIVE ANY DIVER.

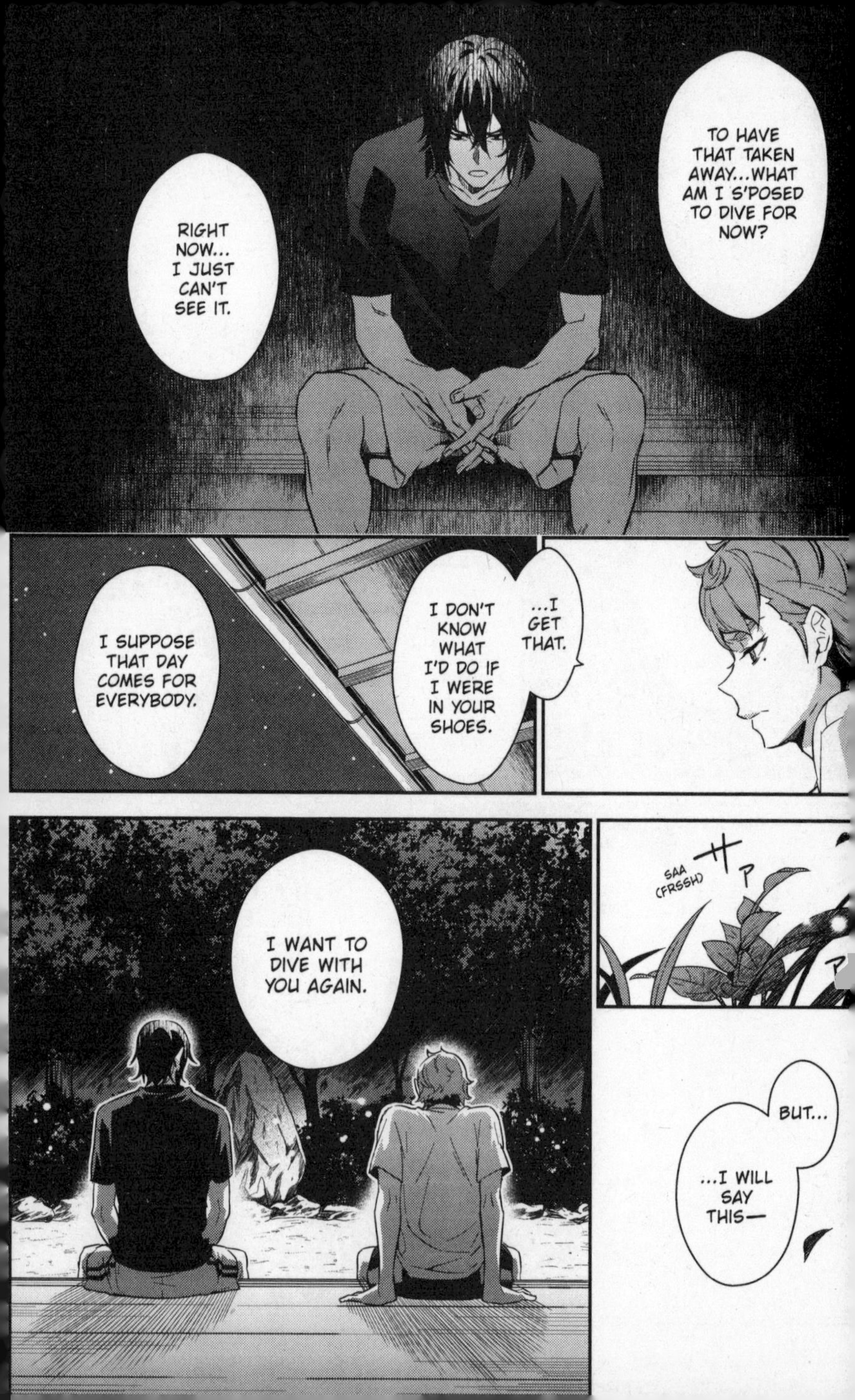
TO HAVE THAT TAKEN AWAY...WHAT AM I S'POSED TO DIVE FOR NOW?
RIGHT NOW... I JUST CAN'T SEE IT.
...I GET THAT.
I DON'T KNOW WHAT I'D DO IF I WERE IN YOUR SHOES.
I SUPPOSE THAT DAY COMES FOR EVERYBODY.
SAA (FRSSH)
BUT...
...I WILL SAY THIS—
I WANT TO DIVE WITH YOU AGAIN.

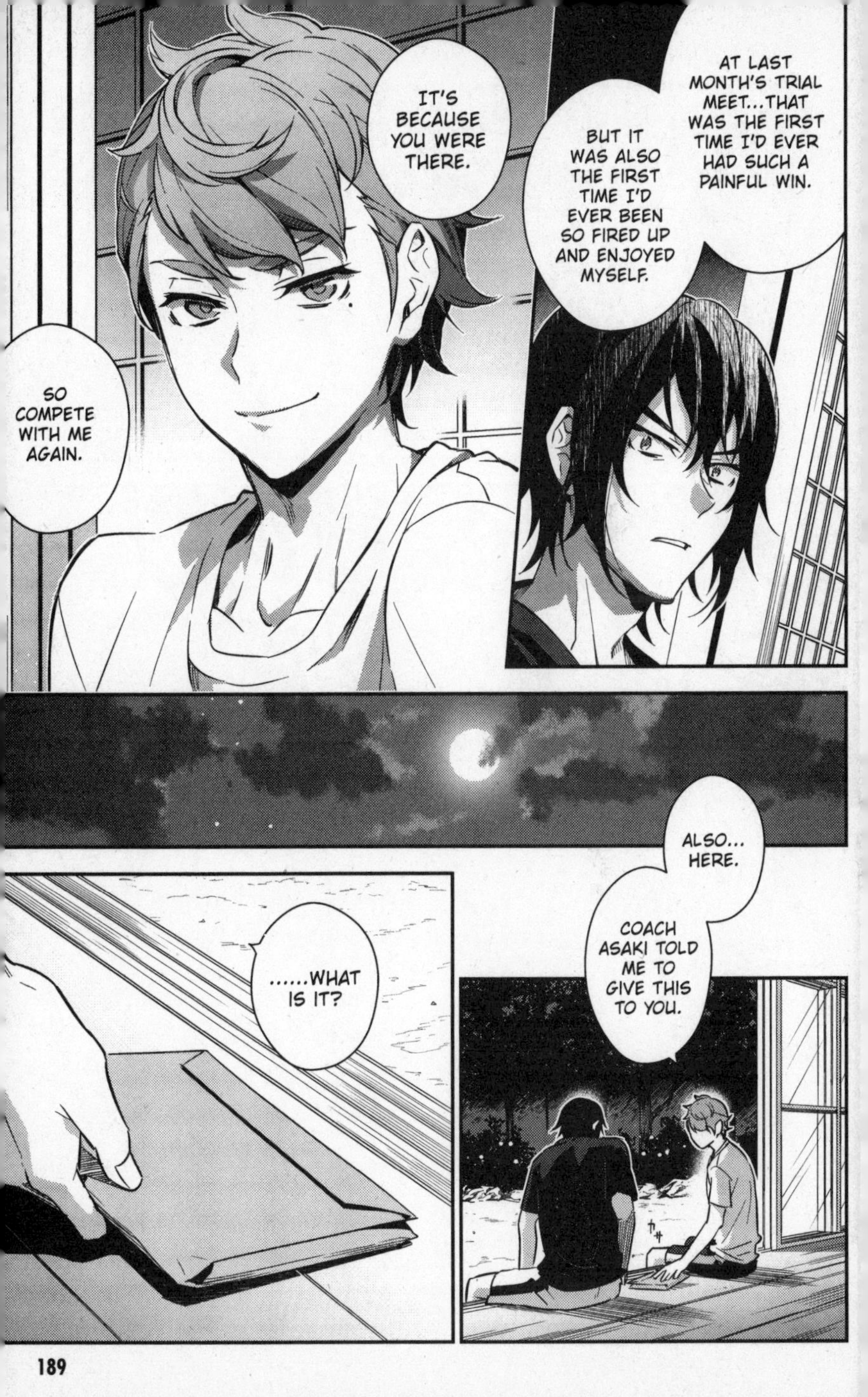
AT LAST MONTH'S TRIAL MEET...THAT WAS THE FIRST TIME I'D EVER HAD SUCH A PAINFUL WIN.
BUT IT WAS ALSO THE FIRST TIME I'D EVER BEEN SO FIRED UP AND ENJOYED MYSELF.
IT'S BECAUSE YOU WERE THERE.
SO COMPETE WITH ME AGAIN.
ALSO... HERE.
COACH ASAKI TOLD ME TO GIVE THIS TO YOU.
......WHAT IS IT?

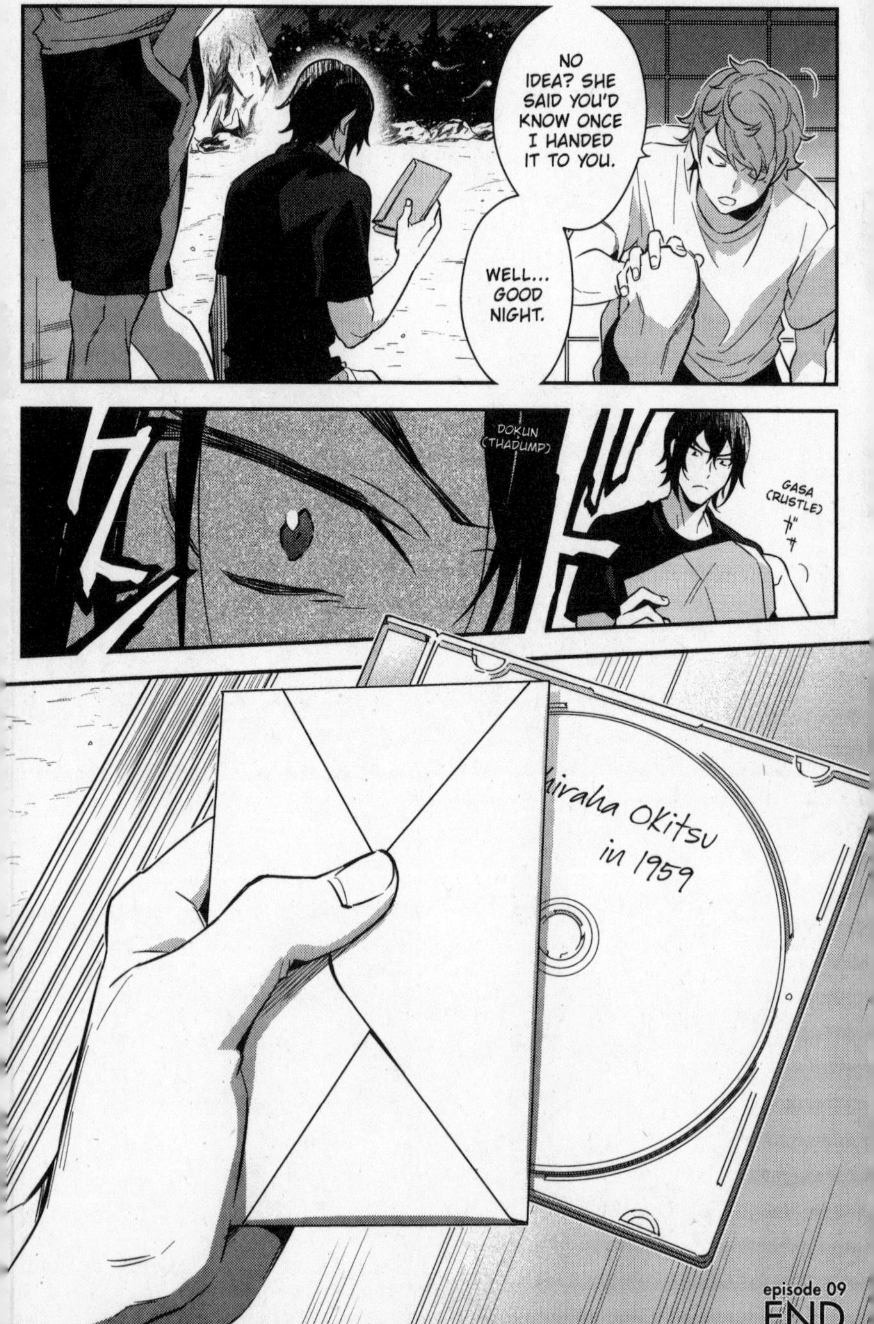
NO IDEA? SHE SAID YOU'D KNOW ONCE I HANDED IT TO YOU.
WELL... GOOD NIGHT.
GASA (RUSTLE)
ザッ
DOKUN (THADUMP)
hiraha Okitsu in 1959
episode 09 END

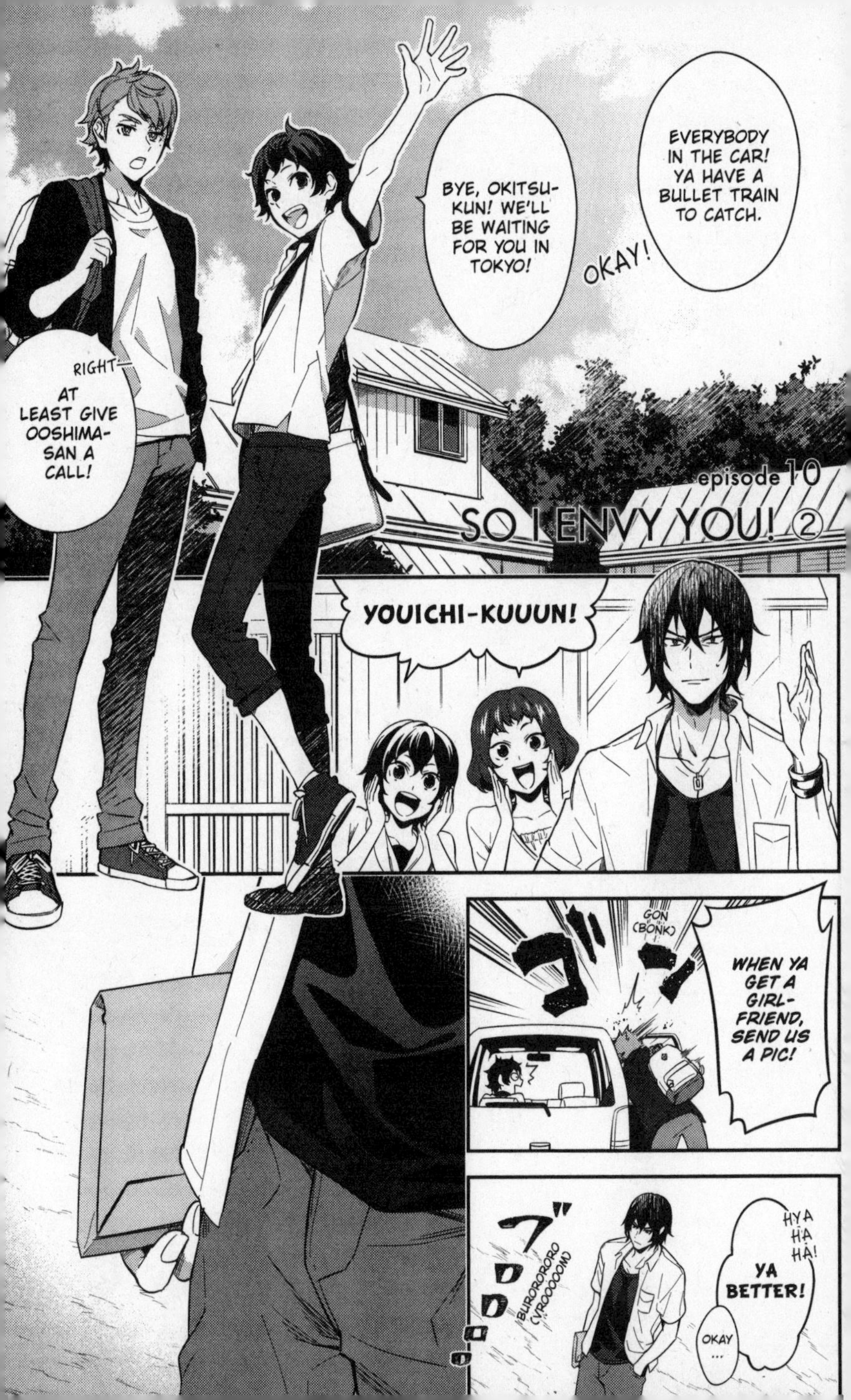
EVERYBODY IN THE CAR! YA HAVE A BULLET TRAIN TO CATCH.
OKAY!
BYE, OKITSU-KUN! WE'LL BE WAITING FOR YOU IN TOKYO!
RIGHT—
AT LEAST GIVE OOSHIMA-SAN A CALL!
episode 10
SO I ENVY YOU! ②
YOUICHI-KUUUN!
GON (BONK)
WHEN YA GET A GIRL-FRIEND, SEND US A PIC!
HYA HA HA!
YA BETTER!
OKAY...
BURORORORO (VROOOOOM)

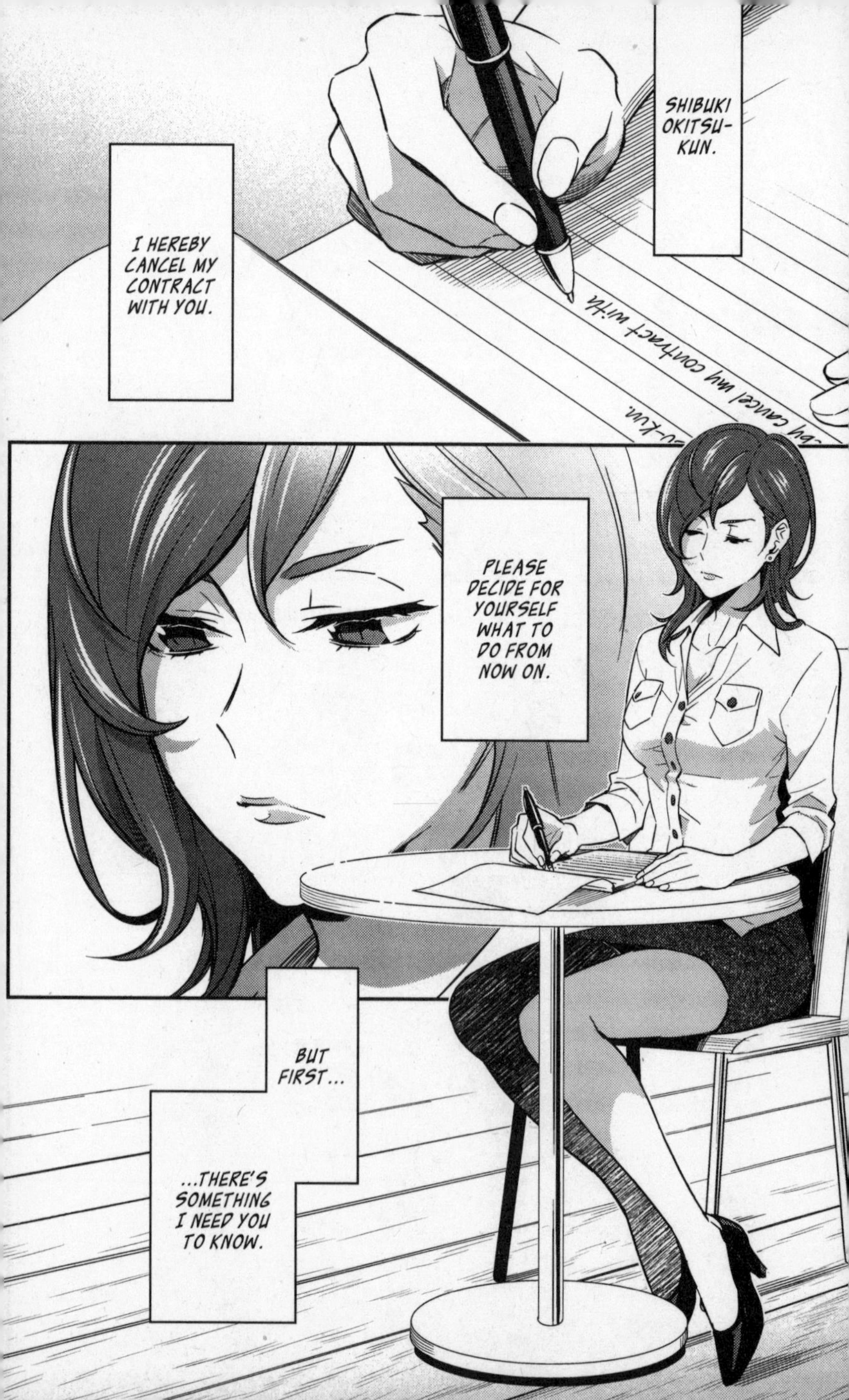
SHIBUKI OKITSU-KUN.
I HEREBY CANCEL MY CONTRACT WITH YOU.
PLEASE DECIDE FOR YOURSELF WHAT TO DO FROM NOW ON.
BUT FIRST...
...THERE'S SOMETHING I NEED YOU TO KNOW.

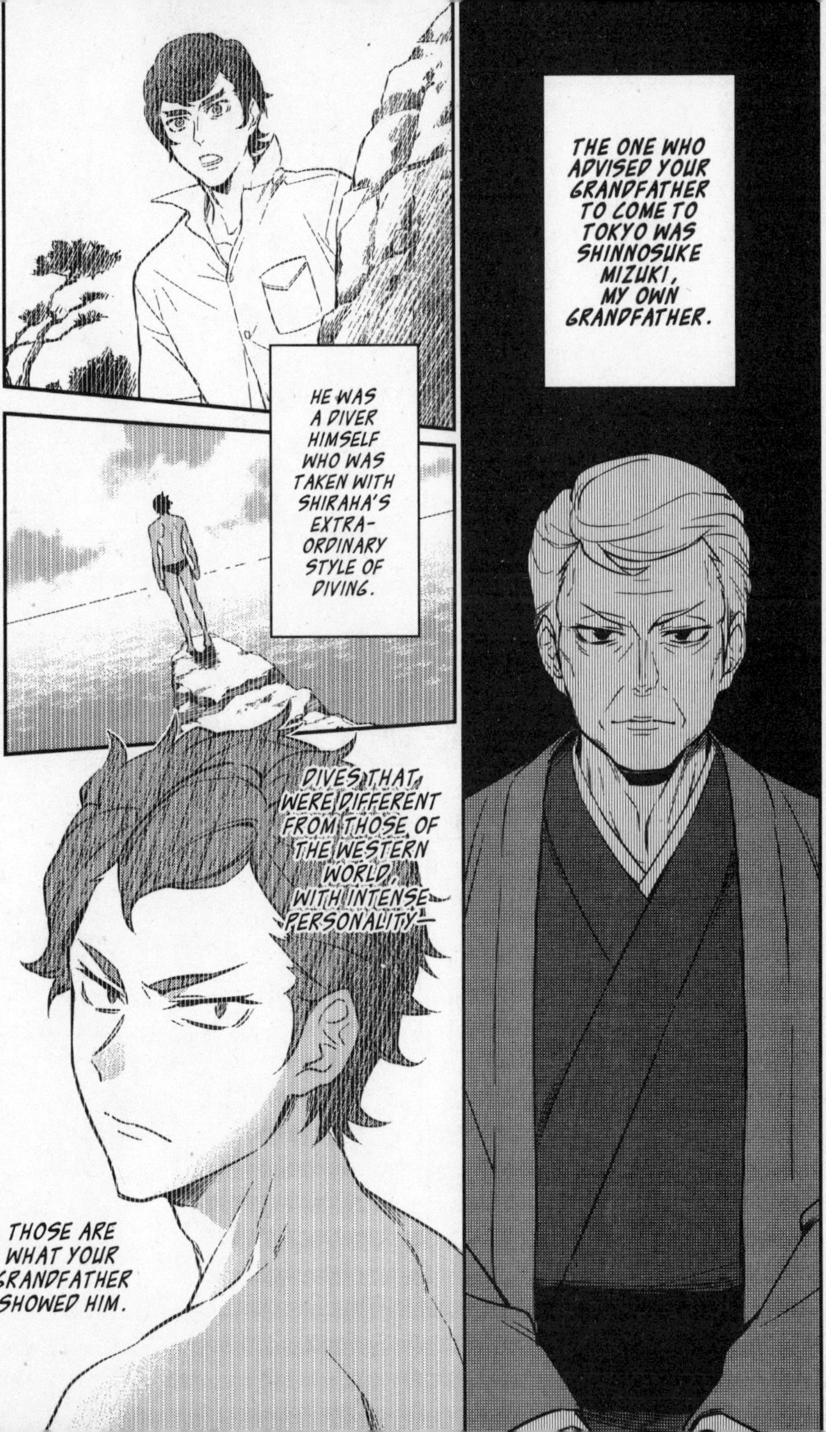
THE ONE WHO ADVISED YOUR GRANDFATHER TO COME TO TOKYO WAS SHINNOSUKE MIZUKI, MY OWN GRANDFATHER.
HE WAS A DIVER HIMSELF WHO WAS TAKEN WITH SHIRAHA'S EXTRA-ORDINARY STYLE OF DIVING.
DIVES THAT WERE DIFFERENT FROM THOSE OF THE WESTERN WORLD, WITH INTENSE PERSONALITY—
THOSE ARE WHAT YOUR GRANDFATHER SHOWED HIM.

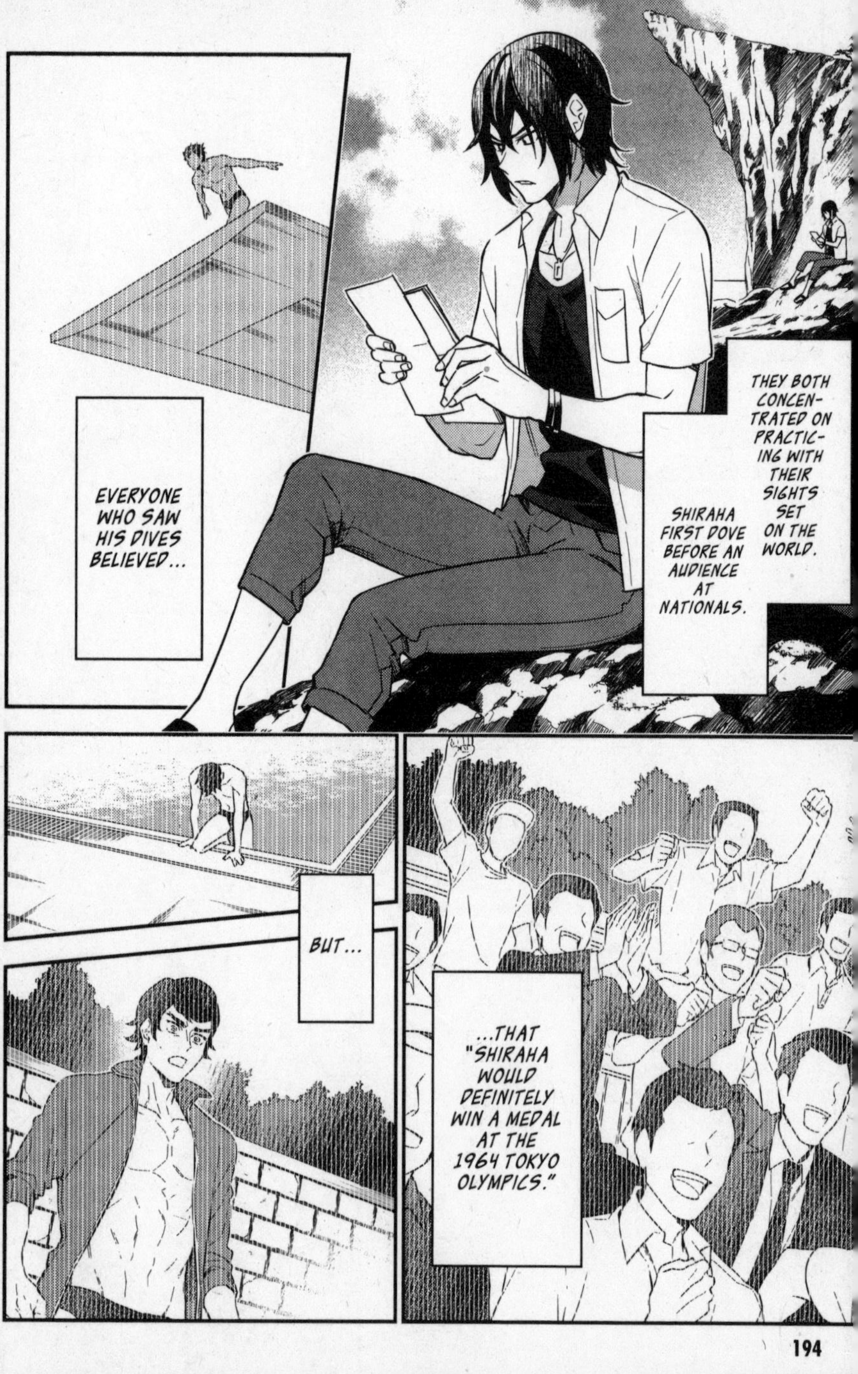
THEY BOTH CONCENTRATED ON PRACTICING WITH THEIR SIGHTS SET ON THE WORLD.
SHIRAHA FIRST DOVE BEFORE AN AUDIENCE AT NATIONALS.
EVERYONE WHO SAW HIS DIVES BELIEVED...
..."THAT "SHIRAHA WOULD DEFINITELY WIN A MEDAL AT THE 1964 TOKYO OLYMPICS."
BUT...

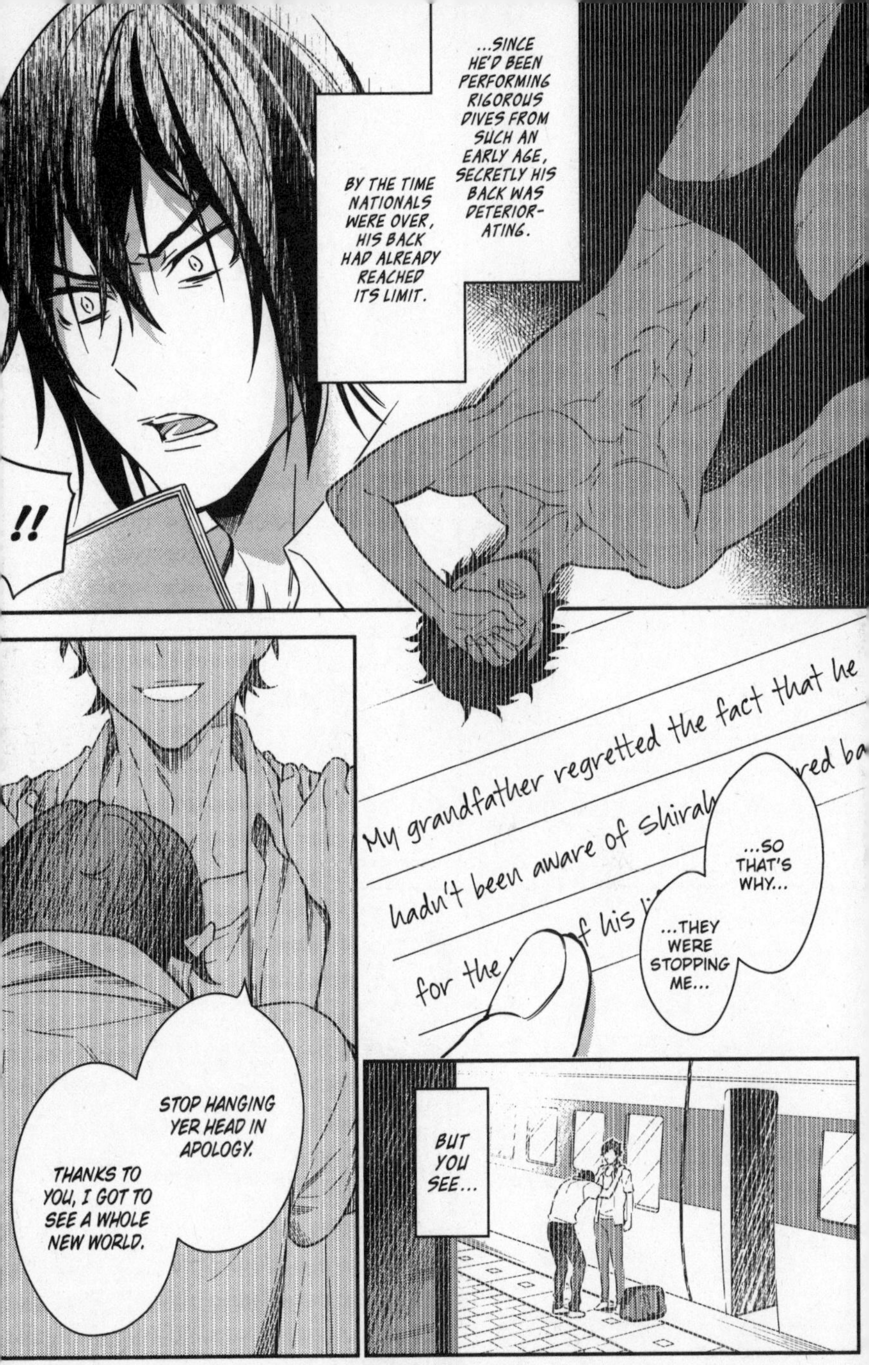
...SINCE HE'D BEEN PERFORMING RIGOROUS DIVES FROM SUCH AN EARLY AGE, SECRETLY HIS BACK WAS DETERIOR-ATING.
BY THE TIME NATIONALS WERE OVER, HIS BACK HAD ALREADY REACHED ITS LIMIT.
!!
My grandfather regretted the fact that he
hadn't been aware of Shirab
for the
...SO THAT'S WHY...
...THEY WERE STOPPING ME...
BUT YOU SEE...
STOP HANGING YER HEAD IN APOLOGY.
THANKS TO YOU, I GOT TO SEE A WHOLE NEW WORLD.

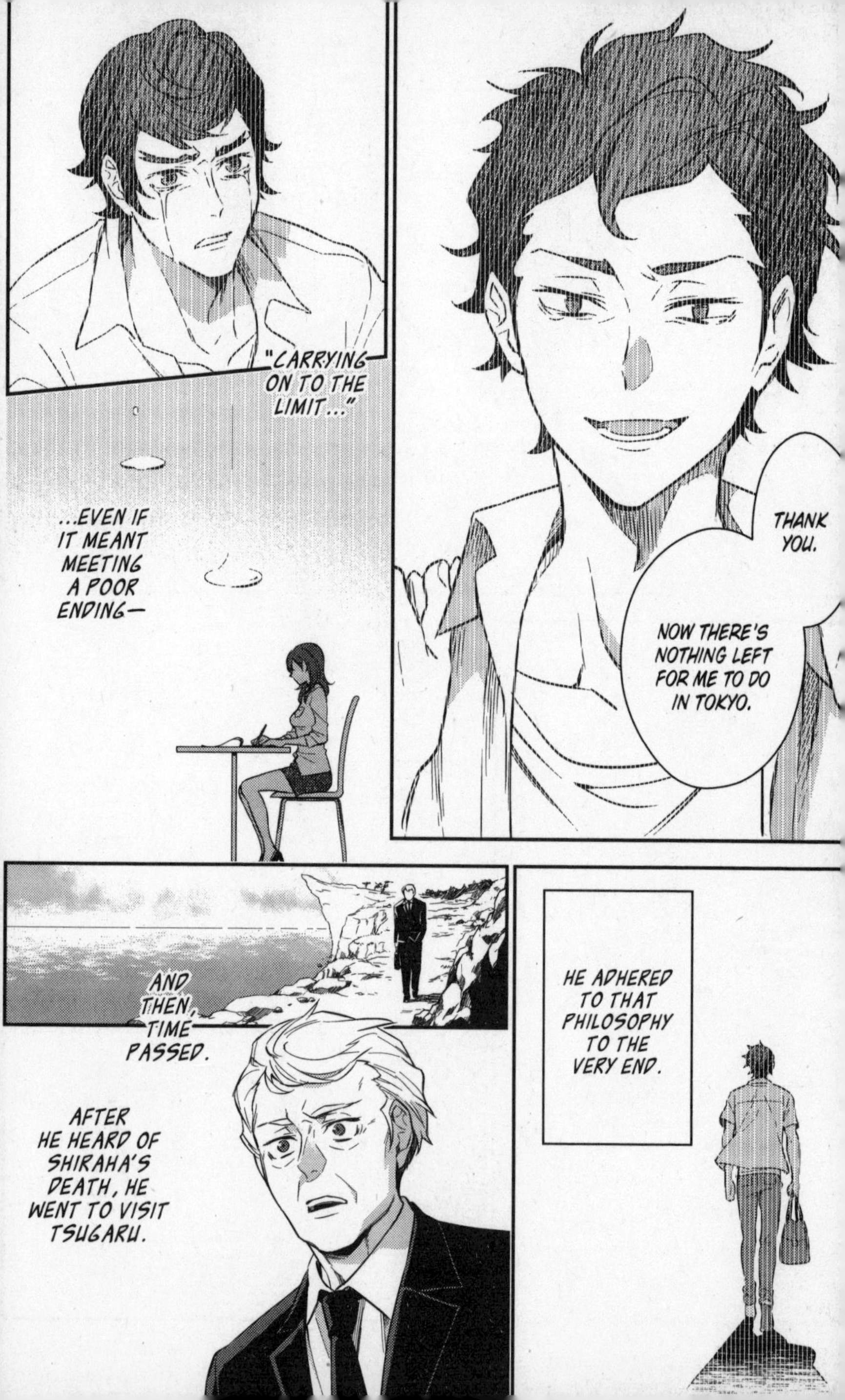
THANK YOU.
NOW THERE'S NOTHING LEFT FOR ME TO DO IN TOKYO.
"CARRYING ON TO THE LIMIT..."
...EVEN IF IT MEANT MEETING A POOR ENDING—
HE ADHERED TO THAT PHILOSOPHY TO THE VERY END.
AND THEN, TIME PASSED.
AFTER HE HEARD OF SHIRAHA'S DEATH, HE WENT TO VISIT TSUGARU.

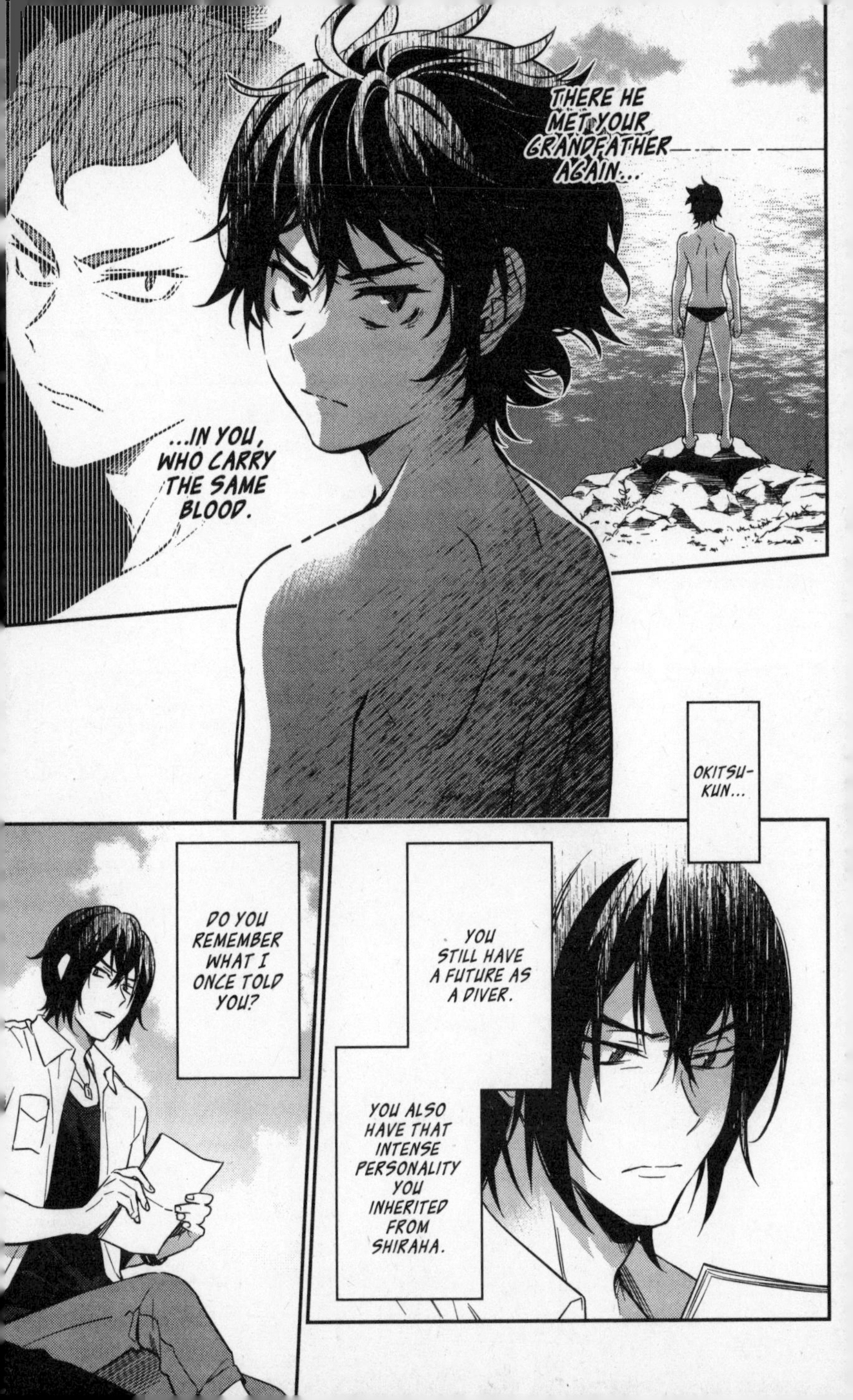

THERE HE MET YOUR GRANDFATHER AGAIN...
...IN YOU, WHO CARRY THE SAME BLOOD.
OKITSU-KUN...
YOU STILL HAVE A FUTURE AS A DIVER.
YOU ALSO HAVE THAT INTENSE PERSONALITY YOU INHERITED FROM SHIRAHA.
DO YOU REMEMBER WHAT I ONCE TOLD YOU?

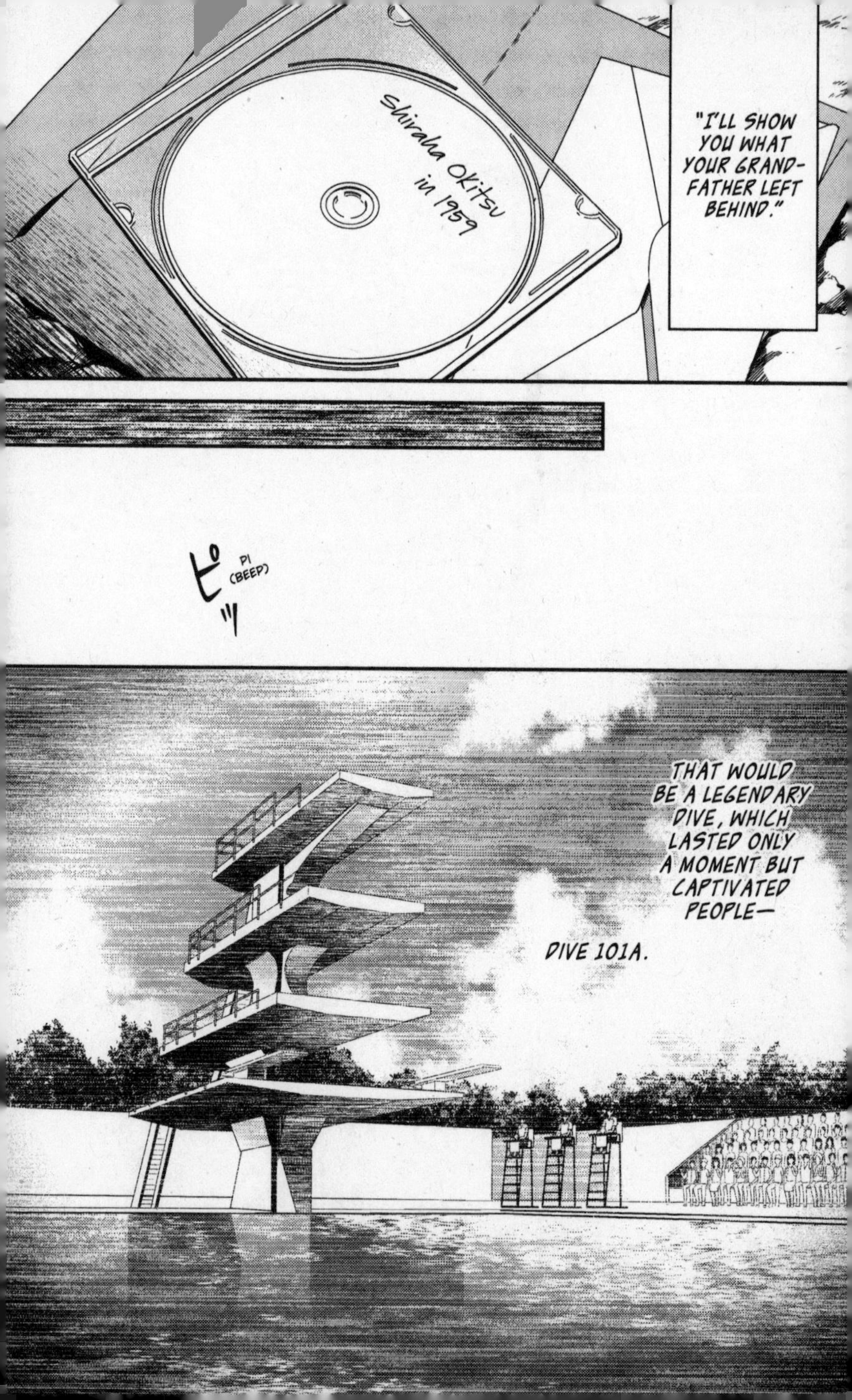
"I'LL SHOW YOU WHAT YOUR GRANDFATHER LEFT BEHIND."
Shiraha Okitsu in 1959
ピッ
PI (BEEP)
THAT WOULD BE A LEGENDARY DIVE, WHICH LASTED ONLY A MOMENT BUT CAPTIVATED PEOPLE—
DIVE 101A.

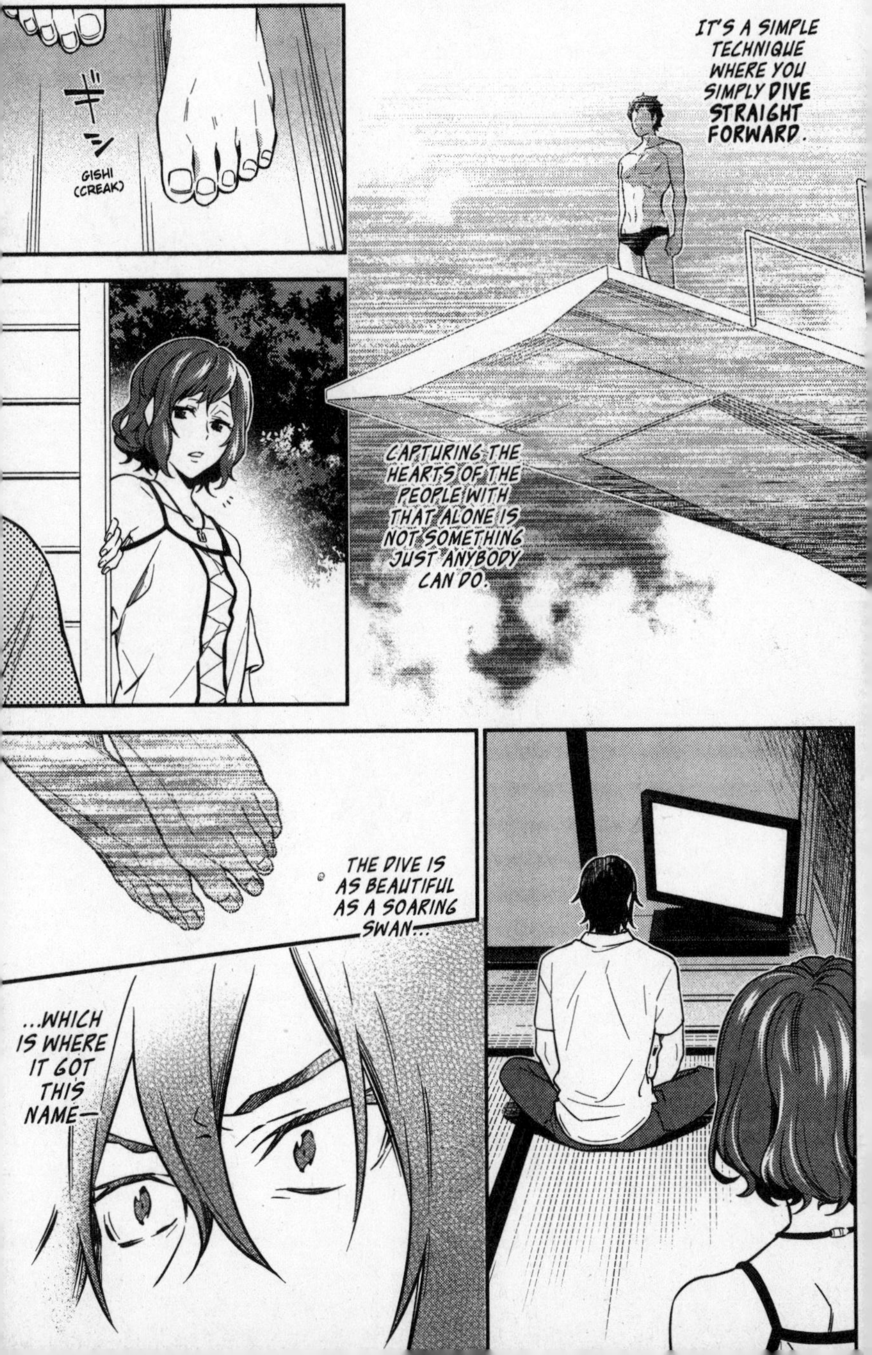
IT'S A SIMPLE TECHNIQUE WHERE YOU SIMPLY DIVE STRAIGHT FORWARD.
CAPTURING THE HEARTS OF THE PEOPLE WITH THAT ALONE IS NOT SOMETHING JUST ANYBODY CAN DO.
ギシ
GISHI (CREAK)
THE DIVE IS AS BEAUTIFUL AS A SOARING SWAN...
...WHICH IS WHERE IT GOT THIS NAME—

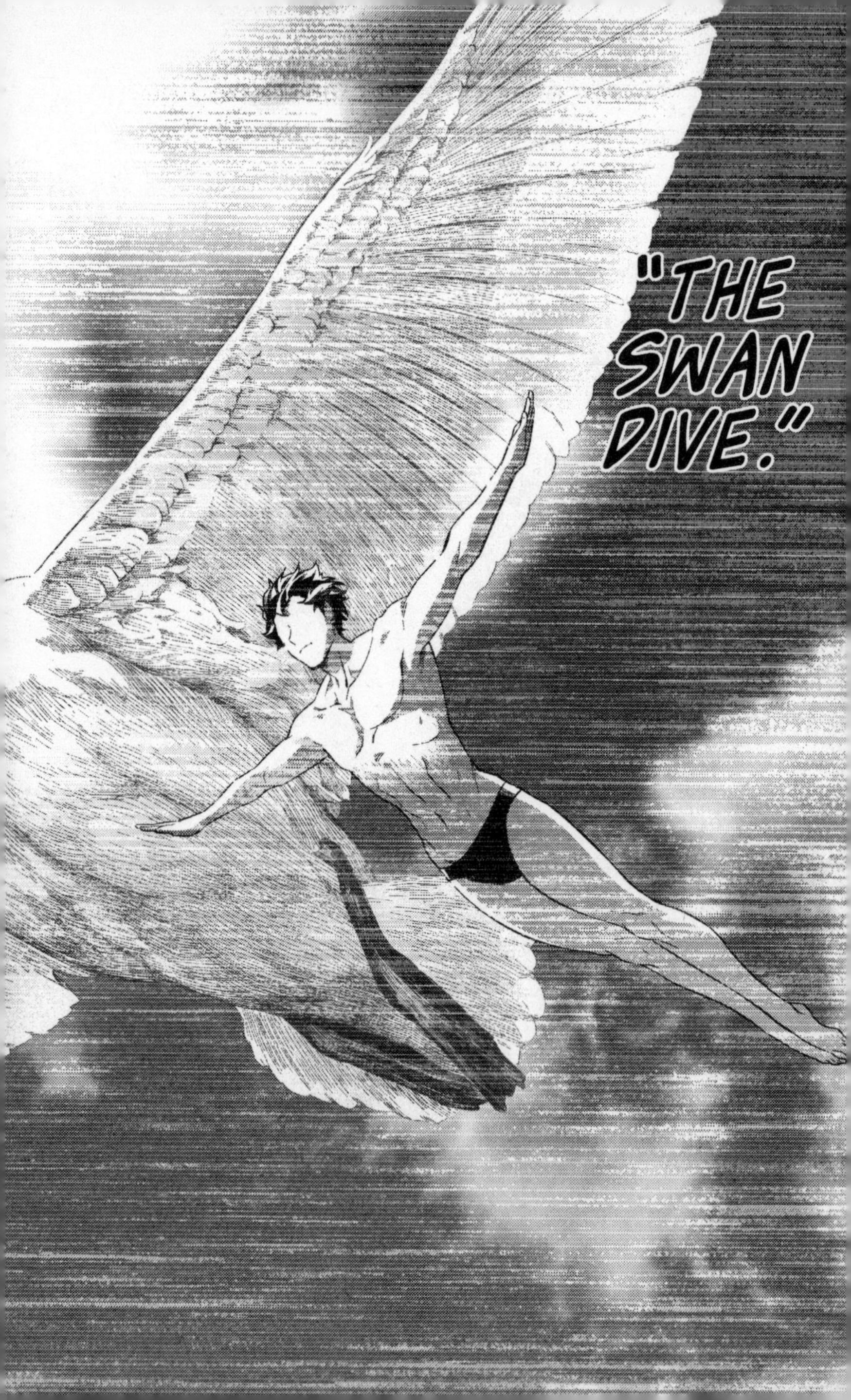
"THE SWAN DIVE."

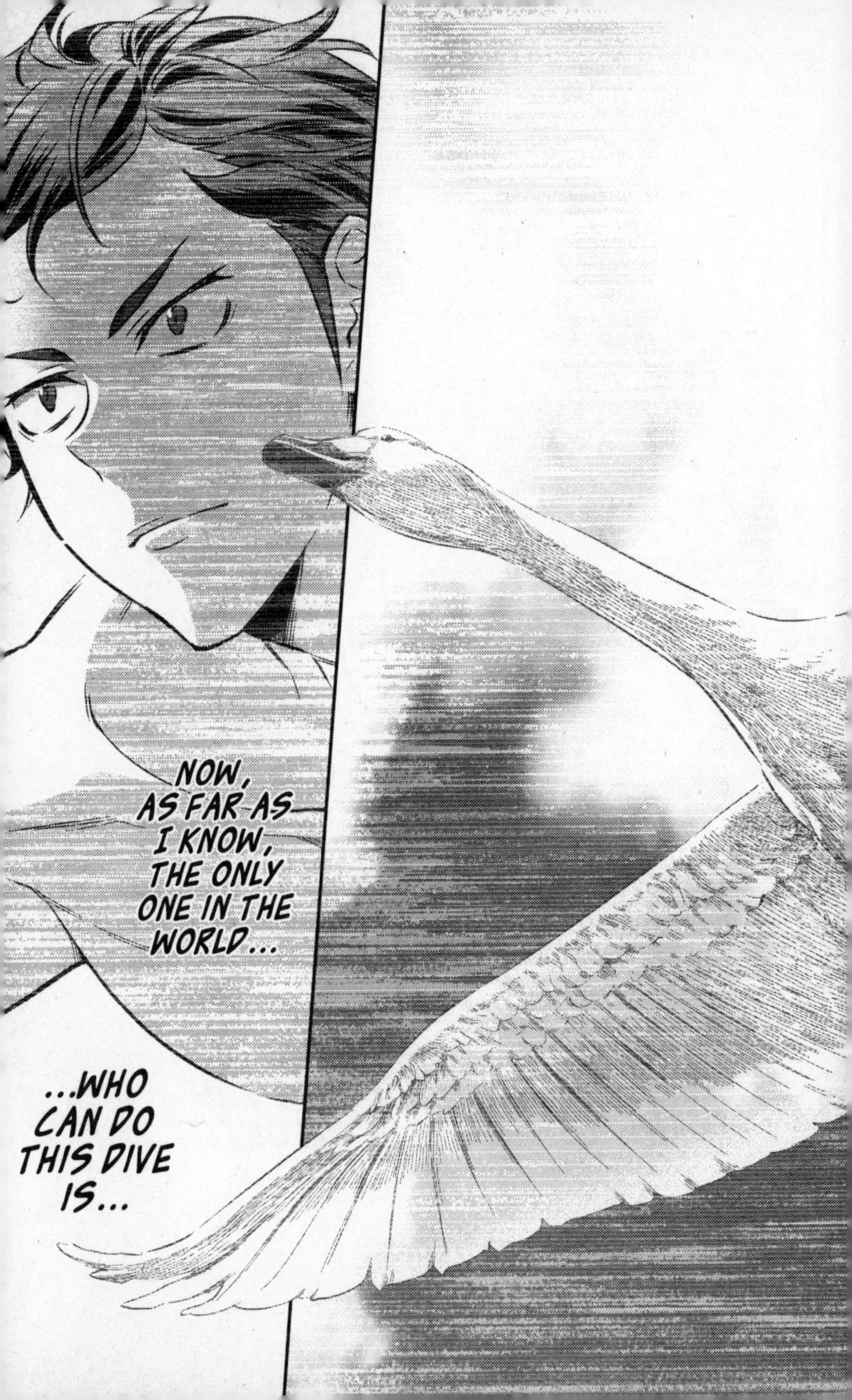
NOW, AS FAR AS I KNOW, THE ONLY ONE IN THE WORLD...
...WHO CAN DO THIS DIVE IS...

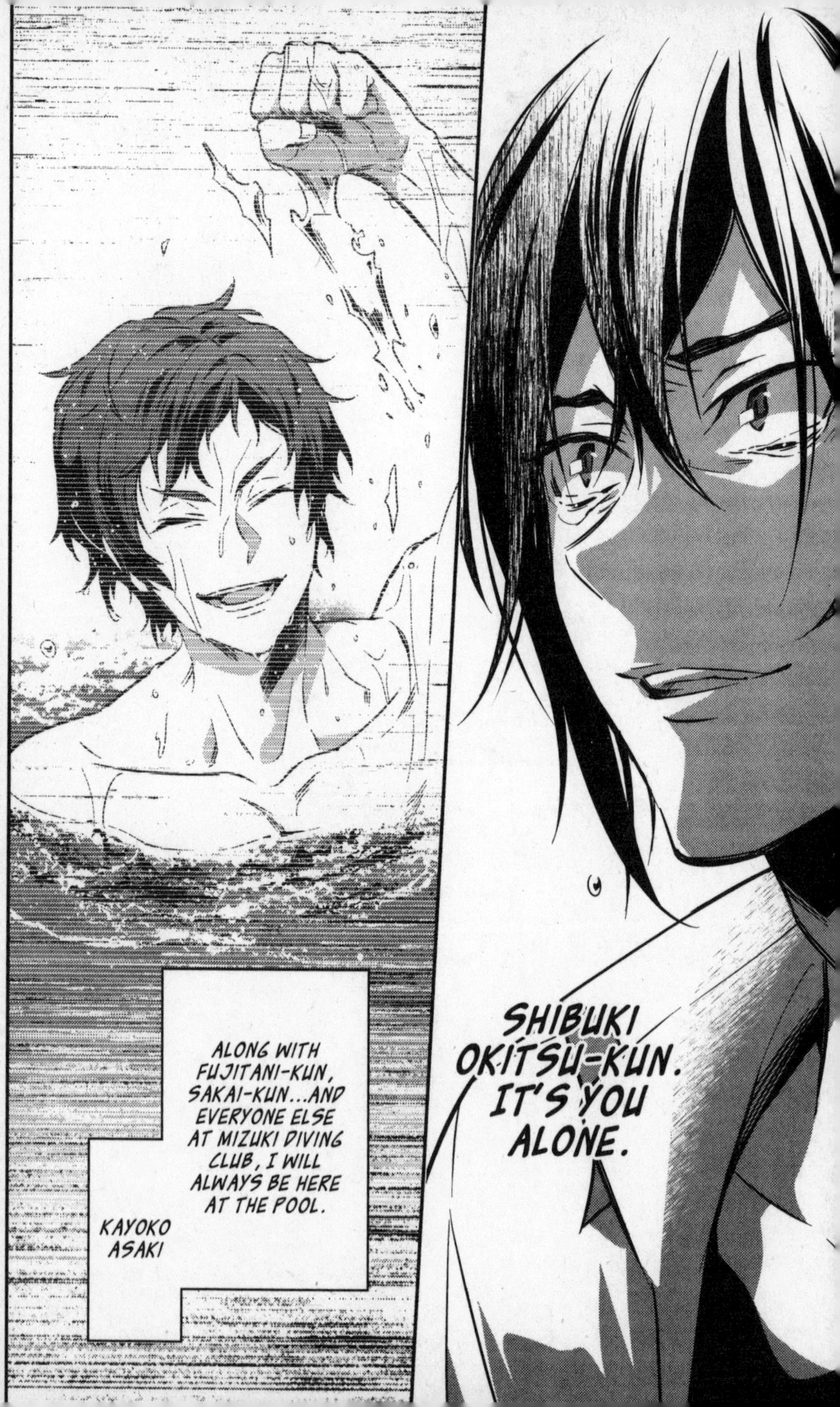
SHIBUKI OKITSU-KUN. IT'S YOU ALONE.
ALONG WITH FUJITANI-KUN, SAKAI-KUN...AND EVERYONE ELSE AT MIZUKI DIVING CLUB, I WILL ALWAYS BE HERE AT THE POOL.
KAYOKO ASAKI

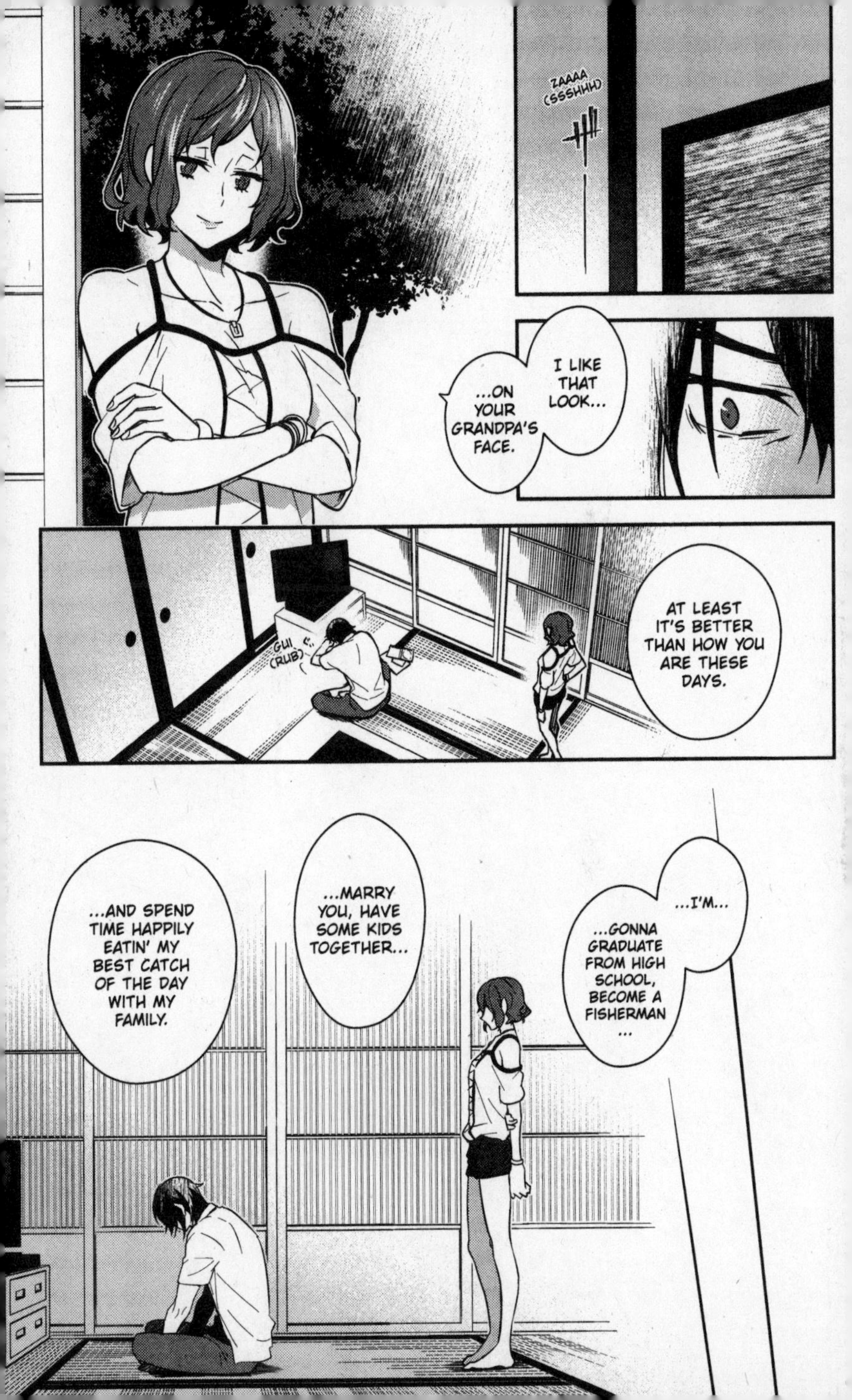
ZAAAA (SSSHHH)
I LIKE THAT LOOK...
...ON YOUR GRANDPA'S FACE.
AT LEAST IT'S BETTER THAN HOW YOU ARE THESE DAYS.
GUI (RUB)
...I'M...
...GONNA GRADUATE FROM HIGH SCHOOL, BECOME A FISHERMAN ...
...MARRY YOU, HAVE SOME KIDS TOGETHER...
...AND SPEND TIME HAPPILY EATIN' MY BEST CATCH OF THE DAY WITH MY FAMILY.

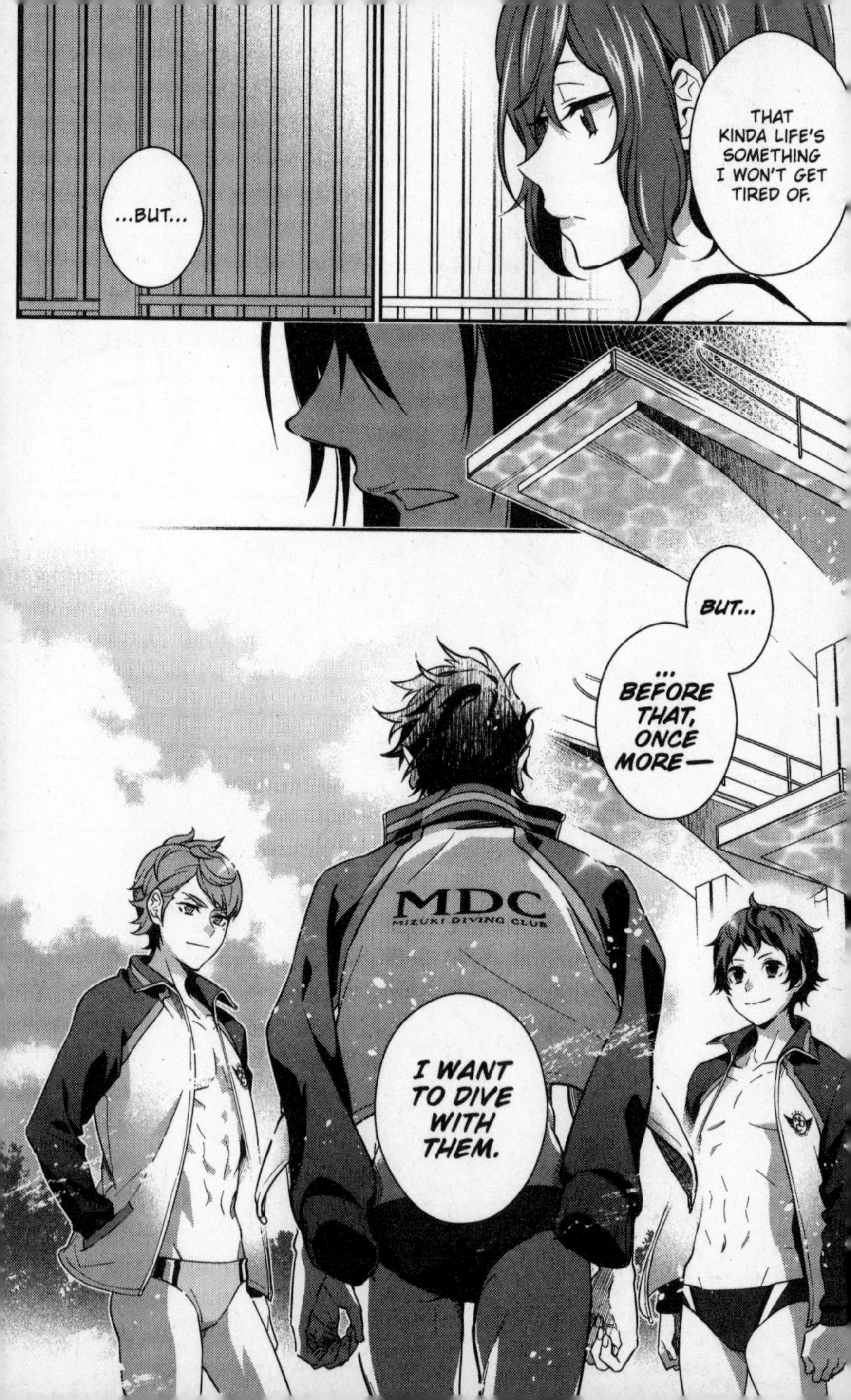
THAT KINDA LIFE'S SOMETHING I WON'T GET TIRED OF.
...BUT...
BUT...
...BEFORE THAT, ONCE MORE—
MDC
MIZUKI DIVING CLUB
I WANT TO DIVE WITH THEM.

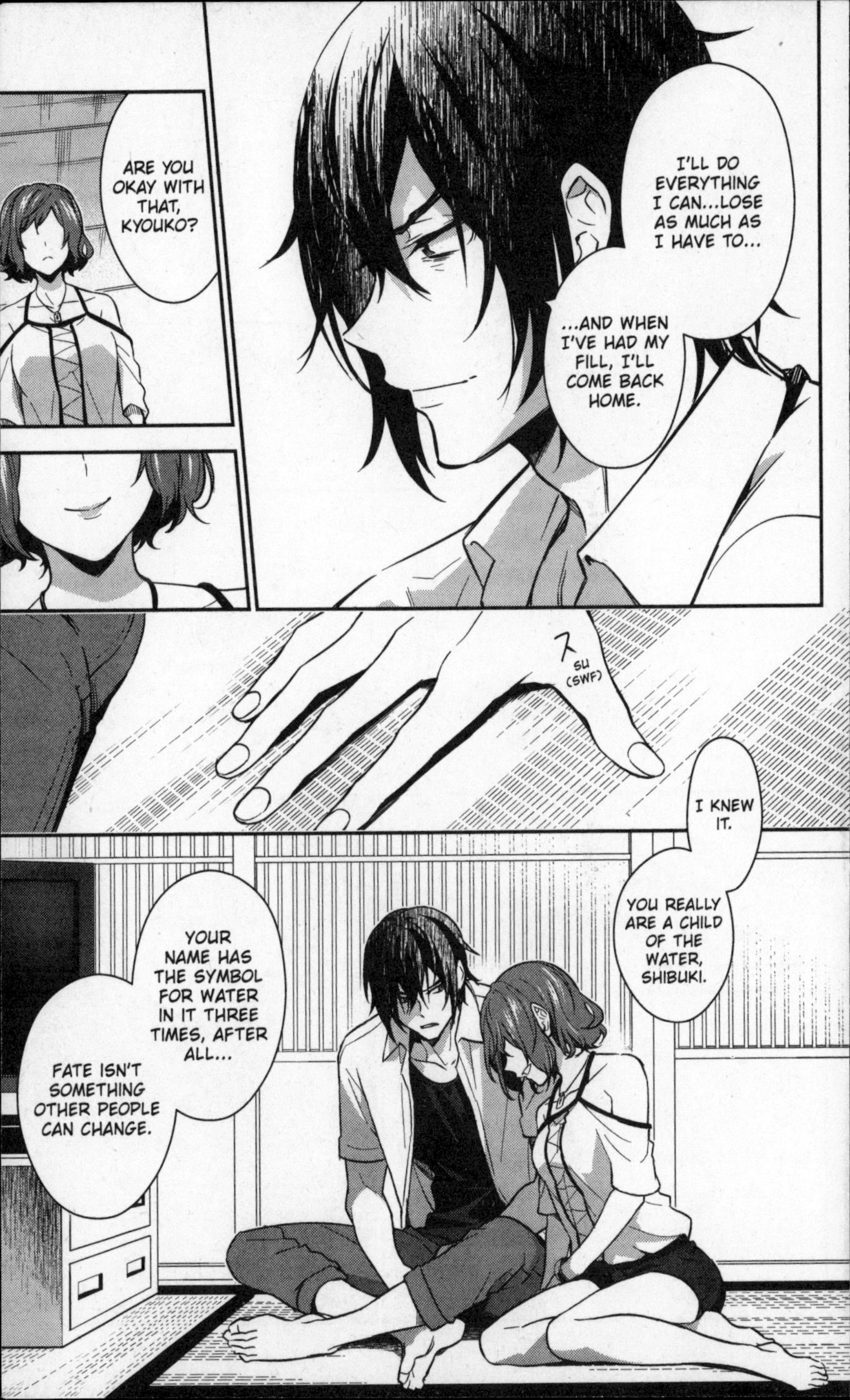
I'LL DO EVERYTHING I CAN...LOSE AS MUCH AS I HAVE TO...
...AND WHEN I'VE HAD MY FILL, I'LL COME BACK HOME.
ARE YOU OKAY WITH THAT, KYOUKO?
ス
SU (SWF)
I KNEW IT.
YOU REALLY ARE A CHILD OF THE WATER, SHIBUKI.
YOUR NAME HAS THE SYMBOL FOR WATER IN IT THREE TIMES, AFTER ALL...
FATE ISN'T SOMETHING OTHER PEOPLE CAN CHANGE.

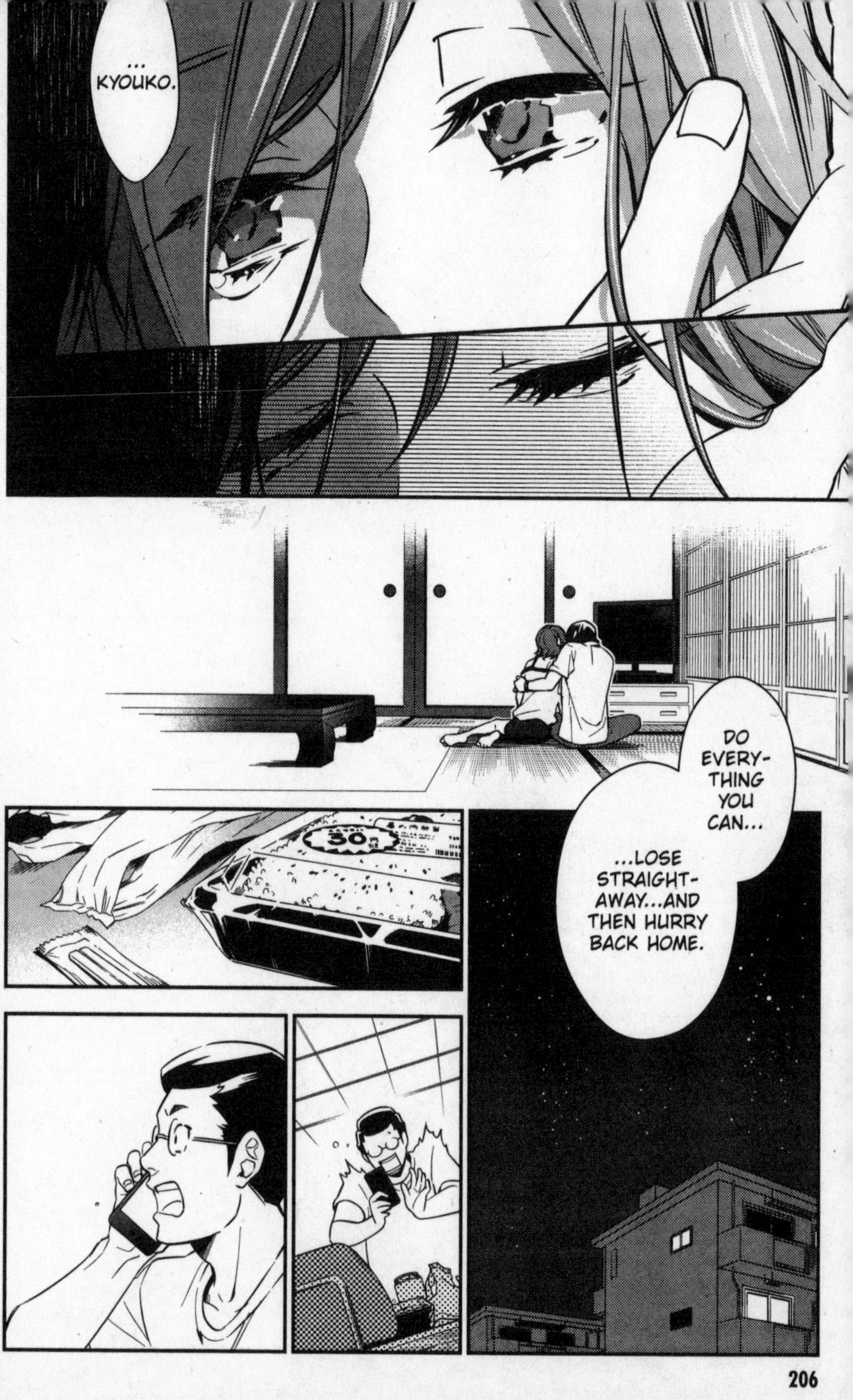
...KYOUKO.
DO EVERY-THING YOU CAN...
...LOSE STRAIGHT-AWAY...AND THEN HURRY BACK HOME.

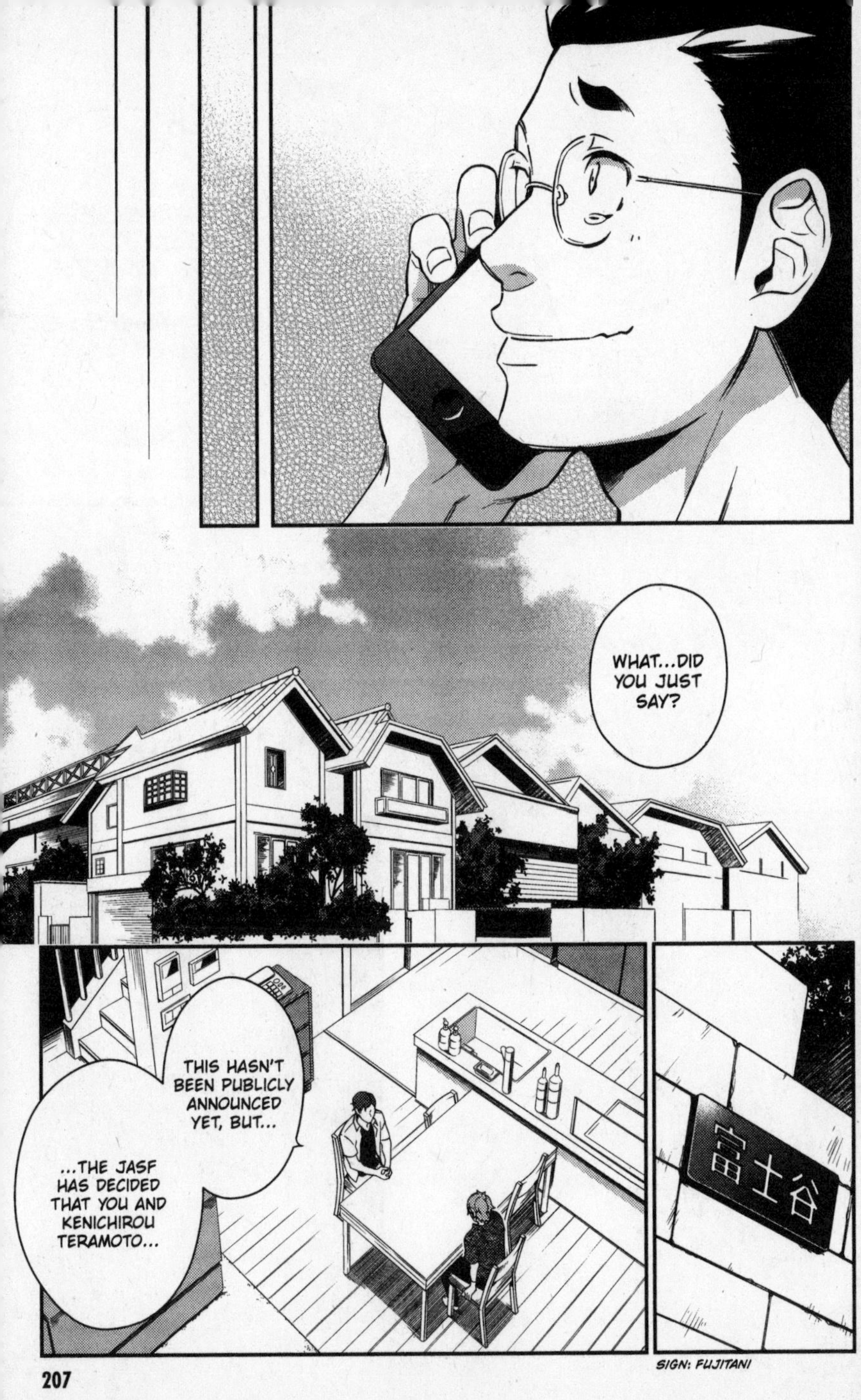
WHAT...DID YOU JUST SAY?
富士谷
THIS HASN'T BEEN PUBLICLY ANNOUNCED YET, BUT...
...THE JASF HAS DECIDED THAT YOU AND KENICHIROU TERAMOTO...
SIGN: FUJITANI

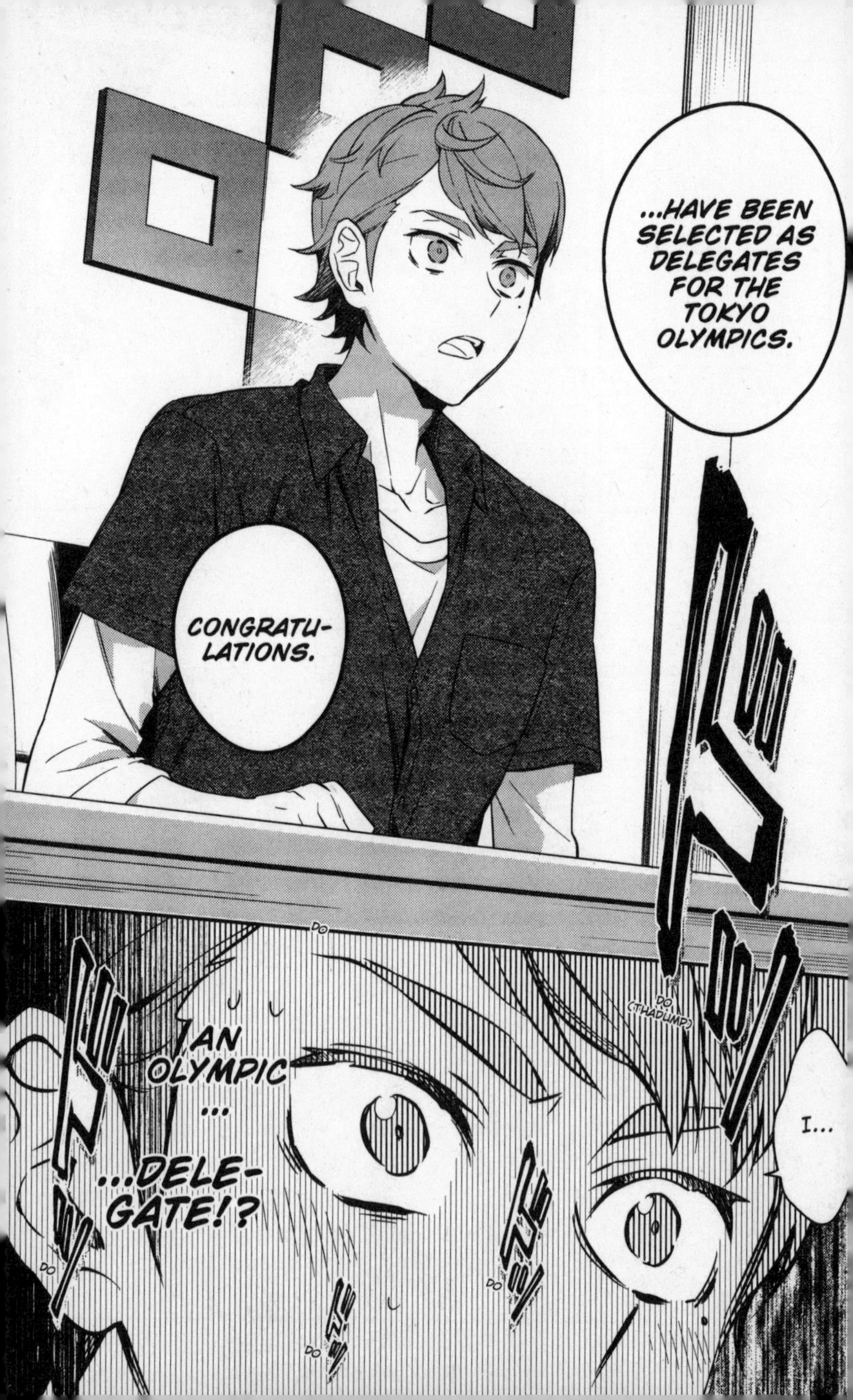
...HAVE BEEN SELECTED AS DELEGATES FOR THE TOKYO OLYMPICS.
CONGRATULATIONS.
DO (THADUMP)
I...
AN OLYMPIC ...
...DELEGATE!?

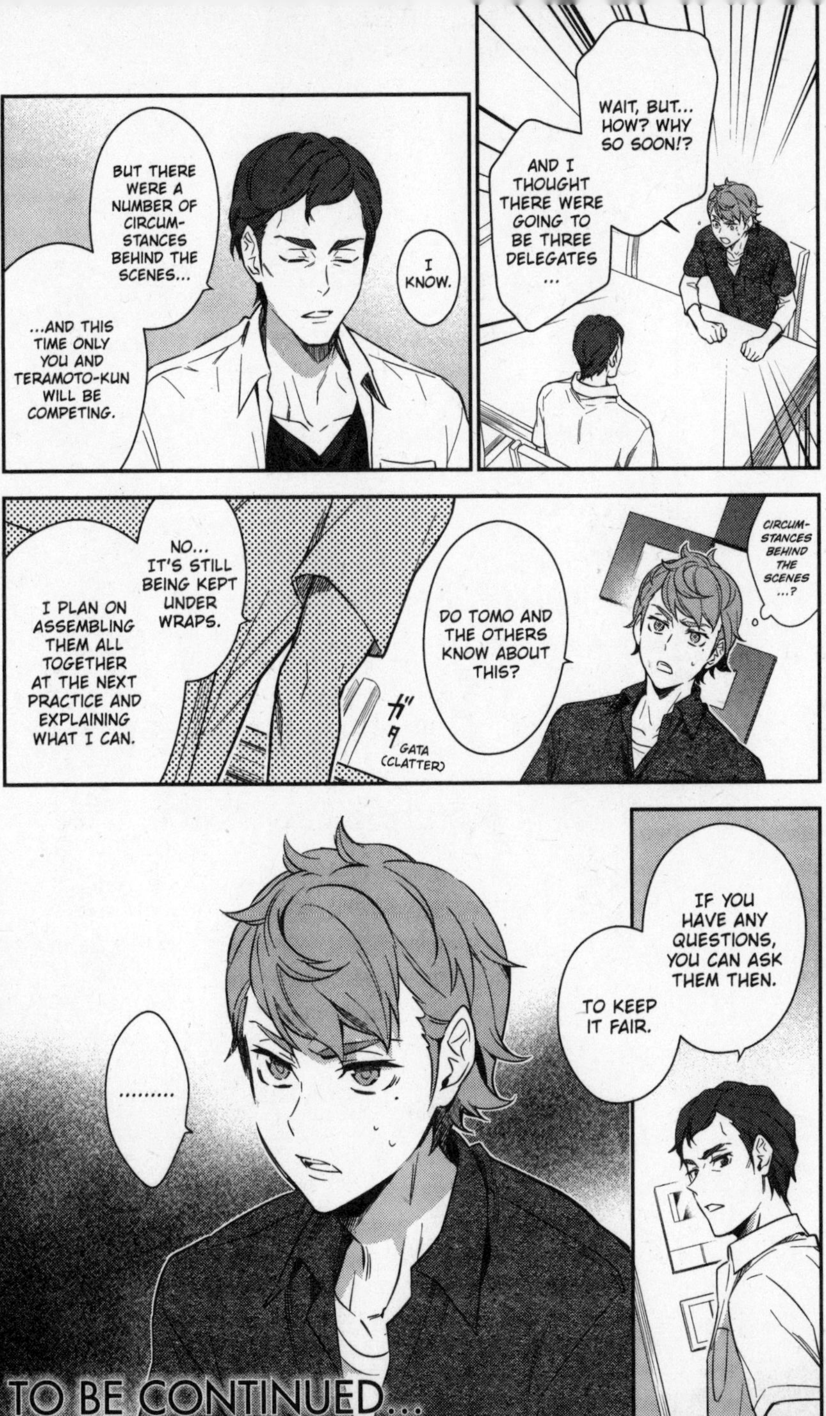
WAIT, BUT... HOW? WHY SO SOON!?
AND I THOUGHT THERE WERE GOING TO BE THREE DELEGATES...
I KNOW.
BUT THERE WERE A NUMBER OF CIRCUM-STANCES BEHIND THE SCENES...
...AND THIS TIME ONLY YOU AND TERAMOTO-KUN WILL BE COMPETING.
CIRCUM-STANCES BEHIND THE SCENES...?
DO TOMO AND THE OTHERS KNOW ABOUT THIS?
ガタ GATA (CLATTER)
NO... IT'S STILL BEING KEPT UNDER WRAPS.
I PLAN ON ASSEMBLING THEM ALL TOGETHER AT THE NEXT PRACTICE AND EXPLAINING WHAT I CAN.
IF YOU HAVE ANY QUESTIONS, YOU CAN ASK THEM THEN.
TO KEEP IT FAIR.
....
TO BE CONTINUED...

STAFF

Art
RUZURU AKASHIBA

Assistant
MUNEHARU MORI

Original Cover Design
SHINJI YAMAGUCHI (R design studio)

TRANSLATION NOTES

COMMON HONORIFICS

no honorific: Indicates familiarity or closeness; if used without permission or reason, addressing someone in this manner would constitute an insult.

-san: The Japanese equivalent of Mr./Mrs./Miss. If a situation calls for politeness, this is the fail-safe honorific.

-kun: Used most often when referring to boys, this indicates affection or familiarity. Occasionally used by older men among their peers, but it may also be used by anyone referring to a person of lower standing.

-chan: An affectionate honorific indicating familiarity used mostly in reference to girls; also used in reference to cute persons or animals of either gender.

Page 68

Tsugaru dialect, or *Tsugaru-ben*, is a dialect very specific to Tsugaru city in Aomori Prefecture. It includes some of its own vocabulary, and many words and phrases are condensed. It is not spoken in other areas of the prefecture, and the accent can be so thick that even people within Aomori can have trouble understanding it.

Page 123

"...stretching himself past his limits!": In Japanese, the word *nobiru* can be used to mean "to stretch" as well as "to improve." Due to this, after Pinky expresses that he will continue to improve, or stretch himself past his limits, Jirou takes the opportunity to poke fun at his tight, or stretched out, clothing.

Page 179

"...would turn to sea-foam.": The phrase used in the Japanese is *mizu no awa*, which literally refers to the bubbles on the surface of water but also is used to refer to something coming to nothing.

Page 205

When Kyouko says Shibuki's name **"has the symbol for water in it three times,"** she is talking about the Chinese characters that make up his full name, Shibuki Okitsu. Out of the five characters that compose his name, three of them contain the radical that carries the meaning of "water." A "radical" is a part of a Chinese character that can be found in multiple characters and is used in classification.

DIVE!! 2

ORIGINAL STORY: **Eto Mori**
ART: **Ruzuru Akashiba**

CHARACTER DESIGN: **Suzuhito Yasuda**

IN COLLABORATION WITH: **Animation DIVE!! Committee**

Translation: Christine Dashiell ○ **Lettering: Alexis Eckerman**

DIVE!! Volume 2
© Eto MORI 2018
© Ruzuru AKASHIBA 2018
© EtoMori, KADOKAWA/Animation DIVE!! Committee
First published in Japan in 2018 by KADOKAWA CORPORATION, Tokyo.
English translation rights arranged with KADOKAWA CORPORATION, Tokyo through
TUTTLE-MORI AGENCY, INC.

English translation © 2019 by Yen Press, LLC

Yen Press
1290 Avenue of the Americas
New York, NY 10104

Visit us at yenpress.com • facebook.com/yenpress • twitter.com/yenpress • yenpress.tumblr.com • instagram.com/yenpress

First Yen Press Edition: April 2019

Yen Press is an imprint of Yen Press, LLC.
The Yen Press name and logo are trademarks of Yen Press, LLC.

The publisher is not responsible for websites (or their content) that are not owned by the publisher.

Library of Congress Control Number: 2018958633

ISBNs: 978-1-9753-0414-0 (paperback)
        978-1-9753-5787-0 (ebook)

10 9 8 7 6 5 4 3 2 1

WOR

Printed in the United States of America